当代国外语言学与应用语言学文库（升级版）

关联性：交际与认知

第二版

Relevance: Communication and Cognition
(Second Edition)

［法］Dan Sperber
［英］Deirdre Wilson   著

何自然 冉永平 导读

外语教学与研究出版社
FOREIGN LANGUAGE TEACHING AND RESEARCH PRESS
北京 BEIJING

WILEY

京权图字：01-2023-0579

图书在版编目 (CIP) 数据

关联性 ：交际与认知 ：第二版 ＝ Relevance: Communication and Cognition (Second Edition) ：英文／（法）达恩·斯佩贝尔（Dan Sperber），（英）戴尔德丽·威尔逊（Deirdre Wilson）著 ；何自然，冉永平导读. －－ 北京 ：外语教学与研究出版社，2023.3
　　（当代国外语言学与应用语言学文库 ：升级版）
　　ISBN 978－7－5213－4322－9

　　Ⅰ. ①关… Ⅱ. ①达… ②戴… ③何… ④冉… Ⅲ. ①语言学－研究－英文 Ⅳ. ①H0

中国国家版本馆 CIP 数据核字 (2023) 第 041941 号

出 版 人　王　芳
项目负责　姚　虹　李亚琦
责任编辑　都楠楠
责任校对　徐　宁
装帧设计　李　高
出版发行　外语教学与研究出版社
社　　址　北京市西三环北路 19 号（100089）
网　　址　https://www.fltrp.com
印　　刷　唐山市润丰印务有限公司
开　　本　650×980　1/16
印　　张　23.5
版　　次　2023 年 3 月第 1 版 2023 年 3 月第 1 次印刷
书　　号　ISBN 978-7-5213-4322-9
定　　价　59.00 元

如有图书采购需求，图书内容或印刷装订等问题，侵权、盗版书籍等线索，请拨打以下电话或关注官方服务号：
客服电话：400 898 7008
官方服务号：微信搜索并关注公众号"外研社官方服务号"
外研社购书网址：https://fltrp.tmall.com

物料号：343220001

记载人类文明
沟通世界文化
www.fltrp.com

当代国外语言学与应用语言学文库

（升级版）

学术委员会

（按姓氏拼音排列）

蔡金亭	陈新仁	程　工	程晓堂	戴曼纯	丁建新
丁言仁	董　洁	董燕萍	范　琳	封宗信	高　远
顾永琦	韩宝成	何莲珍	何　伟	胡建华	胡旭辉
胡壮麟	黄国文	黄友义	贾玉新	姜望琪	金　艳
蓝　纯	李　兵	李福印	李战子	梁晓晖	刘立华
刘润清	刘世生	马秋武	苗兴伟	宁春岩	冉永平
申　丹	施　旭	束定芳	宋　莉	苏　祺	田贵森
田海龙	王初明	王海啸	王克非	王文斌	王　寅
文秋芳	文　旭	吴　霞	吴一安	武尊民	徐　浩
杨信彰	杨延宁	姚小平	于书林	余国兴	张　辉
张绍杰	周晓林				

出版前言

　　"当代国外语言学与应用语言学文库"（以下简称"文库"）从2000年至今已出版近200个品种，深受语言学与应用语言学专业师生和研究者的欢迎，大家既把"文库"视为进入语言学与应用语言学百花园的引路人，又把"文库"视为知识更新的源泉，还把"文库"当成点亮科研之路的明灯。

　　为了追踪相关领域的研究进程，并满足广大读者的需求，外语教学与研究出版社从2020年开始启动了"文库"的更新升级工作，与牛津大学出版社、剑桥大学出版社、劳特利奇出版社等世界知名出版机构合作，推出"文库"（升级版）。

　　"文库"升级的原则如下：

　　1. 对原有经典图书，若无新版，则予以保留，并予以必要修订；若有新版，则以新版代替旧版，并请相关领域学者撰写新版中文导读。

2. 引进语言学与应用语言学领域的新锐力作，进一步拓展学科领域。

3. 用二维码代替CD-ROM，帮助读者更加快捷地获取内容。

"文库"（升级版）定位为一套大型的、开放性的系列丛书，希望它能对我国语言学教学与研究和外语教学与研究起到积极的推动作用。外语教学与研究出版社亦将继续努力，力争把国外最新、最具影响力的语言学与应用语言学著作奉献给广大读者。

外语教学与研究出版社
2021年8月

导　　读

何自然　冉永平

1. 关联理论研究概述

从事语言学与哲学研究的法国学者 Dan Sperber（达恩·斯佩贝尔）和英国学者 Deirdre Wilson（戴尔德丽·威尔逊）合作撰写的著作《关联性：交际与认知》第一版于1986年出版。其目的是"给认知科学打下一个统一的理论基础"（第一版封底）。可见，该著作不是作者特意为语用学而撰写的，它是一本概括性很强、有关交际与认知的著作，不仅涵盖了现代语用学的很多研究课题，还涉及现代交际理论，因此"这可能是你阅读到的有关交际的最好著作"（第二版封底）。第一版面世后，该著作很快就被翻译成法语、俄语、意大利语、西班牙语、日语、朝鲜语、马来语等多种语言。在1995年，Sperber 和 Wilson 又推出了该书的第二版，接着又被翻译成了多种语言。2008年，该著作的中译本《关联：交际与认知》（译者：蒋严）由中国社会科学出版社出版。

从广义的角度来说，话语产出和话语理解是语用学研究的两大主题。Grice（1975）会话含意理论模式以说话人为出发点，提出了意向交际的思想，设想说话等言谈交际应该遵守合作原则，当说话人故意违反合作原则时听话人据此推导交际中的话语含意。后来，有关含意推导的认知阐释路径与理论视角得到了进一步充实、修正与发展。在这些理论模式当中，引发人们注意并产生广泛学术影响的就是Sperber和Wilson在《关联性：交际与认知》中所提出的关联理论（relevance theory）。从该理论提出至今，介绍、评论、应用该理论的研究论文、专辑和专著就一直不断，比如《关联的语义制约》（Blakemore 1987）、《话语中的关联关系》（Blass 1990）、《关联理论：应用与启示》（Carston & Uchida 1997）、《关联理论中的当下议题》（Rouchota & Jucker 1998）、《言据性与关联性》（Ifantidou 2001）、《关联与语言意义：话语标记语的语义与语用》（Blakemore 2002）、《关联、语用学与理解》（Scott, Clark & Carston 2019/2022）等，相关著作还被纳入了John Benjamins出版集团的 *Pragmatics & Beyond* 系列丛书。众多文献资料显示，关联理论引发了有关语言使用与理解的多方面话题研究，包括语境、隐喻、转喻、媒体话语、网络交际等的相关问题，还出现了关联理论视角下的语用能力研究，比如《语用能力与关联》（Ifantidou 2014）等，提出了语言能力使用研究的新思路和新认识，语用能力被看作涉及话语产出与话语理解的认知行为（cognitive performance），这体现了语用能力阐释的认知取向以及语用能力的认知特征。有的研究主要涉及关联理论在相关领域的应用，比如德国学者Gutt（1991）的专著《翻译与关联：认知与语境》将翻译看作与认识紧密相关的过程与结果，因此翻译不是简单的信息处理，而是一种认知取向的行为；也有学者利用关联理论分析广告语等现实生活中的语言使用，比如日本学者Tanaka（1994）的《广告语言》，利用关联理论的主要思想去分析公告语等公共话语，类似研究对商业话语、机构性话语、媒体话语等的研究具有重要启示。关联理论不仅被广泛应用于研究日常的面对面交际，还出现了针对网络交际、网络话语等的专门研究，比如西班牙学者Francisco Yus（2019）的《网络语用学：网络语境中的交际》、英国学者Scott（2022）的《网络语用学》等，都扩展了有关语言使用与理解的研究范围，体现了创新思路。

值得一提的是，Clark（2013）还专门出版了题为《关联理论》的著作，一方面介绍该理论在语义学和语用学领域里的相关研究，另一方面介绍该理论在多个领域里的扩展、应用与批评性讨论。为了帮助大家更好地理解关联理论，该著作提供了有关该理论的系统性框架，包括该理论的核心内容，以及在Grice会话含意理论基础上的缘起、两者之间的相互联系与区别等。

同时，语言学等领域的国际学术期刊，比如*Journal of Pragmatics, Pragmatics, Lingua, Pragmatics and Cognition, Behavioral and Brain Sciences, Cognitive Linguistics, Multilingua, Discourse Processes, Journal of Linguistics* 等均先后刊发了关联理论的研究论文。仅国际语用学期刊Journal of Pragmatics就出现了涉及语用与认知研究的多个专辑，比如Cognitive aspects of language use (vol.12, 1988), Cognitive perspectives of language use (vol.16, 1991), Literary pragmatics: Cognitive metaphor and the structure of the poetic text (vol.25, 1995), On the cognitive aspects of cinematic and visual discourse (vol.26, 1996), Cognition and relevance (vol. 29, 1998)等，其中包括关联理论的理论探索与实践研究。此外，语言学期刊*Lingua*刊载了两期关联理论研究专辑（vol. 87, 1992；vol. 90, 1993），还有很多成果见于交际学、语篇研究、信息处理等方面的国际期刊。在《关联性：交际与认知》中，作者"直接研讨的理论问题涉及语用学、语义学、语篇分析、语言哲学、心理语言学、认知科学和修辞学，但其结论对其他一些学科也有直接的影响：计算语言

学、社会语言学、人工智能、逻辑学、译学、文学理论和交际传播研究"（蒋严 2008：1）。在该理论的应用方面，涉及"语文教学、语言测试、企业传讯公关、广告宣传、论辩实践策划、使用说服性话语设计，如竞选宣传、商品促销、保险经纪和地产租赁、买卖等等"（同上：1-2）。

需要指出的是，英国伦敦大学学院（University College London）特意成立了一个"关联理论研究小组"（Relevance Theory Research Group），一直坚持多年，Wilson教授在退休前带头参与该研讨活动；同时还开辟了"关联理论电邮通讯"（Relevance Theory E-mail List，简称RT List），就认知语用学的一些重大问题展开讨论与交流，或通告与关联理论有关的研讨会、讲习班等，持续至今。后来，西班牙学者Francisco Yus教授一直坚持收集、汇编和补充具有重要参考价值的关联理论研究参考文献，至今每月仍通过网络进行推送，这就是关联理论网络文献（the RT Online Bibliography），汇集了全球学者的主要研究成果，涉及与关联理论研究的很多问题，内容十分丰富。

从20世纪80年代末至今，《外语教学与研究》《外国语》《现代外语》等国内学术期刊也刊发了关联理论的评介文章和研究论文，还出版了研究文集，比如《语用与认知：关联理论研究》（何自然、冉永平 2001）等。有的学术著作涉及关联理论的认知语用思想，比如《认知语用学概论》（熊学亮 1999）等，有的著作涉及该理论的应用，比如《小说交际中言语反讽的认知语用研究》（赵虹 2016）、《语用翻译学》（李占喜 2017）等。不难看出，早期的研究成果主要是该理论的引入与评介，后逐步涉及该理论在语用学等领域里的广泛应用，包括部分博士学位论文。

下面我们介绍《关联性：交际与认知》一书的主要内容，以帮助读者理解关联理论及其交际思想。

2. 主要内容

2.1 全书概貌

本书第二版保留了第一版的主要内容，甚至连页码都一样，只是更正了印刷错误，增加了一些原文注释。两版的主要不同在于，第二版增加了一个长达25页的后记（postface），参考书目也从8页增加到20页。增加的参考书目和后记注释中提及的参考书目都体现了第一版后人们围绕关联理论及其应用研究所取得的一些主要成果。在第二版后记中，作者首先回顾了自关联理论提出以来该理论的发展概况，然后重点列举了对该理论的修正。

本书的第一版和第二版都分成四章，章节布局十分简单清楚。不过，Levinson（1989）指出，此书易读不易懂；整体不是一本容易念的书，讨论范围几乎涉及语用学的所有理论课题，其论证方式又相当复杂微妙乃至艰深（蒋严 2008）。

第一章"交际"，讨论关联理论的来源，综述作者的交际思想。"交际"这一概念是理解关联理论的中心，也是从交际角度理解关联理论的前提。交际涉及两个主要问题：（1）什么是明说信息？（2）哪些是隐含信息？交际的代码或语码模式（code model）只能回答第一个问题，却不能说明第二个问题，甚至纯推理模式（inferential model）也不能对整个交际过程进行合理的解释。因此，我们有必要从一个新的、更为综合的角度去分析交际。那么，交际指什么、它是如何发生的、影响交际的因素有哪些、交际成功的关键是什么等，作者对类似问题进行了全面论述。在20世纪70年代，人们以Grice会话含意理论为基本框架，开展了有关语用推理和自然语言理解的研究，但作为有关交际的一种推理理论，会话含意理论存在一定的解释力缺陷，涉及合作原则及其准则的来源、合理性等一系列问题。Grice努力通过引导人们识别隐含信息，即含意，为此他着力于交际的隐含层面，但如何从明说到隐含，则需要进行更为合理的认知语用阐释。对此类问题，会话含意理论显然存在解释力不足的问题。

Sperber 和 Wilson 对比了交际的代码或语码模式与推理模式，然后分析 Grice 交际理论存在的主要问题，接着讨论交际中的互知（mutual knowledge）假设、认知环境（cognitive environment）、互明（mutual manifestness）等与关联理论相关的重要概念。互知指人们在语言交际中随着交际内容或过程的变化，交际双方必须随时相互知道有关语境的所有信息。其实，在实际交际中这是不可能的。为此，Sperber 和 Wilson 认为互知不合常理，它不能反映交际双方的认知状态，因此主张用"互明"代替互知。认知环境就是交际双方所知道的、由一系列事实或假设所构成的信息集合，互明就是在一定认知环境中交际双方共同明白的类似事实或信息。认知环境的互明是决定交际能否成功的主要因素。

Sperber 和 Wilson 还指出，交际是涉及信息意图（informative intention）和交际意图（communicative intention）的一个明示–推理过程（ostensive-inferential process）。明示与推理是交际过程中的两个方面。从说话人的角度来说，交际是一种明示过程，也就是把信息意图明白地展现出来；从听话人的角度来说，交际又是一个推理过程，推理就是根据说话人的明示行为（比如话语、或非言语行为等），结合语境假设以及可能实现的语境效果，推知说话人的交际意图。

需要强调的是，关联理论的交际观并没有完全抛弃语码或代码模式，相反，认定编码与解码是推理的基础与前提。根据代码或语码模式，交际双方需要对信息进行编码、接收与解码，交际的成功取决于听话人的解码信息是否等同于说话人的编码信息。而推理模式则强调信息接收者对交际意图的推理。单一的代码或语码模式主张语用模块论，也即语用仅是语法规则的延伸与扩展。但 Sperber 和 Wilson 指出，代码或语码是推理的明示线索，是推理说话人交际意图的基础，他们反对将语用问题视为语言模块的延伸。总之，Sperber和Wilson认为，人类交际（语言的或非语言的）是一种认知活动。

第二章"推理"，是本书的难点所在。该章主要讨论了非论证性（non-demonstrative）推理、逻辑式、命题态度与实际假设、假设力度、演绎规则与概念、演绎系统或机制、演绎类型以及演绎在非论证性推理中的作用等。Sperber和Wilson指出，语用推理是非论证性的演绎推理，从一个假设推导出另一个假设，直到找出话语在交际语境下的最佳关联。语用推理不同于一般的逻辑推理，仅借助前提就可以得出正确的结论；在他们看来，语用推理依据的是逻辑信息、百科信息和词汇信息。Sperber和Wilson指出，信息的自动处理过程主要利用的是演绎推理，即利用消除规则（elimination rules），而不是引导规则（introduction rules），因为推理所依据的假设是消除规则的操作对象，也就是，可以排除或放弃原有的假设，从而产生语境下的新假设。这体现了语境中交际信息或交际意图的选择。

Sperber和Wilson的语用推理需要考虑语境，得出具有关联性的逻辑结论，这是一种交际信息的语境依赖。非关联性的逻辑结论不是推理出来的，与语用推理相关的假设，一方面涉及如何从诸如"明天我要考试"等话语，推理出"我不去看电影"之类交际信息的总体过程；另一方面需要考虑该过程中的每个动态环节，比如从一个假设推理出另一个假设的演绎过程中，如何通过推理补足话语的语义表征与其交际信息之间的信息差。在交际中，听话人需要对说话人的信息意图和交际意图进行推理，形成与话语交际目的相关的假设。在非论证性推理中，前提的正确不能保证结论一定是正确的，它只是有可能使结论正确。同时，根据Sperber和Wilson，推理就是进行假设与验证的过程；输入信息的真实与否并不影响其关联性（如小说等文学作品提供的不一定是真实的信息），推理中不同的逻辑分析可能会引发关联性的差异。

本章提出了"语境效果"这一重要概念。当话语的新信息与语境假设之间出现下述情况之一时，就是一种语境效果：

（1）新信息加强了现时的语境假设；

（2）新信息与现时的语境假设相互矛盾或抵触；

（3）新信息与现时的语境假设相结合，引发了一种语境隐含。

后来，Sperber和Wilson把这里的语境效果统称为一种"认知效果"。

第三章"关联性"，是本书的核心部分，也是重点与难点。Sperber和Wilson讨论了关联的条件、关联程度、语境观、语境选择、个人关联、现象与刺激的关联、关联原则以及对明示-推理交际的解释。关联性是制约演绎推理的原则，而语境效果是衡量关联性的一个必要条件，二者之间成正比关系，也就是，在同等条件下语境效果越大，其关联性就越强。然而，语境效果不是衡量关联性的唯一因素，还需要人们处理信息时在心理上付出一定的努力。这样一来，在其他条件相同的情况下，付出努力和关联性之间成反比关系，也就是，付出努力越多，话语的关联性就越弱；如果理解话语时心理上无须付出太多的努力，说明话语具有最大的关联性，就会因而取得最大的语境效果。由于语境效果和心理上付出努力属于思维过程中的非表征部分，关联性也就成了语境效果和付出努力之间的一种关系，它不能运算，不能被量化，只具有一定的心理特征。

关联性可以看作是从交际输入到认知过程中话语、思想、记忆、行为、声音、情景、气味等的一种特性。如果输入信息或内容受到人们的注意，并付出一定努力进行理解或处理，它就具有关联特性。至于什么使输入信息或内容值得人们注意，并付出努力去理解，则要看它是否会取得交际中的语境效果，是否值得在心理上付出努力对该信息进行加工处理，包括最终的信息选择。

关联原则不包括一条一条的准则，也不是交际中说话人可以随意遵循或违反的规定。实际上，关联原则是一条交际原则。根据该原则，语境中每一个明示的交际行为都应设想它本身具有最佳关联性。这是说，明示的每一个行为都存在这样的前提，也就是，它本身具有最佳关联性。当话语具有足够的关联性，值得听话人付出努力去加工理解，特别是当话语具有一定语境下的最大关联性，说话人又愿意并且能把它说出来时，那么该话语就是具有最佳关联性的话语（Wilson 2000）。

需要特别注意的是，Sperber 和 Wilson 提出了不同于传统意义的认知语境观。在关联理论中，语境也称为"语境假设"（contextual assumptions），在交际过程中双方互明的共知环境被视为一种"相互认知环境"（mutual cognitive environment）。在言语交际中，对话语理解起主要作用的是构成听话人认知环境的一系列假设，因此，语境不限于现实环境中的情景或话语本身所在的语言语境；言语交际中的语境不是双方事先知道的，也不是固定不变或静态的，而是动态的。关联理论将语境看作是在互动过程中为了正确理解话语而存在于人们大脑中的一系列假设。理解每一个话语所需要的语境因素是不同的，因此，听话人要在话语理解过程中为每一个话语建构新的语境。由于人们存在不完全相同的认知环境与认知结构，话语理解或信息推理也会因此得出不同的隐含结论，也即，出现不同的理解结果，甚至对同一话语出现误解或错误理解。总之，关联性是人类交际的基本制约，也是交际信息的一种特质，可被看作一个常量。而语境则是一个变量，语言的交际过程离不开认知环境的制约，涉及语境假设的形成、选择与检验。

第四章"言语交际的若干方面"，涉及如何利用关联理论解释交际中的某些语言现象。本章讨论的主要内容包括语言与交际之间的关系、言语交际中的明说与隐含、命题形式与隐含意义的识别、与命题形式及语体有关的预设效果、与隐含意义及语体有关的意境效果或诗意效果（poetic effects）、语言用法的描写与解释功能、刻意（literalness）言谈与隐喻、回声式话语（echoic utterances）与反语，最后分析了言语行为及其关联等问题。

围绕言语交际，Sperber 和 Wilson 重点区分了"明说"（explicature）与隐含（implicature）、刻意话语（literal utterance）与隐喻和反语等随意言谈（loose talk）之间的主要差异。Grice 会话含意理论所涉及的"说出"（saying）与含意（implicature）不完全相同于 Sperber 和 Wilson 提出的"明说"与隐含。Grice 的"说出"指话语直截了当所表达的命题内容，听话人只需对话语进行解码，便可以获取该话语的语义信息；Grice 的含意则与违反合作原则某准则有关，需通过语用推理才能获取话语的隐含信息，即一种交际意义。会话含意理论所关心的主要是隐含交际，而 Sperber 和 Wilson 同样重视交际中的明说和隐含。他们认为，从交际的明说到隐含信息，听话人需要根据说话人的明说得出隐含前提，再据此推理出交际语境中的隐含结论。

在 Grice 看来，交际中的隐喻、反语等是说话人刻意违反合作原则中某准则的语言现象，为此听话人能够推理其在语境中的特定含意。但根据 Sperber 和 Wilson 的说法，含意是语体学上的形象表达，属于随意言谈，并没有违反什么准则。在理解话语的喻意用法（如隐喻、夸张、反语等）时，我们不能只限于从中搜寻恰当的含意，还要努力获知它们产生的复杂效果，比如语体效果或意境效果等。此外，言语行为理论认为，说话是在实施一种行为，它可以是直接的或间接的；但是在很多情况下，对话语的言语行为所作的分析往往会忽略语言形式和命题态度之间可能存在的联系。陈述句、疑问句、祈使句等表达的言语行为只是说话人的信息意图，需要通过寻找关联来理解它们的施为用意（illocutionary force）。

总的来说，本章集中讨论的是关联理论对言语交际的应用价值，以此证明关联理论是一个可以提出问题和解决问题的语用框架。

2.2 关联理论的几个新修正

修订后的《关联性：交际与认知》第二版保留了第一版的基本内容。第二版的两个重要变化是：一方面，增加了一个后记，归纳介绍第一版后关联理论的研究与发展概貌；另一方面，通过增加大量的注释，对第二版的变化与修正进行必要说明。

（1）关联原则

在第一版，Sperber 和 Wilson 提出了一条关联原则，也就是，关联的交际原则。在第二版，该原则被改为了关联的第二原则，并增列了关联的第一原则，也就是，关联的认知原则：

关联的第一原则，即认知原则：人类认知倾向于同最大关联相吻合。

关联的第二原则，即交际原则：每个明示的交际行为都应设想它本身具有最佳关联。

其中，第一原则涉及人类认知，注意关联信息是一种基本的认知原则；第二原则与交际密切相关，在特定交际语境下人们获取的交际信息是该语境下最佳的关联信息。第二原则以第一原则为基础，第一原则可预测人们的认知行为，会对交际起导向作用。Sperber 和 Wilson 将关联原则由原来的一条改为两条，其目的是让大家注意到最大关联与最佳关联之间的差异，明确关联与认知的关系。

人类认知往往与最大关联相吻合，也就是，人们的认知往往始于最容易引起自己注意的信息。但在特定交际中，人们所期待的信息则是该语境下具有最佳关联的信息。在第一版，Sperber 和 Wilson 区分了最大关联和最佳关联。当人们理解话语时，付出尽可能少的努力而获得了最大的语境效果，该信息就具有最大关联；当人们理解话语时付出有效努力，并产生足够的语境效果，该信息就具有最佳关联。第一版只突出了关联的交际原则，因此引发了一些误解，以为 Sperber 和 Wilson 只主张最大关联这条单一原则，从而管束交际和认知的两方面。在第二版，他们改用了两条关联原则，帮助消除类似误解（Higashimori & Wilson 1996）。

（2）关联假设

受制于认知原则（第一原则）的影响，交际中的听话人会对交际信息产生什么样的关联期待呢？在第二版的后记，Sperber 和 Wilson 修改了原有的最佳关联假设，旨在解决第一版未涉及的问题。

不管交际中的听话人等信息接收者存在什么样的交际需求或期待，不能总希望说话人产出具有最大关联的话语，说话人可能不愿意或不可能提供最大关联的话语或以最恰当的方式呈现信息。最佳关联与话语理解所付出的认知努力和可能取得的语境效果紧密相关，最佳关联这一概念的提出是为了探究听话人应该产生什么样的期待。根据关联的交际原则（第二原则），每个明示的交际行为应被视为它本身具有最佳关联。在第一版中，Sperber 和 Wilson 曾指出，寻找关联就是指寻找最低限度的关联（即满足说话人的期待），只要找到关联就不再找了。但在第二版中，他们认识到，话语的关联性可以比期待的关联要大。为了取得特定的语境效果，在寻找关联的过程中，需进一步追求较高层次的关联。于是，他们提出了修改后的最佳关联假设（Sperber & Wilson 1995: 270）：

（a）明示刺激具有足够的关联，因而值得听话人付出努力，加工处理。

（b）明示刺激与说话人的能力和偏爱相一致，因而最具关联性。

相比之下，修改以后的关联假设在某些方面比旧假设更具解释力，更简单。因此，这是第二版在后记中提出的最具实质性的修改（Jucker 1997）。

（3）概念意义和过程意义

在第二版，Sperber 和 Wilson 强调了区分概念编码（conceptual encoding）与过程编码（procedural encoding）的重要性。话语可以对概念意义和过程意义进行编码。它们相当于 Blakemore（1992）所区分的"表述意义"和"过程意义"。前者涉及话语表达的明示信息和隐含意义，并通过增加话语的关联假设，提高明示交际行为的关联性；后者对理解明示信息和推导隐含意义的过程进行制约或指引，以让听话人付出较小的努力获取更大的语境效果。为了保证交际能够取得最佳关联，也就是，保证交际中明示的（非）语言成分（如话语或非言语行为等）有助于取得交际效果，并减少听话人话语理解时所付出的努力（也即，使话语更容易理解），说话人必须让听话人获得足够的关联。为了给听话人理解话语时寻找关联提供指引，Blakemore（1987）提出了关联的语义限制，也就是，通过情态指示语、话语联系语等的语言手段及其限制性作用，对听话人在话语理解中寻找关联，进行关联假设的限制，从而收窄范围，以便获取话语信息理解的最佳关联。这种给听话人的话语理解，提供过程指引，有助于提高明示交际活动的关联性，从而减少为信息理解所付出的努力。

（4）语境效果与语境假设的削弱

在第一版，Sperber 和 Wilson（1986: 108-117）指出，在一定语境下，只要新信息或话语产生任何一种语境效果，就说明它具有关联性：（a）新信息与现存的语境假设相互作用，产生语境含意；（b）新信息加强或证实现存的语境假设；（c）新信息与现存的语境假设相互矛盾或抵触。在第二版（Sperber & Wilson 1995: 294，第2章注释d）中，他们补充了另一种语境效果，也就是，新信息对现存语境假设的削弱（weakening）。他们指出，现存语境假设的加强或削弱都是一种具有关联性的语境效果。但现存语境假设在什么时候削弱呢？这里有两个问题：（a）削弱现存语境假设是否有助于获取话语的关联性？对此，Sperber 和 Wilson 持肯定态度，而且始终认为，现存语境假设的加强或削弱都对获取关联性起一定作用（ibid: 286，注释 26）；（b）与原来的三种语境效果一样，现存语境假设的削弱是否应该被看作第四种语境效果？Sperber 和 Wilson 认为，现存语境假设不可能被直接减损，只能将其当作语境效果的一种副产品（by-product），比如，当现存语境假设出现矛盾或抵触时，就会削弱因该假设而产生的语境隐含。因此，我们不应把现存语境假设的削弱看作一种独立的语境效果，它只对关联性起间接作用。

（5）正面认知效果

Sperber 和 Wilson（1995: 264-266）指出，关联信息是值得保留的信息，而错误信息一般是不值得保留的，因为它会降低认知效率（cognitive efficiency）。为了获知关联性与认知效率之间的直觉联系（intuitive connection），Sperber 和 Wilson 在第一版指出，关联性取决于语境（认知）效果和努力程度：语境效果越大，获取这些语境效果所付出的努力越小，关联性就越强。（无论正确或错误的）关联信息都是人们能够成功处理的信息，它们可以产生正确或错误的结论（一种语境效果）。在第二版后记 3.3.1（ibid: 271）中，他们便提出了以下问题：假设人们存在一定的错误信念（belief），且该错误信念提供的信息可能会被成功处理，进而出现更多的错误信念，那么，这是否会影响认知效率和关联性呢？为此，Sperber 和 Wilson 区分了两种认知效果：（a）正面认知效果（positive cognitive effects），比如正确的信念或认识，有利于提高认知效率，这显然是关联性在起作用；（b）其他认知效果，比如错误信念，就是不值得保留的，因而不具有关联性。在第二版中，作者在对"个人关联"界定时，所依据的就是正面认知效果和话语理解所付出的努力程度：正面认知效果越大，获取这些认知效果所付出的努力越小，关联性就越强。因而，认知效率与努力之间成反比关系。但须注意的是，只要错误信息产生了正面认知效果，它仍可能具有关联性。这就是说，输入信息的真实性既不是关联性的必要条件，也不是其充分条件，起作用的是输出信息的真实性。

3. 关联理论评述

（1）关联理论的理论意义

Grice（1975）提出会话含意理论后，推动了有关语用推理和交际信息理解的诸多研究。该意义理论认为，话语可以传递语义内容以外的信息，听话人能够识别话语的含意，因为人类交际受制于一定的普遍原则，比如他提出的"合作原则"（Grice 1975,1989）。Sperber 和 Wilson（1981: 155）一方面肯定了 Grice 理论的贡献，认为"现代话语理解理论是其'William James 系列讲座'的直接结果"；另一方面他们对 Grice 的语用学说进行了某些质疑和批评（Yus 1998; Schulz 1999）。尽管 Grice 的会话含意理论存在不足，但它为关联理论奠定了基本的思想基础。Sperber 和 Wilson 的交际认知观，特别是针对话语理解过程中的认知分析，既得益于 Grice 的贡献，也超越了 Grice 的会话含意理论学说。

关联理论从语言哲学、认知心理学、交际学等多学科的角度去阐释语言交际，它将认知分析与语用研究结合起来，将语用学研究的重点从话语的产出转移到话语的理解，指出语言交际是一个认知-推理的互明过程，对话语的理解就是一种认知活动。尽管关联理论不专门服务于语用学，但它对 Grice 的理论学说进行了修正和补充，进而丰富了语用学理论，比如，为（非）语言交际提供了认知语用学研究的理论框架。

Sperber 和 Wilson 指出，人类认知往往力求以最小的心理投入获取最大的认知效果。因此，在理解话语时，听话人只会关注并处理具有足够关联的话语，而且倾向于在与这些话语之间存在最大关联的语境中进行处理，并构建与这些话语之间存在足够关联的心理表征。Sperber 和 Wilson 认为交际中的语境是动态的，应被看作一个变项，包含一系列变化中的命题，只有关联性才是一个常项和一种必然。因此，关联理论的语境观不同于传统的语境认识：语境是一个心理建构体（psychological construct），由一系列假设构成；话语理解过程就是在语境假设与新信息之间进行推理的过程，其中对语境假设的选择、调整或证实，始终会受到关联原则的支配。

关联理论吸收了当代认知科学、心理学以及行为科学的研究成果。比如，Sperber 和 Wilson 借鉴 Fodor（1983）等的研究成果，探寻推理的心理机制，并认为认知系统包括逻辑信息、百科信息和词汇信息，它们构成了人们的认知环境。关联理论思想还体现了人类交际行为的"经济原则"（principle of economy）：以最少的投入获取最佳的交际效果。可见，关联理论存在多元化的理论背景，与以往的语言交际理论相比，存在更多的理论支撑或理论基础，因此具有更强的解释力。

（2）关联理论的应用价值

针对交际中的话语理解、信息处理与加工等，关联理论的解释力已得到普遍认可，具有广泛的应用价值。关联理论从一个不同于 Grice 会话含意理论的认知语用视角，对隐喻、转喻、幽默、反语、夸张等随意言谈或非刻意用法进行过较多分析研究，关联理论提出者之一 Deirdre Wilson 对隐喻的早期研究已说明它的应用价值和解释力。此外，借助该理论思想，我们可以探究交际语境中的歧义消除、指称意义选择与确定等，还有助于解释交际语境下词汇意义的收窄、扩充等信息加工；它可对包括语体、时态、情态动词、小品词、话语联系语、语用标记语等进行分析，也可用来分析话语或语篇中的文体特征、指称结构、省略形式等用法。

关联理论还被用来分析文学作品、传媒语篇（比如广告语、宣传语篇）、翻译等的信息处理，提供认知语用阐释。

鉴于交际中的话语使用与信息理解涉及认知环境，交际主体对特定语境下相关信息的认知解读就存在差异，从而导致不同理解。因此，关联理论还被用以分析母语、外语或第二语言中语篇阅读、听力理解等的信息处理或信息加工，就其中信息理解的成功、困难、误解等现象与问题提供认知语用阐释；也可以对跨文化跨语言交际中信息理解的失败与失误，如何扩大或丰富交际双方的认知环境，以取得相互之间的互明，从而实现交际成功等问题，进行关联理论阐释。这些都表明，关联理论对指导语言教学与语言学习等具有重要的理论与实践意义。不仅如此，关联理论还对非语言交际具有解释力。

（3）争鸣与不足

《关联性：交际与认知》出版后，关联理论及其交际观、语境观等就引发了较多肯定，也招致一定的批评或负面评价（Nemo 1988；Levinson 1989）。第二版之后，人们对关联理论的争论仍持续不断，也出现了更多的应用性研究。这正说明该理论的生机与活力。作为一种认知理论，它确实给我们解释交际带来了新视角，也推进了认知语用学的理论研究。不过，与任何别的理论一样，关联理论有其自身的局限性与不完备性，引起争议实属正常。Sperber 和 Wilson 在第二版后记中指出，他们的"交际理论提出以后已得到人们广泛的认可，同时也受到广泛批评与误解"（Sperber & Wilson 1995: 255）。Levinson（1989）很早就说过，《关联性：交际与认知》是一本大胆的、颇具争议的专著。Giora（1997, 1998）认为，关联理论不是管束人类语言交际的唯一理论。在 Giora 看来，关联原则可以解释人类的语言交际，但它并不是有关人类交际的唯一原则。语言交际不限于仅寻找话语的关联性，也需考虑话语的意义连贯等问题。

针对Giora对关联理论的认识与异议，Wilson（1998）认为Giora感兴趣的是话语连贯及其程度，包括话语的规范与恰当，以及话语的可接受程度、意义凸显等问题。但Wilson和Sperber认为，话语连贯恰好取决于关联；只要话语具备了关联，它在意义上就是连贯的。根据Giora，听话人可能觉得话语具有（最大）关联，但会同时认为该话语的意义是不连贯的；另一方面，话语可能不具有最大关联，但听话人却认为它是连贯的。据此，Wilson认为，Giora没有区分最佳关联的交际原则与最大关联的认知原则，将它们混在一起了。她和Sperber坚持认为，我们应该根据最佳关联及关联原则去判断话语的可接受性和连贯性。

在针对关联理论的相关评论中，有些质疑或负面认识是因为误解或不完全理解所导致的。比如，有学者（如Goatly 1994）认为Sperber和Wilson没有重视交际的社会规约，忽略了社会文化制约对寻找话语信息的关联所起的作用。有的甚至认为，仅从认知的角度来解释交际而不考虑社会因素，那是'缺乏社会性的'（asocial）理论模式。Talbot（1997）指出，现实生活中相互交往的人是社会的人，具有一定的社会文化属性，因此语言交际等会受到社会规约的影响与限定。此外，也有学者（如Mey & Talbot 1988; O'Neill 1988-89; Talbot 1993）指出，关联理论将交际者之间的个体差异看作个人的认知环境差异及其相关的认知能力差异，从而忽略了社会文化等共同因素对语言交际和信息处理的普遍影响。针对类似误解，Sperber曾在2000年5月20日通过"关联理论网上通讯"进行了解释，并指出关联理论是一种认识论方面的理论（epistemological theory）。参与网上讨论的学者，如Borsley也指出，持有以上误解的读者往往关注的是交际的社会作用，而不是实现交际的认知过程。Jary（1998）也驳斥过以上误解，指出关联理论并没有忽视社会文化因素的作用，还可以解释一定的社会语言学问题。就关联理论而言，Sperber和Wilson的目的在于阐释人们是如何成功实现交际的，作为交际主体的人是信息的处理者，但他们并没有否认人的社会属性。就交际中语言结构的礼貌特征问题，Jary（ibid）甚至认为关联理论框架下的分析要比 Brown & Levinson（1978）从社会文化角度下的解释更令人信服。Escandell-Vidal（1996）也认为，从认知出发可以分析话语理解等所涉及的社会文化特征及其差异，他还从认知角度探讨了礼貌现象，指出"关联理论可以为礼貌的理论阐释提供一个恰当的框架"（ibid: 638），解释话语理解中礼貌的关联性，说明交际中所产生的（非）礼貌效果。从认知语用的角度出发，Sperber 和Wilson 认为礼貌不是固有形式，礼貌或不礼貌是语言形式和认知环境相互作用的结果。

根据关联理论，交际在于通过明示行为改变双方的认知环境。听话人需要利用互明假设（mutually manifest assumptions），推理出说话人的交际意图。然而，说话人的互明假设本身包含他对交际者的社会地位、人际关系等的所知或推导信息，因此在说话人产出话语之前，实际上已考虑或参照了相关的社会因素等影响交际的非语言制约。可见，关联理论并没有忽略社会文化因素对交际的影响与制约，也就是说，该理论不是一种'缺乏社会性'的理论模式。在话语产出与理解过程中，社会文化等语境信息可为话语的交际信息推理提供某种方向，有助于取得该话语所在语境下的交际效果或认知效果。

诚然，关联理论没有足够重视语言使用的规约性等对话语理解的作用，因该理论过于强调交际主体的能动性、认知语境假设等的制约与调节作用，这样就容易突显关联性和交际信息等的个体差异。不过，常规性与能动性、普遍性与差异性等在话语理解过程中到底是如何相互作用的，这对任何语言交际理论来说都是具有挑战性的问题。对此，Sperber 和Wilson 也没有在《关联性：交际与认知》一书中进行讨论或直接给出答案。

  Sperber 和 Wilson 将话语理解的关联性看作是一种必然，认为话语理解的结果（如交际信息）是由认知主体在具体交际过程中根据语境变项作出的选择与确定。然而，关联理论并没有对该结果的必然性与或然性问题进行阐释，给人们的深入系统研究留下了悬念与空间。关联理论中的"关联（性）"是一个相对的、有程度之分的概念，它取决于话语所取得的语境效果的大小与理解该话语所付出的努力程度。在同等条件下，语境效果越大，其关联性就越强；如果话语理解时所付出的努力越大，其关联性就越小；反之，如果话语理解时所付出的努力越小，其关联性就越强。因此，语境效果与理解时付出的努力是制约关联性的两个正反因素。可是，关联理论似乎又告诉我们，听话人要获取话语所产生的语境效果以决定他需付出多大程度的努力，而语境效果反过来又由努力的程度决定。这样，决定话语关联性的语境效果与为理解付出的努力就陷入了难以自救的矛盾循环之中，二者究竟哪一个因素决定另一个仍显得有些模糊，需进一步明确阐述。

  此外，如果"关联（性）"这一概念不与产生特定交际意义的话语联系起来，也会显得很抽象。综观全书，两位作者 Sperber 和 Wilson 只是根据语境效果和话语理解或信息处理所付出的心理投入或认知努力这两个因素去衡量关联性，却没有给出一个可以明确衡量、容易操作或计算的标准。不过，话语信息产生的语境效果和为之付出的心理投入或认知努力既然是一种心理过程，就是难以准确衡量的，多数情况下只能凭直觉进行判断了，这也是信息处理或话语理解存在个体差异的主要原因。衡量关联性是话语理解的手段与过程，而不是目的，因为根据关联的交际原则，特定语境下的每个话语或明示交际行为应设想它本身具有最佳关联性。至于如何让话语理解的心理过程具有可操作性，也是认知心理学等学科需要共同努力探讨的问题。通过本著作，Sperber 和 Wilson 旨在提出关联理论的框架思路，因此他们没有提供足够的动态语料，来支撑和检验该理论的解释力，这也是导致著作内容难以理解的原因之一。如果Sperber和Wilson能够结合更多真实的交流话语，进行关联理论框架下的理论阐释，就能让读者更加充分地认识该理论的解释力和实用价值。

针对《关联性：交际与认知》的相关缺陷与质疑，Sperber和Wilson在早期经常借助"关联理论网上通讯"进行回应，后来主要通过学术期刊的研究论文阐述自己的见解。当然，与任何语言学理论一样，关联理论尚需进一步发展，最终评价尚不确定，不过它至今仍是一个具有解释力的认知语用学理论框架，已在国际语言学界受到广泛关注与应用。近40年来，综观国际学术刊物发表的有关论文和国际出版社出版的著作，关联理论对语用学等多个领域的学术贡献已得到肯定，这也体现了该理论的生命力。

4. 对关联理论的国际评价

Sperber和Wilson出版的《关联性：交际与认知》"开启了探究人类交际与理解能力的一个新阶段，对认知与其阐释具有更广的重要价值"（Carston, Clark & Scott 2019/2022: 1）。"作者试图将语用学理论的重点转移到认知的一般理论上来"（Levinson 1989: 25）。"关联理论已被证明是一个强大的理论建构，它重新审视了语用推理在话语理解中的作用，及其与认知科学诸多方面的关系"（Horn 1996: 316）。所以，《关联性：交际与认知》是语用学方面最具影响的著作之一（Jucker 1997），给语用学研究提供了新的理论思路。

"关联理论给认知语用学带来了新生"（Yus 1998: 333）。关联理论从认知的角度揭示人类交际的共性。"本著作很可能成为一部经典之作，不仅因为它对语言学、认知心理学及人类学具有潜在影响，而且在于它提出的是一种涉及范围广和具有独创性的理论"（Pascal Engel, *Revue Philosophique*，本书第二版封底）。可见，关联理论不仅是为语用学而提出的，还可用于阐释与人类认知、人际交际、人机交流、网络信息处理等有关的很多问题（Yus 2019; Scott 2022）。

还有很多的类似评价，在此不一一列举。我们向那些"对语言学、语言哲学和语用学感兴趣的人们，当然还包括符号学爱好者，推荐本著作"（Umberto Eco, L'Expresso，本书第二版封底）。同时，"这也可能是你阅读过的有关交际的最佳著作"（*Rhetoric Society Quarterly*）。

参考书目

Blakemore, Diane. 1987. *Semantic Constraints on Relevance.* Oxford: Blackwell.

Blakemore, Diane. 1992. *Understanding Utterances: An Introduction to Pragmatics.* Oxford: Blackwell.

Blakemore, Diane. 2002. *Relevance and Linguistic Meaning: The Semantics and Pragmatics of Discourse Markers.* Cambridge: Cambridge University Press.

Blass, Regina. 1990. *Relevance Relations in Discourse.* New York: Cambridge University Press.

Brown, Penelope & Stephen. Levinson. 1978. Universals in language usage: Politeness phenomena. In E. N. Goody (ed.) *Questions and Politeness.* Cambridge: Cambridge University Press, 56-289.

Carston, Robyn. & Seiji Uchida. 1997. *Relevance Theory: Application and Implications.* Amsterdam: John Benjamins.

Carston, Robyn, Billy Clark & Kate Scott. 2019/2022. Introduction. In Kate Scott, Billy Clark & Robyn Carston (eds.) *Relevance, Pragmatics and Interpretation.* Cambridge: Cambridge University Press, 1-10.

Clark, Billy. 2013. *Relevance Theory.* Cambridge: Cambridge University Press.

Cole, Peter & Jerry Morgan. 1975. *Syntax and Semantics 3: Speech Acts.* New York: Academic Press.

Escandell - Vidal, Victoria. 1996. Towards a cognitive approach to politeness. *Language Sciences* 18: 629-650.

Fodor, Jerry. 1983. *Modularity of Mind.* Cambridge. MA: MIT Press.

Giora, Rachel. 1997. Discourse coherence and theory of relevance: Stumbling blocks in search of a unified theory. *Journal of Pragmatics* 27: 17-34.

Giora, Rachel. 1998. Discourse coherence is an independent notion: A Reply to Deirdre Wilson. *Journal of Pragmatics* 29: 75-86.

Goatly, Andrew. 1994. Register and the redemption of relevance theory: The case of metaphor. *Pragmatics* 4: 139-181.

Goody, Esther. 1978. *Questions and Politeness: Strategies in Social Interaction.* Cambridge: Cambridge University Press.

Grice, Herbert Paul. 1975. Logic and conversation. In Peter Cole & Jerry Morgan (eds.) *Syntax and Semantics* (Vol.3). New York: Academic Press, 41-58.

Grice, Herbert Paul. 1989. *Studies in the Way of Words.* Cambridge, MA: Harvard University Press.

Gutt, Esther. A. 1991. *Translation and Relevance: Cognition and Context.* Oxford: Blackwell.

Higashimori, Isao & Deirdre Wilson. 1996. Questions on

relevance. *Working Papers in Linguistics* 8, University College London.

Horn, Larry. 1996. Presupposition and implication. In Shalom Lappin (ed.) *The Handbook of Contemporary Semantic Theory*. Oxford: Blackwell.

Ifantidou, Elly. 2001. *Evidentials and Relevance*. Amsterdam: John Benjamins.

Ifantidou, Elly. 2014. *Pragmatic Competence and Relevance*. Amsterdam: John Benjamins.

Jary, Mark. 1998. Is relevance theory asocial. *Revista Alicantina de Estudios Ingleses* 11: 157-169.

Jucker, Andreas H. 1997. A review of *Relevance: Communication and Cognition*. *Journal of Pragmatics* 27: 107-119.

Levinson, Stephen. 1989. A review of *Relevance*. *Journal of Linguistics* 25: 455-472.

Mey, Jacob & Mary Talbot. 1988. A review of *Relevance: Communication and Cognition*. *Journal of Pragmatics* 12: 743-789.

Nemo, Francois. 1988. A review of *Relevance: Communication and Cognition*. *Journal of Pragmatics* 12: 791-795.

O'Neill, John, 1988-89. Relevance and pragmatic inference. *Theoretical Linguistics* 15 (1988-89): 241-261.

Rouchota, Villy & Andreas H. Jucker. 1998. *Current Issues in Relevance Theory*. Amsterdam: John Benjamins.

Schulz, Ralph. 1999. Relevance theory and Grice's ideas. Paper presented at the seminar "Relevance Theory", University of Wales, Bangor.

Scott, Kate. 2022. *Pragmatics Online*. London: Routledge.

Scott, Kate, Billy Clark & Robyn Carston. 2019/2022. *Relevance, Pragmatics and Interpretation*. Cambridge: Cambridge University Press.

Sperber, Dan & Deirdre Wilson. 1981. On Grice's theory of conversation. In Paul Werth (ed.) *Conversation and Discourse*. London: Croom Helm, 155-178.

Sperber, Dan & Deirdre Wilson. 1986/1995. *Relevance: Communication and Cognition*. Oxford: Blackwell.

Talbot, Mary. 1993. Relevance theory. In Ron E. Asher (ed.) *The Encyclopedia of Language and Linguistics*. Oxford: Pergamon Press.

Talbot, Mary. 1997. Relevance. In Peter V. Lamarque & Ron E. Asher (eds.) *Concise Encyclopedia of Philosophy of Language*. New York: Pergamon.

Tanaka, Keiko. 1994. *Advertising Language*. London: Routledge.

Wilson, Deirdre. 1998. Discourse, coherence and relevance. *Journal of Pragmatics* 29: 57-74.

Wilson, Deirdre. 2000. 关联与交际。《现代外语》, 第2期: 210-217。

Yus, Francisco. 1998. A decade of relevance theory. *Journal of Pragmatics* 30: 305-345.

Yus, Francisco, 2019,《网络语用学：网络语境中的交际》。上海：上海外语教育出版社。

何自然、冉永平, 2001,《语用与认知：关联理论研究》。北京：外语教学与研究出版社。

蒋严（译）, 2008,《关联：交际与认知》。北京：中国社会科学出版社。

李占喜, 2017,《语用翻译学》。广州：暨南大学出版社。

熊学亮，1999，《认知语用学概论》。上海：上海外语教育出版社。

赵虹，2016，《小说交际中言语反讽的认知语用研究》。济南：山东大学出版社。

Contents

Contents

Preface to Second Edition

In this book, first published nine years ago, we present a new approach to the study of human communication. This approach (outlined in chapter 1) is grounded in a general view of human cognition (developed in chapters 2 and 3). Human cognitive processes, we argue, are geared to achieving the greatest possible cognitive effect for the smallest possible processing effort. To achieve this, individuals must focus their attention on what seems to them to be the most relevant information available. To communicate is to claim an individual's attention: hence to communicate is to imply that the information communicated is relevant. This fundamental idea (developed in chapter 3), that communicated information comes with a guarantee of relevance, is what in the First Edition we called the *principle of relevance* and what we would now call the *Second*, or *Communicative Principle of Relevance* (see the Postface to this Second Edition). We argue that this principle of relevance is essential to explaining human communication, and show (in chapter 4) how it is enough on its own to account for the interaction of linguistic meaning and contextual factors in utterance interpretation.

Here is how this book came about. In 1975, Deirdre Wilson published *Presuppositions and Non-Truth-Conditional Semantics* and Dan Sperber published 'Rudiments de rhétorique cognitive', a sequel to his *Rethinking Symbolism*. In these works, we were both turning to pragmatics – the study of contextual factors in verbal communication – but from different perspectives: Deirdre Wilson was showing how a number of apparently semantic problems could be better solved at a pragmatic level; Dan Sperber was arguing for a view of figures of speech rooted in pragmatics. We then formed the project of writing, in a few months, a joint essay which would cover, at least programmatically, the ground between our two vantage points and show the continuities and discontinuities between semantics, pragmatics and rhetoric. Work did not proceed according to plan. We got involved in carrying out the programme we had merely intended to outline. The months became years. The projected essay became a series of papers and the present book.

This Second Edition preserves the text of the original, except for the correction of typographical errors, removal of obvious mistakes and inconsistencies, updating of existing references, and addition of a few explanatory notes. In a new Postface, we sketch the main developments in the theory since the First Edition was published, and argue for some revisions both of formulation and of substance.

A number of people, who have helped us by their encouragements and criticisms, bear part of the responsibility for our failure to stick to our original plan of writing a short, programmatic sketch: Scott Atran, Regina Blass, Michael Brody, Sylvain Bromberger, Annabel Cormack, Martin Davies, Sue George, Paul Grice, Ernst-August Gutt, Sam Guttenplan, Jill House, Pierre Jacob, Phil Johnson-Laird, Aravind Joshi, Jerry Katz, Stephen Levinson, Rose MacLaran, George A. Miller, Dinah Murray, Stephen Neale, Yuji Nishiyama, Ellen Prince, Anne Reboul, François Récanati, Michael Rochemont, Nicolas Ruwet, Dorota Rychlik, Tzvetan Todorov, Charles Travis and Bonnie Webber. Dan Sperber is particularly grateful to Monique Canto-Sperber, Catherine Cullen and Jenka and Manès Sperber; and Deirdre Wilson to her colleagues Diane Blakemore, Robyn Carston, Ruth Kempson and Neil Smith, and especially her husband, Theodore Zeldin. For this Second Edition, we have benefited from the comments, suggestions and support of the members of the Relevance e-mail group.

List of symbols

P, Q individual assumptions

U an utterance

A   a set of assumptions made manifest by an utterance

C   a set of contextual assumptions

I   a set of assumptions the communicator intended to make manifest

P   a set of newly presented assumptions

1, 2   notes to First Edition

a, b   notes to Second Edition

1

Communication

How do human beings communicate with one another? For verbal communication at least, there is a sort of folk answer, suggested by a variety of metaphors in everyday use: 'putting one's thoughts into words', 'getting one's ideas across', 'putting one's thoughts down on paper', and so on.[1] These make it sound as if verbal communication were a matter of packing a *content* (yet another metaphor) into words and sending it off, to be unpacked by the recipient at the other end. The power of these figures of speech is such that one tends to forget that the answer they suggest cannot be true. In writing this book, we have not literally put our thoughts down on paper. What we have put down on paper are little dark marks, a copy of which you are now looking at. As for our thoughts, they remain where they always were, inside our brains.

Suppose it were physically possible to transport thoughts from one brain to another, as programs and data stored on a magnetic disk can be transported from one computer to another: then communication would be unnecessary (whether it might still be useful, for reasons of speed or economy, is another matter). But thoughts do not travel, and the effects of human communication cannot be achieved by any other means.

Communication is a process involving two information-processing devices. One device modifies the physical environment of the other. As a result, the second device constructs representations similar to representations already stored in the first device. Oral communication, for instance, is a modification by the speaker of the hearer's acoustic environment, as a result of which the hearer entertains thoughts similar to the speaker's own. The study of communication raises two major questions: first, what is communicated, and second, how is communication achieved?

What is communicated? Meanings, information, propositions, thoughts, ideas, beliefs, attitudes, emotions, are some of the answers which have been proposed. More than one of them may well be true.

Certainly, what is communicated by a religious ritual is quite different from what is communicated by a list of stock-exchange rates. Even within the domain of verbal communication, a poem and a legal document seem to communicate profoundly different things. Nonetheless, we will argue in section 11 of this chapter that there is a general answer to this question.

For the time being, we will talk quite informally of the communication of thoughts, assumptions, or information. By *thoughts*, we mean conceptual representations (as opposed to sensory representations or emotional states). By *assumptions*, we mean thoughts treated by the individual as representations of the actual world (as opposed to fictions, desires, or representations of representations). Some authors (e.g. Dretske 1981) use the terms 'information' and 'inform' to talk only of the representation and transmission of facts; for them, all information is by definition true. We will use the terms more broadly, treating as information not only facts, but also dubious and false assumptions presented as factual. In section 8, we will characterise information more precisely. In chapter 2, we will consider the structure of thoughts and assumptions in some detail.

Even more important than the question of what is communicated is the question of how communication is achieved. How can a physical stimulus bring about the required similarity of thoughts, when there is no similarity whatsoever between the stimulus and the thoughts it brings into correspondence? Here again, it is worth considering whether there is a single, general answer. Should there be – can there be – a general theory of communication? Most authors, insofar as they are aware of the issue at all, seem to think that there can, and should.

Let us approach this question in terms of another. Clearly, no one would waste much time trying to invent a general theory of locomotion. Walking should be accounted for in terms of a physiological model, plane flight in terms of an engineering model. While it is true that both walking and plane flight fall under the same physical laws, these laws are much too general to constitute a theory of locomotion either. Thus, locomotion is either too general or not general enough to be the object of an integrated theory. It is worth considering whether this might not be the case for communication too.

There seems to be a general agreement that there can, and should, be a general theory of communication. From Aristotle through to modern semiotics, all theories of communication were based on a single model, which we will call the *code model*. According to the code model, communication is achieved by encoding and decoding messages. Recently, several philosophers, notably Paul Grice and David Lewis, have proposed a quite different model, which we will call the *inferential model*. According to the inferential model, communication is achieved by producing and interpreting evidence.

The code model and the inferential model are not incompatible; they can be combined in various ways. The work of pragmatists, philosophers of language and psycholinguists over the past twenty years has shown that verbal communication involves both coding and inferential processes. Thus both the code model and the inferential model can contribute to the study of verbal communication. However, it is usually assumed that one of the two models must provide the right overall framework for the study of communication in general. Most authors take for granted that a proper theory of communication should be based on the familiar code model; a few philosophers seem tempted to develop the inferential model into an inferential theory of communication.

Against these reductionist views, we maintain that communication can be achieved in ways which are as different from one another as walking is from plane flight. In particular, communication can be achieved by coding and decoding messages, and it can be achieved by providing evidence for an intended inference. The code model and the inferential model are each adequate to a different mode of communication; hence upgrading either to the status of a general theory of communication is a mistake. Both coded communication and inferential communication are subject to general constraints which apply to all forms of information processing, but these are too general to constitute a theory of communication either.

Some modes of locomotion involve the interaction of quite different mechanisms: bicycle riding, for instance, involves both physiology and engineering. Similarly, verbal communication involves both code and inferential mechanisms. In trying to construct an adequate description of these two types of mechanism and their interaction, it is important to realise that they are intrinsically independent of one another, and that communication in general is independent of either.

In sections 1 to 3 of this chapter we will discuss the code theory, and in sections 4 to 7, the inferential theory. In discussing the views of code and inferential theorists, our aim is to contrast two extreme approaches so as to map out the full range of available choices; it is not to do justice to those who have defended subtly qualified, or cautiously vague, versions of either. In sections 8 to 12 of this chapter and in chapters 2 and 3, we will propose what we hope is an improved inferential model. However, we do not regard this model as the basis for a general theory of communication. In chapter 4, we will show instead how it can be combined with a code model to provide an explanatory account of verbal communication.

1 The code model and the semiotic approach to communication

A *code*, as we will use the term, is a system which pairs messages with signals, enabling two information-processing devices (organisms or machines) to communicate. A *message* is a representation internal to the communicating devices. A *signal* is a modification of the external environment which can be produced by one device and recognised by the other. A simple code, such as the Morse code, may consist of a straightforward list of message–signal pairs. A more complex code, such as English, may consist of a system of symbols and rules generating such pairs.

A widely quoted[2] diagram of Shannon and Weaver (1949), slightly adapted in figure 1, shows how communication can be achieved by use of a code:

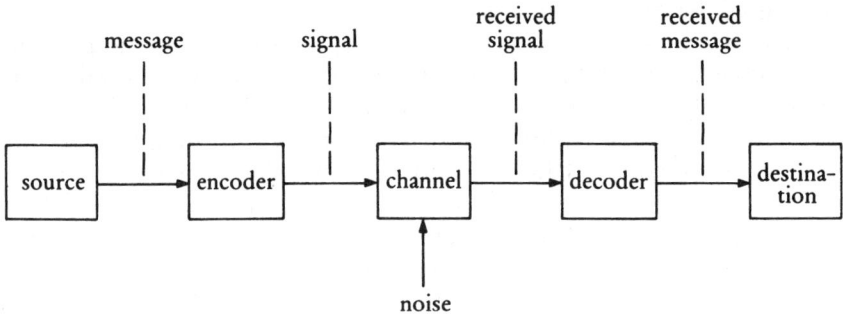

Figure 1

This diagram shows how a message originating in an information source can be duplicated at a destination as the result of a communication process. For instance, the source and the destination could be telecommunications employees, the encoder and the decoder telex machines, the channel an electric wire, the message a text, i.e. a series of letters, and the signal a series of electrical impulses. The message is typed by the source on the encoder's keyboard. The encoder contains a code which associates each letter to a distinct pattern of electrical impulses. The encoder sends these impulses through the channel to the decoder. The decoder contains a duplicate of the encoder's code, and uses it to deliver to the destination the series of letters and signs associated by the code to the electrical impulses it has received.

Communication is achieved by encoding a message, which cannot travel, into a signal, which can, and by decoding this signal at the receiving end. Noise along the channel (electrical disturbances in our example) can destroy or distort the signal. Otherwise, as long as the devices are in order and the codes are identical at both ends, successful communication is guaranteed.

In this example, the communicating devices are neither the telecommunications employees nor the telex machines but the man–machine pairs on both sides. This apparent complication is, in fact, illuminating. It shows what the relevant internal structure of any device capable of coded communication would have to be. Consider the case of honey bees. Von Frisch (1967) has shown that bees can encode into flight patterns (their 'dance') what they have learnt about the location of nectar, so that other bees can decode the information and find the nectar in their turn. To account for this communicative ability, bees must be seen as containing two information-processing sub-devices: a memory (which constitutes the 'source' on the one side and the 'destination' on the other) in which plans for flying towards a supply of nectar can be stored, and an encoder–decoder device which pairs messages consisting of flight plans with signals consisting of dances.

It may seem that a similar model could be proposed for human verbal communication, as shown in figure 2:

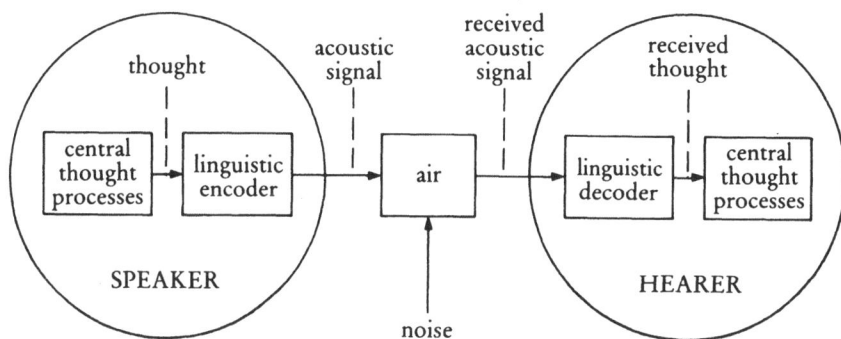

Figure 2

Here the source and the destination are central thought processes, the encoder and the decoder are linguistic abilities, the message is a thought, and the channel is air which carries an acoustic signal. There are two assumptions underlying this proposal: the first is that human languages, such as Swahili or English, are codes; the second is that these codes associate thoughts with sounds.

While Shannon and Weaver's diagram is inspired by telecommunications technology, the basic idea is quite old, and was originally proposed as an account of verbal communication. To give just two examples: Aristotle claimed that 'spoken sounds are symbols of affections in the soul', which are themselves 'likenesses of actual things' (Aristotle, *De Interpretatione*: 43). In our terms, he claimed that utterances encode assumptions. Arnauld and Lancelot in their famous *Grammaire de Port-Royal* describe language as the marvellous invention of composing out of 25 or 30 sounds that infinite variety of words, which tho' they have no natural resemblance to the operations of the mind, are yet the means of unfolding all its secrets, and of disclosing unto those, who cannot see into our hearts, the variety of our thoughts, and our sentiments upon all manner of subjects.

Words therefore may be defined as distinct and articulate sounds, made use of by men as signs, to express their thoughts. (Arnauld and Lancelot, *Grammaire de Port-Royal*: 22)

The view of linguistic communication as achieved by encoding thoughts in sounds is so entrenched in Western culture that it has become hard to see it as a hypothesis rather than a fact. Yet the code model of verbal communication is only a hypothesis, with well-known merits and rather less well-known defects. Its main merit is that it is explanatory: utterances do succeed in communicating thoughts, and the hypothesis that they encode thoughts might explain how this is done. Its main defect, as we will shortly argue, is that it is descriptively inadequate: comprehension involves more than the decoding of a linguistic signal.

The semiotic approach to communication (as Peirce called it and we will call it ourselves), or the semiological approach (as Saussure and his followers called it), is a generalisation of the code model of verbal communication to all forms of communication. Todorov (1977) dates it back to Augustine, who approached the study of grammar, logic, rhetoric and hermeneutics within the unifying framework of a theory of signs. Systems of signs were seen as governing not just the ordinary verbal communication of thoughts, but also the poetic effects of tropes, communication by gestures, religious symbols and rites, and the interpretation of sacred texts.

From a semiotic point of view, the existence of an underlying code is the only possible explanation of how communication is achieved. Here is how the psychologist Vygotsky formulated this 'axiom':

That understanding between minds is impossible without some mediating expression is an axiom for scientific psychology. In the absence of a system of signs, linguistic or other, only the most primitive and limited type of communication is possible. Communication by means of expressive movements, observed mainly among animals, is not so much communication as spread of affect ... Rational, intentional conveying of experience and thought to others requires a mediating system, the prototype of which is human speech. (Vygotsky 1962: 6)

Whenever communication is observed, an underlying system of signs is postulated, and the task of the semiotician is seen as that of reconstructing it. Saussure's formulation of the programme is well known:

> Language is a system of signs that express ideas, and is therefore comparable to a system of writing, the alphabet of deaf-mutes, symbolic rites, polite formulas, military signals, etc. But it is the most important of all these systems.
>   *A science that studies the life of signs within society* is conceivable . . . I shall call it *semiology*. (Saussure 1974: 16)

The semiotic programme has been enthusiastically adopted by a number of linguists, literary theorists, psychologists, sociologists and anthropologists. Here is an anthropologist's endorsement:

> I shall assume that *all* the various non-verbal dimensions of culture, such as style in clothing, village lay-out, architecture, furniture, food, cooking, music, physical gestures, postural attitudes and so on are organised in patterned sets so as to incorporate coded information in a manner analogous to the sounds and words and sentences of a natural language. I assume therefore it is just as meaningful to talk about the grammatical rules which govern the wearing of clothes as it is to talk about the grammatical rules which govern speech utterances. (Leach 1976: 10)

The recent history of semiotics has been one of simultaneous institutional success and intellectual bankruptcy. On the one hand, there are now departments, institutes, associations, congresses and journals of semiotics. On the other, semiotics has failed to live up to its promises; indeed, its foundations have been severely undermined. This is not to deny that many semioticians have done invaluable empirical work. However, it does not follow that the semiotic framework has been productive, let alone theoretically sound; merely that it has not been entirely sterilising, or that it has not been strictly adhered to in practice.[3]

Saussure expected that 'the laws discovered by semiology will be applicable to linguistics, and the latter will circumscribe a well-defined area within the mass of anthropological facts' (1974: 16). What actually happened was that for the few decades in which structuralist linguistics flourished, the semiotic program was taken seriously and spelled out in more detail. Linguists such as Hjelmslev (1928, 1959) and Kenneth Pike (1967) developed ambitious terminological schemes as tools for carrying it out. However, no semiotic law of any significance was ever discovered, let alone applied to linguistics. After the publication in 1957 of Noam Chomsky's *Syntactic Structures*, linguistics took a new turn and did undergo remarkable developments;[4] but these owed nothing to semiotics. As the structure of language became better understood, its *sui generis* nature became more and more striking. The assumption that all systems of signs should have similar structural properties became more and more untenable. Without this assumption, however, the semiotic programme makes little sense.

Saussure made a further prediction:

> By studying rites, customs, etc. as signs, I believe that we shall throw new light on the facts and point up the need for including them in a science of semiology and explaining them by its laws. (1974: 17)

Here again, valiant attempts were made by anthropologists such as Lévi-Strauss or literary theorists such as Barthes to approach cultural or artistic symbolism in semiotic terms. In the course of these attempts, they certainly shed new light on the phenomena, and drew attention to many interesting regularities; but they never came near to discovering an underlying code in the strict sense: that is, a system of signal–message pairs which would explain how myths and literary works succeed in communicating more than their linguistic meaning, and how rites and customs succeed in communicating at all.

This failure is instructive. What a better understanding of myth, literature, ritual, etc., has shown is that these cultural phenomena do not, in general, serve to convey precise and predictable messages. They focus the attention of the audience in certain directions; they help to impose some structure on experience. To that extent, some similarity of representations between the artists or performers and the audience, and hence some degree of communication, is achieved. However, this is a long way from the identity of representations which coded communication is designed to guarantee. It is not clear how the type of communication involved in these cases could be explained in terms of the code model at all.

A semiotician might reply as follows. Granted that the best models we have of human languages are generative grammars: since a generative grammar just is a code which associates phonetic representations of sentences to semantic representations of sentences, it follows that the code model is applicable to verbal communication. Other forms of communication, say those involving Morse signals or traffic lights, are also adequately described in terms of the code model. As for rites, customs and the arts, although the semiotic approach is unable to deal with them yet, there is no well-developed alternative approach either. Hence, the code model is still the only available explanation of how communication is possible at all.

We will try to show that this line of argument is invalid. It is true that a language is a code which pairs phonetic and semantic representations of sentences. However, there is a gap between the semantic representations of sentences and the thoughts actually communicated by utterances. This gap is filled not by more coding, but by inference. Moreover, there is an alternative to the code model of communication. Communication has been described as a process of inferential recognition of the communicator's intentions. We will try to show how this description can be improved and made explanatory.[5]

2 Decoding and inference in verbal comprehension

As already mentioned, a generative grammar is a code which pairs phonetic and semantic representations of sentences. Since an utterance can generally be perceived as a realisation of the phonetic representation of a single sentence (or in the case of phonetic ambiguity, two sentences), it is reasonable to regard the phonetic representations of sentences as corresponding closely to the actual sounds of speech. By contrast, since most sentences can be used to convey an infinite number of different thoughts, the semantic representations of sentences cannot be regarded as corresponding very closely to thoughts. In constructing a general picture of verbal communication, it is thus a legitimate idealisation (though pheneticians might not agree) to ignore the differences between phonetic representations of sentences and acoustic realisations of utterances. However, it is not legitimate to ignore the differences between the semantic representations of sentences and the thoughts that utterances are used to convey.

Crucial here is the difference between *sentences* and *utterances*. An utterance has a variety of properties, both linguistic and non-linguistic. It may contain the word 'shoe', or a reflexive pronoun, or a trisyllabic adjective; it may be spoken on top of a bus, by someone with a heavy cold, addressing a close friend. Generative grammars abstract out the purely linguistic properties of utterances and describe a common linguistic structure, the sentence, shared by a variety of utterances which differ only in their non-linguistic properties. By definition, the semantic representation of a sentence, as assigned to it by a generative grammar, can take no account of such non-linguistic properties as, for example, the time and place of utterance, the identity of the speaker, the speaker's intentions, and so on.

The semantic representation of a sentence deals with a sort of common core of meaning shared by every utterance of it. However, different utterances of the same sentence may differ in their interpretation; and indeed they usually do. The study of the semantic representation of sentences belongs to grammar; the study of the interpretation of utterances belongs to what is now known as 'pragmatics'.[6]

To illustrate, consider sentences (1)–(3):

(1) I'll come tomorrow.
(2) Bill is tall.
(3) Betsy's gift made her very happy.

A generative grammar cannot determine who 'I', 'Bill' and 'Betsy' refer to, and which day 'tomorrow' picks out. It can only provide some very general indications. It might state, for example, that 'I' always refers to the speaker, that 'Bill' and 'Betsy' refer to people or other entities with those names, and that 'tomorrow' picks out the day after the utterance. This is not enough to determine which thought is expressed when sentences such as (1)–(3) are uttered. For instance, if John says (1) on 25 March, it expresses the thought that John will come on 26 March; if Ann says (1) on 30 November, it expresses the thought that Ann will come on 1 December. The grammar can say nothing about how the hearer, using non-linguistic information, determines on a particular occasion what the time of utterance actually is, who the speaker is, which Bill or Betsy the speaker has in mind, etc., and hence which thought is actually being expressed. These aspects of interpretation involve an interaction between linguistic structure and non-linguistic information, only the former being dealt with by the grammar.

Other aspects of the interpretation of (1)–(3) left unspecified by the grammar are where the speaker of (1) is planning to come, by what criteria Bill is tall (since, for instance, a tall dwarf is not a tall person), and in what sense the ambiguous word 'gift' is to be taken. In every case, the grammar can only help determine the possibilities of interpretation. How the hearer sets about narrowing down and choosing among these possibilities is a separate question. It is one that grammarians, but not pragmatists, can ignore: an adequate theory of utterance interpretation must answer it.

Examples (1)–(3) show that as a result of referential indeterminacy such as that of 'Bill', semantic ambiguity such as that of 'gift', and semantic incompleteness such as that of 'tall', a single sentence, with a single semantic representation, can express an unbounded range of thoughts. There are still other factors widening the gap between sentence meaning and utterance interpretation.

The same sentence, used to express the same thought, may sometimes be used to present this thought as true, sometimes to suggest that it is not, sometimes to wonder whether it is true, sometimes to ask the hearer to make it true, and so on. Utterances are used not only to convey thoughts but to reveal the speaker's attitude to, or relation to, the thought expressed; in other words, they express 'propositional attitudes', perform 'speech-acts', or carry 'illocutionary force'.

To illustrate, consider sentences (4) and (5):

(4) You're leaving.
(5) What an honest fellow Joe is.

It makes a difference to the interpretation of (4) whether the speaker is informing the hearer of a decision that he is to leave, making a guess and asking him to confirm or deny it, or expressing outrage at the fact that he is leaving. It makes a difference to the interpretation of (5) whether the speaker is being sincere or ironical, making a literal claim or speaking figuratively. Often, the linguistic structure of the utterance suggests a particular attitude, as, for example, interrogative form most naturally suggests that the utterance is a request for information. However, as examples (4)–(5) show, the hearer is generally left a certain latitude, which he must make up on the basis of non-linguistic information.

Moreover, an utterance which explicitly expresses one thought may implicitly convey others. Whereas a thought that is explicitly expressed must be in some kind of correspondence to the semantic representation of the sentence uttered, those that are implicitly conveyed are under no such constraint. Consider utterances (6) and (7):

(6) Do you know what time it is?
(7) Coffee would keep me awake.

The speaker of (6), while explicitly asking whether the hearer knows the time, might be implicitly suggesting that it is time to go. The speaker of (7), while making an explicit assertion about the effect of coffee, might be implicitly refusing or forestalling an offer of coffee (or in other circumstances, implicitly soliciting or accepting such an offer).

Examples (1)–(7) show a variety of ways in which the semantic representation of the sentence uttered may fall short of being a complete interpretation of an utterance in context. As we have seen, code theorists must show which code it is that makes verbal communication possible. On closer examination, the claim that human languages, as described by grammars which pair phonetic and semantic representations of sentences, are codes of the required type is not borne out. This is not the end of the code model of verbal communication, however. One might still assume that the code involved is more complex than a grammar: rather than being a grammar, it might merely contain a grammar as a sub-part.

To justify the code model of verbal communication, it would have to be shown that the interpretation of utterances in context can be accounted for by adding an extra pragmatic level of decoding to the linguistic level provided by the grammar. Much recent work in pragmatics has assumed, largely without question, that this can be done. Pragmatics has been treated, on the analogy of phonology, syntax and semantics, as a code-like mental device, underlying a distinct level of linguistic ability. It is widely accepted that there are rules of pragmatic interpretation much as there are rules of semantic interpretation, and that these rules form a system which is a supplement to a grammar as traditionally understood.

There are certainly pragmatic phenomena which lend themselves to this sort of approach. For example, a pragmatic device might contain rules of interpretation such as (8) and (9):

(8) Substitute for 'I' a reference to the speaker.
(9) Substitute for 'tomorrow' a reference to the day after the utterance.

Imagine a hearer equipped with such rules and able to recognise that the speaker of (1) is Ann and the date of utterance is 30 November. He could automatically interpret utterance (1) as conveying the thought in (10):

(1) I'll come tomorrow.
(10) Ann will come on 1 December.

However, most aspects of utterance interpretation cannot be handled so easily. Consider (11) and (12):

(11) He's got egg on his tie.
(12) That's interesting.

It presumably follows from the grammar of English that the referent of 'he' must be male and the referent of 'that' must be non-human. However, (11) and (12) are unlike (1) in that on virtually every occasion of utterance, there is more than one referent meeting these conditions. The assignment of actual referents in these cases must clearly involve something much more complicated than rules (8) and (9).

To substantiate the code model of verbal communication, it would have to be shown that every case of reference assignment can be dealt with by rules which automatically integrate properties of the context with semantic properties of the utterance. It would also have to be shown that disambiguation, the recovery of propositional attitudes, figurative inter-pretations and implicit import can be handled along similar lines. Nothing approaching such a demonstration has ever been given.

While still assuming that the code model provides the framework for a general theory of communication, and hence for a theory of verbal communication, most pragmatists have described comprehension as an inferential process. Inferential and decoding processes are quite different. An *inferential process* starts from a set of premises and results in a set of conclusions which follow logically from, or are at least warranted by, the premises. A *decoding process* starts from a signal and results in the recovery of a message which is associated to the signal by an underlying code. In general, conclusions are not associated to their premises by a code, and signals do not warrant the messages they convey.

To illustrate the difference between coding and inferential processes, consider (13)–(15):

(13) (a) Either Mary is early or Bob is late.
  (b) Bob is never late.
(14) [mɛəriːɪzɜːliː]
(15) Mary is early.

That Mary is early, i.e. (15), can be either inferred from the premises in (13) or decoded from the phonetic signal in (14), but the converse is not true: (15) can be neither decoded from (13) nor inferred from (14). It cannot be decoded from (13) because there is no code identifying (13) as a signal and (15) as its associated message. It cannot be inferred from (14) because signals do not by themselves warrant the messages they encode (otherwise any absurdity could be transformed into a warranted assumption merely by uttering it).

The view that utterance interpretation is a largely inferential process squares well with ordinary experience. Consider (16)–(18), for instance:

(16) Jones has bought the *Times*.
(17) Jones has bought a copy of the *Times*.
(18) Jones has bought the press enterprise which publishes the *Times*.

Sentence (16) is ambiguous, and can be understood as conveying either (17) or (18). Ordinary hearers in ordinary circumstances have no trouble choosing one of these two meanings, usually without even realising that they have made a choice. When the ambiguity is pointed out and they are asked to explain how they know which interpretation is correct, they generally offer something that looks like a truncated logical argument: the speaker must have intended this interpretation rather than that, because this is the only interpretation that is true; or the only one that gives the required information; or the only one that makes sense.

For instance, hearers asked why they understood 'Jones has bought the *Times*' to mean 'Jones has bought a copy of the *Times*' rather than 'Jones has bought the press enterprise which publishes the *Times*' might answer: 'because the other interpretation could not be true', or 'because the question was whether I should buy a copy of the *Times* myself'. The assumption behind these truncated arguments is that speakers set themselves certain standards, of truthfulness, informativeness, comprehensibility, and so on, and only try to communicate information that meets the standards set. As long as speakers systematically observe the standards, and hearers systematically expect them to, a whole range of linguistically possible interpretations for any given utterance can be inferentially dismissed, and the task of communication and comprehension becomes accordingly easier. The same types of truncated argument, based on implicit standards, are invoked by hearers to justify their interpretation of referential expressions, illocutionary force, figures of speech and implicit import.

Modern pragmatists, inspired by the work of Grice,[7] have tried to describe these implicit standards of verbal communication more explicitly and show how they are used in comprehension. The mental processes involved have not been described in any detail, but everybody agrees that they are inferential. As we have said, inferential processes are quite different from decoding processes. Does it follow that pragmatists who hold to the code model, and yet describe comprehension in inferential terms, are being inconsistent? Not necessarily: an inferential process can be used as part of a decoding process.

Let us use an artificial example to show how inference can double as decoding. Imagine two partners who know (when nobody else around them knows) that (19) is true, who want to let one another know whether (20) is true, and who do not want bystanders to benefit from the information:

(19) Bob is in Miami.
(20) The speaker will leave the party.

They can use the standard inference rule (21) as a decoding rule, treat utterances (22) and (23) as signals, and thus convey by use of these signals messages (24) and (25) respectively:

(21) *Premises*: If P then Q
$$P$$
Conclusion: Q

(22) If Bob is in Miami, I'll leave the party.
(23) If Bob is in Miami, I won't leave the party.
(24) The speaker will leave the party.
(25) The speaker will not leave the party.

In this example, we have an inferential process simultaneously functioning as a decoding process. However, for this to be possible several conditions have to be fulfilled: first, speaker and hearer must share the tacit premise (19); second, they must share the inference rule (21); and third, they must use that premise and that rule to the exclusion of any other tacit premise or inference rule at their disposal. Otherwise, the signal will not be properly decoded.

Do speakers and hearers in ordinary verbal communication generally achieve a similar parallelism of premises and inference rules? If not, the inferential processes involved in verbal comprehension cannot qualify as decoding processes. To defend the code model of verbal communication, it must be shown, then, how speaker and hearer can come to have not only a common language, but also common sets of premises, to which they apply identical inference rules in parallel ways.

For language, the demonstration is fairly straightforward. The evidence suggests that speakers with quite different linguistic histories may end up with very similar grammars. Any number of different examples will do to illustrate a particular aspect of linguistic structure – say, the relative clause – so that it does not much matter which utterances of the language the child actually hears. It is also clear that after a certain point, the structure of the language has essentially been mastered, so that as new utterances are encountered, the grammar of an adult speaker will hardly change at all. The requirement of a common language thus presents no real difficulty for the code model.

Although the question of inference rules has not been dealt with in the pragmatic literature, it is arguable that the development of inferential abilities is similar in relevant respects to that of linguistic abilities. That is, any application of an inference rule will give grounds for its adoption. Thus different experiences with inferential processes may nevertheless converge on the same logical system. A more serious problem is that logical systems, as described by logicians, allow infinitely many different conclusions to be derived from the same premises. How, then, is the hearer to infer just those conclusions intended by the speaker? A solution to this problem will be proposed in the next chapters.

However, as we will show in the next section, the claim that speaker and hearer can and do restrict themselves to a set of common premises is much harder to maintain.

3 The mutual-knowledge hypothesis

The set of premises used in interpreting an utterance (apart from the premise that the utterance in question has been produced) constitutes what is generally known as the *context*. A context is a psychological construct, a subset of the hearer's assumptions about the world. It is these assumptions, of course, rather than the actual state of the world, that affect the interpretation of an utterance. A context in this sense is not limited to information about the immediate physical environment or the immediately preceding utterances: expectations about the future, scientific hypoth-

eses or religious beliefs, anecdotal memories, general cultural assumptions, beliefs about the mental state of the speaker, may all play a role in
interpretation.

While it is clear that members of the same linguistic community
converge on the same language, and plausible that they converge on the
same inferential abilities, the same is not true of their assumptions about
the world. True, all humans are constrained by their species-specific
cognitive abilities in developing their representation of the world, and all
members of the same cultural group share a number of experiences,
teachings and views. However, beyond this common framework, individuals tend to be highly idiosyncratic. Differences in life history
necessarily lead to differences in memorised information. Moreover, it has
been repeatedly shown that two people witnessing the same event – even a
salient and highly memorable event like a car accident – may construct
dramatically different representations of it, disagreeing not just on their
interpretation of it, but in their memory of the basic physical facts.[8] While
grammars neutralise the differences between dissimilar experiences,
cognition and memory superimpose differences even on common experiences.

Grammars and inferential abilities stabilise after a learning period and
remain unchanged from one utterance or inference to the next. By
contrast, each new experience adds to the range of potential contexts. It
does so crucially in utterance interpretation, since the context used in
interpreting a given utterance generally contains information derived
from immediately preceding utterances. Each new utterance, while
drawing on the same grammar and the same inferential abilities as previous
utterances, requires a rather different context. A central problem for
pragmatic theory is to describe how, for any given utterance, the hearer
finds a context which enables him to understand it adequately.

A speaker who intends an utterance to be interpreted in a particular way
must also expect the hearer to be able to supply a context which allows that
interpretation to be recovered. A mismatch between the context envisaged
by the speaker and the one actually used by the hearer may result in a
misunderstanding. Suppose, for example, that the speaker of (7) wants to
stay awake, and therefore wants to accept his host's offer of coffee,
whereas the host assumes that the speaker does not want to stay awake,
and thus interprets (7) as a refusal:

(7) Coffee would keep me awake.

Clearly, this difference between actual and envisaged contexts will lead to
a misunderstanding. Of course such misunderstandings do occur. They
are not attributable to noise in the acoustic channel. The question is
whether they happen because the mechanisms of verbal communication

are sometimes improperly applied, or because these mechanisms at best make successful communication probable, but do not guarantee it. We will pursue this second alternative. Most pragmatists opt for the first: they try to describe a failsafe mechanism which, when properly applied and not disrupted by noise, would guarantee successful communication.

The only way to make sure that misunderstandings such as the one described above could not arise would be to make sure that the context actually used by the hearer was always identical to the one envisaged by the speaker. How can this be done? Since any two people are sure to share at least a few assumptions about the world, they should use only these shared assumptions. However, this cannot be the whole answer, since it immediately raises a new question: how are the speaker and hearer to distinguish the assumptions they share from those they do not share? For that, they must make second-order assumptions about which first-order assumptions they share; but then they had better make sure that they share these second-order assumptions, and that calls for third-order assumptions. Some pragmatists stop here (e.g. Bach and Harnish 1979) and consider it of no practical importance that in principle, as noticed by others (Schiffer 1972; Clark and Marshall 1981), the same problem arises for third-order assumptions, calling for fourth-order assumptions, and so on indefinitely.

Consider a relevant example from the literature on reference assignment:

> On Wednesday morning Ann and Bob read the early edition of the newspaper, and they discuss the fact that it says that *A Day at the Races* is showing that night at the Roxy. When the late edition arrives, Bob reads the movie section, notes that the film has been corrected to *Monkey Business*, and circles it with his red pen. Later, Ann picks up the late edition, notes the correction, and recognizes Bob's circle around it. She also realizes that Bob has no way of knowing that she has seen the late edition. Later that day Ann sees Bob and asks, 'Have you ever seen the movie showing at the Roxy tonight?' (Clark and Marshall 1981: 13)

The question is, which film should Bob take Ann to be referring to? As Clark and Marshall point out, although Ann and Bob both know that the film showing at the Roxy is *Monkey Business*, and Ann knows that Bob knows that it is, this degree of shared knowledge is not enough to guarantee successful communication. Bob might reason that although he knows that the film actually showing is *Monkey Business*, Ann might still think it is *A Day at the Races*, and be referring to that. Or he might decide that she must have seen the marked correction, have realised that he knows the film is *Monkey Business*, and be referring to that. Or perhaps he might think that though she must have seen the correction, she will realise that he has no way of knowing that she has, so she will in fact be referring to *A Day at the Races*. Or maybe she has seen the correction and expects him to realise that she has seen it, but is not sure he will realise that she will realise that he will realise that she has seen it; and so on *ad infinitum*.

Clark and Marshall conclude that the only way to guarantee successful communication is for Ann not only to know what the film showing at the Roxy actually is, but to know that Bob knows what it is, and that Bob knows that she knows what it is, and that he knows that she knows that he knows what it is, and so on indefinitely. Similarly, Bob must not only know what the film showing at the Roxy actually is, but know that Ann knows what it is, and that she knows that he knows what it is, and that she knows that he knows that she knows what it is, and so on indefinitely. Knowledge of this infinitely regressive sort was first identified by Lewis (1969) as *common knowledge*, and by Schiffer (1972) as *mutual knowledge*.[9] The argument is that if the hearer is to be sure of recovering the correct interpretation, the one intended by the speaker, every item of contextual information used in interpreting the utterance must be not only known by the speaker and hearer, but mutually known.

Within the framework of the code model, mutual knowledge is a necessity. If the only way to communicate a message is by encoding and decoding it, and if inference plays a role in verbal communication, then the context in which an utterance is understood must be strictly limited to mutual knowledge; otherwise inference cannot function as an effective aspect of decoding. But as virtually everyone who has touched on the topic has noticed, it is hard to see how the requirement of mutual knowledge could ever be built into a psychologically adequate account of utterance production and comprehension. Someone who adopts this hypothesis is thus inevitably forced to the conclusion that when human beings try to communicate with each other, they are aiming at something they can never, in fact, achieve.

If mutual knowledge is necessary for communication, the question that immediately arises is how its existence can be established. How exactly do the speaker and hearer distinguish between knowledge that they merely share, and knowledge that is genuinely mutual? To establish this distinction, they would have, in principle, to perform an infinite series of checks, which clearly cannot be done in the amount of time it takes to produce and understand an utterance. Hence, even if they *try* to restrict themselves to what is mutually known, there is no guarantee that they will succeed.

Many pragmatists have accepted this conclusion and argued that mutual knowledge is not a reality but 'an ideal people strive for because they . . . want to avoid misunderstanding whenever possible' (Clark and Marshall 1981: 27). Now while it is true that people sometimes go to great lengths to avoid misunderstanding, such efforts are the exception and not the rule. In legal proceedings, for instance, there really is a serious attempt to establish mutual knowledge among all the parties concerned: all laws and precedents are made public, all legitimate evidence is recorded, and only legitimate evidence can be considered, so that there is indeed a restricted domain of mutual knowledge on which all parties may call, and within which they must remain. There is no evidence of any such concern in normal conversation, however serious or formal it is. All sorts of risks are taken, assumptions and guesses made. There is no indication that any particular striving after mutual knowledge goes on.

Enormous energy has been spent on trying to develop an empirically defensible approximation to the mutual knowledge requirement. It has been argued that in certain circumstances, speaker and hearer are justified in assuming that they have mutual knowledge, even though its existence cannot be conclusively established. For example, if two people can see each other looking at the same thing, they have grounds for assuming mutual knowledge of its presence. If some information has been verbally given in their joint presence, they are justified in assuming mutual knowledge of it. If some fact is known to all members of a community, two people who think they recognise each other as members of that community have grounds for assuming mutual knowledge of that fact. In none of these cases, though, can there be any certainty of mutual knowledge. People may look at the same object and yet identify it differently; they may impose different interpretations on information that they are jointly given; they may fail to recognise facts. In all these cases, the individual would be wrong in assuming mutual knowledge.

There is a paradox here. Since the assumption of mutual knowledge may always be mistaken, the mutual-knowledge hypothesis cannot deliver the guarantees it was set up to provide. If Bob may be mistaken in assuming that he and Ann have mutual knowledge of the fact that the film playing at the Roxy is *Monkey Business*, he cannot be sure of having correctly understood which film she is referring to. Bob's painstaking but inconclusive attempt at ascertaining mutual knowledge does not really protect him from the risk of misunderstanding. So why go to all that trouble?

There is yet another paradox in the idea that speaker and hearer might reasonably come to assume, but with something less than certainty, that they have mutual knowledge of some fact. By the very definition of mutual knowledge, people who share mutual knowledge *know* that they do. If you do not *know* that you have mutual knowledge (of some fact, with someone), then you do not have it. Mutual knowledge must be certain, or else it does not exist; and since it can never be certain it can never exist.

The apparent fallback position for the code theorist would be to replace the requirement of mutual knowledge by that of mutual probabilistic assumptions. This more realistic proposal raises an obvious problem. In general, the higher the order of the assumptions involved in such a scheme, the less likely they are to be true. Bob may know for a fact that *Monkey Business* is the film playing tonight; in the absence of compelling evidence, he should feel less certain that Ann assumes that he knows it, and even less certain that she assumes that he assumes that she assumes that he knows it, and so on. The assumption of mutuality itself, which is the highest ordered one, will have the weakest probability. How, then, could restricting the context to mutual assumptions ensure the identity or near-identity of premises which the code model requires?

Another problem with the mutual-knowledge hypothesis is that even if it defines a class of *potential* contexts for use in utterance interpretation, it says nothing about how an actual context is selected, nor about the role of context in comprehension. Take the following utterance:

(26) The door's open.

Speaker and hearer might have shared knowledge of hundreds of different doors; the mutual-knowledge requirement does nothing to explain how the choice of an actual referent is made.

Bach and Harnish (1979: 93) spend some time justifying their particular version of the mutual-knowledge hypothesis, but add that their pragmatic theory says little about 'the specific strategy the hearer uses to identify a particular communicative intent. It gives no indication of how certain mutual beliefs are activated or otherwise picked out as relevant, much less how the correct identification is made.' But in that case, the adoption of the mutual-knowledge hypothesis is just whistling in the dark. Until we know something about how contexts are actually selected and used in utterance interpretation, the belief that they must be restricted to mutual knowledge has no justification apart from the fact that it follows from the code model.[10]

Pragmatists have no positive argument that individuals engaging in verbal communication can and do distinguish mutual from non-mutual knowledge. Their only argument is a negative one: if mutual knowledge does not exist in the form required by the code model of verbal communication, then the code model is wrong. Since they see the code model as the only possible explanation of communication, they cling to the mutual-knowledge hypothesis.

Instead of adopting the code model, seeing that it commits us to the mutual-knowledge hypothesis, and then having to worry about how this hypothesis can be empirically justified, we want to approach things the other way around. We see the mutual-knowledge hypothesis as untenable. We conclude, therefore, that the code theory must be wrong, and that we had better worry about possible alternatives.

4 Grice's approach to 'meaning' and communication

In 1957, Paul Grice published an article, 'Meaning', which has been the object of a great many controversies, interpretations and revisions.[11] In this article, Grice proposed the following analysis of what it is for an individual S to mean something by an utterance x (where 'utterance' is to be understood as referring not just to linguistic utterances but to any form of communicative behaviour):

'[S] meant something by x' is (roughly) equivalent to '[S] intended the utterance of x to produce some effect in an audience by means of the recognition of this intention'. (Grice 1957/1971: 58)

Strawson's reformulation of this analysis (Strawson 1964a/1971: 155; see also Schiffer 1972: 11) separates out the three sub-intentions involved. To mean something by x, S must intend

(27) (a) S's utterance of x to produce a certain response r in a certain audience A;
    (b) A to recognise S's intention (a);
    (c) A's recognition of S's intention (a) to function as at least part of A's reason for A's response r.

This analysis can be developed in two ways. Grice himself used it as the point of departure for a theory of 'meaning', trying to go from the analysis of 'speaker's meaning' towards such traditional semantic concerns as the analysis of 'sentence meaning' and 'word meaning'. For reasons which should become apparent, we doubt that very much can be achieved in this direction. However, Grice's analysis can also be used as the point of departure for an inferential model of communication, and this is how we propose to take it. In the rest of this section we will show how this analysis applies to the description of communication. In the next three sections we will consider some of the objections and reformulations which have been proposed. Finally, in the last five sections of this chapter, we will develop our own model.

There are situations in which the mere fact that an intention is recognised may lead to its fulfilment. Suppose that Mary intends to please

Peter. If Peter becomes aware of her intention to please him, this may in itself be enough to please him. Similarly, when the inmates of a prison recognise their warder's intention to make them fear him, this may be enough in itself to make them fear him. There is one type of intention for which this possibility, rather than being exceptional, is regularly exploited: intentions to inform are quite generally fulfilled by being made recognisable.

Suppose that Mary intends to inform Peter of the fact that she has a sore throat. All she has to do is let him hear her hoarse voice, thus providing him with salient and conclusive evidence that she has a sore throat. Here, Mary's intention can be fulfilled whether or not Peter is aware of it: he could realise that she has a sore throat without also realising that she intends him to realise that she has one. Suppose now that Mary intends, on 2 June, to inform Peter (truly or falsely) that she had a sore throat on the previous Christmas Eve. This time she is unlikely to be able to produce *direct* evidence of her past sore throat. What she can do, though, is give him direct evidence, not of her past sore throat, but of her present intention to inform him of it. How can she do this, and what good will it do? One way she can do it is by uttering (28), and the good it will do is to give Peter *indirect*, but nevertheless strong, evidence that she had a sore throat on the previous Christmas Eve:

(28) I had a sore throat on Christmas Eve.

In our first example, Mary's hoarse voice is most likely to have been caused by her sore throat. The fact that she has spoken hoarsely is thus direct evidence for the assumption that she has a sore throat. Mary's utterance of (28) on 2 June is not directly caused by her having had a sore throat on the previous Christmas Eve. Hence her utterance is not direct evidence for the assumption that she had a sore throat on the previous Christmas Eve. However, her utterance *is* directly caused by her present intentions. Although she might have had various intentions in uttering (28), it is most likely that she intended to inform Peter that she had a sore throat on the previous Christmas Eve. This makes Mary's utterance direct evidence of her present intention to inform Peter of her past sore throat.

Suppose now that Peter assumes that Mary is sincere and is likely to know whether or not she had a sore throat on the previous Christmas Eve. Then for Peter, the fact that Mary intends to inform him that she had a sore throat on that date provides conclusive evidence that she had. In these quite ordinary conditions, Mary's intention to inform Peter of her past sore throat can be fulfilled by making Peter recognise her intention. This is not an exceptional way of fulfilling an intention to inform an audience. Let us assume that it is precisely how Mary intends to have her intention fulfilled. Then she does have all three sub-intentions of the Grice–Strawson definition (27), as shown in (29):

(29) Mary intends
    (a) her utterance (28) to produce in Peter the belief that she had a sore throat the previous Christmas Eve;
    (b) Peter to recognize her intention (a);
    (c) Peter's recognition of her intention (a) to function as at least part of his reason for his belief.

Mary's intentions in this example are quite similar in structure to those we all have when we communicate, verbally or otherwise.

We have shown two different ways of conveying information. One way is to provide direct evidence for the information to be conveyed. This should not be regarded as a form of communication: any state of affairs provides direct evidence for a variety of assumptions without necessarily *communicating* those assumptions in any interesting sense. Another way of conveying information is to provide direct evidence of one's intention to convey it. The first method can only be used with information for which direct evidence can be provided. The second method can be used with any information at all, as long as direct evidence of the communicator's intentions can be provided. This second method is clearly a form of communication; we will call it, for the time being, *inferential communication* (and, in section 10, *ostensive–inferential communication*): it is inferential in that the audience infers the communicator's intention from evidence provided for this precise purpose.

The description of communication in terms of intentions and inferences is, in a way, commonsensical. We are all speakers and hearers. As speakers, we intend our hearers to recognise our intention to inform them of some state of affairs. As hearers, we try to recognise what it is that the speaker intends to inform us of. Hearers are interested in the meaning of the sentence uttered only insofar as it provides evidence about what the speaker means. Communication is successful not when hearers recognise the linguistic meaning of the utterance, but when they infer the speaker's 'meaning' from it. This is shown by the following easily verifiable observation: when hearers realise that the speaker has misused a word or made a slip of the tongue, they generally discount the wrong meaning. The meaning they discount, however, need not be ill-formed or undecodable; it is 'wrong' only in that it provides misleading evidence about the speaker's intentions.

From a psychological point of view, the description of communication in terms of intentions and inferences also makes good sense. The attribution of intentions to others is a characteristic feature of human cognition and interaction. Humans typically conceptualise human and animal behaviour, not in terms of its physical features, but in terms of its underlying intentions. For instance, an ordinary-language concept such as *give*, *take*, *attack* or *defend* applies to various forms of behaviour which do not fall under any characteristic physical description, and have in common only the kind of intention which governs them. Human interaction is largely determined by the conceptualisation of behaviour in intentional rather than physical terms. The idea that communication exploits this ability of humans to attribute intentions to each other should be quite intelligible, and even appealing, to cognitive and social psychologists.

So it seems that we all know – semioticians included – that communication involves the publication and recognition of intentions. Yet until Grice, the significance of this truism was generally ignored;[12] attempts to describe and explain communication continued to be based on one form or another of the code model. Grice's original idea, as presented in his 1957 paper, can thus be seen as an attempt to rehabilitate a commonsense view of communication and spell it out in theoretically acceptable terms. However, the elaboration of this idea in the work of Grice himself, Strawson, Searle, Schiffer and others has often taken the form of a move away from common sense, away from psychological plausibility, and back to the code model. This unfortunate development resulted from the discovery of part spurious, part genuine problems with Grice's original formulation.

5 Should the code model and the inferential model be amalgamated?

We have now looked at two models of communication. According to the code model, communication is achieved by encoding and decoding messages. According to the inferential model, communication is achieved by the communicator providing evidence of her[13] intentions and the audience inferring her intentions from the evidence. Several questions come to mind. Are these two different models of the same thing? If so, must we choose between them, or can they be amalgamated in some way? Or are they, as we have hinted, models of two quite different things? If so, how are these things related?

Most theorists see communication as a unitary phenomenon, to be described by a single model. The code model is very well entrenched in the Western scholarly tradition. The inferential model appeals to common sense. When an appealing new approach is put forward, the temptation is to treat it not as an alternative to the old approach but as an elaboration of it. This is what most pragmatists have done, almost unconsciously, with

Grice's analysis. John Searle at least takes the trouble to justify this reaction.[14] He claims that Grice's analysis

> fails to account for the extent to which meaning can be a matter of rules and conventions. This account of meaning does not show the connection between one's meaning something by what one says, and what that which one says actually means in the language. (Searle 1969: 43)

Searle wants to improve on Grice's account by showing the connection between speaker's meaning and linguistic meaning. His first step is to restrict the application of this account to the domain of 'literal meaning'. This he defines in terms of the speaker's intentions, including the intention to have her intentions recognised, but adds a rider: the speaker should intend the hearer to recognise her intentions 'in virtue of his knowledge of the rules for the sentence uttered' (Searle 1969: 48). In other words, the speaker should intend the hearer to understand her by *decoding* her utterance.

This reduces Grice's analysis to a commonsense amendment of the code model. The code model is reintroduced as the basic explanation of communication, but in the case of human communication, the message that is encoded and decoded is regarded as a communicator's intention. If Searle's revision is justified, then Grice's analysis is not a genuine alternative to the code model after all.

Grice's greatest originality was not to suggest that human communication involves the recognition of intentions. That much, as already pointed out, is common sense. It was to suggest that this characterisation is sufficient: as long as there is some way of recognising the communicator's intentions, then communication is possible. Recognition of intentions is an ordinary human cognitive endeavour. If Grice is right, the inferential abilities that humans ordinarily use in attributing intentions to each other should make communication possible even in the absence of a code. And of course it *is* possible.

For example, Peter asks Mary,

(30) How are you feeling today?

Mary responds by pulling a bottle of aspirin out of her bag and showing it to him. Her behaviour is not coded: there is no rule or convention which says that displaying a bottle of aspirin means that one is not feeling well. Similarly, her behaviour affords only the weakest kind of direct evidence about her feelings: maybe she always carries a bottle of aspirin in her bag. On the other hand, it is strong direct evidence of her intention to inform

Peter that she does not feel well. Because her behaviour enables Peter to recognise her intention, Mary successfully communicates with him, and does so without the use of any code.[15]

Even Searle does not deny the existence of purely inferential communication. However, he insists that it is rare, and that most human communication crucially involves the use of a language or code:

> Some very simple sorts of illocutionary acts can indeed be performed apart from any use of conventional devices at all, simply by getting the audience to recognize certain of one's intentions in behaving in a certain way. . . One can in certain special circumstances 'request' someone to leave the room without employing any conventions, but unless one has a language one cannot request of someone that he, e.g., undertake a research project on the problem of diagnosing and treating mononucleosis in undergraduates in American universities. (Searle 1969: 38)

It may be true that most human communication involves the use of language, that cases of communication clearly achieved without the use of a code are rare, and that the thoughts so communicated tend to be rather simple. But the very existence of such cases is incompatible with the code model. On the other hand, it is predicted by the inferential model. Searle's dismissal of these cases as unimportant misses the point. They may be unimportant as examples of human interaction, but they are important as evidence for or against theories.

Since purely inferential communication exists, the inferential model is adequate by itself to account for at least some forms of communication. On the other hand, there is no doubt that most cases of communication involve the use of a code. Someone who takes the strong view that all human communication must be accounted for in inferential terms is then faced with the task of redescribing coding and decoding in inferential terms. Here is how it might be done. Regard a code as a set of conventions (in the sense of Lewis 1969) shared by all participants in the communication process. Members of the audience use their knowledge of these conventions on the one hand, and their knowledge of the signal and of the context on the other, to infer the message. This is a reasonably good description of what often happens when artificial codes are devised and used.

For example, Romeo and Juliet agree between them that a white kerchief tied to the rail of her balcony means that he can come up. Romeo sees the white kerchief, uses as a premise his knowledge of the convention they have devised, i.e. his knowledge that a white kerchief means that he can come up, and indeed *infers* that he can come up. When this account is generalised, all decoding, linguistic decoding included, is seen as an ordinary inferential process distinguished only by the fact that it involves premises based on knowledge of linguistic conventions.

We believe, and will argue in a later chapter, that the strong inferential theory of communication is empirically inadequate. There are coding–decoding processes, and there are inferential processes, and the two types of process are essentially distinct (even though, under rather artificial conditions, inference can mimic decoding, or decoding can mimic inference). A variety of species, from bees to humans, have codes which are to a greater or lesser extent genetically determined. These differ from inferential systems in two main respects: first, the representations they relate need not be conceptual, and second, the rules relating these representations need not be inferential. Human natural languages are cases in point. If we are right, then linguistic knowledge does not contribute to the comprehension process in the way described above: by providing premises for inference.[16]

We maintain, then, that there are at least two different modes of communication: the coding–decoding mode and the inferential mode. If we are right, from the fact that a particular communication process involves the use of a code, it does not follow that the whole process must be accounted for in terms of the code model. Complex forms of communication can combine both modes. Inferential communication, for example, might involve the use of coded signals which fall short of encoding the communicator's intentions and merely provide incomplete evidence about them. It becomes an empirical question whether the code model can provide a full account of a given communication process. It is not enough to show that a code is being used; one must also be able to show that what is communicated is actually being encoded and decoded. Otherwise, all that can be reasonably maintained is that the use of a code plays some role in this particular communication process, without perhaps wholly explaining it.

Verbal communication is a complex form of communication. Linguistic coding and decoding is involved, but the linguistic meaning of an uttered sentence falls short of encoding what the speaker means: it merely helps the audience infer what she means. The output of decoding is correctly treated by the audience as a piece of evidence about the communicator's intentions. In other words, a coding–decoding process is subservient to a Gricean inferential process.

Searle saw the fact that almost all human communication involves the use of codes as an objection to Grice's analysis. However, this fact is easy to explain on the assumption that the code and inferential modes of communication can combine. People who are in a position to communicate with one another usually share a language (and various minor codes);

as a result, they can produce much subtler and stronger evidence about their intentions than they could in the absence of a shared code. They are unlikely, then, to go to the trouble of communicating inferentially without these powerful tools, just as modern humans are unlikely to go to the trouble of making fire without matches or lighters. Still, just as no one would want to define fire as necessarily produced by the use of matches or lighters, it would be unreasonable to define communication as necessarily achieved by the use of codes.

The reduction of Grice's analysis to an amendment of the code model destroys not just its originality, but also many of its empirical implications and justifications. The elevation of the inferential model into a general theory of communication ignores the diversity of forms of communication, and the psychological evidence that much decoding is non-inferential (to be discussed in chapter 4).

6 Problems of definition

Most discussions of Grice's 1957 article have had to do with the definition of 'meaning' or 'communication' and have been highly philosophical. In this section, we will single out two genuinely empirical issues for discussion. Our aim is simply to highlight these relevant issues, not to write a history or an evaluation of the surrounding debates.

Grice characterises 'meaning' in terms of a communicator's intentions. Conversely, an act of communication (in an appropriately restricted sense of the term) might be characterised as one that fulfils these Gricean intentions. However, as Searle (1969: 46–8; 1971: 8–9) points out, a communicator can mean something, and successfully communicate it, without all these Gricean intentions being fulfilled. Recall Strawson's reformulation (27) of Grice's analysis. To mean something by an utterance x, an individual S must intend

(27) (a) S's utterance of x to produce a certain response r in a certain audience A;
  (b) A to recognise S's intention (a);
  (c) A's recognition of S's intention (a) to function as at least part of A's reason for A's response r.

Now it is easy to see that once intention (b) is fulfilled, the communicator has succeeded in communicating what she meant, whether or not intentions (a) and (c) are also fulfilled. For example, when Mary utters (28), her specific intention (29a) is to produce in Peter the belief that she had a sore throat on the previous Christmas Eve. Suppose Peter recognises this intention, but does not believe Mary. Then only her intention (29b) is fulfilled; intentions (29a) and (29c) are not. Nonetheless, although Mary has failed to convince Peter, she has succeeded in communicating to him what she meant.

Since communication can succeed without intention (27a) being fulfilled, intention (27a) is not an intention to communicate at all. It is better described as an intention to inform, or as we will call it, an *informative intention*.[17] The true *communicative intention* is intention (27b): that is, the intention to have one's informative intention recognised.

What about intention (27c): that the recognition by the audience of the communicator's intention (27a) shall function as at least part of the audience's reason for fulfilling intention (27a)? By definition, intention (27c) cannot be fulfilled when the informative intention (27a) is not. Since the fulfilment of (27a) is not necessary for successful communication, the fulfilment of (27c) cannot be necessary either. What Grice has convincingly shown is that the recognition of an informative intention can lead to its fulfilment. Very often, it is because this possibility exists that the communicator engages in communication at all. However to turn this possibility into a definitional necessity requires some justification. For the time being, we will drop intention (27c) from the characterisation of inferential communication without further discussion, and re-examine Grice's motivations on this point in section 10.[18]

We are now almost ready to propose a modified version of Grice's analysis, highlighting the difference between the informative and communicative intentions. However, we must first get rid of a confusing terminological idiosyncrasy. Grice and Strawson use the term 'utterance' to refer not just to linguistic utterances, or even to coded utterances, but to any modification of the physical environment designed by a communicator to be perceived by an audience and used as evidence of the communicator's intentions. This usage seems to us to introduce a bias into the identification of communicative behaviour. It encourages the view that utterances in the usual linguistic sense can be taken as the paradigm of communicative behaviour in general. Psychologists use the term 'stimulus' for any modification of the physical environment designed to be perceived. We will do the same. An utterance in the usual sense is, of course, a special case of a stimulus. Let us say, then, that communication involves producing a certain stimulus intending thereby

(31) *Informative intention*: to inform the audience of something;
  Communicative intention: to inform the audience of one's informative intention.

Note that the communicative intention is itself a second-order informative intention: the communicative intention is fulfilled once the first-order informative intention is recognised. In ordinary situations, if all goes well, the recognition of the informative intention will itself lead to the fulfilment of that intention, so that as a result of an act of communication, both the communicative and the informative intention will be fulfilled. However, a communicative intention can be fulfilled without the corresponding informative intention being fulfilled. Hence our reformulation is not open to the objections to Grice's and Strawson's formulation that we have so far considered.

While Grice's conditions on communication are too restrictive in some respects, in others they are not restrictive enough. One tends to think of communication as something done overtly: either your behaviour makes it clear that you are communicating, or else you are not truly communicating at all. In other words, communication should be distinguished from covert forms of information transmission.

Suppose, for instance, that Mary wants Peter to mend her broken hair-drier, but does not want to ask him openly. What she does is begin to take her hair-drier to pieces and leave the pieces lying around as if she were in the process of mending it. She does not expect Peter to be taken in by this staging; in fact, if he really believed that she was in the process of mending her hair-drier herself, he would probably not interfere. She does expect him to be clever enough to work out that this is a staging intended to inform him of the fact that she needs some help with her hair-drier. However, she does not expect him to be clever enough to work out that she expected him to reason along just these lines. Since she is not really asking, if Peter fails to help, it will not really count as a refusal either.

This example fits both Grice's original analysis of speaker's meaning and the reformulations in (27) and (31). Mary does intend Peter to be informed of her need by recognising her intention to inform him of it. Yet there is an intuitive reluctance to say that Mary *meant* that she wanted Peter's help, or that she was *communicating* with Peter in the sense we are trying to characterise. This reluctance, which we believe is well-founded, has to do with the fact that Mary's second-order intention to have her first-order informative intention recognised is hidden from Peter.

To deal with such counterexamples, Strawson (1964a), who first drew attention to the problem, argued that the Gricean analysis must be enriched: true communication must be characterised as *wholly overt*. The question then is how to modify the analysis of inferential communication to include this requirement of overtness; in other words, how should the intuitive and rather vague notion of overtness be made more precise? Answers to this question have been highly technical.

Strawson's own solution was to add to the analysis of speaker's meaning a third-order intention to have the second-order intention recognised by the audience; a meta-communicative intention, so to speak, was added to the informative and communicative intentions. As Strawson envisaged, and as Schiffer (1972: chapter 2) showed, this is not enough: examples can be constructed where the third-order meta-communicative intention is present but hidden from the audience, and the resulting interaction lacks the required overtness. Adding a fourth-order meta-meta-communicative intention that the third-order meta-communicative intention should itself be recognised by the audience may not be enough either: in principle, for any *n*th-order intention of this type, you need an *n*+1th-order intention to the effect that the *n*th-order intention be recognised. In other words you need an infinity of such intentions to explicate the intuitive notion of overtness along those lines.

There are ways of making logical sense of an infinity of intentions, and of analysing speaker's meaning or communication in terms of such an infinity.[19] But the results have little psychological plausibility. From the psychological point of view, intentions are mental representations capable of being realised in the form of actions. No psychologist would want to analyse an utterance as the realisation of an infinity of intentions so understood.[20]

The intuitive idea that communicative intentions must be overt can be worked out in another way, using the notion of mutual knowledge. This solution, proposed by Schiffer (1972), essentially involves the assumption that a true communicative intention is not just an intention to inform the audience of the communicator's informative intention, but an intention to make the informative intention *mutually known* to the communicator and the audience. By this criterion, the counterexample of Mary trying to get Peter to repair her hair-drier without openly asking him is not a case of true communication. Although Mary wants Peter to recognise her informative intention, she does not want this informative intention to become mutually known to both of them. More complex examples built on the same pattern would similarly be ruled out by this mutual-knowledge requirement.[21]

We have already argued (in section 3) that the appeal to 'mutual knowledge' lacks psychological plausibility. Hence to rely on it in explicating the notion of overtness is to turn one's back on psychology once more. Thus, all the solutions to the overtness problem proposed so far replace vagueness by one inadequate formalism or another. What we believe is a satisfactory solution will be proposed in section 8 and developed in section 12. In the meantime, we turn to further problems with Grice's analysis, problems this time not of definition but of explanation.

7 Problems of explanation: Grice's theory of conversation

The Gricean analysis of communication has been discussed almost exclusively by philosophers,[22] whose main concern has been to define the terms 'meaning' or 'communication'. From our current, more psychological point of view, defining communication is not a primary concern. For one thing, communication does not necessarily involve a distinct and homogeneous set of empirical phenomena. Our aim is to identify underlying mechanisms, rooted in human psychology, which explain how humans communicate with one another. A psychologically well-founded definition and typology of communication, if possible at all, should follow from a theoretical account of these underlying mechanisms. We see Grice's analysis as a possible basis for such a theoretical account. From this perspective, the main defect of Grice's analysis is not that it defines communication too vaguely, but that it explains communication too poorly.

The code model has the merit of explaining how communication could in principle be achieved. It fails not on the explanatory but on the descriptive side: humans do not communicate by encoding and decoding thoughts. The inferential model, despite the technical problems discussed in the last section, provides a description of human communication which rings true. By itself, however, it explains very little. The temptation to return to the code model will remain powerful as long as the inferential model is not developed into a plausible explanatory account of communication. However, the basis for such an account is suggested by another work of Grice's, his *William James Lectures*, in which he puts forward the view that communication is governed by a 'co-operative principle' and 'maxims of conversation'.[23]

According to the inferential model, communication is achieved by the audience recognising the communicator's informative intention. However, it is not enough to point out, as we have done, that recognising intentions is a normal feature of human cognition. The recognition of informative intentions presents problems which the recognition of other human intentions does not.

How does one recognise another individual's intentions? One observes his behaviour; using one's knowledge of people in general and of the individual in particular, one infers which of the effects of this behaviour he could have both predicted and desired; one then assumes that these predictable and desirable effects were also intended. In other words, one infers the intention behind the behaviour from its independently observed or inferred effects. This pattern of inference is generally not available to an audience trying to recognise a communicator's informative intention. As we have seen, the informative effects of communication are normally achieved, if at all, via recognition of the informative intention. Hence, it seems, the audience cannot *first* observe or infer these effects, and *then* use them to infer the informative intention.

However, the problem is not that it is hard to come up with hypotheses about what the communicator might have intended to convey: it is that too many hypotheses are possible. Even a linguistic utterance is generally full of semantic ambiguities and referential ambivalences, and is open to a wide range of figurative interpretations. For non-coded behaviour there is, by definition, no predetermined range of information it might be used to communicate. The problem, then, is to choose the right hypothesis from an indefinite range of possible hypotheses. How can this be done? First, it is easy enough to infer that a certain piece of behaviour is communicative. Communicative behaviour has at least one characteristic effect which is achieved before the communicator's informative intention is recognised: it overtly claims the audience's attention.

Grice's fundamental idea in his *William James Lectures* is that once a certain piece of behaviour is identified as communicative, it is reasonable to assume that the communicator is trying to meet certain general standards. From knowledge of these general standards, observation of the communicator's behaviour, and the context, it should be possible to infer the communicator's specific informative intention. Grice, talking only of verbal communication, argues,

> Our talk exchanges ... are characteristically, to some degree at least, cooperative efforts; and each participant recognizes in them, to some extent, a common purpose or set of purposes, or at least a mutually accepted direction. .... at each stage, *some* possible conversational moves would be excluded as conversationally unsuitable. We might then formulate a rough general principle which participants will be expected (*ceteris paribus*) to observe, namely: Make your conversational contribution such as is required, at the stage at which it occurs, by the accepted purpose or direction of the talk exchange in which you are engaged. (Grice 1975: 45)

This Grice calls the *co-operative principle*. He then develops it into nine *maxims* classified into four categories:

Maxims of quantity
1 Make your contribution as informative as is required (for the current purposes of the exchange).
2 Do not make your contribution more informative than is required.

Maxims of quality
Supermaxim: Try to make your contribution one that is true.
1 Do not say what you believe to be false.
2 Do not say that for which you lack adequate evidence.

Maxim of relation
Be relevant.

Maxims of manner
Supermaxim: Be perspicuous.
1 Avoid obscurity of expression.
2 Avoid ambiguity.
3 Be brief (avoid unnecessary prolixity).
4 Be orderly.

   This account of the general standards governing verbal communication makes it possible to explain how the utterance of a sentence, which provides only an incomplete and ambiguous representation of a thought, can nevertheless express a complete and unambiguous thought.[24] Of the various thoughts which the sentence uttered could be taken to represent, the hearer can eliminate any that are incompatible with the assumption that the speaker is obeying the co-operative principle and maxims. If only one thought is left, then the hearer can infer that it is this thought that the speaker is trying to communicate. Thus, to communicate efficiently, all the speaker has to do is utter a sentence only one interpretation of which is compatible with the assumption that she is obeying the co-operative principle and maxims.

   Recall, for instance, our example (16)–(18):

(16) Jones has bought the *Times*.
(17) Jones has bought a copy of the *Times*.
(18) Jones has bought the press enterprise which publishes the *Times*.

There might be situations where only interpretation (17) of the utterance in (16) would be compatible with the assumption that the speaker does not say what she believes to be false (first maxim of quality). There might be situations where only interpretation (18) would be compatible with the assumption that the speaker is being relevant (maxim of relation). In those situations, the intended interpretation of (16) can easily be inferred. Hence the maxims and the inferences they give rise to make it possible to convey an unambiguous thought by uttering an ambiguous sentence.

   Grice's approach to verbal communication also makes it possible to explain how utterances can convey not just explicit but also implicit thoughts. Consider dialogue (32):

(32) *Peter*: Do you want some coffee?
     Mary: Coffee would keep me awake.

Suppose that Peter is aware of (33). Then from the assumption explicitly expressed by Mary's answer, together with assumption (33), he could infer conclusion (34):

(33) Mary does not want to stay awake.
(34) Mary does not want any coffee.

In just the same way, if Peter is aware of (35), he could infer conclusion (36):

(35) Mary's eyes remain open when she is awake.
(36) Coffee would cause Mary's eyes to remain open.

Now in ordinary circumstances, Mary would have wanted to communicate (34) but not (36), although both are inferable in the same way from the thought she has explicitly expressed. This is easily explained on the assumption that Mary obeys Grice's maxims. The explicit content of her utterance does not directly answer Peter's question; it is therefore not relevant as it stands. If Mary has obeyed the maxim 'be relevant', it must be assumed that she intended to give Peter an answer. Since he can obtain just the expected answer by inferring (34) from what she said, she must have intended him to draw precisely this conclusion. There is no parallel reason to think that she intended Peter to infer (36). Hence, just as the Gricean maxims help the hearer choose, from among the senses of an ambiguous sentence, the one which was intended by the speaker, so they help him choose, from among the implications of the explicit content of an utterance, the ones which are implicitly conveyed.

Suppose now that the exchange in (32) takes place in the same circumstances as before, except that Peter has no particular reason beforehand to assume that Mary does not want to stay awake. Without this assumption, no answer to his question is derivable from Mary's utterance, and the relevance of this utterance is not immediately apparent. One of Grice's main contributions to pragmatics was to show how, in the event of such an apparent violation of the co-operative principle and maxims, hearers are expected to make any additional assumptions needed to dispose of the violation. Here Peter might first adopt (33) as a specific assumption jointly suggested by the utterance, his knowledge of Mary, and the general assumption that Mary is trying to be relevant. He might then infer, as in the previous example, that she does not want any coffee. To eliminate the apparent violation of the maxims, Peter would have to assume that Mary had intended him to reason just as he did: that is, that she was intending to convey implicitly both assumption (33) and conclusion (34).

Grice calls additional assumptions and conclusions such as (33) and (34), supplied to preserve the application of the co-operative principle and maxims, *implicatures*. Like his ideas on meaning, Grice's ideas on implicature can be seen as an attempt to build on a commonsense view of verbal communication by making it more explicit and exploring its implications. In his *William James Lectures*, Grice took one crucial step away from this commonsense view towards theoretical sophistication;

but of course one step is not enough. Grice's account retains much of the vagueness of the commonsense view. Essential concepts mentioned in the maxims are left entirely undefined. This is true of *relevance*, for instance: hence appeals to the 'maxim of relation' are no more than dressed-up appeals to intuition. Thus, everybody would agree that, in ordinary circumstances, adding (33) and (34) to the interpretation of Mary's answer in (32) makes it relevant, whereas adding (35) and (36) does not. However, this fact has itself to be explained before it can be used in a genuine explanation of how Mary's answer is understood.

Grice's view of implicature raises even more basic questions. What is the rationale behind the co-operative principle and maxims? Are there just the nine maxims Grice mentioned, or might others be needed, as he suggested himself? It might be tempting to add a maxim every time a regularity has to be accounted for.[25] However, this would be entirely *ad hoc*. What criteria, then, do individual maxims have to meet? Could the number of maxims be not expanded but reduced?[26]

How are the maxims to be used in inference? Grice himself seems to think that the hearer uses the assumption that the speaker has observed the maxims as a premise in inference. Others have tried to reinterpret the maxims as 'conversational postulates' (Gordon and Lakoff 1975), or even as code-like rules which take semantic representations of sentences and descriptions of context as input, and yield pragmatic representations of utterances as output (Gazdar 1979). The flavour of such proposals can be seen from the following remarks:

> The tactic adopted here is to examine some of the data that would, or should be, covered by Grice's quantity maxim and then propose a relatively simple formal solution to the problem of describing the behaviour of that data. This solution may be seen as a special case of Grice's quantity maxim, or as an alternative to it, or as merely a conventional rule for assigning one class of conversational meanings to one class of utterance. (Gazdar 1979: 49)

The pragmatic phenomena amenable to this sort of treatment are rather limited: they essentially arise when the utterance of a certain sentence is so regularly correlated with a certain pragmatic interpretation that it makes sense to set up a rule linking the one to the other. For example, the utterance of (37) regularly suggests (38), the main exception being when it is already assumed that (38) is, or might be, false:

(37) Some of the arguments are convincing.
(38) Not all of the arguments are convincing.

The proposal is to deal with this by setting up a general rule associating

(37) with the pragmatic interpretation (38), and effectively blocking its application in contexts where it is assumed that (38) is, or might be, false (Gazdar 1979: 55–9). However, in most cases of implicature, as for instance in example (32)–(34), the context does much more than filter out inappropriate interpretations: it provides premises without which the implicature cannot be inferred at all. The translation of Grice's maxims into code-like rules would thus reduce them to dealing with a narrow set of interesting but quite untypical examples of implicature.

What, then, are the forms of inference involved in the normal operation of the maxims? If, as seems plausible, non-demonstrative (i.e. non-deductive) inference is involved, how does it operate? Without pursuing these questions in any depth, most pragmatists have adopted one form or another of the Gricean approach to implicatures, and are otherwise content to explain the explicit core of verbal communication in terms of the code model. The results are as can be expected. Although based on an insight which seems quite correct, and although somewhat more explicit and systematic than the intuitive reconstructions supplied by unsophisticated speakers, the analyses of implicature which have been proposed by pragmatists have shared with these intuitive reconstructions the defect of being almost entirely *ex post facto*.

Given that an utterance in context was found to carry particular implicatures, what both the hearer and the pragmatic theorist can do, the latter in a slightly more sophisticated way, is to show how in very intuitive terms there was an argument based on the context, the utterance and general expectations about the behaviour of speakers, that would justify the particular interpretation chosen. What they fail to show is that on the same basis, an equally convincing justification could not have been given for some other interpretation that was not in fact chosen. There may be a whole variety of interpretations that would meet whatever standards of truthfulness, informativeness, relevance and clarity have been proposed or envisaged so far. The theory needs improving at a fundamental level before it can be fruitfully applied to particular cases.

In his *William James Lectures*, Grice put forward an idea of fundamental importance: that the very act of communicating creates expectations which it then exploits. Grice himself first applied this idea and its elaboration in terms of the maxims to a rather limited problem of linguistic philosophy: do logical connectives ('and', 'or', 'if . . . then') have the same meaning in natural languages as they do in logic? He argued that the richer meaning these connectives seem to have in natural languages can be explained in terms not of word meaning but of implicature. He then suggested that this approach could have wider applications: that the task of linguistic semantics could be considerably simplified by treating a large array of problems in terms of implicatures. And indeed, the study of implicature along Gricean lines has become a major concern of pragmatics.[27] We believe that the basic idea of Grice's *William James Lectures* has even wider implications: it offers a way of developing the analysis of inferential communication, suggested by Grice himself in 'Meaning' (1957), into an explanatory model. To achieve this, however, we must leave aside the various elaborations of Grice's original hunches and the sophisticated, though empirically rather empty debates they have given rise to. What is needed is an attempt to rethink, in psychologically realistic terms, such basic questions as: What form of shared information is available to humans? How is shared information exploited in communication? What is relevance and how is it achieved? What role does the search for relevance play in communication? It is to these questions that we now turn.

8 Cognitive environments and mutual manifestness

We have argued that mutual knowledge is a philosopher's construct with no close counterpart in reality. This is not to deny that humans do, in some sense, share information. In the first place, the communication process itself gives rise to shared information; in the second place, some sharing of information is necessary if communication is to be achieved. Any account of human communication must thus incorporate some notion of shared information. In this section, we want to go beyond both the empirically inadequate notion of 'mutual knowledge' and the conceptually vague notion of 'shared information'. We will discuss in what sense humans share information, and to what extent they share information about the information they share.

All humans live in the same physical world. We are all engaged in a lifetime's enterprise of deriving information from this common environment and constructing the best possible mental representation of it. We do not all construct the same representation, because of differences in our narrower physical environments on the one hand, and in our cognitive abilities on the other. Perceptual abilities vary in effectiveness from one individual to another. Inferential abilities also vary, and not just in effectiveness. People speak different languages, they have mastered different concepts; as a result, they can construct different representations and make different inferences. They have different memories, too, different theories that they bring to bear on their experience in different ways. Hence, even if they all shared the same narrow physical environment, what we propose to call their *cognitive environments* would still differ.

To introduce the notion of a cognitive environment, let us consider a parallel case. One human cognitive ability is sight. With respect to sight, each individual is in a visual environment which can be characterised as the set of all phenomena visible to him. What is visible to him is a function both of his physical environment and of his visual abilities.

In studying communication, we are interested in conceptual cognitive abilities. We want to suggest that what visible phenomena are for visual cognition, manifest facts are for conceptual cognition. Let us define:

(39) A fact is *manifest* to an individual at a given time if and only if he is capable at that time of representing it mentally and accepting its representation as true or probably true.

(40) A *cognitive environment* of an individual is a set of facts that are manifest to him.

To be manifest, then, is to be perceptible or inferable.[28] An individual's total cognitive environment is the set of all the facts that he can perceive or infer: all the facts that are manifest to him. An individual's total cognitive environment is a function of his physical environment and his cognitive abilities. It consists of not only all the facts that he is aware of, but also all the facts that he is capable of becoming aware of, in his physical environment. The individual's actual awareness of facts, i.e. the knowledge that he has acquired, of course contributes to his ability to become aware of further facts. Memorised information is a component of cognitive abilities.

We want to elaborate the notion of what is manifest in two ways: first, we want to extend it from facts to all assumptions; and second, we want to distinguish degrees of manifestness. Our point of view here is cognitive rather than epistemological. From a cognitive point of view, mistaken assumptions can be indistinguishable from genuine factual knowledge, just as optical illusions can be indistinguishable from true sight. Just as illusions are 'visible', so any assumption, whether true or false, may be manifest to an individual. An assumption, then, is manifest in a cognitive environment if the environment provides sufficient evidence for its adoption, and as we all know, mistaken assumptions are sometimes very well evidenced.

Anything that can be seen at all is visible, but some things are much more visible than others. Similarly, we have defined 'manifest' so that any assumption that an individual is capable of constructing and accepting as true or probably true is manifest to him. We also want to say that manifest assumptions which are more likely to be entertained are more manifest. Which assumptions are more manifest to an individual during a given period or at a given moment is again a function of his physical environment on the one hand and his cognitive abilities on the other.

Human cognitive organisation makes certain types of phenomena (i.e. perceptible objects or events) particularly salient. For instance, the noise of an explosion or a doorbell ringing is highly salient, a background buzz or a ticking clock much less so. When a phenomenon is noticed, some assumptions about it are standardly more accessible than others. In an environment where the doorbell has just rung, it will normally be strongly manifest that there is someone at the door, less strongly so that whoever is at the door is tall enough to reach the bell, and less strongly still that the bell has not been stolen. The most strongly manifest assumption of all is the assumption that the doorbell has just rung, the evidence for which is both salient and conclusive. We will have more to say, in chapter 3, about the factors which make some assumptions more manifest than others in a given situation. For the moment it is the fact rather than the explanation that matters.

Our notion of what is manifest to an individual is clearly weaker than the notion of what is actually known or assumed. A fact can be manifest without being known; all the individual's actual assumptions are manifest to him, but many more assumptions which he has not actually made are manifest to him too. This is so however weakly the terms 'knowledge' and 'assumption' are construed. In a strong sense, to know some fact involves having a mental representation of it. In a weaker sense, to say that an individual knows some fact is not necessarily to imply that he has ever entertained a mental representation of it. For instance, before reading this sentence you all knew, in that weak sense, that Noam Chomsky never had breakfast with Julius Caesar, although until now the thought of it had never crossed your mind. It is generally accepted that people have not only the knowledge that they actually entertain, but also the knowledge that they are capable of deducing from the knowledge that they entertain. However, something can be manifest without being known, even in this virtual way, if only because something can be manifest and false, whereas nothing can be known and false.

Can something be manifest without being actually assumed? The answer must again be yes. Assumptions are unlike knowledge in that they need not be true. As with knowledge, people can be said to assume, in a weak sense, what they are capable of deducing from what they assume. However, people do not assume, in any sense, what they are merely capable of inferring non-demonstratively – that is, by some creative process of hypothesis formation and confirmation – from what they assume. Although it presumably followed non-demonstratively from what you knew and assumed before you read this sentence that Ronald Reagan and Noam Chomsky never played billiards together, this was not, until now, an assumption of yours: it was only an assumption that was manifest to you. Moreover, something can be manifest merely by being perceptible, and without being inferable at all from previously held knowledge and assumptions. A car is audibly passing in the street. You have not yet paid any attention to it, so you have no knowledge of it, no assumptions about it, even in the weakest sense of 'knowledge' and 'assumption'. But the fact that a car is passing in the street is manifest to you.

We will now show that because 'manifest' is weaker than 'known' or 'assumed', a notion of mutual manifestness can be developed which does not suffer from the same psychological implausibility as 'mutual knowledge' or 'mutual assumptions'.

To the extent that two organisms have the same visual abilities and the same physical environment, the same phenomena are visible to them and they can be said to share a visual environment. Since visual abilities and physical environments are never exactly identical, organisms never share their total visual environments. Moreover, two organisms which share a visual environment need not actually see the same phenomena; they are merely capable of doing so.

Similarly, the same facts and assumptions may be manifest in the cognitive environments of two different people. In that case, these cognitive environments intersect, and their intersection is a cognitive environment that these two people share. The total shared cognitive environment of two people is the intersection of their two total cognitive environments: i.e. the set of all facts that are manifest to them both. Clearly, if people share cognitive environments, it is because they share physical environments and have similar cognitive abilities. Since physical environments are never strictly identical, and since cognitive abilities are affected by previously memorised information and thus differ in many respects from one person to another, people never share their total cognitive environments. Moreover, to say that two people share a cognitive environment does not imply that they make the same assumptions: merely that they are capable of doing so.

One thing that can be manifest in a given cognitive environment is a characterisation of the people who have access to it. For instance, every Freemason has access to a number of secret assumptions which include the assumption that all Freemasons have access to these same secret assumptions. In other words, all Freemasons share a cognitive environment which contains the assumption that all Freemasons share this environment. To take another example, Peter and Mary are talking to each other in the same room: they share a cognitive environment which consists of all the facts made manifest to them by their presence in this room. One of these facts is the fact that they share this environment.

Any shared cognitive environment in which it is manifest which people share it is what we will call a *mutual cognitive environment*. In a mutual cognitive environment, for every manifest assumption, the fact that it is manifest to the people who share this environment is itself manifest. In other words, in a mutual cognitive environment, every manifest assumption is what we will call *mutually manifest*.

Consider, for example, a cognitive environment E shared by Peter and Mary, in which (41) and (42) are manifest:

(41) Peter and Mary share cognitive environment E.
(42) The phone is ringing.

In this environment, (43)–(45) and indefinitely many assumptions built on the same pattern are also manifest:

(43) It is manifest to Peter and to Mary that the phone is ringing.
(44) It is manifest to Peter and to Mary that it is manifest to Peter and to Mary that the phone is ringing.
(45) It is manifest to Peter and to Mary that it is manifest to Peter and to Mary that it is manifest to Peter and to Mary that the phone is ringing.

The more complex assumptions of type (43)–(45) get, the less likely they are actually to be made. However, in such a series, assumption n does not have to be actually made by the individuals it mentions for assumption $n+1$ to be true. There is therefore no cut-off point beyond which these assumptions are likely to be false rather than true; they remain manifest throughout, even though their degree of manifestness tends asymptotically toward zero. (41)–(45) and all the assumptions in E are not only manifest to Peter and Mary; they are mutually manifest.

The notion of a mutually manifest assumption is clearly weaker than that of a mutual assumption (and *a fortiori* than that of mutual knowledge). Consider assumptions (46)–(48) and all the further assumptions that can be built on the same pattern:

(46) Peter and Mary assume that the phone is ringing.
(47) Peter and Mary assume that Peter and Mary assume that the phone is ringing.
(48) Peter and Mary assume that Peter and Mary assume that Peter and Mary assume that the phone is ringing.

As before, the more complex assumptions of type (46)–(48) get, the less likely they are actually to be made. In this case, however, assumption n does have to be made by Peter and Mary for assumption $n + 1$ to be true. Moreover, there is sure to be some point – quite soon actually – at which Mary does *not* assume that Peter assumes that she assumes that he assumes, etc. At this point and beyond, all the assumptions in this series are false, and mutuality of assumptions is not achieved. Another way of seeing that mutuality of assumptions is stronger than mutual manifestness is to notice that

(43) may be true when (46) is not, (44) may be true when (47) is not, (45) may be true when (48) is not, and so on, while the converse is not possible.

Mutual manifestness is not merely weaker than mutual knowledge or mutual assumption; it is weaker in just the right way. On the one hand, it is not open to the same psychological objections, since the claim that an assumption is mutually manifest is a claim about cognitive environments rather than mental states or processes. On the other hand, as we will show in section 12, the notion of mutual manifestness is strong enough to give a precise and interesting content to the notion of overtness discussed in section 6. However, by rejecting the notion of mutual knowledge and adopting the weaker notion of mutual manifestness, we deprive ourselves of a certain type of explanation in the study of communication.

Communication requires some degree of co-ordination between communicator and audience on the choice of a code and a context. The notion of mutual knowledge is used to explain how this co-ordination can be achieved: given enough mutual knowledge, communicator and audience can make symmetrical choices of code and context. A realistic notion of mutual manifestness, on the other hand, is not strong enough to explain such symmetrical co-ordination. However, before concluding that mutual manifestness is too weak after all, ask yourself what are the grounds for assuming that responsibility for co-ordination is equally shared between communicator and audience, and that both must worry, symmetrically, about what the other is thinking. Asymmetrical co-ordination is often easier to achieve, and communication is an asymmetrical process anyhow.

Consider what would happen in ballroom dancing if the responsibility for choosing steps was left equally to both partners (and how little help the mutual-knowledge framework would be for solving the resulting co-ordination problems in real time). Co-ordination problems are avoided, or considerably reduced, in dancing, by leaving the responsibility to one partner who leads, while the other has merely to follow. We assume that the same goes for communication. It is left to the communicator to make correct assumptions about the codes and contextual information that the audience will have accessible and be likely to use in the comprehension process. The responsibility for avoiding misunderstandings also lies with the speaker, so that all the hearer has to do is go ahead and use whatever code and contextual information come most easily to hand.

Suppose Mary and Peter are looking at a landscape where she has noticed a distant church. She says to him,

(49) I've been inside that church.

She does not stop to ask herself whether he has noticed the building, and whether he assumes she has noticed, and assumes she has noticed he has noticed, and so on, or whether he has assumed it is a church, and assumes she assumes it is, and so on. All she needs is reasonable confidence that he will be able to identify the building as a church when required to: in other words, that a certain assumption will be manifest in his cognitive environment at the right time. He need not have accessed this assumption before she spoke. In fact, until she spoke he might have thought the building was a castle: it might be only on the strength of her utterance that it becomes manifest to him that the building is a church.

Inspired by the landscape, Mary says,

(50) It's the sort of scene that would have made Marianne Dashwood swoon.

This is an allusion to Jane Austen's *Sense and Sensibility*, a book she knows Peter has read. She does not stop to think whether he knows she has read it too and knows she knows he has read it, and so on. Nor is she unaware of the fact that they may well have reacted to the book in different ways and remember it differently. Her remark is based on assumptions that she does not mention and that he need never have made himself before she spoke. What she expects, rightly, is that her utterance will act as a prompt, making him recall parts of the book that he had previously forgotten, and construct the assumptions needed to understand the allusion.

In both these examples Mary makes assumptions about what assumptions are, or will be, manifest to Peter. Peter trusts that the assumptions he spontaneously makes about the church and about *Sense and Sensibility*, which help him understand Mary's utterances, are those she expected him to make. To communicate successfully, Mary had to have some knowledge of Peter's cognitive environment. As a result of their successful communication, their mutual cognitive environment is enlarged. Note that symmetrical co-ordination and mutual knowledge do not enter into the picture at all.

The most fundamental reason for adopting the mutual-knowledge framework, as for adopting the code model, is the desire to show how successful communication can be guaranteed, how there is some failsafe algorithm by which the hearer can reconstruct the speaker's exact meaning. Within this framework the fact that communication often fails is explained in one of two ways: either the code mechanism has been imperfectly implemented, or there has been some disruption due to 'noise'. A noiseless, well-implemented code mechanism should guarantee perfect communication.

In rejecting the mutual-knowledge framework, we abandon the possibility of using a failsafe algorithm as a model of human communication. But since it is obvious that the communication process takes place at a risk, why assume that it is governed by a failsafe procedure? Moreover, if there is one conclusion to be drawn from work on artificial intelligence, it is that most cognitive processes are so complex that they must be modelled in terms of heuristics rather than failsafe algorithms. We assume, then, that communication is governed by a less-than-perfect heuristic. On this approach, failures in communication are to be expected: what is mysterious and requires explanation is not failure but success.

As we have seen, the notion of mutual manifestness is not strong enough to salvage the code theory of communication. But then, this was never one of our aims. Instead of taking the code theory for granted and concluding that mutual knowledge must therefore exist, we prefer to look at what kind of assumptions people are actually in a position to make about each other's assumptions, and then see what this implies for an account of communication.

Sometimes, we have direct evidence about other people's assumptions: for instance, when they tell us what they assume. More generally, because we manifestly share cognitive environments with other people, we have direct evidence about what is manifest to them. When a cognitive environment we share with other people is mutual, we have evidence about what is mutually manifest to all of us. Note that this evidence can never be conclusive: the boundaries of cognitive environments cannot be precisely determined, if only because the threshold between very weakly manifest assumptions and inaccessible ones is unmarked.

From assumptions about what is manifest to other people, and in particular about what is strongly manifest to them, we are in a position to derive further, though necessarily weaker, assumptions about what assumptions they are actually making. From assumptions about what is mutually manifest to all of us, we are in a position to derive further, and weaker, assumptions about the assumptions they attribute to us. And essentially, this is it. Human beings somehow manage to communicate in situations where a great deal can be assumed about what is manifest to others, a lot can be assumed about what is mutually manifest to themselves and others, but nothing can be assumed to be truly mutually known or assumed.

The situations which establish a mutual cognitive environment are essentially those that have been treated as establishing mutual knowledge.[29] We have argued that assumptions of mutual knowledge are never truly warranted. Examples (49) and (50) are anecdotal evidence that they are unnecessary. The detour via mutual knowledge is superfluous: mutual cognitive environments directly provide all the information needed for communication and comprehension.[a]

The notions of cognitive environment and of manifestness, mutual or otherwise, are psychologically realistic, but by themselves shed little light on what goes on in human minds. A cognitive environment is merely a set of assumptions which the individual is capable of mentally representing and accepting as true. The question then is: which of these assumptions will the individual actually make? This question is of interest not only to the psychologist, but also to every ordinary communicator. We will argue that when you communicate, your intention is to alter the cognitive environment of your addressees; but of course you expect their actual thought processes to be affected as a result. In the next section we will argue that human cognition is relevance-oriented, and that as a result, someone who knows an individual's cognitive environment can infer which assumptions he is actually likely to entertain.

9 Relevance and ostension

An individual's cognitive environment is a set of assumptions available to him. Which particular assumptions is he most likely to construct and process? There may, of course, be no general answer to this question. We want to argue that there is. This book is essentially an exploration of the idea that there is a single property – relevance – which makes information worth processing for a human being. Chapter 3 will contain a relatively technical discussion of relevance. In this section, we simply want to characterise the notion in very general, informal terms, and to make some suggestions about the role of relevance in communication.

Human beings are efficient information-processing devices. This is their most obvious asset as a species. But what is efficiency in information processing?

Efficiency can only be defined with respect to a goal. Some goals, such as catching a prey, winning a game or solving a problem, are absolute: they consist in bringing about a particular state of affairs which at any given moment either exists or does not exist. Other goals, such as multiplying one's offspring, improving one's backstroke, or understanding oneself, are relative: they consist in raising the value of some variable, and can thus only be achieved to a degree. Efficiency with respect to absolute goals is simply a matter of reaching them with the smallest possible expenditure of whatever resource (time, money, energy . . .) it takes. Efficiency with respect to relative goals is a matter of striking a balance between degree of achievement and expenditure. In the special case where the expenditure is fixed – say all the time available is going to be spent anyhow – efficiency consists in achieving the goal to the highest possible degree.

Most discussions of information processing, whether in experimental psychology or in artificial intelligence, have been concerned with the realisation of absolute goals. 'Problem solving' has become the paradigm of information processing. The problems considered have a fixed solution; the goal of the information-processing device is to find this solution; efficiency consists in finding it at the minimal cost. However, not all cognitive tasks fit this description; many tasks consist not in reaching an absolute goal, but in improving on an existing state of affairs. Hence, cognitive efficiency may have to be characterised differently for different devices.

Simpler information-processing devices, whether natural, such as a frog, or artificial, such as an electronic alarm system, process only very specific information: for example, metabolic changes and fly movements for frogs, noises and other vibrations for alarm systems. Their information-processing activity consists in monitoring changes in the values of a few variables. They could be informally described as engaged in answering a few set questions: 'Is there a fly-like object within reach?', 'Is there a large body moving in the room?' More complex information-processing devices, by contrast, can define and monitor new variables or formulate and answer new questions.

For the simpler devices, efficiency consists in answering their set questions at the minimal processing cost. Efficiency cannot be so easily defined for more complex devices such as human beings. For such devices, efficient information processing may involve formulating and trying to answer new questions despite the extra processing costs incurred. Formulating and answering specific questions must then be seen as subservient to a more general and abstract goal. It is in relation to this general goal that the efficiency of complex information-processing devices must be characterised.

On the general goal of human cognition, we have nothing better to offer than rather trivial speculative remarks. However, these remarks have important and non-trivial consequences. It seems that human cognition is aimed at improving the individual's knowledge of the world. This means adding more information, information that is more accurate, more easily retrievable, and more developed in areas of greater concern to the individual. Information processing is a permanent life-long task. An individual's overall resources for information processing are, if not quite fixed, at least not very flexible. Thus, long-term cognitive efficiency consists in improving one's knowledge of the world as much as possible given the available resources.

What, then, is short-term cognitive efficiency – efficiency, say, in the way your mind spends the next few seconds or milliseconds? This is a more concrete question, and one that is harder to answer. At every moment, many different cognitive tasks could be performed, and this for two reasons: first, human sensory abilities monitor much more information than central conceptual abilities can process; and second, central

abilities always have plenty of unfinished business. The key problem for
efficient short-term information processing is thus to achieve an optimal
allocation of central processing resources. Resources have to be allocated
to the processing of information which is likely to bring about the greatest
contribution to the mind's general cognitive goals at the smallest
processing cost.

Some information is old: it is already present in the individual's
representation of the world. Unless it is needed for the performance of a
particular cognitive task, and is easier to access from the environment than
from memory, such information is not worth processing at all. Other
information is not only new but entirely unconnected with anything in the
individual's representation of the world. It can only be added to this
representation as isolated bits and pieces, and this usually means too much
processing cost for too little benefit. Still other information is new but
connected with old information. When these interconnected new and old
items of information are used together as premises in an inference process,
further new information can be derived: information which could not
have been inferred without this combination of old and new premises.
When the processing of new information gives rise to such a multiplication effect, we call it *relevant*. The greater the multiplication effect, the
greater the relevance.

Consider an example. Mary and Peter are sitting on a park bench. He
leans back, which alters her view. By leaning back, he modifies her
cognitive environment; he reveals to her certain phenomena, which she
may look at or not, and describe to herself in different ways. Why should
she pay attention to one phenomenon rather than another, or describe it to
herself in one way rather than another? In other words, why should she
mentally process any of the assumptions which have become manifest or
more manifest to her as a result of the change in her environment? Our
answer is that she should process those assumptions that are most relevant
to her at the time.

Imagine, for instance, that as a result of Peter's leaning back she can see,
among other things, three people: an ice-cream vendor who she had
noticed before when she sat down on the bench, an ordinary stroller who
she has never seen before, and her acquaintance William, who is coming
towards them and is a dreadful bore. Many assumptions about each of
these characters are more or less manifest to her. She may already have
considered the implications of the presence of the ice-cream vendor when
she first noticed him; if so, it would be a waste of processing resources to
pay further attention to him now. The presence of the unknown stroller is
new information to her, but little or nothing follows from it; so there
again, what she can perceive and infer about him is not likely to be of much
relevance to her. By contrast, from the fact that William is coming her

way, she can draw many conclusions from which many more conclusions will follow. This, then, is the one truly relevant change in her cognitive environment; this is the particular phenomenon she should pay attention to. She should do so, that is, if she is aiming at cognitive efficiency.

Our claim is that all human beings automatically aim at the most efficient information processing possible. This is so whether they are conscious of it or not; in fact, the very diverse and shifting conscious interests of individuals result from the pursuit of this permanent aim in changing conditions. In other words, an individual's particular cognitive goal at a given moment is always an instance of a more general goal: maximising the relevance of the information processed. We will show that this is a crucial factor in human interaction.

Among the facts made manifest to Mary by Peter's behaviour is the very fact that he has behaved in a certain way. Suppose now that she pays attention to this behaviour, and comes to the conclusion that it must have been deliberate: perhaps he is leaning back more rigidly than if he were merely trying to find a more comfortable position. She might then ask herself why he is doing it. There may be many possible answers; suppose that the most plausible one she can find is that he is leaning back in order to attract her attention to some particular phenomenon. Then Peter's behaviour has made it manifest to Mary that he intends to make some particular assumptions manifest to her. We will call such behaviour – behaviour which makes manifest an intention to make something manifest – *ostensive* behaviour or simply *ostension*. Showing someone something is a case of ostension. So too, we will argue, is human intentional communication.

The existence of ostension is beyond doubt. What is puzzling is how it works. Any perceptible behaviour makes manifest indefinitely many assumptions. How is the audience of an act of ostension to discover which of them have been intentionally made manifest? For instance, how is Mary to discover which of the phenomena which have become manifest to her as a result of Peter's behaviour are the ones he intended her to pay attention to?

Information processing involves effort; it will only be undertaken in the expectation of some reward. There is thus no point in drawing someone's attention to a phenomenon unless it will seem relevant enough to him to be worth his attention. By requesting Mary's attention, Peter suggests that he has reason to think that by paying attention, she will gain some relevant information. He may, of course, be mistaken, or trying to distract her attention from relevant information elsewhere, as the maker of an assertion may be mistaken or lying; but just as an assertion comes with a tacit guarantee of truth, so ostension comes with a tacit guarantee of relevance[b].

This guarantee of relevance makes it possible for Mary to infer which of the newly manifest assumptions have been intentionally made manifest. Here is how the inference process might go. First, Mary notices Peter's behaviour and assumes that it is ostensive: i.e. that it is intended to attract her attention to some phenomenon. If she has enough confidence in his guarantee of relevance, she will infer that some of the information which his behaviour has made manifest to her is indeed relevant to her. She then pays attention to the area that has become visible to her as a result of his leaning back, and discovers the ice-cream vendor, the stroller, this dreadful William, and so on. Assumptions about William are the only newly manifest assumptions relevant enough to be worth her attention. From this, she can infer that Peter's intention was precisely to draw her attention to William's arrival. Any other assumption about his ostensive behaviour is inconsistent with her confidence in the guarantee of relevance it carries.

Mary has become aware not only that there is someone coming who she wants to avoid, but also that Peter intended her to become aware of it, and that he is aware of it too. On the basis of his observable behaviour, she has discovered some of his thoughts.

Ostensive behaviour provides evidence of one's thoughts. It succeeds in doing so because it implies a guarantee of relevance. It implies such a guarantee because humans automatically turn their attention to what seems most relevant to them. The main thesis of this book is that an act of ostension carries a guarantee of relevance, and that this fact – which we will call the *principle of relevance* – makes manifest the intention behind the ostension.[c] We believe that it is this principle of relevance that is needed to make the inferential model of communication explanatory.

10 Ostensive–inferential communication

Ostension provides two layers of information to be picked up: first, there is the information which has been, so to speak, pointed out; second, there is the information that the first layer of information has been intentionally pointed out. One can imagine the first layer being recovered without the second. For example, as a result of Peter's leaning back, Mary might notice William coming their way, even if she paid no attention to Peter's intentions. And as for Peter, he might not care much whether Mary recognises his intention, as long as she notices William.

In general, however, recognising the intention behind the ostension is necessary for efficient information processing: someone who fails to recognise this intention may fail to notice relevant information. Let us modify our example slightly and suppose that William is in the distance, barely visible in a crowd. If Mary pays no attention to the fact that Peter's behaviour is ostensive, she might well look in the right direction and yet not notice William. If she pays attention to the ostension, she will be inclined to take a closer look and find out what information Peter thought might be relevant to her.

In our modified example, what Peter's ostension mostly does is make much more manifest some information which would have been manifest anyhow, though very weakly so. Sometimes, however, part of the basic information will not be manifest at all unless the intention behind the ostension is taken into account. Suppose a girl is travelling in a foreign country. She comes out of the inn wearing light summer clothes, manifestly intending to take a stroll. An old man sitting on a bench nearby looks ostensively up at the sky. When the girl looks up, she sees a few tiny clouds, which she might have noticed for herself, but which she would normally have paid no further attention to: given her knowledge – or lack of knowledge – of the local weather, the presence of these tiny clouds is not relevant to her. Now, however, the old man is drawing her attention to the clouds in a manifestly intentional way, thus guaranteeing that there is some relevant information to be obtained.

The old man's ostensive behaviour opens up for the girl a whole new strategy of processing. If she accepts his guarantee of relevance, she has to find out what makes him think that the presence of the clouds would be relevant to her. Knowing the area and its weather better than she does, he might have reason to think that the clouds are going to get worse and turn to rain. Such an assumption is of a very standard sort and would probably be the first to come to mind. The old man can thus be reasonably confident that, prompted by his behaviour, she will have no difficulty in deciding that this is what he believes. If it were not manifest to the old man that it was going to rain, it would be hard to explain his behaviour at all. The girl thus has reason to think that in drawing her attention to the clouds, he intended to make manifest to her that he believed it was going to rain. As a result of this act of ostension, she now has some information that was not available to her before: that he thinks it is going to rain, and hence that there is a genuine risk of rain.

In this example, the state of affairs that the old man drew the girl's attention to had been partly manifest to her, and partly not. The presence of the clouds and the fact that clouds may always turn to rain had been manifest and merely became more so. However, until that moment she had regarded the fact that the weather was beautiful as strong evidence that it would not rain. The risk of rain in that particular situation was not manifest to her at all. In other words, the clouds were already evidence of oncoming rain, but evidence that was much too weak. The old man made that evidence much stronger by pointing it out; as his intentions became manifest, the assumption that it would rain became manifest too.

Sometimes, all the evidence displayed in an act of ostension bears directly on the agent's intentions. In these cases, only by discovering the agent's intentions can the audience also discover, indirectly, the basic information that the agent intended to make manifest. The relation between the evidence produced and the basic information conveyed is arbitrary. The same piece of evidence can be used, on different occasions, to make manifest different assumptions, even mutually inconsistent assumptions, as long as it makes manifest the intention behind the ostension.

Here is an example. Two prisoners, from different tribes with no common language, are put in a quarry to work back to back breaking rocks. Suddenly, prisoner A starts putting some distinct rhythm into the sound of his hammer – one–two–three, one–two, one–two–three, one–two – a rhythm that is both arbitrary and noticeable enough to attract the attention of prisoner B. This arbitrary pattern in the way the rocks are being broken has no direct relevance for B. However, there are grounds for thinking that it has been intentionally produced, and B might ask himself what A's intentions were in producing it. One plausible assumption is that this is a piece of ostensive behaviour: that is, that A intended B to notice the pattern. This would in turn make manifest A's desire to interact with B, which in the circumstances would be relevant enough.

Here is a more substantial example. Prisoners A and B are at work in their quarry, each with a guard at his shoulder, when suddenly the attention of the guards is distracted. Both prisoners realise that they have a good chance of escaping, but only if they can co-ordinate their attack and overpower their guards simultaneously. Here, it is clear what information would be relevant: each wants to know when the other will start the attack. Prisoner A suddenly whistles, the prisoners overpower their guards and escape. Again, there is no need for a pre-existing code correlating a whistle with the information that now is the moment to attack. The information is obvious enough: it is the only information that A could conceivably have intended to make manifest in the circumstances.

Could not the repetition of such a situation lead to the development of a code? Imagine that the two prisoners, caught again, find themselves in the same predicament: again a whistle, again an escape, and again they are caught. The next time, prisoner B, who has not realised that both guards are distracted, hears prisoner A whistle: this time, fortunately, B does not have to infer what the whistle is intended to make manifest: he knows. The whistle has become a signal associated by an underlying code to the message 'Let us overpower our guards now!'

Inferential theorists might be tempted to see language as a whole as having developed in this way: to see conventional meanings as growing out of natural inferences.[30] This is reminiscent of the story of how Rockefeller became a millionaire. One day, when he was young and very poor, Rockefeller found a one-cent coin in the street. He bought an apple, polished it, sold it for two cents, bought two apples, polished them, sold them for four cents... After one month he bought a cart, after two years he was about to buy a grocery store, when he inherited the fortune of his millionaire uncle. We will never know how far hominid efforts at conventionalising inference might have gone towards establishing a full-fledged human language. The fact is that the development of human languages was made possible by a specialised biological endowment.

Whatever the origin of the language or code employed, a piece of coded behaviour may be used ostensively – that is, to provide two layers of information: a basic layer of information, which may be about anything at all, and a second layer consisting of the information that the first layer of information has been intentionally made manifest. When a coded signal, or any other arbitrary piece of behaviour, is used ostensively, the evidence displayed bears directly on the individual's intention, and only indirectly on the basic layer of information that she intends to make manifest. We are now, of course, dealing with standard cases of Gricean communication.

Is there a dividing line between instances of ostension which one would be more inclined to describe as 'showing something', and clear cases of communication where the communicator unquestionably 'means something'? One of Grice's main concerns was to draw such a line: to distinguish what he called 'natural meaning' – smoke meaning fire, clouds meaning rain, etc. – from 'non-natural meaning': the word 'fire' meaning fire, Peter's utterance meaning that it will rain, etc. Essential to this distinction was the third type of communicator's intention Grice mentioned in his analysis: a true communicator intends the recognition of his informative intention to function as at least part of the audience's reason for fulfilling that intention. In other words, the first, basic, layer of information must not be entirely recoverable without reference to the second.

What we have tried to show so far in this section is that there are not two distinct and well-defined classes, but a continuum of cases of ostension ranging from 'showing', where strong direct evidence for the basic layer of information is provided, to 'saying that', where all the evidence is indirect. Even in our very first case of Peter leaning back ostensively to let Mary see William approaching, it is arguable that some of the basic information is made manifest indirectly, through Peter's intention being made manifest. Someone who engages in any kind of ostensive behaviour intentionally draws some attention to himself and intentionally makes manifest a few assumptions about himself: for instance, that he is aware of the basic information involved, and that he is trying to be relevant. Peter's ostension might make it manifest not just that William is approaching, but also that Peter expects Mary to be concerned, and that he is concerned too.

Would we want to say, though, that Peter 'meant something' by his behaviour? Like most English speakers, we would be reluctant to do so; but this is irrelevant to our pursuit, which is not to analyse ordinary language usage, but to describe and explain forms of human communication. Our argument at this stage is this: either inferential communication consists in providing evidence for what the communicator means, in the sense of 'meaning' which Grice calls 'non-natural meaning', and in that case inferential communication is not a well-defined class of phenomena at all; or else showing something should be considered a form of inferential communication, on a par with meaning something by a certain behaviour, and inferential communication and ostension should be equated.

There are two questions involved here. One is substantive: which domains of facts are to be described and explained together? Our answer is that ostension is such a domain, and that inferential communication narrowly understood (i.e. understood as excluding cases of ostension where talk of 'meaning' would be awkward) is not. The second question is terminological (and hence not worth much argument): can the term 'communication' be legitimately applied to all cases of ostension? Our answer is yes, and from now on we will treat ostensive communication, inferential communication, and ostensive–inferential communication as the same thing. Inferential communication and ostension are one and the same process, but seen from two different points of view: that of the communicator who is involved in ostension and that of the audience who is involved in inference.

Ostensive–inferential communication consists in making manifest to an audience one's intention to make manifest a basic layer of information. It can therefore be described in terms of an informative and a communicative intention. In the next two sections, we want to reanalyse the notions of informative and communicative intention in terms of manifestness and mutual manifestness, and to sketch in some of the empirical implications of this reformulation.

11 The informative intention

We began this chapter by pointing out that any account of communication must answer two questions: first, what is communicated; and second, how is communication achieved? Up to now, we have considered only the second question. In this section, we return to the first. The generally accepted answer is that what is communicated is a meaning. The question then becomes, what is a meaning? And there is no generally accepted answer any more.

However much they differ, all answers to the what-is-a-meaning question share the view that the paradigm example of meaning is what is explicitly expressed by a linguistic utterance. The verbal communication of an explicit meaning is then taken as the model of communication in general. This is true of semiotic approaches, which are not only generalisations of a linguistic model, but are also based on the assumption that to communicate is always, in Saussure's terms, to trasmit a 'signified' by use of a 'signifier'. It is true of inferential approaches, which regard all communicative acts as 'utterances' in an extended sense, used to convey an 'utterer's meaning'.

We believe that the kind of explicit communication that can be achieved by the use of language is not a typical but a limiting case. Treating linguistic communication as the model of communication in general has led to theoretical distortions and misperceptions of the data. The effects of most forms of human communication, including some of the effects of verbal communication, are far too vague to be properly analysed along these lines. Moreover, there is not a dichotomy but a continuum of cases, from vaguer to more precise effects.

Let us first illustrate this point with two examples of non-verbal communication. Mary comes home; Peter opens the door. Mary stops at the door and sniffs ostensively; Peter follows suit and notices that there is a smell of gas. This fact is highly relevant, and in the absence of contextual counterevidence or any obvious alternative candidate, Peter will assume that Mary intended to make it manifest to him that there was a smell of gas. Here, at least part of what is communicated could be reasonably well paraphrased by saying that there is a smell of gas; and it could be argued that this is what Mary *means*. She could indeed have achieved essentially the same result by speaking rather than sniffing ostensively.

Contrast this with the following case. Mary and Peter are newly arrived at the seaside. She opens the window overlooking the sea and sniffs appreciatively and ostensively. When Peter follows suit, there is no one particular good thing that comes to his attention: the air smells fresh, fresher than it did in town, it reminds him of their previous holidays, he can smell the sea, seaweed, ozone, fish; all sorts of pleasant things come to mind, and while, because her sniff was appreciative, he is reasonably safe in assuming that she must have intended him to notice at least some of them, he is unlikely to be able to pin her intentions down any further. Is there any reason to assume that her intentions were more specific? Is there a plausible answer, in the form of an explicit linguistic paraphrase, to the question, what does she mean? Could she have achieved the same communicative effect by speaking? Clearly not.

Examples like the one of Mary smelling gas, where it is reasonable to impute a meaning to the communicator, are the only ones normally considered in discussions of communication; examples like the one of Mary at the seaside – clearly communicating, but what? – are generally ignored. Yet these examples do not belong to distinct classes of phenomena, and it is easy enough to imagine intermediate cases: say, a guest sniffing appreciatively and ostensively when the stew is brought to the table, etc.

The distortions and misperceptions introduced by the explicit communication model are also found in the study of verbal communication itself. Some essential aspects of implicit verbal communication are overlooked. Pragmatists assume that what is communicated by an utterance is a speaker's meaning, which in the case of an assertion is a set of assumptions. One of these assumptions is explicitly expressed; the others (if any) are implicitly conveyed, or implicated. The only difference between the explicit content of an utterance and its implicatures is supposed to be that the explicit content is decoded, while the implicatures are inferred. Now we all know, as speakers and hearers, that what is implicitly conveyed by an utterance is generally much vaguer than what is explicitly expressed, and that when the implicit import of an utterance is explicitly spelled out, it tends to be distorted by the elimination of this often intentional vagueness. The distortion is even greater in the case of metaphor and other figures of speech, whose poetic effects are generally destroyed by being explicitly spelled out.

In an effort to minimise the distortion, pragmatists have tended to focus on examples such as (32), where the implicit import is fairly precise, and to ignore equally ordinary cases of implicit vagueness such as (51):

(32) *Peter*: Do you want some coffee?
    Mary: Coffee would keep me awake.

(51) *Peter*: What do you intend to do today?
    Mary: I have a terrible headache.

In (32), Mary implicates that she doesn't want coffee (or, in some circumstances, that she does) and that her reason for not wanting it is that it would keep her awake. Here the implicatures can be spelled out without distortion. In (51), what does Mary implicate? That she will not do anything? That she will do as little as possible? That she will do as much as she can? That she does not yet know what she will do? There is no precise assumption, apart from the one explicitly expressed, which she can be said to intend Peter to share. Yet there is more to her utterance than its explicit content: she manifestly intends Peter to draw some conclusions from what she said, and not just any conclusions. Quite ordinary cases such as (51) are never discussed in the pragmatic literature.

Pragmatists tend to take for granted that a meaning is a proposition combined with a propositional attitude, though they may diverge considerably in the way they present and develop this view. In other words, they treat the communicator's informative intention as an intention to induce in an audience certain attitudes to certain propositions. With assertions, often taken to be the most basic case, the informative intention is treated as an intention to induce in an audience the belief that a certain proposition is true.

There is a very good reason for anyone concerned with the role of inference in communication to assume that what is communicated is propositional: it is relatively easy to say what propositions are, and how inference might operate over propositions. No one has any clear idea how inference might operate over non-propositional objects: say, over images, impressions or emotions. Propositional contents and attitudes thus seem to provide the only relatively solid ground on which to base a partly or wholly inferential approach to communication. Too bad if much of what is communicated does not fit the propositional mould.

At first sight, it might look as if semioticians had a more comprehensive view. They have an *a priori* account of how any kind of representation, propositional or not, might be conveyed: namely, by means of a code. However, studies by semioticians of what they call 'connotation', i.e. the vaguer aspect of what is communicated, are highly programmatic and do not offer the beginnings of a psychologically adequate account of the type of mental representation involved.[31] The semiotic approach is more comprehensive only by being more superficial.

The only people who have been quite consistently concerned with the vaguer aspects of communication are the Romantics, from the Schlegel brothers and Coleridge to I. A. Richards, and their many acknowledged or unacknowledged followers, including many semioticians such as Roman Jakobson in some of his writings, Victor Turner, or Roland Barthes. However, they have all dealt with vagueness in vague terms, with metaphors in metaphorical terms, and used the term 'meaning' so broadly that it becomes quite meaningless.

We see it as a major challenge for any account of human communication to give a precise description and explanation of its vaguer effects. Distinguishing meaning from communication, accepting that something can be communicated without being strictly speaking *meant* by the communicator or the communicator's behaviour, is a first essential step – a step away from the traditional approach to communication and most modern approaches. Once this step is taken, we believe that the framework we propose, unlike the others we have discussed, can rise to this challenge.

Accounts of communication either are not psychological at all, and avoid all talk of thoughts, intentions, etc., or else they assume that a communicator's intention is to induce certain specific thoughts in an audience. We want to suggest that the communicator's informative intention is better described as an intention to modify directly not the thoughts but the cognitive environment of the audience. The actual cognitive effects of a modification of the cognitive environment are only partly predictable. Communicators – like human agents in general – form intentions over whose fulfilment they have some control: they can have some controllable effect on their audience's cognitive environment, much less on their audience's actual thoughts, and they form their intentions accordingly.

We therefore propose to reformulate the notion of an informative intention along the following lines. A communicator produces a stimulus intending thereby

(52) *Informative intention*: to make manifest or more manifest to the audience a set of assumptions I.

We take an intention to be a psychological state, and we assume that the content of the intention must be mentally represented. In particular, the communicator must have in mind a representation of the set of assumptions I which she intends to make manifest or more manifest to the audience. However, to have a representation of a set of assumptions it is not necessary to have a representation of each assumption in the set. Any individuating description may do.

When the communicator's intention is to make manifest some specific assumptions, then, of course, her representation of I may be in the form of a list of assumptions which are members of I. Consider dialogue (53), for instance:

(53) *Passenger*: When does the train arrive at Oxford?
Ticket-collector: At 5:25.

Here the ticket-collector's informative intention is to make manifest to the passenger the single assumption that the train arrives at 5:25. Examples of this type, where the communicator wants to communicate one or more specific assumptions which she actually has in mind, are the only ones usually considered. Our characterisation (52) of informative intentions fits these cases quite straightforwardly, but unlike other approaches, is not limited to them.

Consider, at the other extreme, the vaguest forms of communication. Here the communicator may have a representation of I in which none of the assumptions in I is directly listed. For instance, Mary's informative intention when sniffing the seaside air might be that all the assumptions which became manifest to her when she opened the window and took a deep breath should, as a result of her ostensive behaviour, become manifest or more manifest to Peter. She need not intend to communicate any particular one of these assumptions.

If asked what she wanted to convey, one of the best answers Mary could give is that she wanted to share an impression with Peter. What is an impression? Is it a type of mental representation? Can it be reduced to propositions and propositional attitudes? What we are suggesting is that an impression might be better described as a noticeable change in one's cognitive environment, a change resulting from relatively small alterations in the manifestness of many assumptions, rather than from the fact that a single assumption or a few new assumptions have all of a sudden become very manifest. It is quite in line with common sense to think of an impression as the sort of thing that can be communicated, and yet this intuition is unexplainable within current theories of communication. In the model of ostensive–inferential communication we are trying to develop, impressions fall squarely within the domain of things that can be communicated, and their very vagueness can be precisely described.

In many – perhaps most – cases of human communication, what the communicator intends to make manifest is partly precise and partly vague. She may have in mind a characterisation of I based on a representation of some but not all of the assumptions in I. For instance, in (51), Mary's informative intention in saying that she has a headache might be described as follows: she intends to make manifest to Peter the assumption that she has a headache and all the further assumptions manifestly required to make this a relevant answer to Peter's question. Similarly, Mary's informative intention when sniffing the smell of gas might be to make manifest to Peter not only the assumption that there is a smell of gas, but also all the further assumptions that this initial assumption makes mutually manifest.

Instead of treating an assumption as either communicated or not communicated, we have a set of assumptions which, as a result of communication, become manifest or more manifest to varying degrees. We might think of communication itself, then, as a matter of degree. When the communicator makes strongly manifest her informative intention to make some particular assumption strongly manifest, then that assumption is strongly communicated. An example would be answering a clear 'Yes' when asked 'Did you pay the rent?' When the communicator's intention is to increase simultaneously the manifestness of a wide range of assumptions, so that her intention concerning each of these assumptions is weakly manifest, then each of them is weakly communicated. An example would be sniffing ecstatically and ostensively at the fresh seaside air. There is, of course, a continuum of cases in between. In the case of strong communication, the communicator can have fairly precise expectations about some of the thoughts that the audience will actually entertain. With weaker forms of communication, the communicator can merely expect to steer the thoughts of the audience in a certain direction. Often, in human interaction, weak communication is found sufficient or even preferable to the stronger forms.

Non-verbal communication tends to be relatively weak. One of the advantages of verbal communication is that it gives rise to the strongest possible form of communication; it enables the hearer to pin down the speaker's intentions about the explicit content of her utterance to a single, strongly manifest candidate, with no alternative worth considering at all. On the other hand, what is implicit in verbal communication is generally weakly communicated: the hearer can often fulfil part of the speaker's informative intention by forming any of several roughly similar but not identical assumptions. Because all communication has been seen as strong communication, descriptions of non-verbal communication have been marred by spurious attributions of 'meaning'; in the case of verbal communication, the difference between explicit content and implicit import has been seen as a difference not in what gets communicated but merely in the means by which it is communicated, and the vagueness of implicatures and non-literal forms of expression has been idealised away. Our account of informative intentions in terms of manifestness of assumptions corrects these distortions without introducing either *ad hoc* machinery or vagueness of description.

12 The communicative intention

When we introduced the notion of a communicative intention in section 6, we drew attention to a problem first discussed by Strawson (1964a). Strawson pointed out that a communicator's intentions must be 'overt' in a sense which is easy enough to illustrate and grasp intuitively, but hard to spell out precisely. One type of solution, proposed by Strawson himself, is to regard an intention as overt when it is backed by a series of further intentions, each to the effect that the preceding intention in the series should be recognised. Schiffer (1972) proposed another solution: he analysed 'overt' as meaning mutually known. We argued that both types of solution are psychologically implausible.

Our solution, which is closer to Schiffer's than Strawson's, though without suffering from the defects of either, is to replace the vague 'overt' by the more precise 'mutually manifest'. We therefore redefine a communicative intention as follows. To communicate intentionally by ostension is to produce a certain stimulus with the aim of fulfilling an informative intention, and intending moreover thereby

(54) *Communicative intention*: to make it mutually manifest to audience and communicator that the communicator has this informative intention.

This takes care of the types of example which Strawson and Schiffer used to show that, in order to communicate, it is not quite enough to inform an audience of one's informative intention. For instance, in our example in section 6, Mary leaves the pieces of her broken hair-drier lying around, intending thereby to inform Peter that she would like him to mend it. She wants this informative intention to be manifest to Peter, but at the same time, she does not want it to be 'overt'. In our terms, she does not want her informative intention to be mutually manifest. Intuitively, what she does is not quite communicate. Our redefinition of a communicative intention accounts for this intuition.

What difference does it make whether an informative intention is merely manifest to the audience or mutually manifest to audience and communicator? Should this really be a criterion for distinguishing communication from other forms of information transmission? Is it more than a technicality designed to take care of implausible borderline cases dreamed up by philosophers? Our answer is that there is indeed an essential difference.

Consider first a more general question: why should someone who has an informative intention bother to make it known to her audience that she has this intention? In other words, what are the reasons for engaging in ostensive communication? Grice discussed only one of these reasons: sometimes, making one's informative intention known is the best way, or the only way, of fulfilling it. We have shown that people sometimes engage in ostensive communication even though the informative intention could be fulfilled without being made manifest: for example, by providing direct evidence for the information to be conveyed. However, even in these cases, ostension helps focus the attention of the audience on the relevant information, and thus contributes to the fulfilment of the informative intention. This is still the Gricean reason for engaging in communication, just slightly extended in scope.

However, we want to argue that there is another major reason for engaging in ostensive communication, apart from helping to fulfil an informative intention. Mere informing alters the cognitive environment of the audience. Communication alters the mutual cognitive environment of the audience and communicator. Mutual manifestness may be of little cognitive importance, but it is of crucial social importance. A change in the mutual cognitive environment of two people is a change in their possibilities of interaction (and, in particular, in their possibilities of further communication).

Recall, for instance, the case of Peter leaning back to let Mary see William coming their way. If, as a result of his behaviour, it becomes mutually manifest to them that William is coming, that they are in danger of being bored by his conversation, etc., then they are in a position to act efficiently: i.e. promptly. All Mary may have to do is say, 'Let's go!'; she can feel confident that Peter will understand her reasons, and, if he shares them, will be ready to act without question or delay.

In the case of the broken hair-drier, if Mary had made mutually manifest her wish that Peter would mend it, one of two things would have happened. Either he would have mended it, thus granting her wish and possibly putting her in his debt; or he would have failed to mend it, which would have amounted to a refusal or rejection. Mary avoids putting herself in his debt or meeting with a refusal by avoiding any modification of their mutual cognitive environment. If Peter mends the hair-drier, he is being kind on his own initiative, and she does not owe him anything. If Peter decides not to mend the hair-drier, he might reason as follows: she doesn't know I know she intended to inform me of her wish, so if I ignore it, she will attribute this to her failure to inform me; she may find me stupid, but not unkind. As for Mary, she may have intentionally left this line of reasoning open to Peter. If he does not mend her hair-drier, she will find him unkind, but not hostile. His failure to grant her wish will not be in the nature of a rebuff. They will stand in exactly the same social relationship to each other as before. This shows how ostensive communication may have social implications that other forms of information transmission do not.

By making her informative intention mutually manifest, the communicator creates the following situation: it becomes mutually manifest that the fulfilment of her informative intention is, so to speak, in the hands of the audience. If the assumptions that she intends to make manifest to the audience become manifest, then she is successful; if the audience refuses to accept these assumptions as true or probably true, then she has failed in her informative intention. Suppose – we will soon see how this may happen – that the audience's behaviour makes it mutually manifest that the informative intention is fulfilled. Then the set of assumptions I that the communicator intended to make manifest to the audience becomes, at least apparently, mutually manifest. We say 'at least apparently' because, if the communicator is not sincere and some of the assumptions in I are not manifest to her, then by our definition of mutual manifestness, these assumptions cannot be mutually manifest to her and others.[32]

A communicator is normally interested in knowing whether or not she has succeeded in fulfilling her informative intention, and this interest is mutually manifest to her and her audience. In face-to-face communication, the audience is generally expected to respond to this interest in fairly conventional ways. Often, for instance, the audience is expected to communicate its refusal to accept the information communicated, or else it becomes mutually manifest that the communicator's informative intention is fulfilled.

Where communication is non-reciprocal, there are various possible situations to be taken into account. The communicator may be in a position of such authority over her audience that the success of her informative intention is mutually manifest in advance. Journalists, professors, religious or political leaders assume, alas often on good grounds, that what they communicate automatically becomes mutually manifest. When the communicator lacks that kind of authority, but still wants to establish a mutual cognitive environment with her audience, all she has to do is adapt her informative intentions to her credibility. For instance, in writing this book we merely intend to make mutually manifest that we have developed certain hypotheses and have done so on certain grounds. That is, we take it as mutually manifest that you will accept our authority on what we actually think. The mutual cognitive environment thus created is enough for us to go on to communicate further thoughts which we would otherwise have been unable to communicate. (Of course we would also like to convince you, but we hope to do this by the force of our arguments, and not by making you recognise our informative intentions.)

We began this chapter by asking how human beings communicate with one another. Our answer is that they use two quite different modes of communication: coded communication and ostensive–inferential communication. However, the two modes of communication are used in fundamentally different ways. Whereas ostensive–inferential communication can be used on its own, and sometimes is, coded communication is only used as a means of strengthening ostensive–inferential communication. This is how language is used in verbal communication, as we will argue in chapter 4.

Ostensive–inferential communication can be defined as follows:

(55) *Ostensive–inferential communication*: the communicator produces a stimulus which makes it mutually manifest to communicator and audience that the communicator intends, by means of this stimulus, to make manifest or more manifest to the audience a set of assumptions I.

As this definition stands, it does not exclude the possibility of unintentional communication: that is, a stimulus merely intended to inform might make mutually manifest the intention to inform, and this, by our definition, would count as communication. For instance, suppose Mary yawns, intending to inform Peter that she is tired, and hoping that her yawn will look natural. She does not do it too well: it is all too obvious that her yawn is artificial — and her informative intention becomes mutually manifest. We see no reason for refusing to call this a case of unintended ostensive communication. It would be easy enough, though, to modify definition (55) and make intentionality a defining feature of communication.

In any case, most human communication is intentional, and it is intentional for two good reasons. The first reason is the one suggested by Grice: by producing direct evidence of one's informative intention, one can convey a much wider range of information than can be conveyed by producing direct evidence for the basic information itself. The second reason humans have for communicating is to modify and extend the mutual cognitive environment they share with one another.

What we have offered so far is a good enough description of ostensive–inferential communication. However, we have not explained how it works. We have suggested that the explanation is to be sought in a principle of relevance. To make this principle truly explanatory, we must first make the notion of relevance much more explicit, and to do this we must consider how information is mentally represented and inferentially processed. This, then, is the programme for the next two chapters.

2

Inference

1 Non-demonstrative inference

In the last chapter, we outlined a model of ostensive–inferential communication, looking more closely at the ostensive nature of the communicator's behaviour than at the inferential nature of comprehension. In this chapter, we will outline a model of the inferential abilities involved in comprehension. Here, we have already made two broad hypotheses on which we hope to build. First, we implicitly assumed that the process of inferential comprehension is non-demonstrative: even under the best of circumstances, we argued, communication may fail. The addressee can neither decode nor deduce the communicator's communicative intention. The best he can do is construct an assumption on the basis of the evidence provided by the communicator's ostensive behaviour. For such an assumption, there may be confirmation but no proof.

Second, we explicitly assumed that any conceptually represented information available to the addressee can be used as a premise in this inference process. In other words, we assumed that the process of inferential comprehension is 'global' as opposed to 'local': where a local process (e.g. deductive reasoning from fixed premises or auditory perception) is either context-free or sensitive only to contextual information from some set domain, and a global process (e.g. empirical scientific reasoning) has free access to all conceptual information in memory.

A non-demonstrative inference process with free access to conceptual memory: this sounds, appropriately enough, like an ordinary central thought process. A distinction between 'central' processes and 'input', 'perceptual' or 'peripheral' processes is assumed in much of current cognitive psychology. Roughly speaking, input processes are relatively specialised decoding processes, whereas central processes are relatively unspecialised inferential processes. The distinction will be discussed and illustrated below.

We do maintain that inferential comprehension involves no specialised mechanisms. In particular, we will argue that the inferential tier of verbal comprehension involves the application of central, unspecialised inference processes to the output of specialised, non-inferential linguistic processes. It seems, then, that our undertaking – and the whole pragmatic enterprise if our understanding of it is correct – should fall (and we use the word advisedly) under Fodor's First Law of the Nonexistence of Cognitive Science, which goes, 'the more global . . . a cognitive process is, the less anybody understands it' (Fodor 1983: 107).[a]

Fodor points out that while something is known about the operation of the perceptual systems, very little is known about the so-called central thought processes, which integrate information derived from the perceptual systems with information stored in memory, and perform a variety of inferential tasks. As a typical example of a central thought process, he takes scientific theorising. The construction and confirmation of a scientific theory is a global operation in the sense that there is no piece of evidence, however remote, no hypothesis, however implausible, that might not turn out to have a bearing on its outcome. It is the global nature of scientific theorising, Fodor suggests, that makes it so unamenable to study. To the extent that other central processes share this property, they are likely to prove equally resistant to investigation:

> the reason that there is no serious psychology of central processes is the same as the reason there is no serious philosophy of scientific confirmation. Both exemplify the significance of global factors in the fixation of belief, and nobody begins to understand how such factors have their effects. (Fodor 1983: 129)

If inferential comprehension is a central thought process, the wish to construct an adequate theory of ostensive–inferential communication appears to lead into very deep waters indeed.

We do not entirely share this pessimism. We doubt that scientific theorising is the most appropriate model of a central cognitive process. Inferential comprehension, which we are claiming is also a central process, differs from scientific theorising in a number of relevant respects. First, although both processes are global in Fodor's sense, they operate on very different time-scales. Because the construction and evaluation of a scientific theory may take all the time in the world, the range of hypotheses that can be considered, and the range of evidence that can be taken into account, can be enormous, not just in theory but in practice. By contrast, ordinary utterance comprehension is almost instantaneous, and however much evidence *might* have been taken into account, however many hypotheses *might* have been considered, in practice the only evidence and hypotheses considered are those that are immediately accessible.

In the second place, the data for scientific theorising come from nature, which is not actively involved in helping humans build correct scientific theories. By contrast, the data for the comprehension process come from a helpful source. People would not communicate ostensively if they did not want their communicative intentions to be recognised, and they devise their stimuli accordingly. Moreover, while it is quite conceivable that it is beyond the power of humans to construct a fully adequate scientific theory, successful inferential comprehension is demonstrably within the grasp of the normal intellect. Verbal comprehension in particular, with its well-described linguistic stimuli and relatively clear criteria of success, is much more amenable to investigation than scientific theorising. Precisely because it is a central process, and is not a separate, purpose-built ability like the visual or grammatical abilities, an adequate account of inferential comprehension should shed light on other central processes, about which, as Fodor rightly emphasises, so little is so far known.

As we will show in chapter 3, the fact that verbal comprehension is almost instantaneous, and is achieved with the active help of the information source, i.e. the speaker, makes the hearer's choice of a context from the whole of conceptual memory more amenable to study. However, the richness of the accessible information is only one of the two main obstacles to investigation of the central cognitive processes. The other has to do with the nature of the inference processes that this information undergoes. Although logic provides us with several models of demonstrative inference, it is agreed that the inference processes involved in comprehension are non-demonstrative. While it is generally assumed that non-demonstrative inference must be based on inductive rules of some kind, there is no well-developed system of inductive logic that would provide us with a plausible model of the central cognitive processes.

Moreover, humans may be capable of controlling more than one technique for performing non-demonstrative inference. A scientist self-consciously applying explicit standards of confirmation to each piece of available evidence may well be using a quite different system from those we all use – scientists included – in making spontaneous, instantaneous and unconscious inferences about the movements of other vehicles while driving a car, about what some appetising food might taste like, or about a speaker's communicative intention. Here, we are only concerned with spontaneous non-demonstrative inference, which we take to be of more general psychological significance than the painstakingly acquired inferential techniques of the scientist.

Even the claim that a proper model of spontaneous non-demonstrative inference is to be found in a system of inductive logic is open to question. Inference is the process by which an assumption is accepted as true or probably true on the strength of the truth or probable truth of other assumptions. It is thus a form of fixation of belief. There are other forms: perception, for instance, is a process by which an assumption is accepted as true or probably true on the strength of a non-conceptual cognitive experience. Demonstrative inference, the only form of inference that is well understood, consists in the application of deductive *rules* to an initial set of premises. There is thus a temptation to think of non-demonstrative inference as the application of non-deductive inference rules. However, this temptation is based on analogy rather than argument. In fact, there is reason to doubt that spontaneous non-demonstrative inference, as performed by humans, involves the use of non-deductive inference rules.

Deductive inference rules generate all the interesting conclusions logically implied by a set of premises.[1] It is generally recognised that non-demonstrative inference rules cannot be expected to *generate* all the interesting conclusions non-demonstratively supported by a set of premises. For instance, the theory of relativity could not have been generated by applying inference rules to the results of Eddington's experiment. Instead, the process of reaching valid non-demonstrative conclusions is generally broken down into two distinct stages: hypothesis formation and hypothesis confirmation. Eddington's experiment provided the first empirical confirmation of Einstein's theory, but did not in any sense imply it. Hypothesis formation, it is argued, is a matter of creative imagination; hypothesis confirmation, on the other hand, can be seen as a purely logical process governed by inference rules.

The function of inference rules is to guarantee the logical *validity* of the inferences they govern. In a valid demonstrative inference, the application of deductive rules to true premises guarantees the truth of the conclusions. Similarly, in a valid non-demonstrative inference, hypothesis confirmation could be seen as governed by logical rules. These confirmation rules might apply jointly to the premises, or 'evidence', and the tentative conclusions, or 'assumptions', and assign a degree of confirmation to the assumptions on the basis of the evidence. It is tempting to move from these logical considerations to psychological speculation.

Humans are rather good at non-demonstrative reasoning; otherwise the species would be extinct. This might be because they have logical rules which constrain the confirmation of assumptions in the way just described. However, this is not much of an explanation, since we have no clear idea of what these rules might be. Also, at this level of vagueness, other explanations are possible. For all we know, human inferential successes might be attributable not so much to logical constraints on confirmation as to cognitive constraints on hypothesis formation.

The constraints on human conceptual systems might be such that the only spontaneously devisable hypotheses are those which, if false, are very likely to be contradicted by perceptually fixed beliefs. In fact, there are independent reasons for assuming that human conceptual systems are so constrained. For instance, no human language contains a word such as 'grue', the troublesome term invented by Nelson Goodman (1955) which applies to anything which is either green and examined before some time t, or blue and examined after t. If t is the year 3000 and all the emeralds you have ever seen have been green, then you have evidence that all emeralds are grue, and therefore that all emeralds examined after year 3000 will be blue. Moreover, the hypothesis that all emeralds are grue rather than green could not be falsified by any empirical evidence available before the year 3000. It is quite remarkable that natural language predicates prevent such paradoxes from arising.

We are suggesting, then, that non-demonstrative inference, as spontaneously performed by humans, might be less a logical process than a form of suitably constrained guesswork. If so, it should be seen as successful or unsuccessful, efficient or inefficient, rather than as logically valid or invalid. We would like to pursue this idea and make an even stronger claim: that the only logical rules spontaneously accessible to the human mind are *deductive* rules. Deductive rules, we will argue, play a crucial role in non-demonstrative inference. Of course, the validity of a deductive inference does not guarantee the validity of the overall non-demonstrative inference of which it forms a part. Human spontaneous non-demonstrative inference is not, overall, a logical process. Hypothesis formation involves the use of deductive rules, but is not totally governed by them; hypothesis confirmation is a non-logical cognitive phenomenon: it is a by-product of the way assumptions are processed, deductively or otherwise.

By its very definition, a non-demonstrative inference cannot *consist* in a deduction. Many authors seem to make the much stronger and unwarranted hypothesis that a non-demonstrative inference cannot *contain* a deduction as one of its sub-parts. The recovery of implicatures, for example, is a paradigm case of non-demonstrative inference, and it is becoming a commonplace of the pragmatic literature that deduction plays little if any role in this process. Leech (1983: 30-1) claims that the process by which implicatures are recovered 'is not a formalised deductive logic, but an informal rational problem-solving strategy', and that 'all implicatures are probabilistic'. Levinson (1983: 115-16) suggests that in certain respects implicatures 'appear to be quite unlike logical inferences, and cannot be directly modelled in terms of some semantic relation like entailment'. Bach and Harnish (1979: 92-3) argue that the form of inference by which implicatures are recovered 'is not deductive but what might be called an inference to a plausible explanation'. Brown and Yule (1983: 33) say, more generally,

> It may be the case that we are capable of drawing a specific conclusion . . . from specific premises . . . via deductive inference, but we are rarely asked to do so in the everyday discourse we encounter. . . . We are more likely to operate with a rather loose form of inferencing.

Similar views are expressed by de Beaugrande and Dressler (1981: 93–4):

> Humans are evidently capable of intricate reasoning processes that traditional logics cannot explain: jumping to conclusions, pursuing subjective analogies, and even reasoning in the absence of knowledge. . . . The important standard here is not that such a procedure is logically unsound, but rather that the procedures work well enough in everyday affairs.

However, those pragmatists who express scepticism about the role of deductive reasoning in comprehension generally have little positive to say about the nature of the inference processes involved. Bach and Harnish comment, (1979: 93),

> Our empirical thinking in general is rife with generalizations and inference principles that we are not conscious of when we use them, if we are conscious of them at all. It would take us well beyond present-day cognitive psychology to speculate on the details of any of this. Whatever these processes are, whatever activates them, whatever principles or strategies are involved, they work, and work well.

But the fact that these procedures work well enough in everyday utterance comprehension does not absolve us from saying what they are. If anything, the lack of any existing framework for describing them should make us more, not less interested in their nature.[2]

Pragmatic theory in general is condemned to vagueness if it says nothing more about the inference processes involved in comprehension than that they are non-demonstrative, a purely negative characterisation. Moreover pragmatic theories in which some notion of relevance plays a role (i.e. most pragmatic theories) need some account of non-demonstrative inference for a second reason: one common way of achieving relevance consists in providing the addressee with evidence which bears on some assumption of his. Consider the following dialogue, for instance:

(1) *Peter*: According to the weather forecast, it's going to rain.
   Mary (standing at the window): It certainly looks like it.

Mary's remark does not prove that it will rain, but it confirms Peter's belief and achieves relevance thereby. Relevant information, we have suggested, is information that modifies and improves an overall representation of the world. Confirmation of an assumption by a non-demonstrative inference process is a case in point.

It seems, then, that the comprehension process may involve confirmation of assumptions in two quite different ways, or on two quite different levels. On the one hand, as we saw in chapter 1, understanding a piece of ostensive behaviour involves constructing and confirming a hypothesis about the communicator's informative intention. On the other, as we have just suggested, the most relevant effect of ostension may be to confirm some previous assumption of the audience. A clearer account of non-demonstrative inference processes should thus shed light on the role of relevance in both communication and cognition: on what is involved in constructing and confirming a hypothesis about the communicator's intentions; on what it is for a representation of the world to be modified and improved; and on the relation between the two.

We will suggest an approach to non-demonstrative inference which we hope will go some way towards resolving these issues. But first we must specify the domain of spontaneous non-demonstrative inference and say a little more about what it is to have an overall representation of the world.

2 Logical forms, propositional attitudes and factual assumptions

Following Fodor (1983), we see the mind as a variety of specialised systems, each with its own method of representation and computation. These systems are of two broad types. On the one hand there are the input systems, which process visual, auditory, linguistic and other perceptual information. On the other hand there are the central systems, which integrate information derived from the various input systems and from memory, and perform inferential tasks.[b]

We assume that each input system has its own method of representation and computation, and can process only information in the appropriate representational format. Auditory perception can process only acoustic information, and the processes involved in auditory perception differ from those involved in olfactory perception, etc. One of the functions of the input systems is to transform 'lower level' sensory representations into 'higher level' conceptual representations, which are all in the same format regardless of the sensory modality from which they derive. It is because they operate over such modality-neutral conceptual representations that the central processes can integrate and compare information derived from the various input systems and from memory.

The fact that many central processes are inferential puts an important constraint on the conceptual representation system. Conceptual representations must have logical properties: they must be capable of implying or contradicting one another, and of undergoing deductive rules. However, not all properties of a conceptual representation are logical properties. A conceptual representation is both a mental state and a brain state.[3] As a mental state, it can have such non-logical properties as being happy or sad. As a brain state, it can have such non-logical properties as being located in a certain brain at a certain time for a certain duration. Let us abstract away from all these non-logical properties, and call the remaining logical properties of a conceptual representation its *logical form*. It is in virtue of its logical form that a conceptual representation is involved in logical processes and enters into relations such as contradiction or implication with other conceptual representations.

A logical form is a well-formed formula, a structured set of constituents, which undergoes formal logical operations determined by its structure. As we have already said, what distinguishes logical operations from other formal operations is that they are truth-preserving: a deduction from a true representation P yields a true representation Q. By contrast, deleting the first constituent of a representation, say, is a formal operation but not a logical one. Given this relationship between truth and logic, it might seem that only a conceptual representation which is capable of being true or false can have a logical form. We see things rather differently. In essence, we will argue that for a representation to be amenable to logical processing, all that is necessary is for it to be well formed, whereas to be capable of being true or false, it must also be semantically complete: that is, it must represent a state of affairs, in a possible or actual world, whose existence would make it true. We take it that an incomplete conceptual structure can nevertheless be well formed, and can undergo logical processing.

Let us say that a logical form is *propositional* if it is semantically complete and therefore capable of being true or false, and *non-propositional* otherwise. A formal example of a non-propositional logical form is a predicate calculus formula containing a free variable: this may be syntactically well formed without being fully propositional. A psychological example of a non-propositional logical form is the sense of a sentence. Given that 'she' and 'it' in (2) below do not correspond to definite concepts, but merely mark an unoccupied place where a concept might go, sentence (2) is neither true or false:

(2) She carried it in her hand.

In spite of its non-propositionality, (2) has obvious logical properties. For instance, it implies (3), which is equally non-propositional, and it contradicts (4), which is, or can be understood as, propositional:

(3) She held something in her hand.
(4) No one ever carried anything.

Incomplete logical forms play an important role in cognition. In the first place, we will argue that they may be stored in conceptual memory as assumption schemas, which can be completed into full-fledged assumptions on the basis of contextual information. In the second place, as we have just seen, the sense of a sentence is often an incomplete logical form. We will show in chapter 4 that when a natural-language sentence is uttered, the linguistic input system automatically decodes it into its logical form (or in the case of an ambiguous sentence a set of logical forms), which the hearer is normally expected to complete into the fully propositional form that the speaker intended to convey.[4]

However, while non-propositional logical forms may play an important role in intermediate stages of information processing, only fully propositional forms represent definite states of affairs. It is these that constitute the individual's encyclopaedic knowledge, his overall representation of the world.

The mind does not just construct and store logical forms: it entertains them in different ways. A philosopher would say that the mind is capable of different propositional attitudes; a cognitive psychologist might say that different representations are processed and stored in different ways. For instance, a propositional form can be entertained as a description of an actual state of affairs, as a description of a desirable state of affairs, or as a good rendering (e.g. a summary) of some other representation. An individual encyclopaedic memory consists not merely of a stock of conceptual representations but of a stock of representations with propositional or non-propositional logical forms, entertained in different ways, as objects of different attitudes such as belief and desire.

Utterances, too, convey different attitudes to the representations they express. Some basic attitudes are conveyed by syntactic means, in particular by the mood of the verb. In English, for instance, there is a correspondence between indicative mood and the attitude of belief, and between imperative mood and the attitude of desire. Other attitudes are expressed by lexical means: that is, the speaker's attitude is made explicit in a main clause, as in (5), or a parenthetical clause, as in (6):

(5) I wish that P.
(6) P, I suppose.

The attitudes which can be expressed lexically are much more numerous and varied than those which can be expressed syntactically. Arguably, similar alternatives exist in the conceptual representation system, the language of thought. That is, there may be one or two basic formats for distinguishing, say, the attitudes of belief and desire, together with a range of conceptual resources for expressing or recording a wide range of further attitudes. We would like to pursue this possibility.

Let us assume that there is a basic memory store[5] with the following property: any representation stored in it is treated by the mind as a true description of the actual world, a fact. What this means is that a fundamental propositional attitude of belief or assumption is pre-wired into the very architecture of the mind. As a result, a representation can be entertained as an assumption without the fact that it is an assumption being explicitly expressed. Such basic assumptions, entertained as true descriptions of the world, but not explicitly represented as such, we will call *factual assumptions*.

The human internal representation system is clearly rich enough to allow for second-order representations of representations. In other words, the language of thought acts as its own meta-language: we are capable not only of entertaining assumptions but also of thinking about them and about other representations. It is thus possible not merely to entertain the belief that P, but to represent to oneself the fact that one believes that P, or that someone else believes that P, or that one believes that someone else believes that P, and so on. The belief or assumption that P can thus be held in two different ways: either as the basic factual assumption that P, or as the factual assumption *I believe that P*.[6]

Conceivably, the attitude of desire might parallel the attitude of belief in having its own basic memory store or storage format. This would mean that desire, like belief, was pre-wired into the architecture of the human cognitive system. It would follow that the desire that P could be held in two different ways: either as the basic desire that P, or as the factual assumption *I desire that P*. Alternatively, there might be only a single basic memory store, the one used for factual assumptions. In that case desires could play a cognitive role only by being represented in factual assumptions of the form *I desire that P*.

As far as we can see, factual assumption is the only obvious case of an attitude marked off by a special form of storage, and desire is the only other plausible case. It seems unlikely that other propositional attitudes – e.g. doubting that P, regretting that P, fearing that P, pretending that P – have their own basic memory stores. If we are right, these attitudes can play a cognitive role only via factual assumptions of the form *It is dubious that P, I regret that P, I am afraid that P*, and so on.

A representation of the world, then, may be regarded without too much oversimplification as a stock of factual assumptions, some basic, others expressing attitudes to embedded propositional or non-propositional representations. Factual assumptions are the domain *par excellence* of spontaneous non-demonstrative inference processes. Each newly acquired factual assumption is combined with a stock of existing assumptions to undergo inference processes whose aim, we have suggested, is to modify and improve the individual's overall representation of the world.[7]

When a representation is stored not as a basic factual assumption but by being embedded under an expression of attitude, it is often processed in a self-conscious, non-spontaneous way. This is true of representations used in problem-solving tasks of the kind familiar from experimental psychology. It is true of speculatively held opinions, religious beliefs, or scientific hypotheses. The largely conscious reasoning processes which these indirectly held representations undergo are of great intrinsic interest, but we see it as a mistake to extrapolate from them to the spontaneous and essentially unconscious inference processes used in most ordinary thinking, and in particular in ordinary verbal comprehension.

The model of inferential communication and the notion of relevance we are developing are not tied to any particular form of inference. We assume, for instance, that the lengthy and highly self-conscious processes of textual interpretation that religious or literary scholars engage in are governed just as much by considerations of relevance as is spontaneous utterance comprehension. However, in this book we want to focus on the latter. Spontaneous inference plays a role even in scholarly interpretation, whereas scholarly thinking is a rather exceptional human endeavour, even for scholars. The study of spontaneous inference is thus a necessary prerequisite to a proper investigation of all forms of human inference, including inferential communication.

3 Strength of assumptions

Factual assumptions are entertained with greater or lesser confidence; we think of them as more or less likely to be true. We do so consciously in two main types of situation. First, we may have to choose between contradictory assumptions, as when I assumed that Bob would be out of town, and now I assume that I am seeing him walking down the street: of the two assumptions, the one I regard as more likely to be true will displace the other. Second, we may have to choose between different courses of action, as when I want to buy some petrol, and I assume that both the petrol station up the street and the one down the street are open: if I regard the assumption that the station down the street is open as more likely to be true, that is where I will go.

When our more confident assumptions are those which are in fact more likely to be true, we tend to make the right choices of assumptions and courses of action. In other words, the adequacy of our representation of the world depends not only on which assumptions we hold, but also on our degree of confidence in them: an adequate representation is one in which there is a good match between the assumptions we regard as well confirmed and those that actually are well confirmed. Improvements in our representation of the world can be achieved not only by adding justified new assumptions to it, but also by appropriately raising or lowering our degree of confidence in them, the degree to which we take them to be confirmed.

'Confirmation' is a term taken from a relatively undeveloped branch of logic (which itself took it from commonsense psychology). How should it be adapted for use in cognitive psychology? Two very different answers can be given. On one approach, the logical concept of confirmation makes a good psychological concept as it stands; the logician's system is, on the whole, an adequate psychological model. All that is needed is to replace the objective notion of confirmation with some subjective analogue: for example, a system assigning *subjective probability values* to representations. Call this the *logical* view.

On another approach, the logical concept of confirmation should be not adapted but rejected. The ability to judge an assumption as more or less likely to be true is to be explained not in terms of a system which assigns subjective probability values to assumptions, but in terms of a non-logical property of assumptions: what, metaphorically, we will call their *strength*. Call this the *non-logical*, or *functional*, view. This is the approach that we would like to pursue.

According to the logical view, every factual assumption consists of two representations. The first is a representation of a state of affairs – for instance (7a); the second is a representation of the confirmation value of the first representation – for instance (7b):

(7) (a) Jane likes caviar.
    (b) The confirmation value of (a) is 0.95.

How are these two representations arrived at? The first, so the story goes, is the output of a non-logical cognitive process of assumption formation. The second is the output of a process of logical computation which takes as input the assumption to be confirmed, on the one hand, and the available evidence, on the other. When new evidence becomes available, a new logical computation may take place, as a result of which the confirmation value of an assumption may be raised or lowered. On this view, the notion of a confirmation value is basic, and the strength of an assumption – if this is worth talking about at all – is determined by its confirmation value.

According to the functional view, a factual assumption consists of a single representation, such as (7a). The strength of this assumption is a result of its processing history, and cannot be accounted for in terms of the logical concept of confirmation. Understood in this way, the strength of an assumption is a property comparable to its accessibility. A more accessible assumption is one that is easier to recall. For instance, for most of our readers who assume (8) and (9), (8) is more accessible than (9):

(8) Cairo is the capital of Egypt.
(9) Thebes was the capital of Egypt under the 20th dynasty.

Clearly, this difference is not to be explained by an appeal to two second-order representations assigning different degrees of accessibility to (8) and (9). A more plausible claim is that, as a result of some kind of habituation, the more a representation is processed, the more accessible it becomes. Hence, the greater the amount of processing involved in the formation of an assumption, and the more often it is accessed thereafter, the greater its accessibility.

Similarly, the initial strength of an assumption may depend on the way it is acquired. For instance, assumptions based on a clear perceptual experience tend to be very strong; assumptions based on the acceptance of somebody's word have a strength commensurate with one's confidence in the speaker; the strength of assumptions arrived at by deduction depends on the strength of the premises from which they were derived. Thereafter, it could be that the strength of an assumption is increased every time that assumption helps in processing some new information, and is reduced every time it makes the processing of some new information more difficult. On this account, these variations in strength are neither the object nor the output of a special logical computation. They arise, rather, as by-products of various cognitive processes, deductive and non-deductive.

Here is an informal illustration. Jane told me herself that she likes caviar, and I have no reason to doubt her word; so I hold assumption (7a) quite strongly. On one occasion, I observe Jane eating caviar with a big smile; my assumption helps me understand this fact and becomes even stronger as a result. On another occasion, though, I see Jane turning down an offer of caviar; accessing my assumption that she likes caviar not only does not help, but makes this fact more difficult to understand; as a result, the assumption becomes weaker. At no point do I process a representation of the confirmation value of (7a). The strength of (7a) is established and varies as a by-product of other processes, and need not be represented at all in order to exist and vary.

However, this is not the whole story. Functional properties of representations, such as accessibility or strength, need not be represented in the mind in order to exist, vary and affect cognitive processes, but they *can* be represented. People have intuitions about the accessibility of different assumptions; we appealed to such intuitions about example (8)–(9) above. Similarly, people have intuitions about the strength of their assumptions. They may express these intuitions in different ways. They may say such things as

(10) I am quite certain that Jane likes caviar.
(11) I firmly believe that Jane likes caviar.
(12) What I have seen confirms my assumption that Jane likes caviar.
(13) It seems more probable to me that Jane likes caviar than that she likes oysters.

Behind these forms of expression lies a tacit hypothesis. We take for granted that there is a good match between the strength of our assumptions and the likelihood that they are true. That is, we trust our cognitive mechanisms to strengthen or weaken our assumptions in a way that is epistemologically sound: we trust our representation of the world to be adequate in this respect, as in others. As a result, intuitions about the strength of our assumptions are expressed as intuitions about their degree of confirmation. Such intuitions *are* assumptions about assumptions, and can be processed as such. More often than not, they are assumptions about changes in the strength of a single assumption, as in (12), or about the relative strength of pairs of assumptions, as in (13). In some cases, it seems plausible that such assumptions play a genuine cognitive role: for instance, in conscious attempts to resolve a contradiction by working out which of the contradictory assumptions is the more likely to be true.

According to the logical view, the soundness of our assumptions depends on our ability to carry out a computational check on the confirmation value of each assumption. According to the functional view, the soundness of our assumptions – to the extent that they are sound – depends on our having cognitive mechanisms so attuned to the world we live in that the strength of our assumptions tends to match the likelihood that they are true. On the logical view, a representation of the confirmation value of an assumption is an aspect of that assumption; it is the outcome of a logical process which every assumption undergoes. On the functional view, a representation of the degree of confirmation of an assumption is another assumption; it is generally the product of an intuition about one of the effects of the processing history of that assumption. Assumptions can exist without their degree of confirmation ever being represented.

Neither the logical nor the functional view has been developed to a point where they could be effectively tested. Nonetheless, they are different enough for some empirical comparisons to be made. We will try to show that these comparisons favour the functional view.

Our conscious intuitions about the strength of assumptions yield only the grossest kinds of *absolute* judgement. We may think of a given assumption as certain (true), very strong (very well confirmed), strong (well confirmed), weak (poorly confirmed), but the boundaries between these categories are fuzzy. Unless we have been trained in inductive logic, we have no sub-categories to express more precise absolute judgements. On the other hand, we can often make much finer *comparative* judgements. For instance, we may be aware that some new piece of evidence has strengthened an assumption even though it remains in the same absolute category: say it was strong before and is still strong, but we think of it as stronger than before. However, not all comparative judgements are equally easy. If two assumptions are utterly unrelated, and if they belong to the same gross category, say *strong*, they become well nigh impossible to compare. Consider (14) and (15):

(14) Jane likes caviar.
(15) There are more Indian restaurants than Chinese restaurants in Chelsea.

Someone who quite strongly believes (14) and (15) might find it difficult or impossible to answer the question, 'Do you think it is more likely that Jane likes caviar than that there are more Indian restaurants than Chinese restaurants in Chelsea?'

It seems to us implausible that humans might have a system for computing and representing the strength of assumptions which is both wholly unconscious and radically more sophisticated than anything that is reflected in their conscious intuitions. We therefore reject the possibility that an individual might unconsciously assess confirmation values through the kind of numerical computations suggested by logicians, when he is incapable of doing so consciously.[8] We conclude, more generally, that the strength of an assumption cannot be quantitatively assessed: in the terms of Carnap (1950), it is a comparative rather than a quantitative value.

In his 1950 treatise on subjective probability (another term for estimated degree of confirmation), Carnap contrasts classificatory, comparative and quantitative concepts along the following lines.

A *classificatory* concept sets up a necessary and sufficient condition for class membership. For example, an integer either is prime (if it can be evenly divided by no other whole number than itself and 1), or it is not.

A *comparative* concept is one that figures in comparative judgements. For example, some things feel warmer than others, some sounds seem louder than others, some foods taste nicer than others, and so on. Some classificatory concepts have comparative counterparts, but not all of them do. *Caffeinated* is both a classificatory concept (a substance either does or does not contain caffeine) and a comparative one (some substances contain more caffeine than others). On the other hand, *prime* does not have a comparative interpretation: numbers cannot be more or less prime.

Carnap's third type of concept, the *quantitative* concept, is one that figures in numerical comparisons. For example, *distance* is a quantitative concept because we can not only say that London is further from Edinburgh than it is from Oxford, but also measure the distance in miles or kilometres, and hence say how much further London is from Edinburgh than it is from Oxford. However, as Carnap points out, not every comparative concept has a quantitative counterpart. Though we might know that one food tastes better than another, there is no obvious way of measuring how good a food tastes, and therefore of measuring how much better one food tastes than another.

The existence of an objective numerical scale makes it easy to formulate precise absolute judgements and to compare unlike objects: say the ages of a child and a car, or the distance from Trafalgar Square to Buckingham Palace and from the foot of Mount Qomolangma to the top. Where no numerical scale exists, absolute judgements become gross, and comparison of unlike objects becomes much harder. For example, someone might be able to say that one champagne tastes better than another, or that one caviar tastes better than another, but be quite unable to say whether or not a certain champagne tastes better than a certain caviar.

Even where an objective numerical scale exists, it does not follow that some internal analogue of it is used in mental comparison. For example, when a suitcase feels heavier the longer it is carried, this feeling is presumably not based on any assumption that the suitcase is actually gaining ounces or pounds as the journey proceeds. Similarly, comparisons of the warmth of unlike objects, such as a liquid with a solid, or a solid with a gas, are much harder than comparisons of the warmth of like objects. This strongly suggests that ordinary judgements of warmth are not based on an internal analogue of a temperature scale.

Difficulties in comparing unlike objects are hard to explain on the assumption that a numerical scale is being used. Where such difficulties arise, it seems more reasonable to assume that what is being used is not a numerical scale but rather a heuristic (based for instance on matching procedures), which applies only to like objects: comparing, for example, the taste of several samples of caviar, the warmth of various liquids, the strength of several assumptions of related content.

The performance of humans in comparing the strength of unlike assumptions is thus a powerful indication that strength, as a basic psychological concept applied to assumptions, is comparative rather than quantitative. This fits much better with the functional view than with the logical view. On the functional view, judgements and comparisons of strength are introspective intuitions, just like judgements and comparisons of taste, pain or accessibility, all of which are clearly comparative. Of course, this does not explain how these judgements and comparisons are made; but it makes the problem of degrees of confirmation one among many: no new problem is created. The logical view, on the other hand, implies that each assumption is assigned an absolute quantitative confirmation value. This raises two new problems: since fine comparisons are possible in some cases, why aren't they *always* possible? And why are our conscious absolute judgements of strength so gross?

Other arguments for the functional view could be derived from a study of the logical mistakes that subjects make in evaluating degrees of confirmation.[9] We are aware that neither these further arguments nor those we have put forward are conclusive. What we hope to have shown so far is that the functional view has some initial plausibility and may be worth pursuing.

On the functional approach, the successes of human non-demonstrative inference must be explained by appealing not to logical processes of assumption confirmation, but to constraints on the formation and exploitation of assumptions. Factual assumptions are acquired from four sources: perception, linguistic decoding, assumptions and assumption schemas stored in memory, and deduction. In the rest of this section we will look briefly at how assumptions from these four sources are formed, and at how they acquire an initial degree of strength.

Perceptual mechanisms assign to a sensory stimulus a conceptual identification of that stimulus, e.g.

(16) This is an orchid.
(17) The doorbell is ringing.
(18) The pavement is wet.

Under normal conditions of perception, these elementary descriptions of stimuli become strong assumptions. That these assumptions are generally correct is due to the fact that human perceptual mechanisms are the outcome of a long biological evolutionary process, and are well adapted to the task.

The linguistic input mechanisms assign to a particular type of sensory stimulus a logical form. We have seen that the logical forms recovered by decoding fall short of being fully propositional, and that even when completed into propositional forms they fall short of being factual assumptions. However, the propositional form arrived at by completing the logical form of an uttered sentence can be integrated by a standard procedure into an assumption about what the speaker said. For instance, if Peter is heard uttering (19) at time t, his utterance will be decoded as having the logical form of sentence (20), which can be completed to yield the propositional form (21), which can in turn be integrated into the assumption schema in (22) to yield assumption (23):

(19) [aɪhævəhedeɪk]
(20) I have a headache.
(21) Peter has a headache at time t.
(22) Peter says that ——.
(23) Peter says that Peter has a headache at time t.

The processes by which assumptions such as (23) are formed and exploited, and the empirical adequacy of these assumptions, will be discussed extensively in chapter 4.

Conceptual memory is a huge repertory of assumptions such as (24)–(28):

(24) The car is in the garage.
(25) Larry is a philosopher.
(26) Orchids are rare flowers.
(27) When the outside temperature is below five degrees centigrade, the pond is frozen.
(28) Philosophers are entertaining.

We assume that memory also contains assumption schemas, i.e. logical forms which can be completed to yield propositional forms in the format appropriate for factual assumptions.[10] Thus, assumption schema (29) might be completed to yield assumption (30), and assumption schema (31) might be completed to yield assumption (32):

(29) The outside temperature is —— degrees centigrade.
(30) The outside temperature is minus six degrees centigrade.
(31) —— is (a bachelor/married/divorced/a widower).
(32) Larry is a bachelor.

It also appears that when available assumptions correspond to a certain schema, related schemas are used to derive further assumptions. For instance, when assumptions of the form (33) are made, it seems that assumptions of the form (34) or (35) are standardly considered:

(33) If P then Q.
(34) If (not P) then (not Q).
(35) If Q, then (Q because P).

Thus, the formation of assumption (36) would standardly lead to a consideration of assumptions (37) or (38):

(36) If Fido is pleased, then he wags his tail.
(37) If Fido is not pleased, then he does not wag his tail.
(38) If Fido wags his tail, then he does so because he is pleased.

Assumptions retrieved from memory come with a certain degree of strength. Assumptions constructed by completing assumption schemas come with an initial plausibility which may make them worth processing; their subsequent strength depends on their subsequent processing history.

Given a set of assumptions as premises, further assumptions can be derived as conclusions of a deductive process. For instance, from (16) and (26), assumption (39) can be derived:

(16) This is an orchid.
(26) Orchids are rare flowers.
(39) This is a rare flower.

Similarly, (40) can be derived from assumptions (25) and (28):

(25) Larry is a philosopher.
(28) Philosophers are entertaining.
(40) Larry is entertaining.

Assumption (41) can be derived from (27) and (30):

(27) When the outside temperature is below zero centigrade, the pond is frozen.
(30) The outside temperature is minus six degrees centigrade.
(41) The pond is frozen.

We will argue that the formation of assumptions by deduction is the key process in non-demonstrative inference, and show how new assumptions inherit their strength from the assumptions used in deriving them. But first we must give some thought to the deductive process itself.

4 Deductive rules and concepts

The deductive processing of information has much of the automatic, unconscious, reflex quality of linguistic decoding and other input processes. What distinguishes the deductive system from the input systems is that it applies to conceptual rather than to perceptual representations: that is, to representations with a logical or propositional form. What distinguishes it from other central systems is the type of computation it performs.

Deductive arguments can be looked at from a syntactic (computational) or a semantic point of view. Let us say that a semantic relation of *entailment* holds between two assumptions P and Q if and only if every conceivable state of affairs which would make P true would also make Q true: that is, if and only if there is no conceivable state of affairs in which P would be true and Q false. The relation is a semantic one in that it involves reference to the states of affairs which particular assumptions represent: that is, the states of affairs which constitute their semantic interpretations. By this definition, (42) entails (43), since there is no conceivable state of affairs in which (42) would be true and (43) false:

(42) Apples grow in orchards and grapes grow in vineyards.
(43) Apples grow in orchards.

Let us say that a syntactic relation of *logical implication* holds between two assumptions P and Q with respect to a certain deductive system if and only if one is deducible from the other by the deductive rules of that system. A deductive rule is a computation which applies to assumptions in virtue of their logical form. Logical implication is a syntactic relation in that it holds purely in virtue of the formal properties of assumptions, and involves no reference to their semantic properties. For example, most standard logics have a rule of *and*-elimination which applies to assumptions of the form (P *and* Q) to yield conclusions of the form P, or conclusions of the form Q. In a system with such a rule, (42) logically implies (43).

There is a necessary connection between logical implication and entailment in at least the following sense: the notion of a deductive rule itself cannot be properly explicated without appeal to the semantic notion of entailment. Formally, a deductive rule is a computation like any other. What distinguishes it from other computations is the fact that it is a truth-preserving operation: that is, when it applies to an assumption, the conclusion it yields stands in a semantic entailment relation to the premise. Hence, all logical implications are also entailments. However, the reverse relation does not necessarily hold.

Although most standard logics in principle aim at completeness, which means that they aim at a system in which every assumed entailment is also a logical implication, in practice they ignore entailments which do not hinge on the meanings of a small class of 'logical particles' such as *and, or, not, some* and *all*. For example, there is no deductive rule in standard logics which would derive (45) from (44), even though (44) entails (45):

(44) All bachelors are happy.
(45) All unmarried men are happy.

Nor is there any reason why there should be from the purely logical point of view. There is no contradiction in the idea of an incomplete logic, as there is in the idea of a logic whose rules are not at least partial reconstructions of assumed entailment relationships.

The question of whether humans have deductive rules as part of their basic mental equipment, and if so, which rules they have, is of no particular interest to pure logicians. Logicians are concerned with the nature of conceivable deductive systems, whether psychologically realised or not. However, it is a question of considerable interest for cognitive psychology in general and pragmatic theory in particular. We assume, as do most others working in the area, that there is a set of deductive rules which are spontaneously brought to bear in the deductive processing of information. This is an empirical assumption, which might be justifiable along the following lines.

First, for any organism which represents the world in conceptual terms, that is, in terms of a set of assumptions, a deductive system would effect an important economy of storage. Given a set of deductive rules, the logical implications of any set of assumptions would be recoverable from it by means of the deductive rules, and would not need to be separately stored. Second, for any organism interested in improving its conceptual representation of the world, it would provide a tool not only for working out the consequences of adding a new assumption to an existing representation of the world, but for guaranteeing the accuracy of any conclusions deduced from initially accurate premises. Third, for any organism interested in the accuracy of its conceptual representation of the world, it would provide a tool for exposing inconsistencies, and hence inaccuracies, in any existing representation. No other system of inference with similar powers has ever been developed with a degree of explicitness comparable to that of a deductive system.[11c]

We assume, then, that at the heart of the human ability to perform spontaneous demonstrative inference is a set of deductive rules: a set of computations which take account of the semantic properties of assumptions only insofar as these are reflected in their form.[12] We have so far said little about the form of assumptions, in virtue of which they undergo deductive rules. In what follows, we will sketch an account which, though speculative, is as far as we know compatible with the available empirical evidence. Some of these speculations have the sole function of showing that our general claims about verbal comprehension could in principle be psychologically realised; others are more substantive.

It seems reasonable to regard logical forms, and in particular the propositional forms of assumptions, as composed of smaller constituents to whose presence and structural arrangements the deductive rules are sensitive. These constituents we will call *concepts*. An assumption, then, is a structured set of concepts.

Concepts, like the logical forms that contain them, are psychological objects considered at a fairly abstract level. Formally, we assume that each concept consists of a label, or address, which performs two different and complementary functions. First, it appears as an address in memory, a heading under which various types of information can be stored and retrieved. Second, it may appear as a constituent of a logical form, to whose presence the deductive rules may be sensitive. These functions are complementary in the following sense: when the address of a certain concept appears in a logical form being processed, access is given to the various types of information stored in memory at that address.

The information that may be stored in memory at a certain conceptual address falls into three distinct types: logical, encyclopaedic and lexical. The *logical entry* for a concept consists of a set of deductive rules which apply to logical forms of which that concept is a constituent. The *encyclopaedic entry* contains information about the extension and/or denotation of the concept: that is, about the objects, events and/or properties which instantiate it. The *lexical entry* contains information about the natural-language counterpart of the concept: the word or phrase of natural language which expresses it. On this approach, a conceptual address is thus a point of access to the logical, encyclopaedic and linguistic information which may be needed in the processing of logical forms containing that address. We consider each type of entry in turn.

A logical entry consists of a set of deductive rules, each formally describing a set of input and output assumptions: that is, a set of premises and conclusions. Our first substantive claim is that the only deductive rules which can appear in the logical entry of a given concept are *elimination rules* for that concept. That is, they apply only to sets of premises in which there is a specified occurrence of that concept, and yield only conclusions from which that occurrence has been removed.

Standard logics invariably contain such rules. For example, the standard logical rule of *and*-elimination takes as input a single conjoined premise and yields as output one of its constituent conjuncts:

(46) *And-elimination*
    (a) *Input*: (P and Q)
       Output: P
    (b) *Input*: (P and Q)
       Output: Q

That is, it applies only to premises containing a designated occurrence of the concept *and*, and yields conclusions from which that occurrence has been removed. The standard rule of *modus ponendo ponens* takes as input a pair of premises, one a conditional and the other the antecedent of that conditional, and yields as output the consequent of the conditional:

(47) *Modus ponendo ponens*
    Input: (i) P
             (ii) (If P then Q)
    Output: Q

That is, it applies only to premises containing a designated occurrence of the concept *if ... then*, and yields conclusions from which that occurrence has been removed. The standard rule of *modus tollendo ponens* takes as input a pair of premises, one a disjunction and the other the negation of one disjunct, and yields as output the other disjunct:

(48) *Modus tollendo ponens*
    (a) *Input*: (i) (P or Q)
                (ii) (not P)
       Output: Q
    (b) *Input*: (i) (P or Q)
                (ii) (not Q)
       Output: P

That is, it applies only to premises containing a designated occurrence of the concept *or*, and yields conclusions from which that occurrence has been eliminated. We assume that some version of these rules is contained in the logical entries for the concepts *and, if . . . then* and *or*, respectively.

Standard logics make a radical distinction between concepts such as *and, if . . . then*, and *or*, which are regarded as proper logical concepts, and concepts such as *when, know, run, bachelor*, which are considered non-logical. Following another tradition,[13] we regard these other concepts as also determining logical implications. Which concepts do or do not have logical entries, which rules these entries contain, and which natural classes concepts fall into from a cognitive point of view, are all matters for empirical investigation. So far we have simply suggested, as an empirical hypothesis, a general restriction on the form of logical entries. These questions will be taken up in section 5.

The second type of entry attached to a concept, its encyclopaedic entry, contains information about its extension and/or denotation: the objects, events and/or properties which instantiate it. For example, the encyclopaedic entry for the concept *Napoleon* would contain a set of assumptions about Napoleon, the encyclopaedic entry for the concept *cat* would contain a set of assumptions about cats, and the encyclopaedic entry for the concept *argue* would contain a set of assumptions about arguing. Quite a lot of work has been done in the last ten or fifteen years on the organisation of conceptual information in memory, and various models have been proposed to describe what we are calling encyclopaedic entries. These models are intended to answer questions about the structure of the entries, the relations between the various types of assumption contained in them, and the relations among the entries themselves. Many of the models that have been proposed incorporate such notions as *schema, frame, prototype* or *script.*[14]

The idea behind these notions is that humans are disposed to develop stereotypical assumptions and expectations about frequently encountered objects and events. For example, I have an idea of a typical pet, which includes dogs and cats but excludes elephants and spiders. It is thought that these schematic assumptions and expectations are stored and accessed as a unit or 'chunk', that they are highly accessible, and that they will be used in default of any more specific information in processing utterances about the associated objects or events. Thus, when I hear that my neighbour has bought a pet, I will assume that it is something like a dog or a cat rather than an elephant or a spider, unless given specific information to the contrary. We do not want to argue for or against any particular one of these models. We share the basic hypothesis which is common to all of them: in our terms, that encyclopaedic information contains not only factual assumptions but also assumption schemas which an appropriate context may convert into full-fledged assumptions.

Intuitively, there are clear-enough differences between encyclopaedic and logical entries. Encyclopaedic entries typically vary across speakers and times: we do not all have the same assumptions about Napoleon or about cats. They are open-ended: new information is being added to them all the time. There is no point at which an encyclopaedic entry can be said to be complete, and no essential minimum without which one would not say that its associated concept had been mastered at all. Logical entries, by contrast, are small, finite and relatively constant across speakers and times. There is a point at which the logical entry for a concept is complete, and before which one would not say that the concept had been mastered at all. Suppose, for example, that a child has not yet realised that *X knows that P* implies *P*, and so uses *know* interchangeably with *believe*. We would say that he had not yet mastered the concept. On the other hand, if he has grasped this logical point but is unable to think of a single instance of something he is prepared to call knowledge, we would regard this as a failure of memory or experience (or a mark of philosophical potential) rather than of understanding.

The distinction between logical and encyclopaedic entries corresponds in many ways to the traditional distinction between analytic and synthetic truths, which has been a notorious subject of dispute. However, our claim is not so much that there is a fundamental difference between two types of truth, two types of information content, as that information must be representable in two different forms, and function in two different ways, if successful communication is to take place. This claim seems to us incontrovertible, at least within the current climate of research.

The whole framework of current cognitive psychology rests on a distinction between representation and computation, of which our distinction between encyclopaedic assumptions and deductive rules is a special case. The information in encyclopaedic entries is representational: it consists of a set of assumptions which may undergo deductive rules. The information in logical entries, by contrast, is computational: it consists of a set of deductive rules which apply to assumptions in which the associated concept appears. It is not that the same item of information may not be stored now in one form, now in another, or in both forms simultaneously. For example, rules (46a–b) above (the rules of *and*-elimination) could be put into the propositional form in (49), and it is quite possible that, on reflection, one might produce (49) as a description of one's own computational practice:

(49) From a conjunction as premise it is valid to infer either conjunct as conclusion.

The point is that representation and computation are two formally distinct and complementary processes, neither of which can exist without the other, and both of which are necessary for comprehension to take place. It is this distinction that is reflected in our distinction between logical and encyclopaedic entries.

It is also common practice in current cognitive psychology to distinguish between the content of a particular item of information (in this case an assumption) and the context in which it is processed. Our suggestion is that, broadly speaking, the content of an assumption is constrained by the logical entries of the concepts it contains, while the context in which it is processed is, at least in part, determined by their encyclopaedic entries. Again, the point is not that the same piece of information could not function, now as part of the content of an assumption, now as part of the context in which it is processed; indeed there is reason to think that just such overlaps do occur. The point is that in order to make sense of the claim that assumptions are processed in a context – and in particular of our claim that the relevance of an assumption is analysed in terms of the modification that it brings to the context in which it is processed – it must be possible in principle to distinguish between the content of an assumption and its context. This distinction is reflected in our distinction between logical and encyclopaedic entries.

The distinction between logical and encyclopaedic entries is thus quite fundamental to our framework, and indeed to any framework that seems to us remotely plausible. However, it is primarily a formal and functional distinction, and does not necessarily imply that there are two fundamentally different kinds of truth.

The third type of entry for a concept, its lexical entry, contains information about the natural-language lexical item used to express it. We assume that this entry includes the sort of syntactic and phonological information that would be contained in the lexical entry for that item in a generative grammar: information about its syntactic category membership and co-occurrence possibilities, phonological structure, and so on.

The fact that concepts have both logical and lexical entries provides a point of contact between input and central processes, between the linguistic input system and the deductive rules of the central conceptual system. Recovery of the content of an utterance involves the ability to identify the individual words it contains, to recover the associated concepts, and to apply the deductive rules attached to their logical entries.

We assume, then, that the 'meaning' of a word is provided by the associated concept (or, in the case of an ambiguous word, concepts). This allows us to maintain a somewhat ecumenical view of lexical semantics. Most theories of lexical semantics assume that all words, with the possible exception of proper names, have meanings of the same format. They then differ as to what this universal format is. We recognise the possibility that different words may have meanings of different formats.

A classical view is that the meaning of a word is provided by a definition which expresses the individually necessary and jointly sufficient conditions for the word to apply. For instance, the definition of 'mother' could be *female parent*. If this is so, it can be represented by assigning 'mother' as the lexical entry for the concept *female parent*, or by associating with the concept *mother* the elimination rule in (50) (where X and Y stand for possibly empty strings of constituents):

(50) *Mother-elimination rule*
    Input: $(X - \text{mother} - Y)$
    Output: $(X - \text{female parent} - Y)$

On this classical view, proper names, for which necessary and sufficient conditions of application cannot be given, are radically different from other words: they have reference but no meaning. 'Homer', for instance, cannot be defined as *the author of the Iliad and the Odyssey*, since there is no inconsistency in denying that he is their author; he cannot be defined as *a Greek man* (a grossly incomplete definition anyhow), since there is no inconsistency in denying that he was Greek or that he was a man, and so on. If that is so, if there are words which have reference but no logical conditions attached, again, our approach can handle them easily by associating them with concepts which have an empty logical entry.

Against the classical view, it has been argued, by Saul Kripke and Hilary Putnam in particular,[15] that proper names are far from being unique. Their reference is fixed by an initial act of 'baptism' and maintained by a causal chain which relates each of their particular uses to this initial act. The same is true, they argue, at least for natural kind terms such as 'salt' or 'giraffe': you learn the meaning of 'salt' by being shown typical samples of salt and being told that they are called 'salt'; your teacher learned in the same way, and all adequate uses of 'salt' are linked by a causal chain to some initial 'baptism'. True, a chemist might provide a definition of 'salt', but it is not necessary to know this scientific definition in order to use the term 'salt' properly. When this definition is known at all, it is better regarded as belonging to the encyclopaedic entry of the concept, as knowledge of what salt is, rather than as knowledge of what 'salt' means. If this 'causal theory of reference' is entirely correct, then the meaning of natural kind terms could be represented in our framework in terms of concepts with empty logical entries and appropriate encyclopaedic entries.

According to various versions of 'prototype theory',[16] again, the meaning of a word is determined not by a set of logical properties, but by a mental model of the thing the word is used to refer to. You have a mental model of a prototypical giraffe, say, and you use the word 'giraffe' to refer to things which resemble your model. If the meaning of some words is so characterised, then, in our framework, they will have an empty logical entry and an encyclopaedic entry containing the required model.[17]

It seems to us, though, that both the causal theory and the prototype theory might well tell only part of the story, and that even in their pet cases – giraffes etc. – logical properties may still play a role. This makes us feel closer to the view advocated by Fodor and his colleagues,[18] that the meaning of most words cannot be defined in terms of, or decomposed into, more primitive concepts: 'mother', 'bachelor' and a few often-quoted cases are exceptional rather than typical in this respect. Take 'yellow'; assume that it can be defined in terms of more primitive concepts: one of the concepts would undoubtedly be *colour*; what would be the other(s)? Take 'giraffe'; assume that a giraffe is by definition an animal; make it even by definition a quadruped, if you want: how do you then complete the definition? The best you can do, it seems, is to define 'yellow' as *the colour yellow*, 'giraffe' as *animal* (or *quadruped*) *of the giraffe species*, but these are not proper definitions since they make use of the very concepts they purport to define. The conclusion is that the meaning of a word such as 'yellow', 'giraffe' or 'salt' is an irreducible concept. Such concepts have logical properties, but these do not amount to a definition of the concept. Fodor et al. propose representing these logical properties in terms of meaning postulates; they can as easily be represented in terms of elimination rules, e.g.

(51) *Salt-elimination rule*
   Input: $(X - \text{salt} - Y)$
   Output: $(X - \text{substance of a certain kind} - Y)$
(52) *Giraffe-elimination rule*
   Input: $(X - \text{giraffe} - Y)$
   Output: $(X - \text{animal of a certain species} - Y)$
(53) *Yellow-elimination rule*
   Input: $(X - \text{yellow} - Y)$
   Output: $(X - \text{colour of a certain hue} - Y)$

Our framework allows for empty logical entries, logical entries which amount to a proper definition of the concept, and logical entries which fall anywhere between these two extremes: that is, which provide some logical specification of the concept without fully defining it. We assume that this range of possibilities actually exists in the human mind; how exactly it is exploited, to what extent actual concepts are logically specified, we see as a matter for empirical research. What is at issue in the case of each concept is: what deductive inferences are made possible by its presence in an assumption?[19]

In this section we have argued that the rules used in spontaneous deductive inference are elimination rules attached to concepts. We have treated concepts as triples of entries, logical, lexical and encylopaedic, filed at an address. In one sense, the distinction between address and entry is a distinction between form and content, the address being what actually appears in logical forms, and the various entries spelling out its logical, lexical and encyclopaedic content. In another sense, though, everything discussed in this section has been purely formal. Logical entries are sets of deductive rules: that is, formal operations on logical forms; encyclopaedic entries are sets of assumptions: that is, representations with logical forms; and lexical entries are representations with linguistic forms. All three types of entry are thus available for use in a computational account of comprehension.

Occasionally, an entry for a particular concept may be empty or lacking. For example, a concept such as *and*, which has no extension, may lack an encylopaedic entry. We saw that proper names and other concepts could be seen as having an empty logical entry. Finally, there may be concepts which have encyclopaedic and logical entries and play a role in cognitive processes, but which are not lexicalised and which therefore have an empty lexical entry. For example, it seems reasonable to assume that corresponding to the general concept lexicalised as 'the military' or 'the armed forces', we have a particular concept of a soldier/sailor/airman, which lacks a lexical entry.

Although the boundaries between logical and encyclopaedic entries are not always easy to draw, we have tried to show that there are principled differences between them, and that they may be expected to play different roles in comprehension. In the next section we continue our account of spontaneous inference by looking at the deductive process itself.

5 The deductive device

To the extent that deduction has been considered at all in the pragmatic literature, it has been tacitly modelled on informal (natural) deduction systems of the type familiar from introductory logic texts (e.g. Lemmon 1965, Thomason 1970, McCawley 1980). An informal deduction system consists of a smallish set of deductive rules dealing with inferences which hinge on the presence of such concepts as *and, or, if . . . then*, etc. Rules (46)–(48) above (the rules of *and*-elimination, *modus ponendo ponens* and *modus tollendo ponens*) are examples. Typically, no instructions are given about how the rules are to be applied, in what order, or to what set of assumptions as premises. Constructing a logical derivation in an informal system is a matter of deciding what combination of rules and premises might lead to interesting results. There is no way of predicting in advance which premises will be chosen, which rules will be applied, and hence which conclusions drawn.

Despite the widespread scepticism about the role of deductive reasoning in comprehension, many existing pragmatic theories, especially those built on Gricean lines, seem to be based on informal systems of just this type. When a certain inference or implicature is drawn, it can be shown *ex post facto* how the hearer could have derived it from the premises available at that point in the conversation by the use of available deductive rules. However, it would almost invariably have been possible, from the same set of premises, using the same set of rules, to derive quite different conclusions, which would not in practice have been either intended or drawn.

An informal system thus leaves an important part of the deductive process unspecified: it is left to the intelligent user of the system to decide how best to exploit it. In trying to construct a model of the mind, or the part of the mind used in utterance comprehension, it is not legitimate to rely on informal systems of this type, precisely because they leave an important part of the comprehension process unexplained. Formal systems (effective procedures, automata, algorithms) differ from informal systems in just this respect: their procedures can be carried out by an automaton whose decisions are predetermined at every stage. With a formal system, it is decided in advance what assumptions are to be used as premises; a set of assumptions are provided which, for the purposes of this deduction at least, are to constitute the axioms or initial theses of the system (hence such systems are often called axiomatic deduction systems). It is also fully specified in advance which operations may or must apply. Nothing is left to the intuitions of the user: all the information necessary for performing a deduction, all decisions involved in it, are fully specified by the system itself.

The importance of formal systems for modelling mental abilities has become increasingly apparent since Chomsky first used them in the study of language. Chomsky insisted on the difference between informal, traditional grammars and explicit, generative grammars. Informal grammars rely heavily on the intuitions of the user, and are intended to supplement rather than account for these intuitions. They do not try to make explicit what every speaker of a human language already knows, or to rule out what no speaker of a human language would think of doing. Just as informal deduction systems rely on the logical capabilities of the user, so informal grammars presuppose a user with a considerable amount of tacit linguistic knowledge which they make no attempt to explain.

Generative grammars, by contrast, are intended to give an explicit, exhaustive account of the linguistic knowledge of the individual. A generative grammar consists of a set of rules or principles designed to provide a complete description of every sentence in a language, leaving nothing about the structure of these sentences up to the intuitions of the individual. Hence they are formal in the sense just described, and they explain the individual's linguistic intuitions in a way that informal grammars do not. It is not just that generative grammars, and more generally formal systems, provide one way of modelling mental abilities. There is no other way of modelling them known today; no other way of accounting for intuitions than by providing a formal system that can itself be operated without appeal to intuition.

What we want to offer here is the general outline of a formal deduction system intended to model the system used by human beings in spontaneous inference, and in normal utterance comprehension in particular. We are not proposing a fully described system but simply stating some of its general properties. Nor, for that matter, has a fully described formal grammar for a natural language ever been proposed: in both cases the complexity of the phenomena to be described and the number of theoretical choices to be made is enormous. What seems to us important at this stage is to provide a general framework within which more detailed hypotheses can eventually be produced and evaluated.

The device we envisage is an automaton with a memory and the ability to read, write and erase logical forms, compare their formal properties, store them in memory, and access the deductive rules contained in the logical entries for concepts. Deductions proceed as follows. A set of assumptions[20] which will constitute the axioms, or initial theses, of the deduction are placed in the memory of the device. It reads each of these assumptions, accesses the logical entries of each of its constituent concepts, applies any rule whose structural description is satisfied by that assumption, and writes the resulting assumption down in its memory as a derived thesis. Where a rule provides descriptions of two input assumptions, the device checks to see whether it has in memory an appropriate pair of assumptions; if so, it writes the output assumption down in its memory as a derived thesis. The process applies to all initial and derived theses until no further deductions are possible.

The system monitors for redundancies and contradictions in its derivations in the following way. Before writing an assumption down in its memory, it checks to see whether that assumption or its negation is already there. If the assumption itself is there, the device refrains from writing it down again, and marks the theses and deductive rules used in deriving it so that the derivation will not be repeated. If the negation of the assumption is already there, the device halts, and the deductive process is suspended until the contradiction is resolved; a method of resolving contradictions will be considered below. Subject to these constraints, the device continues to operate until no new theses can be derived.

The move to formal systems raises questions about the capacity of the deductive device which are sometimes overlooked when informal systems are proposed. Most informal systems – at least those invented by logicians– aim at completeness: that is, they aim to provide deductive rules which will derive as logical implications all the entailments (or all those that hinge on the logical properties of *and*, *or*, etc.) of a given set of assumptions. It is easy to show that this set of entailments is infinite for any finite set of premises. For example, a single arbitrary assumption P entails each of the following conclusions:

(54) (a) $(P$ and $P)$
    (b) $(P$ or $Q)$
    (c) $(\text{not } (\text{not } P))$
    (d) $(\text{If } (\text{not } P) \text{ then } Q)$
    (e) $(\text{If } Q \text{ then } P)$

These are all entailments of P in the sense that there are no conceivable states of affairs in which P would be true and any of (54a–e) false. Logicians aiming at completeness will therefore set up deductive rules enabling each of (54a–e) to be derived as logical implications of P. (54a) is standardly derived by the rule of *and*-introduction, which takes two arbitrary assumptions, in this case *P* and *P*, as premises, and derives their conjunction as conclusion:

(55) *And-introduction*
    Input: (i) *P*
          (ii) *Q*
    Output: (*P* and *Q*)

(54b) is standardly derived by the rule of *or*-introduction, which takes an arbitrary assumption as premise, and derives its disjunction with any other arbitrary assumption as conclusion:

(56) *Or-introduction*
    Input: *P*
    Output: (*P* or *Q*)

(54c) is standardly derived by the rule of double negation, which takes an arbitrary assumption as premise and derives the negation of its negation as conclusion:

(57) *Double Negation*
    Input: *P*
    Output: (not (not *P*))

Similar, though more complex, derivations yield (54d–e).

In informal systems, the existence of such rules creates no serious problems, because it is left to the intelligent user to decide which line of reasoning to pursue, and when to abandon it. However, in a formal system of the type just described, the assumption is that although the rules may be accessed and tested in a certain order, every rule applies obligatorily whenever it is accessed and its input description is met. In such a system, each of the above rules, once set in motion, would reapply indefinitely to its own output, and the derivation would never stop.

Let us define an *introduction rule* as a rule whose output assumption contains every concept contained in its input assumption(s), and at least one further concept. We take the correct conclusion to be that introduction rules play no part in the spontaneous deductive processing of information, the processing which our deductive device is designed to describe. The only deductive rules available for use in the spontaneous processing of information – the only rules which in any interesting sense form part of the basic deductive equipment of humans – are elimination rules.

This is a substantial claim, and one that most people working on the psychology of deduction have been reluctant to make. If they consider the problem at all, their solution is generally to make use of introduction rules, but to constrain their functioning in some way so that indefinite reapplication is avoided. We will discuss their reasons below. Note, however, that our rejection of introduction rules is not based on the sole desire to avoid indefinite reapplication. Our claim is that introduction rules are *never* used in the spontaneous processing of information. For example, no speaker would utter (58) expecting any of the conclusions in (59a–e) to be drawn on the basis of this utterance alone, and no hearer would draw such conclusions on the basis of this utterance alone:

(58) The Prime Minister has resigned.

(59) (a) The Prime Minister has resigned and the Prime Minister has resigned.
  (b) Either the Prime Minister has resigned or it's a little warmer today.
  (c) It's not true that the Prime Minister hasn't resigned.
  (d) If the Prime Minister hasn't resigned, the tiger will become extinct.
  (e) If it's the Queen's birthday, the Prime Minister has resigned.

The conclusions in (59a–e), and others derived by use of introduction rules, are in some intuitive sense trivial. The intuition of triviality relates to the fact that they leave the content of their input assumptions unchanged except for the addition of arbitrary material; they can in no sense be regarded as analysing or explicating the content of their input assumptions. Elimination rules, by contrast, are genuinely interpretive: the output assumptions explicate or analyse the content of the input assumptions. Our hypothesis is that the human deductive device has access only to elimination rules, and yields only non-trivial conclusions, defined as follows:

(60) *Non-trivial logical implication*
  A set of assumptions **P** *logically and non-trivially implies* an assumption Q if and only if, when **P** is the set of initial theses in a derivation involving only elimination rules, Q belongs to the set of final theses.

In other words, the human deductive device is a system which explicates the content of any set of assumptions submitted to it.

Psychologists who have proposed models of the human deductive system have rarely come to this conclusion. In fact, most of them are concerned less with the study of spontaneous comprehension than with performance on specific reasoning tasks: syllogistic reasoning, distinguishing valid from invalid arguments, and so on. The fact that these are finite rather than open-ended tasks, and that many of the models proposed are informal rather than formal, has meant that the problem of trivial implication is often overlooked. Where it is not, the conclusion has almost invariably been that introduction rules cannot be entirely dispensed with, for two sorts of reasons. First, it is claimed that certain types of spontaneous deduction which are regularly and straightforwardly performed require the use of introduction rules. For example, it is intuitively clear that given premises (61a–c), conclusion (62) would be spontaneously derived, and that given premises (63a-b), conclusion (64) would be spontaneously derived (subject to the usual limitations on memory and attention):

(61) (a) If the trains are on strike and the car has broken down, there is no way of getting to work.
     (b) The trains are on strike.
     (c) The car has broken down.

---

(62) There is no way of getting to work.

(63) (a) If the boiler needs repairing or the electricity has been cut off, the house will be uninhabitable.
     (b) The boiler needs repairing.

---

(64) The house will be uninhabitable.

These examples have been seen as clearly demonstrating the need for at least some version of the rules of *and*-introduction and *or*-introduction in any account of the human deductive device.

The assumption is that the only way, or the only psychologically plausible way, to derive (62) from (61) or (64) from (63) is by the use of introduction rules. The derivation of (62) would involve a step of *and*-introduction at (d) below, followed by a step of *modus ponens* based on (a) and (d) to reach the desired conclusion:

(61) (a) If the trains are on strike and the car has broken down, there is no way of getting to work. [Premise]
     (b) The trains are on strike. [Premise]
     (c) The car has broken down. [Premise]
     (d) The trains are on strike and the car has broken down. [By *and*-introduction from (b) and (c)]

---

(62) There is no way of getting to work. [By *modus ponens* from (a) and (d)]

Similarly, the derivation of (64) is seen as involving a step of *or*-introduction at (c) below, followed by a step of modus ponens based on (a) and (c) to reach the desired conclusion:

(63) (a) If the boiler needs repairing or the electricity has been cut off, the house will be uninhabitable. [Premise].
  (b) The boiler needs repairing. [Premise]
  (c) The boiler needs repairing or the electricity has been cut off. [By *or*-introduction from (b)]

---

(64) The house will be uninhabitable. [By *modus ponens* from (a) and (c)]

These are, of course, the simplest derivations available in most standard logics using primitive rules alone.

However, to show that the rules of *and*-introduction and *or*-introduction are necessary, it would first have to be shown that there is no alternative derivation using only elimination rules, or that any such alternative derivation was psychologically unmotivated. As regards the first point, alternative derivations undoubtedly exist. Any standard logic would permit the use of the following derived rules:

(65) *Conjunctive modus ponens*
  (a) *Input*:   (i)   (if (P and Q) then R)
                   (ii) P
      Output: (If Q then R)
  (b) *Input*:   (i)   (If (P and Q) then R)
                   (ii) Q
      Output: (If P then R)
(66) *Disjunctive modus ponens*
  (a) *Input*:   (i)   (If (P or Q) then R)
                   (ii) P
      Output: R
  (b) *Input*:   (i)   (If (P or Q) then R)
                   (ii) Q
      Output: R

These rules, like *modus ponens* itself, are elimination rules, and as will be seen below, there is good reason to think that they play a role in the spontaneous deductive processing of information. We assume that some version of rule (65) is attached to the logical entry for *and*, and some version of rule (66) is attached to the logical entry for *or*.

Rules (65) and (66) make it possible to derive (62) from (61) and (64) from (63) without the use of introduction rules. The derivation of (62) from (61) would go as in (61′) below, with a step of conjunctive *modus ponens* at (b′), followed by a step of regular *modus ponens*:

(61′) (a) If the trains are on strike and the car has broken down, there is no way of getting to work. [Premise]

    (b) The trains are on strike. [Premise]
    (b′) If the car has broken down, there is no way of getting to work.
        [From (a) and (b) by conjunctive *modus ponens*]
    (c) The car has broken down. [Premise]

---

(62) There is no way of getting to work. [From (b′) and (c) by *modus ponens*]

The derivation of (64) from (63) would go as in (63′) below, with a step of disjunctive *modus ponens* deriving the conclusion directly from the premises:

(63′) (a) If the boiler needs repairing or the electricity has been cut off, the house will be uninhabitable. [Premise]
      (b) The boiler needs repairing. [Premise]

---

(64) The house will be uninhabitable. [From (a) and (b) by disjunctive *modus ponens*]

There is thus no question that alternative derivations exist.

    The psychological plausibility of these derivations depends on the psychological plausibility of rules (65) and (66) themselves. Rips (1983) has experimental evidence that rule (66), the rule of disjunctive *modus ponens*, is not only psychologically real but is one of the most highly accessible rules, more accessible than the rule of *modus ponens* itself. His evidence also shows that the rule of *or*-introduction is one of the least accessible rules, and is indeed rejected by many subjects. The fact that derivations such as (63)–(64) are regularly and easily performed strongly suggests that no step of *or*-introduction is involved.

    We know of no experimental evidence on rule (65), the rule of conjunctive *modus ponens*. However, in a relevance-based framework, both conjunctive and disjunctive *modus ponens* would be highly valued for the following reason. When some item of information is presented in the form of a complex conditional with a conjunctive or disjunctive antecedent, the chances of finding the whole conjunctive or disjunctive antecedent ready-stored in memory are clearly much smaller than those of finding just one of its constituent conjuncts or disjuncts. What the rules of conjunctive and disjunctive *modus ponens* do is allow inferences to be drawn on the basis of a single conjunct or disjunct, rather than requiring the whole conjunctive or disjunctive antecedent to be supplied. They thus increase the chances of the presented information interacting with the individual's existing representation of the world to enable new conclusions to be drawn. For an organism interested in improving its representation of the world, rules (65) and (66) would thus have considerable value.

The other justification for introduction rules found in the psychological literature is based on subjects' performance on specific reasoning tasks: in particular, in checking the validity of arguments. Thus, the fact that almost all subjects say that (67a–b) entails (68), and some say that (69) entails (70), is seen as evidence that the rules of *and*-introduction and *or*-introduction are psychologically real:[21]

(67) (a) Snow is white.
    (b) Grass is green.
(68) Snow is white and grass is green.

(69) The world is round.
(70) The world is round or the world is flat.

Psychologists aware of the problem of trivial implication then assume that the functioning of these rules is constrained in one way or another to avoid iterative application. One solution is to allow the system to formulate goals, and to allow introduction rules to operate only when (i) their input descriptions are met and (ii) the system has the specific goal of deriving a conjunctive or disjunctive conclusion, say, because it is checking the validity of an argument such as (67)–(68) or (69)–(70). Rules which operate under such constraints are called 'backwards' rules and distinguished from the regular 'forwards' rules which simply apply whenever their input descriptions are met.[22]

We do not doubt that hearers sometimes want to derive a particular conclusion from an utterance, and have to have some procedure for obtaining it. What we do doubt is that such a procedure is likely to involve entirely different deductive rules from those used in normal comprehension: that is, that a set of deductive rules exists whose sole function is to confirm conclusions which they cannot spontaneously generate. It seems much more likely that 'backwards reasoning' is merely the search for a set of premises from which the desired conclusion can be derived using the regular deductive rules: in other words that it is a retrieval strategy rather than a distinct form of reasoning. And if, as in the cases (67)–(70) above, there is no elimination rule which will directly derive the desired conclusion from the set of available premises, then that conclusion is simply not directly derivable.

However, there is no reason to think that the only method individuals have of checking the validity of arguments is by direct derivation. An argument is valid if and only if the premises entail the conclusion: that is, if and only if the conclusion must be true whenever the premises are true. We have argued that the human deductive device is incomplete in the sense that there are valid arguments whose conclusions are not directly derivable by the rules of the deductive device; (67)–(68) and (69)–(70) are cases in point. We would therefore expect the deductive device to be complemented with some non-deductive, or not directly deductive, procedures for checking validity whenever the deductive machinery is insufficient. And in that case, from the fact that subjects make correct judgements of validity, it does not follow that these judgements have been arrived at by direct derivation.

Our deductive device offers such an indirect procedure based on the fact that it monitors contradictions. One way of showing that an argument is valid is to show that it is inconsistent to assert the premises while denying the conclusion. For instance, if (67a–b) and the negation of (68), or (69) and the negation of (70), were the initial theses of a derivation, the deductive device would reveal the inconsistencies involved, and thus establish that (67a–b) entails (68) and that (69) entails (70).

We therefore reject two extreme views of the human deductive ability. We do not believe that *all* deductive inference must be accounted for purely in terms of deductive rules (the position tacitly adopted in Rips 1983). On the other hand, we do believe that a deductive rule system is an extremely efficient device for reducing the number of assumptions that have to be separately stored in memory, for accessing the conclusions of arguments, for drawing out the implications of newly acquired conceptual information, and for increasing the impact of this information on a stored conceptual representation of the world. We therefore reject the claim made by Johnson-Laird (1982b, 1983) that there are no mentally represented deductive rules at all:

> The crux of the matter is that a system of inference may perform in an entirely logical way even though it does not employ rules of inference, inferential schemata, meaning postulates, or any other sort of machinery conventionally employed in a logical calculus. (Johnson-Laird 1982b: 20)

It seems reasonable to assume, with Johnson-Laird, that subjects use various heuristics that are not directly derivational in performing certain types of reasoning tasks; but it does not follow that there are no mentally represented deductive rules at all, any more than it follows from the fact that subjects perform correctly on certain reasoning tasks that they must be using deductive rules.

We are suggesting, then, a mixed view of human deductive abilities. Our hypothesis is that when presented with a set of assumptions, subject to the usual limitations of memory and attention,[23] the device should directly and automatically compute the full set of non-trivial implications defined by its deductive rules, as part of its regular working procedure. Trivial implications, by contrast, are not directly computed. The procedures for accessing and checking the validity of trivial implications are quite different from the automatic procedures for deriving the available non-trivial ones: they are in a sense less natural, they may take more time and be subject to different types of mistakes. In other words, performance with the two types of implication should be significantly different, and this might be experimentally checked.

In this section we have described in very general terms a deductive device which might be used in the spontaneous processing of information. The function of the device is essentially to analyse and manipulate the conceptual content of assumptions, this function being performed by the elimination rules attached to the logical entries for concepts. Our central claim has been that in normal circumstances the deductive processing of an assumption involves computation of its non-trivial implications, never of its trivial ones. When an assumption is processed in a context of other assumptions, again we claim that in normal circumstances only non-trivial implications are computed. Since, if we are right, trivial implications play no role in the comprehension process, we will not be concerned with them in the rest of the book. From now on, unless otherwise stated, when we talk of implications or logical implications, we will mean non-trivial implications as defined above.

To restrict the class of implications that could in principle be computed by the human deductive device is not, of course, to say everything about the deductive processing of information. Quite apart from the need to establish which deductive rules actually exist, there is the fact that the implications of a given set of assumptions must be accessed in some order, and we have as yet said nothing about how this order is imposed. Moreover, information is invariably processed in a context of other assumptions, and we have as yet said nothing about how the context is selected. What we have done is merely place an upper bound on the set of implications that could in principle be derived from a given set of assumptions. How the premises are chosen, and in what order the implications are computed, will be the subject of later chapters. In the next section we want to consider, in rather more general terms, what types of deduction can be performed when a chosen propositional content and context are brought together in the memory of the deductive device.

6 Some types of deduction

We have claimed that the relevance of new information to an individual is to be assessed in terms of the improvements it brings to his representation of the world. A representation of the world is a stock of factual assumptions with some internal organisation. We would now like to suggest that the improvements brought by new information to an existing representation of the world can be traced via the workings of the deductive device.

When a set of assumptions is placed in the memory of the deductive device, all the deductive rules in the logical entries attached to their constituent concepts are accessed. As can be seen from the examples given above, these rules are of two formally distinct types, which we will call *analytic* and *synthetic*. An analytic rule takes only a single assumption as input; a synthetic rule takes two separate assumptions as input. For example, *and*-elimination (rules (46a–b) above), which takes a single, conjoined assumption as input, is an analytic rule, and *modus ponendo ponens* (rule (47) above), which takes a conditional assumption and its antecedent as input, is a synthetic rule.

Let us say that any conclusion obtained from an initial set of assumptions by a derivation in which only analytic rules are used is *analytically implied* by that set of assumptions:

(71) *Analytic implication*
   A set of assumptions **P** *analytically implies* an assumption Q if and only if Q is one of the final theses in a deduction in which the initial theses are **P**, and in which only analytic rules have applied.

Notice that by this definition every assumption analytically implies itself.
   Then any implication which is not analytic is *synthetic*:

(72) *Synthetic implication*
   A set of assumptions **P** *synthetically implies* an assumption Q if and only if Q is one of the final theses in a deduction in which the initial theses are **P**, and Q is not an analytic implication of **P**.

In practice, this means that a synthetic implication is the result of a derivation in which at least one synthetic rule has applied.

Inferential approaches to comprehension have sometimes been charged with a failure to distinguish understanding an assumption or an utterance from grasping its logical consequences. Since we have denied the distinction between 'logical' and 'non-logical' terms and conflated 'logical' with 'semantic' deductive rules, we might seem particularly vulnerable to this charge. In fact, the problem is already partly solved by our distinction between trivial and non-trivial implications, and our claim that only the latter are involved in the comprehension process. However, there is still an intuition that even among non-trivial implications, some are more intimately connected with understanding a set of assumptions and others with working out its logical consequences. This intuition can be explained in terms of our distinction between analytic and synthetic implications.

The analytic implications of a set of assumptions are those that are necessary and sufficient for understanding it, for grasping its content. Someone who claims to understand an assumption but denies one of its analytic implications cannot be said to have understood it at all. Failure to grasp the synthetic implications of a set of assumptions, by contrast, is not a failure to understand the information being offered, but a failure to exploit it to the full.

The synthetic implications of a given set of assumptions are those whose derivations involve the application of at least one synthetic rule. For example, (73a–c) synthetically implies (74a–b), the synthetic rule in question being *modus ponens*:

(73) (a) There's a bus coming.
    (b) If there's a bus coming, we'll get to work on time.
    (c) If we get to work on time, it won't matter that we overslept.
(74) (a) We'll get to work on time.
    (b) It won't matter that we overslept.

Or, to give a 'non-logical' example, (75a–c) synthetically implies (76a–c) the synthetic rule involved being something like the rule of containment shown in (77):

(75) (a) The ticket is in the wallet.
    (b) The wallet is in the suitcase.
    (c) The suitcase is in the car.
(76) (a) The ticket is in the suitcase.
    (b) The ticket is in the car.
    (c) The wallet is in the car.
(77) *Containment rule*[24]
    Input: (i) $(X - \text{is} - \text{in} - Y)$
           (ii) $(Y - \text{is} - \text{in} - Z)$
    Output: $(X - \text{is} - \text{in} - Z)$

The ability to understand the set of assumptions (75a–c) certainly involves the ability to grasp such analytic implications as (78a–f):

(78) (a) The ticket is somewhere.
    (b) Something is in the wallet.
    (c) The wallet is somewhere.
    (d) Something is in the suitcase.
    (e) The suitcase is somewhere.
    (f) Something is in the car.

Someone who accepted (75a–c) but denied any of (78a–f) would be guilty of a failure not of logic but of understanding. On the other hand, someone could quite well understand (75a–c) without having computed the synthetic implications (76a–c). Suppose you acquired each of these assumptions at a different time and in different circumstances, so that you never happened to bring them together and compute their synthetic implications (76a–c). This omission would not mean that you had understood each individual assumption any the less. We all have hundreds of thousands of assumptions stored in memory, from which hundreds of thousands of synthetic implications could be computed if only they could all be brought together in the memory of the deductive device. The fact that they never have been, and indeed never will be, does not mean that each individual assumption has not been properly understood.

Notice that what makes a synthetic implication synthetic is not the form in which its premises are presented but the nature of the rules used in deriving it. There is no reason why a single complex assumption should not have synthetic implications. For example, the conjoined assumption in (79) synthetically implies (76a), just as the separate assumptions (75a) and (75b) do:

(79) The ticket is in the wallet and the wallet is in the suitcase.
(75) (a) The ticket is in the wallet.
     (b) The wallet is in the suitcase.
(76) (a) The ticket is in the suitcase.

The only difference in the way this implication is derived from (75a–b) on the one hand and from (79) on the other is that (79) must undergo *and*-elimination before rule (77) can apply. Otherwise the derivations are identical, and what is a synthetic implication in one case remains a synthetic implication in the other.

We have now reached the point where a single assumption can have three types of logical implication: trivial implications, which are not directly computed by our device; analytic implications, which are necessary and sufficient for understanding it; and synthetic implications, which have to do not so much with grasping the information being offered as with exploiting this information to the full. Our framework thus sheds some light on the rather hazy pretheoretical distinction between 'semantic' and 'logical' implication, between intrinsic meaning and wider import.

The distinction between analytic and synthetic implications has an important practical consequence. The analytic implications of a given assumption are intrinsic to it: they are recoverable as long as the assumption itself is recoverable, simply by reprocessing it through the deductive device. Synthetic implications, by contrast, are not intrinsic to any single member of the set of assumptions from which they are derived (barring the case of conjunctions such as (79)). A synthetic implication is necessarily based on two distinct elementary assumptions, and deriving it is not just a matter of having these assumptions somewhere in memory: they have to be brought together in the small working memory of the deductive device. Once there, there is no guarantee that they will ever be brought together again, and their synthetic implications may well be lost for ever if not computed on the spot.

We assume, as do most current models of memory, that information is broken down as far as possible into smaller units before being stored in memory, so that a conjoined assumption, for example, is not stored as a unit but is broken down into its constituent conjuncts, which may end up in different encyclopaedic entries. Any organism interested in improving its overall representation of the world must therefore be interested in recovering as many synthetic implications as possible from any set of assumptions it is currently processing, before the set is dismantled for separate storage. Analytic implications, by contrast, are only worth recovering as a means to an end, the end being the recovery of further synthetic implications.

As we have seen, assumptions entering the memory of the deductive device have four possible sources: they can come from perception, linguistic decoding or encyclopaedic memory, or they can be added to the memory of the device as a result of the deductive process itself. In an intuitive sense, assumptions derived or retrieved from encyclopaedic entries are old information, whereas assumptions derived from perception or linguistic decoding, i.e. from input systems, are newly presented information, and become old in the course of being processed. In this book, we are concerned with the effect of newly presented information, in particular of assumptions derived via the linguistic input system, on old information drawn from an existing representation of the world.

We want to look, then, at the effect of deductions in which the set of initial theses placed in the memory of the deductive device can be partitioned into two subsets, **P** and **C**, where **P** may be thought of as new information, and **C** as old information. Let us call a deduction based on the union of **P** and **C** as premises a *contextualisation of* **P** *in the context* **C**. The contextualisation of **P** in **C** may yield new conclusions not derivable from either **P** or **C** alone. These we will call the *contextual implications* of **P** in **C**:

(80) *Contextual implication*

A set of assumptions **P** *contextually implies* an assumption Q in the context **C** if and only if

(i) the union of **P** and **C** non-trivially implies Q,

(ii) **P** does not non-trivially imply Q, and

(iii) C does not non-trivially imply Q.

A contextual implication is new information in the sense that it could not have been derived from C, the stock of existing assumptions, alone; however, it is not *just* new information, since it is neither an analytic nor a synthetic implication of P, the newly presented information, alone. It is a synthesis of old and new information, a result of interaction between the two.

From a logical point of view, the only slightly unusual feature of this definition of contextual implication is that it partitions the premises of a synthetic implication into two distinct subsets, one subset being treated as carrying the implication in the context of the other. Logically speaking, of course, the two subsets are on a par: it is the union of P and C which synthetically implies Q, and the distinction between the two subsets is a pragmatic rather than a logical one. Newly presented information is seen as adding to, and interacting with, information drawn from an existing representation of the world.

The addition of new information to a context of old information brings not only contextual implications but also analytic, and perhaps synthetic, implications of its own. However, these implications, unlike contextual implications, are context-independent. It is mainly in terms of contextual implications that the effect of context on utterance interpretation, and the rationale for processing information in one context rather than another, must be seen. The notion of contextual implication will play a major role in the remainder of this book.

A central function of the deductive device is thus to derive, spontaneously, automatically and unconsciously, the contextual implications of any newly presented information in a context of old information. Other things being equal, the more contextual implications it yields, the more this new information will improve the individual's existing representation of the world.[25]

The deductive device is also at the centre of spontaneous non-demonstrative inference: it is a major source of assumptions, and its processes affect the strength of both the initial and final theses of the deductions it performs. It is to these aspects of inference that we now turn.

7 Contextual effects: the role of deduction in non-demonstrative inference

Recall that a deduction based on the union of new information P and old information C is a *contextualisation* of P in C. Such a contextualisation may give rise to what we will call *contextual effects*. In this section we will introduce the notion of a contextual effect. In chapter 3 we will argue that relevance can be characterised in terms of contextual effects.

The intuitive idea behind the notion of a contextual effect is the following. To modify and improve a context is to have some effect on that context – but not just any modification will do. As we have seen, the addition of new information which merely duplicates old information does not count as an improvement; nor does the addition of new information which is entirely unrelated to old information. The sort of effect we are interested in is a result of interaction between new and old information. One such effect has already been described. Contextual implications are contextual effects: they result from a crucial interaction between new and old information as premises in a synthetic implication.

Intuitively, in the sort of framework we have been describing, there should be two more types of contextual effect. On the one hand, new information may provide further evidence for, and therefore strengthen, old assumptions; or it may provide evidence against, and perhaps lead to the abandonment of, old assumptions. In the last three sections, we have largely ignored the fact that assumptions placed in the memory of the deductive device come with varying degrees of strength, and that a deduction may result in a contradiction. We now want to look at these two aspects of deduction and the type of contextual effects they give rise to. We will then propose a general characterisation of the notion of a contextual effect.

How does the relative strength of the premises in a deduction affect the strength of the conclusions? This question can be approached from either a logical or a cognitive point of view. A better understanding of the logical issue should help with the cognitive one.

Consider the set of premises (81a–d) and their synthetic implication (82):

(81) (a) If Peter, Paul and Mary came to the party, the party was a success.
  (b) Peter came to the party.
  (c) Paul came to the party.
  (d) Mary came to the party.
(82) The party was a success.

Consider (83), which is the conjunction of (81a–d), and which therefore also entails (82):

(83) If Peter, Paul and Mary came to the party, the party was a success, and Peter, Paul and Mary came to the party.

If we could assign a confirmation value to (83), it would be easy to show that, from a logical point of view, the confirmation value of (82) must be at least as high as that of (83), which entails it. It could not be lower, since this would mean that conceivably (83) might be true and (82) false, and this is ruled out by the fact that (83) entails (82). On the other hand, if there is any possibility that the party was a success without Peter, or Paul, or Mary being there, then the confirmation value of (82) should be even higher than that of (83).

From a logical point of view, then, there is a lower limit to the confirmation value of a conclusion: it cannot be less than the confirmation value of the conjunction of the premises. From a cognitive point of view, the question now becomes: how can the deductive device assess that lower limit, given that (as we are assuming) it can neither derive the conjunction of the premises nor *compute* its confirmation value? Further logical considerations must be taken into account before this cognitive question can be answered.

We are considering, then, how the confirmation value of the conjunction (83) might be assessed. The confirmation value of a conjunction of assumptions depends on the values of its conjuncts. From a logical point of view, it cannot be higher than the value of the weakest, i.e. least confirmed, conjunct. Suppose it is certain that Peter and Paul came to the party, but doubtful that Mary did. It is equally doubtful, then, that Peter, Paul and Mary all came to the party. On the other hand, the confirmation value of a conjunction can be lower than that of its weakest conjunct. Suppose that (81b–d) are are all strongly confirmed, but less than certain. Generally, the likelihood of all three assumptions being true is less than the likelihood of any single one of them being true. The confirmation value of a conjunction should therefore be lower than that of any of its individual conjuncts. In fact, the greater the number of conjuncts, and the lower their confirmation values, the lower the confirmation value of the conjunction.

There is thus an upper limit to the confirmation value of the conjunction of premises used in a deduction, and this can be assessed without either deriving that conjunction or computing its confirmation value. The upper limit of the confirmation value of a conjunction is the confirmation value of its weakest conjunct; to assess that, no computation is required.

Notice that in a single deduction, different conclusions may be derived on the basis of different premises. Only those premises actually used in the derivation of a particular conclusion should affect its confirmation value. For instance, let us add to (81) one further premise (81e):

(81) (e) If Paul and Mary came to the party, Roger left early.

Now, from the set of premises (81a–e), another conclusion follows:

(84) Roger left early.

Clearly, we do not want the confirmation value of (84) to be affected by that of (81a) or (81b), nor do we want the confirmation value of (82) to be affected by that of (81e). Thus, a particular conclusion should inherit its confirmation value only from the set of premises actually used in its derivation.

All this suggests a cognitive account, based on the working of the deductive device, of the relation between the strength of the premises and the strength of the conclusions in a deduction. Such an account could be implemented along the following lines. The deductive device might operate in such a way that when an analytic rule is applied, the conclusion inherits the strength of the premise. When a synthetic rule applies, there are three possibilities. Either both premises are certain, in which case the conclusion is also certain; or one of the premises is certain and the other is not, in which case the conclusion inherits the strength of the weaker premise; or neither premise is certain, in which case the strength inherited by the conclusion is lower than that of the weaker premise.

The effect on derivations involving the application of more than one rule would be as follows. When all the premises actually used in the derivation of a particular conclusion are certain, the conclusion is also certain. When all the premises but one are certain, the conclusion inherits the strength of the less-than-certain premise. When more than one premise is less than certain, then the conclusion is weaker than the weakest premise. Conclusions derived from several weak premises inherit a value that is very weak and vague. However, inherited degrees of strength are lower limits: generally speaking, conclusions are more likely to be true than the conjunction of the premises from which they are deduced.

We are crediting the deductive device with the ability to reproduce degrees of strength, and to raise or lower them. These are much more modest abilities than would be needed for computing quantitative confirmation values. As expected, these procedures do not determine absolute confirmation values except of the grossest kind (e.g. *weakly confirmed, certain*), but by pushing the strength of a given assumption above or below that of other assumptions, it makes some comparisons possible.

When a conclusion is derived from several less-than-certain premises, its value will be very vague. This would be a great defect if we were trying to develop an optimal *logical* system. But we are actually trying to model a *cognitive* system. The inability of our model to determine precisely the strength of a conclusion derived from several uncertain assumptions corresponds well enough to introspective evidence. We are not aware of any other evidence showing that the human mind is equipped with a more powerful and precise way of spontaneously determining the strength of its factual assumptions.

Returning to our discussion of contextual effects, consider first how contextual implication, our original example of a contextual effect, fares when the strength of assumptions is taken into account. Contextual implication is a sub-type of synthetic implication. Consider, then, the relation between a synthetic implication and the premises actually used in deriving it. A synthetic implication is not logically implied by any one of its premises: it cannot be demonstratively inferred from any one of its premises. On the other hand, take away any one of the premises, and the conclusion can no longer be derived from the remaining premises. It could thus be said that each premise is an argument for the conclusion, or evidence for the conclusion, in the context of the other premises; or, as we propose to say, each of the premises actually used in the derivation of a synthetic implication strengthens the conclusion which they jointly imply. The contribution of each individual premise to the strength of this joint conclusion is a function of its own degree of strength.

Contextual implication, as we have defined it, is a relation between a synthetic implication and one of the premises used in deriving it. A contextual implication Q cannot be demonstratively inferred from an assumption P that contextually implies it in context C; but it can be demonstratively inferred from the union of P and C; or it can be non-demonstratively inferred from P, by assuming C. Here, then, is a case of non-demonstrative inference in which the only logical rules involved are deductive. These rules contribute not only to the formation of a new assumption on the basis of existing assumptions, but also to the determination of its strength.

We see the relation of contextual implication, then, as a special case of *contextual strengthening*. It might be called *dependent* strengthening, in the sense that the strength of the conclusion depends not only on the added premises P but also on the context C: P affects, but does not fully determine, the strength of its contextual implication. Dependent strengthening contrasts, of course, with the better known case of *independent* strengthening – the cognitive counterpart of independent confirmation – to which we now turn.

Independent strengthening arises when a single conclusion is independently implied by two different sets of premises. Consider the set of premises (85a–b):

(85) (a) If the party broke up late, then it was a success.
    (b) The party broke up late.

This logically implies (82), a conclusion which, as we saw, is also implied by the set of premises (81a–d):

(81) (a) If Peter, Paul and Mary came to the party, the party was a success.

(b) Peter came to the party.
(c) Paul came to the party.
(d) Mary came to the party.
(82) The party was a success.

Suppose, now, that (85a–b) is contextualised in (81a–d): will that contextualisation have any effect?

We said that the deductive device has the following procedure for avoiding redundancies: before writing an assumption down in its memory, it checks whether that assumption is already there. If so, it refrains from writing the assumption down again, and marks the theses and deductive rules used in deriving it so that the derivation will not be repeated. However, this discussion of what happens when the device meets the same assumption twice did not take into account the possibility that the two occurrences of this assumption may differ in strength. It is in the handling of such cases that significant effects might occur.

The question, then, is how the strength of an assumption already present in the memory of the deductive device, or deducible from the theses present in it, should be affected when the device meets a second occurrence of the same assumption, derived from different premises. Let us call the strength that (82) inherits from (81a–d) alone $S1$, the strength that it inherits from (85a–b) $S2$, and the strength it inherits from the union of (81a–d) and (85a–b) $S3$. The question then is how $S3$ is related to $S1$ and $S2$.

Both intuitively and logically speaking, $S3$ should be greater than both $S1$ and $S2$ (unless, of course, $S1$ or $S2$ is certain, in which case $S3$ should be certain too). The reason for this is straightforward. First, whichever of $S1$ and $S2$ is the greater provides the lower limit for $S3$: if $S3$ fell below this limit, it would fail to reflect the amount of support that each set of premises independently brings to their common conclusion. Second, if $S3$ were merely identical to whichever of $S1$ and $S2$ were the greater, that is, if it merely reflected the amount of support that one set of premises brought to their common conclusion, it would entirely fail to reflect the support that the other set of premises independently brings to it. Hence $S3$ should be greater than both $S1$ and $S2$. In other words, (82) should inherit from the union of (81a–d) and (85a–b) a degree of strength greater than the one it inherits from either (81a–d) or (85a–b) independently. There is no difficulty in implementing this logical condition through the working of the deductive device as we have described it.

Dependent and independent strengthening can combine. Suppose that (86a–b) is contextualised in (81a–d), and that (81d) is the weakest of all the premises:

(86) (a) Either Bob came to the party or Mary came to the party.
    (b) Bob did not come to the party.

(86a–b) logically implies (87):

(87) Mary came to the party.

This leads to an independent strengthening of (81d), which is identical in content to (87). Since (81d) is also an argument for (82) in the context of (81a–c), (82) is in turn dependently strengthened by (81d). The contextualisation of (86) in (81) thus strengthens both (81d) and (82).

We have so far considered two types of contextual effect: the addition of contextual implications and the strengthening of previously held assumptions. But a significant improvement of one's representation of the world can also result from the elimination of false assumptions. This highly significant contextual effect may be brought about when there is a contradiction between new and old information.

In our account of the working of the deductive device, we said that when it encounters a contradiction, it halts until the contradiction is resolved. Suppose, for example, that (88a–b) is contextualised in (89):

(88) (a) If Jennifer came, the party was a success.
    (b) Jennifer came.
(89) (a) If Bill came, the party was not a success.
    (b) Bill came.
    (c) The party was not a success.
    (d) If the party was not a success, we won't have another party.
    (e) We won't have another party.

(88a–b) logically implies (90), the negation of (89c):

(90) The party was a success.

On deriving (90), we said, the device will attempt to resolve this contradiction. In resolving a contradiction, the strength of the two contradictory assumptions must be taken into account.

The deductive device has the power not only to read and write assumptions in its memory, but also to erase them. Let us assume that when two assumptions are found to contradict each other, if it is possible to compare their strengths, and if one is found to be stronger than the other, then the device automatically erases the weaker assumption. When an assumption is erased, the device also erases any assumption which analytically implies it, and the weaker of any pair of assumptions which synthetically imply it; this procedure applies recursively until no more erasures can take place. When such a procedure is possible, the contradiction is eliminated at the root, and the deductive process can be resumed.

Suppose, for example, that (90) is stronger than (89c). On discovering the contradiction, the device would erase (89c). It would then check to see whether it has in memory any assumption which analytically implies (89c), or any pair of assumptions which synthetically imply it; it would discover that (89c) is synthetically implied by (89a) and (89b), and would erase the weaker of these two assumptions.

Notice now that (89c) and (89d) synthetically imply (89e): that is, (89c) is an argument for (89e) in the context of assumption (89d). What happens to (89e) when (89c) is erased? Clearly, (89e) should lose whatever strength it gained by dependent strengthening from (89c). It may be independently strengthened by other assumptions; in which case it should remain in the memory of the device with a degree of strength commensurate with that independent support. Or it may have no other source of strength, having received all its support from (89c) and (89d); in which case the loss of this support should reduce it from the status of an assumption with some degree of strength to the status of a mere unsupported possibility.

There are situations where this straightforward method of resolving contradictions yields no result: for instance because the device is unable to compare the strength of the two contradictory assumptions, or because they are equally strong. We assume that in these situations the contradiction is resolved by other means: for example, by a conscious search for further evidence for or against one of the contradictory assumptions. This seems to correspond to the introspective evidence that some contradictions are resolved by an apparently immediate and automatic rejection of the faulty premises, while other contradictions require deliberation.

The contextualisation of a new assumption in a context which contradicts it can result in the rejection, not of an assumption already present in the context, but of some or all of the new information itself. In this case, there will be no significant contextual effect. Contextual effects are achieved only when, as in the case just described, the new assumption displaces an assumption already present in the context, with subsequent weakening or erasure of other contextual assumptions linked to it by relations of analytic or synthetic implication. If (90) had been weaker than (89c), for example, (90) itself would have been erased, and the contextualisation of (88a–b) in (89a–e) would have had no effect at all.

We have now described the various types of possible contextual effects: contextual implications, strengthenings, and contradictions resulting in the erasure of premises from the context.[d] We have so far considered two types of strengthening: dependent and independent, in both of which the strength of a conclusion is determined by the strength of the premises used in deriving it. Before leaving the subject, we would like to suggest that there is another type of strengthening, which we will call *retroactive* strengthening. Here, the assumptions actually used in a contextualisation may be strengthened by the fact that the contextualisation has had some expected result. Anticipating the next chapters, we will briefly outline how such retroactive strengthening can occur in verbal comprehension, and consider whether a similar effect could be occurring in spontaneous inference generally.

In verbal communication, the hearer is generally led to accept an assumption as true or probably true on the basis of a guarantee given by the speaker. Part of the hearer's task is to find out which assumptions the speaker is guaranteeing as true. Our hypothesis is that the hearer is guided by considerations of relevance in carrying out this task. He expects the information the speaker intended to convey, when processed in the context the speaker expected it to be contextualised in, to be relevant: that is, to have a substantial contextual effect, at a low processing cost. Thus, if the hearer assumes (91),

(91) The speaker intends to assert P

and P turns out to be relevant in the expected way, assumption (91) is strengthened; moreover, if the hearer trusts the speaker to be truthful, assumption P is strengthened too. If P turns to be relevant in the expected way only when assumption Q is added to the context, then assumption (92) is strengthened:

(92) The speaker intends the hearer to assume Q

and again, if the hearer trusts the speaker, then assumption Q is strengthened.

What makes these retroactive strengthenings generally valid is the following. It is generally unlikely that any arbitrary assumption would be relevant enough to be worth the individual's attention; hence any interpretation of an utterance that achieves a satisfactory level of relevance is very likely to be correct. In other words, the hearer who arrives at an adequately relevant interpretation can be fairly confident that it is the one the speaker intended to convey. This point will be discussed in more detail in chapter 4.

Now it might seem that the case of verbal understanding is unique and significantly different from other uses of inferential abilities. The speaker wants to be understood and is actively helping the hearer, whereas, so the argument goes, the environment is not helping observers understand it. In fact this argument is not as compelling as it looks. Much of the environment is man-made and is full of intentional cues to help people perceive it adequately. You might grant that and still ask, what about the natural environment? Surely nature is not helping humans understand it? Well again, that is not so sure.

Human cognitive abilities are a part of nature; they are well adapted as a result of natural evolution. It could be that of the assumptions which come most spontaneously to a human mind, those that are true are more likely to be relevant than those that are false, so that when relevance is achieved it provides generally valid retroactive strengthening. If that is so, then Fodor's suggestion that scientific thinking can be taken as typical of central thought processes is dead wrong. Nature helps humans develop a genuine but limited understanding of it – perfectly suited, say, to palaeolithic hunters and gatherers. Science is an attempt to understand nature more thoroughly but without nature's help, and hence without the benefit of automatic retroactive strengthening.

Discussions by logicians of hypothesis formation and confirmation have generally been inspired by the form these processes seem to take in science. Yet scientific thinking may be quite different in relevant respects from ordinary conceptual thinking. At least we would argue that it is different from verbal understanding. In verbal understanding, non-demonstrative inference can be described without invoking any logical rules apart from deductive rules; the strength of an assumption is a by-product of the way it is formed and used, a by-product, in particular, of the way it is deductively processed.

Having surveyed the various types of possible contextual effects, we are now in a position to generalise. If all a contextualisation does is add all, some or none of the new information to the context without otherwise altering the context at all, then this contextualisation has no contextual effect. Otherwise, there is some contextual effect, in the form of an erasure of some assumptions from the context, a modification of the strength of some assumptions in the context, or the derivation of contextual implications.[26]

In this chapter, we have presented a broad outline of the inferential abilities which we assume are involved in spontaneous inference and, in particular, in verbal understanding. We are very aware of its sketchiness, and of the many questions it raises and leaves unanswered. It seems to us, though, that these questions are not intractable, and that, on the bases we suggest, the psychological study of non-demonstrative inference is an interesting problem rather than an unfathomable mystery. We have also characterised a notion of contextual effect around which, in the next chapter, we will build an explicit notion of relevance.

3

Relevance

1 Conditions for relevance

In the last chapter, we introduced the notion of a contextual effect and discussed a variety of such effects: contextual implications, contradictions, and strengthenings. The notion of a contextual effect is essential to a description of the comprehension process. As a discourse proceeds, the hearer retrieves or constructs and then processes a number of assumptions. These form a gradually changing background against which new information is processed. Interpreting an utterance involves more than merely identifying the assumption explicitly expressed: it crucially involves working out the consequences of adding this assumption to a set of assumptions that have themselves already been processed. In other words, it involves seeing the contextual effects of this assumption in a context determined, at least in part, by earlier acts of comprehension.

At each point in a discourse, the hearer has in the forefront of his attention a different set of assumptions, which he may never have processed together before, and may never process together again. By working out the synthetic implications of this set of assumptions, he can acquire new information which may be lost forever when that particular set is dismantled and its constituent assumptions are either forgotten or stored in their separate locations in the hearer's encyclopaedic memory.

It is not just that these assumptions come together in the hearer's mind for what may be the only time. They also come together in a certain sequence, and are presumably processed in that sequence, so that each new assumption is processed in the context of a set of assumptions many of which have themselves just been processed. The notion of a contextual effect helps describe these two essential properties of utterance comprehension: comprehension involves the joint processing of a set of assumptions, and in that set some assumptions stand out as newly presented information being processed in the context of information that has itself been previously processed.

The notion of a contextual effect is essential to a characterisation of relevance. We want to argue that having contextual effects is a necessary condition for relevance, and that other things being equal, the greater the contextual effects, the greater the relevance.

Before embarking on this project, we would like to make clear what we are trying, and what we are not trying to do. We are not trying to define the ordinary English word 'relevance'. 'Relevance' is a fuzzy term, used differently by different people, or by the same people at different times. It does not have a translation in every human language. There is no reason to think that a proper semantic analysis of the English word 'relevance' would also characterise a concept of scientific psychology.

We do believe, though, that scientific psychology needs a concept which is close enough to the ordinary language notion of relevance; in other words, we believe that there is an important psychological property – a property of mental processes – which the ordinary notion of relevance roughly approximates, and which it is therefore appropriate to call relevance too, using the term now in a technical sense. What we are trying to do is to describe this property: that is, to define *relevance* as a useful theoretical concept.

We assume that people have intuitions of relevance: that they can consistently distinguish relevant from irrelevant information, or in some cases, more relevant from less relevant information. However, these intuitions are not very easy to elicit or use as evidence. The fact that there is an ordinary language notion of relevance with a fuzzy and variable meaning is a hindrance rather than a help. Moreover, intuitions of relevance are relative to contexts, and there is no way of controlling exactly which context someone will have in mind at a given moment. Asking people to restrict themselves to explicit, artificially constructed contexts goes so much against natural procedures for context construction that the resulting intuitions are of questionable value.

Despite these difficulties, we intend to invoke intuitions of relevance. We should make clear, first, that when we claim that one assumption is intuitively relevant and another not, or that one assumption is more relevant than another, we merely expect you to perceive some difference; whether you would ordinarily use the word 'relevance' to describe it is beside the point. Second, we see these intuitive judgements of relevance as suggestive and worth paying attention to, but we do not regard them as conclusive. They will provide us with a starting point, but are certainly not to be treated as a unique and final criterion. The value of our theoretical notion of relevance will ultimately depend on the value of the psychological models which make use of it, and, in particular, on the value of the theory of verbal comprehension that it allows us to formulate. Intuitions of relevance are not the only kinds of intuition involved in comprehension.

If you take a particular set of assumptions C and add to it some arbitrarily chosen assumption *P*, there is little reason to expect *P* to be relevant at all in the context C, or to have any contextual effect in it either. For instance, take C to be the set of assumptions you have in mind while reading this sentence. Suppose we were now to tell you,

(1) 5 May 1881 was a sunny day in Kabul.

The assumption explicitly expressed by (1) is not likely to have any contextual effect in C, or to be relevant (in any sense) in C. It is intuitively obvious that the assumption expressed by (1) is irrelevant in C. We can account for this by pointing out that (1) has no contextual effect in C: there is no assumption in the context with which (1) might combine to yield contextual implications; nor does it affect the strength of any assumption already present in the context. This is because (1) is utterly unrelated to the context in question.

There are other ways in which an assumption may lack contextual effects. Suppose we were now to tell you,

(2) You are now reading a book.

The assumption explicitly expressed by (2) is likely to be irrelevant in the context of whatever assumptions you had in mind immediately before reading it; this can again be accounted for by pointing out that it has no contextual effect in that context. You were presumably already aware of the fact that you were reading a book, so that any implications which (2) would have had in that context would already have been computed. Moreover, you presumably held this assumption as certain, so that its strength could not be increased.

To take a third example, which is irrelevant for different reasons still, suppose we were now to tell you,

(3) You are fast asleep.

The assumption explicitly expressed by (3) is inconsistent with a number of unshakable assumptions which you currently have in mind. You are presumably aware not only of the fact that you are now reading a book, but also of the fact that this is an activity which is incompatible with being fast asleep. Since, however much you trust us, on this question you would rightly trust yourself more, the contradiction which results when the assumption expressed by (3) is added to the present context would lead to the erasure of (3), as described in the last chapter. In other words, (3) would have no contextual effect in the present context, and this is why it is intuitively felt to be irrelevant.

There are thus three types of case in which an assumption may lack contextual effects, and be irrelevant, in a context. In the first, illustrated by (1), the assumption may contribute new information, but this information does not connect up with any information present in the context. In the second, illustrated by (2), the assumption is already present in the context and its strength is unaffected by the newly presented information; this newly presented information is therefore entirely uninformative and, *a fortiori*, irrelevant. In the third type of case, illustrated by (3), the assumption is inconsistent with the context and is too weak to upset it; processing the assumption thus leaves the context unchanged.

It should be stressed that in all these examples it is only the assumption explicitly expressed by the utterance that lacks contextual effects and is irrelevant: the fact that someone chooses to express an irrelevant assumption may itself be highly relevant. For instance, it may be a way of making manifest a desire to change the subject, and this desire may well be relevant. Or, to take an actual example, we have expressed the irrelevant assumptions (1)–(3) in an attempt to make what we hope were relevant remarks. Relevance may be achieved by expressing irrelevant assumptions, as long as this expressive behaviour is itself relevant.

On the basis of these examples, we want to claim that an assumption which has no contextual effect in a given context is irrelevant in that context. In other words, having some contextual effect in a context is a necessary condition for relevance.

The next question seems to be whether having contextual effects might be not only a necessary condition for relevance but also sufficient. There is a certain amount of evidence that it is. For example, consider the following (attested) exchange:

(4) *Flag-seller*: Would you like to buy a flag for the Royal National Lifeboat Institution?
Passer-by: No thanks, I always spend my holidays with my sister in Birmingham.

To see the relevance of the passer-by's response, the hearer must be able to supply something like the premises in (5), and derive something like the contextual implication in (6):

(5) (a) Birmingham is inland.
(b) The Royal National Lifeboat Institution is a charity.
(c) Buying a flag is one way of subscribing to a charity.
(d) Someone who spends his holidays inland has no need of the services of the Royal National Lifeboat Institution.

  (e) Someone who has no need of the services of a charity cannot be expected to subscribe to that charity.
(6) The passer-by cannot be expected to subscribe to the Royal National Lifeboat Institution.

What is interesting about the passer-by's reply is the very close connection that exists between seeing its relevance (or, more precisely, the relevance its speaker intended it to have) and being able to derive some contextual implication from it. It seems clear that someone who is unable to supply something like the context in (5) and derive something like the contextual implication in (6) will be unable to see the intended relevance of this reply, and that, conversely, anyone who sees this implication will agree that this reply is relevant in the appropriate context. Perceiving some contextual effect of an assumption seems to be sufficient for judging it relevant.

It might be tempting, then, to propose the following definition:

(7) *Relevance*
An assumption is relevant in a context if and only if it has some contextual effect in that context.

This definition captures the intuition that to be relevant in a context, an assumption must connect up with that context in some way. It clarifies this intuition by specifying the nature of the connection required. For example, it predicts that the passer-by's reply in (4) is relevant in the context (5a–e) because it connects up with this context to yield the contextual implication (6). In real life, of course, (6) would in turn be processed in a context in which it would have further contextual implications and other contextual effects: for example, strengthening or weakening various assumptions of the hearer, thus ensuring the relevance of the reply in a wider context.

Although the definition in (7) accords with some intuitive judgements of relevance, we would expect there to be others which seem to go against it, and particularly against the claim that having any contextual effect, however small, is a sufficient condition for relevance. Intuitions about the proper use of 'relevance' are like intuitions about the proper use of, say, 'flexibility': the more difficult it is to bend some object, the less willing we are to call it flexible, even though we might recognise that, if an object can be bent at all, then technically it is flexible. Intuitions about 'relevance' go the same way: the weaker the contextual effects of an assumption, the less willing we are to call it relevant, even though it can be argued that, if an assumption has any contextual effect at all, then technically it is relevant.

Suppose, for instance, that we were to inform you now of (8):

(8) It took us a long time to write this book.

At first sight, the assumption expressed by (8) seems irrelevant in the context of the thoughts you have in mind if you are attending to the present discussion of the notion of relevance. That it took us a long time to write this book is not the kind of consideration you would expect at this point.

However, we hope you share our intuition that (8) is not *quite* as irrelevant as (1)–(3) (and if you do not, rest assured that nothing essential hinges on it and just skip the rest of this paragraph). This can be related to the fact that (8), unlike (1)–(3), has *some* contextual effect in a context that you are likely to have accessible. For instance, you might already have suspected that it took us a long time to write this book. In that case, we are independently strengthening this suspicion of yours, as well as any implication you might already have derived from it. Or this might be brand new information for you, in which case you might combine it with whatever opinions you have already formed about the book and derive some contextual implications: say, if you do not like the book, the implication that we have been wasting a lot of time. Some contextual effect, some relevance.

There are reasons, though, for trying to go beyond definition (7) which are more compelling than debatable intuitions about the relevance or irrelevance of (8). The intuitions of relevance that it is essential to account for are intuitions not about the simple presence or absence of relevance, but about degrees of relevance. It is to these that we now turn.

2 Degrees of relevance: effect and effort

The definition of relevance just proposed is insufficient for at least two reasons: first, because relevance is a matter of degree, and we have said nothing about how degrees of relevance are determined; second, because we have defined relevance as a relation between an assumption and a context, but have said nothing about how the context is determined. At the moment, then, we have simply defined a formal property, whose relation to psychological reality has been left undescribed.

Consider first the question of degrees of relevance. At a very general level, we want to compare the concept of relevance to concepts such as *productivity* or *yield*, which involve some form of cost-benefit analysis. A firm with output of any value, however small, is productive to some degree, just as we have claimed that an assumption with any contextual effects at all, however limited, is relevant to some degree. However, where the output is very small, there is some initial reluctance to say that the firm is productive at all, even though, when compared to a firm with genuinely zero output, it is obviously productive to some degree: the parallel with relevance is clear.

The output of the firm, i.e. the value of the goods produced, is not the only factor to be taken into account in assessing its productivity. Imagine two firms which achieve the same output, but on the basis of different inputs, i.e. at different production costs: the one with the lower production costs would be considered the more productive. Production cost is the second factor to be taken into account in assessing productivity. It is a negative factor: other things being equal, the higher the production cost, the lower the productivity.

Similar remarks apply to the assessment of relevance. The contextual effects of an assumption in a given context are not the only factor to be taken into account in assessing its degree of relevance. Contextual effects are brought about by mental processes. Mental processes, like all biological processes, involve a certain effort, a certain expenditure of energy. The processing effort involved in achieving contextual effects is the second factor to be taken into account in assessing degrees of relevance. Processing effort is a negative factor: other things being equal, the greater the processing effort, the lower the relevance.

In the last section we considered a definition of relevance expressed in terms of necessary and sufficient conditions. That is, *relevance* was defined as a classificatory concept. We also suggested that such a definition, although not incorrect, missed the fact that *relevance* is also, and more importantly, a comparative concept.[1]

Comparative concepts are best defined in terms of what might be called 'extent' conditions. Consider, for instance, the ordinary language concept *flexible*. First, an object is not just flexible, it is more or less so; in other words *flexibility* is not just a classificatory but also a comparative concept. Second, degrees of flexibility depend on (at least) two logically independent factors, reflected in the following definition:

(9) *Flexibility*
   Extent condition 1: an object is flexible to the extent that it is easy to bend.
   Extent condition 2: an object is flexible to the extent that the shape it can be bent into differs from its initial shape.

If an object can be bent at all, then conditions 1 and 2 are satisfied to some extent, and conversely. These two extent conditions, therefore, logically imply a necessary and sufficient condition: an object is flexible if and only if it can be bent. Since this necessary and sufficient condition is implied by definition (9), it need not be stated independently.

Definition (9) makes comparisons possible only in some cases: other things being equal, if object A is easier to bend than object B, then it is more flexible; or, other things being equal, if object A can be bent further than object B, then it is more flexible. But if A is easy to bend into a not very different shape and impossible to bend any further, and B can be bent only with difficulty but can then be bent much further, definition (9) does not allow a comparative judgement to be made; and this seems to reflect the limitations of ordinary usage. Incidentally, if we wanted to give an adequate representation of the logical entry of the ordinary language concept of flexibility, we would reformulate the extent conditions of definition (9) as inference rules, which could be done in several different ways. But our reason for discussing degrees of flexibility is not to shed light on ordinary comparative concepts; it is to illustrate the form that a *theoretical* comparative concept might take.

We are trying to develop a theoretical concept of relevance, for use in the study of communication and cognition. We expect this theoretical concept to help predict people's intuitions, but not necessarily their use of the word 'relevance' or of similar ordinary language terms. We can improve on definition (7) of relevance by adopting an extent-conditions format of the type just illustrated:

(10) *Relevance*

> *Extent condition 1*: an assumption is relevant in a context to the extent that its contextual effects in this context are large.
> *Extent condition 2*: an assumption is relevant in a context to the extent that the effort required to process it in this context is small.

This definition implies the necessary and sufficient condition of definition (7), which therefore need not be stated independently.

The assessment of relevance, like the assessment of productivity, is a matter of balancing output against input: here contextual effects against processing effort. Definition (10) of relevance, like definition (9) of flexibility, makes clear comparisons possible only in some cases: other things being equal, an assumption with greater contextual effects is more relevant; and, other things being equal, an assumption requiring a smaller processing effort is more relevant.

Let us now illustrate this comparative notion of relevance with a few artificial examples; artificial in particular in the sense that the contexts we are using are much smaller and more arbitrary than contexts used in real-life comprehension. Readers should try to resist the natural tendency to supply much richer and more appropriate contexts, a tendency which will be discussed at length later on.

Consider a context consisting of assumptions (11a–c):

(11) (a) People who are getting married should consult a doctor about possible hereditary risks to their children.

(b) Two people both of whom have thalassemia should be warned against having children.

(c) Susan has thalassemia.

Consider the effects that assumptions (12) and (13), both by hypothesis equally strong, would have in this context:

(12) Susan, who has thalassemia, is getting married to Bill.
(13) Bill, who has thalassemia, is getting married to Susan.

Both (12) and (13) have some contextual effects in context (11), and are therefore relevant by definition (10). In particular, both (12) and (13) carry the contextual implication (14):

(14) Susan and Bill should consult a doctor about possible hereditary risks to their children.

This corresponds to a first intuition that both assumptions are relevant in this context.

However, there is a further intuition that, in this context, (13) is more relevant than (12). We can account for this on the basis of definition (10). In this context, (13) has a contextual implication which (12) lacks:

(15) Susan and Bill should be warned against having children.

But what about processing effort? (12) and (13) have the same conceptual structure, and thus make the same deductive rules available to the deductive device. By hypothesis, they are also being processed in the same context. May we assume, then, that they require the same processing effort? Yes, but only after having clarified a point.

Having to write down and process the contextual implication (15) involves some processing effort. This effort will have to be made in the processing of (13), which carries implication (15), but not in the processing of (12), which does not. However, this processing effort is unavoidable if any contextual effect at all is to be achieved. If the benefits of achieving a contextual effect were never enough to offset the cost of the processing effort needed to implement it, then a positive degree of relevance could never be achieved. Thinking would not be worth the effort.

Except when they are in a state of utter exhaustion, humans find thinking worth the effort. We can therefore draw the empirical conclusion that the processing effort needed simply to write down a contextual implication or to raise or lower the strength of an assumption is not enough to offset the contribution thereby made to relevance. Moreover, since this processing effort is always in proportion to the effects it implements, it can be altogether ignored in assessments of relevance. Presumably the mind itself only worries about avoidable processing effort. We too will consider only processing effort which *results in* a contextual effect, and will discount processing effort which *results from* the fact that a contextual effect has been obtained.

With this clarification, we can now say that (12) and (13) take exactly the same processing effort when they are processed in the same context. Moreover, since (13) has greater contextual effects than (12) in the context (11a–c), our definition predicts that it should be more relevant, and this prediction is intuitively correct.

To illustrate now how relative relevance is affected by processing effort, compare (13) and (16):

(13) Bill, who has thalassemia, is getting married to Susan.
(16) Bill, who has thalassemia, is getting married to Susan, and 1967 was a great year for French wines.

When (13) and (16) are processed in the context (11a–c), they have exactly the same contextual effects: the extra information conveyed by (16) is utterly unrelated to the context and has no contextual effect whatsoever. However, this extra information requires some extra processing effort: (16) introduces more conceptual material, and hence more deductive rules and matching procedures. By our definition of relevance, (16) should thus be less relevant than (13), which achieves the same contextual effects with a smaller processing effort. This prediction is again intuitively correct.

The examples discussed so far have involved only one kind of contextual effect: contextual implication. Let us now take an example where different kinds of contextual effect are simultaneously achieved. Consider context (17a–g), where the strength of each assumption is indicated on the right:

(17)(a) Peter is richer than Sam.   [*certain*]
    (b) Sam is richer than Bill.   [*certain*]
    (c) Bill is richer than Jim.   [*certain*]
    (d) Jim is richer than Charles.   [*certain*]
    (e) Sam is richer than Sue.   [*strong*]
    (f) Sue is richer than Jim.   [*very weak*]
    (g) Sue is richer than Charles.   [*strong*]

Suppose that a hearer who has context (17a–g) in mind takes everything the speaker says as *certain*. Suppose that the speaker is in a position to assert either (18) or (19):

(18) Sue is richer than Jim.
(19) Sue is richer than Peter.

Intuitively, the assumption expressed by (19) is the more relevant, and is the one which, other things being equal, the speaker should choose to express.

This is easily accounted for in terms of our definition of relevance. Assumption (18) has only two contextual effects in the context (17a–g): first, it raises the strength of (17f) from *very weak* to *certain*, since it is identical in content to (17f) and is itself *certain*; second, it raises the strength of (17g) from *strong* to *certain*, since (17g) is synthetically implied by (17d) and (17f), which are now both *certain*.

Assumption (19) has five contextual effects. It contextually implies (20) and (21):

(20) Sue is richer than Sam.   [*certain*]
(21) Sue is richer than Bill.   [*certain*]

Assumption (20) contradicts assumption (17e), and since (20) is stronger (*certain* versus *strong*), (17e) is erased from the memory of the deductive device, a third contextual effect. Assumption (19) also raises the strength of (17f) and (17g) to *certain*, a fourth and fifth contextual effect. These last two effects are identical to the only two effects achieved by (18).

Since (19) has greater contextual effects than (18), and since they both require exactly the same processing effort (discounting, as we said, the extra effort needed to implement the contextual effects themselves), then, by our definition, (19) should be more relevant than (18), which is intuitively correct.

Suppose now that the hearer accepts the assumptions expressed by (18) and (19) merely as *weak*. Our definition predicts that in this case, (18) should be more relevant than (19), reversing the previous order. The hearer, who very weakly believed that Sue is richer than Jim, would have his belief marginally independently strengthened from *very weak* to *weak* by the assertion of (18). Thus (18) would achieve a modicum of relevance. On the other hand, if the speaker expressed assumption (19), the hearer would disbelieve it, since it contradicts his firm conviction that Sam is richer than Sue. Assumption (19) would then be erased and would achieve no relevance at all. This corresponds to the intuition that an unacceptably exaggerated claim is irrelevant, while a modest and acceptable claim may achieve some relevance, merely by confirming one's own assumptions.

Note, however, that the fact that an exaggerated claim is being made may itself be relevant, which makes intuitions about such examples harder to handle. For instance, the hearer might disbelieve (19), and nevertheless reason that the speaker must have had some ground for believing that Sue is rich; he might then see this as independently strengthening his own assumptions (17f) and (17g). For this line of reasoning to be possible, the context (17a–g) would have to be enriched, and in any case relevance would be achieved on the basis not of assumption (19) but of assumption (22):

(22) The speaker believes (19).

Still supposing that the hearer accepts the speaker's assertions only as *weak*, consider (23):

(23) Sue is richer than Peter or she is richer than Jim.

The assumption expressed by (23) would have exactly the same contextual effect as (18), i.e. it would strengthen (17f) from *very weak* to *weak*. However, it would achieve this effect at a greater processing cost: a series of deductive steps would be needed to reject the first disjunct of (23), which is identical to (19), and accept as *weak* the second disjunct, which is identical to (18). After this initial effort, the processing of (23) would be the same as for (18). Our definition of relevance therefore predicts that (23) should be less relevant than (18), a prediction which seems once more to be intuitively correct.[2]

Definition (10) of relevance does not make it possible to compare any odd pair of assumptions in any arbitrary context. Imagine, for instance, a very large and disparate context, consisting, say, of the contents of this morning's *Times*, and two assumptions which both have substantial but quite different contextual effects in that context. What procedure could be used to compare the resulting contextual effects?

Or consider (24) and (25):

(24) Your garden will be a riot of colour in the spring if you plant these beautiful bulbs.
(25) It has often been claimed that chlorinated water is less pleasant than seawater to swim in.

What procedure could be used to compare the effort needed to process these two assumptions, either in isolation from any context, or in any selected context? More generally, could such procedures for assessing contextual effects, processing effort and relevance be fully specified?

There is another way of putting essentially the same question: could *relevance* be defined not just as a comparative but as a quantitative concept? Our answer is: yes, it could. It is also quite conceivable that such a quantitative notion of relevance would be of some interest to logicians. However, it is not the kind of notion psychologists should be trying to develop.

At an abstract level, the notion of relevance applies not just to human beings, but to any information-processing device which is not simply involved in achieving a fixed goal at a fixed cost. For instance, one might want to characterise relevance for some abstract automaton. Suppose our automaton is capable of achieving only one kind of contextual effect, namely contextual implications. Then the contextual effects achieved by adding an assumption to a context could be measured by counting contextual implications. Contextual effects involving changes in confirmation value could also be measured, as long as these values too were quantitative, i.e. of the kind favoured by logicians.

Suppose further that all the operations of our automaton can be analysed as combinations of equally simple elementary operations; in this case the processing effort needed for a certain task, e.g. achieving certain contextual effects, could be measured by counting the elementary operations involved. Or, if the automaton were implemented in the form of a computer program, processing effort could be measured in terms of the time taken to achieve particular effects. Then it would just be a matter of deciding, in a principled or arbitrary way, how contextual effects and processing effort should be weighted against one another, and relevance for this automaton could be quantitatively defined.

Things go differently when it comes to assessing contextual effects achieved by human minds, and the processing effort needed to achieve them. On the contextual-effects side, we have argued that non-quantitative confirmation values are involved. If so, then these effects cannot be measured. On the processing-effort side, the prospects for quantitative assessment are no better. For example, we do not know what elementary operations complex thought processes reduce to. We do know that the duration of a mental process is not an adequate indicator of its cost for the organism: time spent in high mental concentration involves greater effort than equal time spent in relaxed daydreaming.

The problems involved in measuring contextual effects and processing effort are, of course, by no means specific to relevance theory or to pragmatics. They affect psychology as a whole. However, for relevance theory these problems take on a more specific form. Within relevance theory, the problem is not so much to assess contextual effects and processing effort from the outside, but to describe how the mind assesses its own achievements and efforts from the inside, and decides as a result to pursue its efforts or reallocate them in different directions.

Here is one line of possible speculation: contextual effects and mental effort, just like bodily movements and muscular effort, must cause some symptomatic physico-chemical changes. We might assume that the mind assesses its own efforts and their effects by monitoring these changes. Although we have nothing to say on the neuro-physics or neuro-chemistry involved, this is not an empty assumption. It contrasts with another conceivable view,[3] on which contextual effects would be assessed by actually counting contextual implications, and processing effort by actually counting inferential steps. There are many reasons for rejecting this view: counting each step means adding one operation at each step, which should considerably increase the effort involved in every mental process. This in turn would be paradoxical, since presumably the point of assessing effort is to be better able to reduce it. Moreover, if the assessment of contextual effects and processing effort were the result of such a computation, people should be able to make absolute judgements and compare the contextual effects and processing effort involved in any pair of mental performances, however unrelated; this expectation does not seem to be borne out.

Contextual effects and processing effort are non-representational dimensions of mental processes. They exist whether or not the individual is consciously assessing them, whether or not they are conceptually represented. When they are represented, we claim that they are represented in the form of comparative judgements. These judgements are intuitive; they have their basis in the monitoring of physico-chemical parameters.

People have not only retrospective intuitions about effects already achieved and effort already incurred, but also prospective intuitions. That is, they have intuitions about the effort some task would take and the effects it might achieve (just as they have intuitions about the effort some future bodily movement would take, and about its possible effects). Prospective intuitions must be based not on the monitoring of physico-chemical parameters, but on factors which systematically modify the value of these parameters.

It is easy enough to identify a variety of factors that might make it possible to predict which information will have the greatest contextual effects. For instance, other things being equal, stronger assumptions have greater contextual effects. Similarly, a variety of factors may make it possible to predict how the processing effort needed to perform particular pairs of tasks would compare. For instance, processing more information in the same context, or the same information in a larger context, involves a greater effort. People can take advantage of these comparative abilities in trying to maximise the relevance of the information they process.

How are the two factors governing assessments of relevance balanced: which effects are worth which effort? In a purely formal system, this would be a matter for stipulation rather than discovery. In a computer used for economic benefit, effort and effect could be assessed, say, in dollars and cents. In the case of psychological processes, the problem seems unamenable to any general solution, but then, on closer examination, it need not have a *general* solution at all.

It is extremely unlikely that the relative importance of effect and effort stays constant across all circumstances and individuals. For instance, changes in alertness may well alter one's willingness to incur a certain processing effort: at some times the hope of achieving a given level of contextual effect will suffice, and at others, not. Then, some people are generally alert, and everything that is relevant at all will be more relevant for them than for duller people. Speakers who are not aware of their hearers' disposition in the matter risk asking them for too much effort or providing them with too few effects.

Mental effects and effort are non-representational properties of mental processes. Relevance, which is a function of effect and effort, is a non-representational property too. That is, relevance is a property which need not be represented, let alone computed, in order to be achieved. When it is represented, it is represented in terms of comparative judgements and gross absolute judgements, (e.g. 'irrelevant', 'weakly relevant', 'very relevant'), but not in terms of fine absolute judgements, i.e. quantitative ones.

Since we are interested in relevance as a psychological property, we have no reason to aim for a quantitative definition of relevance. What we have to do is add empirical substance to our comparative definition by considering how relevance is sought and achieved in mental processes, and particularly in processes of verbal comprehension. Our first task is to move from a purely formal characterisation of a context to a more empirical one, and to consider the implications of such a move.

3 Is the context given or chosen?

We have suggested that the context used to process new assumptions is, essentially, a subset of the individual's old assumptions, with which the new assumptions combine to yield a variety of contextual effects. We have also proposed two criteria for comparing the relevance of different assumptions in a given context. However, we still have to face the serious problem of how the context is determined: how some particular subset of the individual's assumptions is selected. For ease of exposition, we will discuss this problem with reference to a particular case: that of a hearer processing an assumption explicitly asserted by a speaker. In section 6, we will generalise our account to deal with the assumptions made manifest by any kind of stimulus.

In this section, we will look at various approaches which take for granted that, at any given moment, there is only one context available to the individual, and try to show that they fail precisely because of this underlying hypothesis. In the next section we will suggest an alternative approach.

In much of the literature, it is explicitly or implicitly assumed that the context for the comprehension of a given utterance is not a matter of choice; at any given point in a verbal exchange, the context is seen as uniquely determined, as given.⁴ Moreover, it is generally assumed that the context is determined in advance of the comprehension process. The assumption explicitly expressed by an utterance is seen as combining with a context present in the hearer's mind at the start of the act of utterance. The simplest version of this view is the hypothesis that the context for the comprehension of a given utterance is the set of assumptions explicitly expressed by preceding utterances in the same dialogue or discourse. This first hypothesis would seem to be borne out by the following exchange:

(26) (a) *Peter*: I'm tired.
　　(b) *Mary*: If you're tired, I'll make the meal.

It is easy to imagine a situation in which Mary's answer would be intuitively relevant. In a discourse context consisting of the assumption expressed by Peter, the assumption expressed by Mary would contextually imply (27), and the fact that it is relevant would seem to be thereby explained:

(27) Mary will make the meal.

However, consider another version of the dialogue:

(28) (a) *Peter*: I'm tired.
　　(b) *Mary*: I'll make the meal.

Intuitively, there is very little difference between Mary's answer in (26) and her answer in (28): both are relevant in more or less the same way. Yet if the context for comprehension were just the assumption explicitly expressed by Peter, we would have to treat Mary's two answers quite differently: (28b), unlike (26b), has no contextual effect whatsoever in such a context, and should therefore not be relevant at all.

Let us then consider, as a second hypothesis, the claim that the context for comprehension contains not only all the assumptions explicitly expressed by preceding utterances in the discourse, but also all the implicatures of these utterances. We can reasonably assume that in a situation where Peter's remark was relevant, it would have implicated something like (29):

(29) Peter wishes Mary would make the meal.

With (29) as part of the context, both (26b) and (28b) contextually imply (30):

(30) Mary will do what Peter wishes.

They will thus both be relevant in this context, and relevant in similar ways. Although (26b) has two contextual implications while (28b) has only one, this is offset by the fact that (26b) has a more complex logical form than (28b), and needs more processing. The fact that the two answers are intuitively similar in relevance could thus be straightforwardly explained.

Consider, however, a third version of the dialogue:

(31) (a) *Peter*: I'm tired.
   (b) *Mary*: The dessert is ready. I'll make the main course.

Neither of the hypotheses considered so far can account for the fact that Mary's answer (31b) is relevant in roughly the same way as her answers in the two earlier versions of the dialogue. (31b) has no contextual effect in a context consisting of either the assumptions explicitly expressed in previous discourse, or the assumptions previously expressed and implicated. To account for the relevance of (31b), the context used by the hearer would have to include a premise such as (32):

(32) A meal consists of at least a main course and a dessert.

With (32) added to the context, contextual implication (33) can be derived from (31b):

(33) Mary will make the meal.

Then from (33) and (29) (*Peter wishes Mary would make the meal*), contextual implication (30) (*Mary will do what Peter wishes*) can be derived, just as it was derivable, in a more restricted context, from (26b) or (28b).

It is plain common sense to assume that a contextual premise such as (32) would be used in processing Mary's answer (31b). However, this is incompatible with the hypothesis that the context for comprehension is the set of assumptions expressed or implicated by previous utterances. Peter's remark that he is tired does not assert or imply that a meal consists of at least a main course and a dessert. Assumption (32) has to be specially retrieved from the encyclopaedic entry of the concept of a meal.

We might then consider, as a third hypothesis, the claim that the context for comprehension consists not only of the assumptions expressed or implicated by preceding utterances, but also of the encyclopaedic entries attached to any concepts used in these assumptions. For instance, if Peter's initial remark implicates that he wishes Mary would make the meal, then the encyclopaedic entry of the concept of a meal, and in particular assumption (32) (*A meal consists of a main course and a dessert*), is automatically added to the context in which Mary's answer will be interpreted. With this third hypothesis, the relevance of (31b) is accounted for.

However, consider a fourth version of the dialogue:

(34) (a) *Peter*: I'm tired.
   (b) *Mary*: The dessert is ready. I'll make an osso-bucco.

Intuitively there is little difference between the relevance of Mary's fourth answer (34b) and her third answer (31b). The obvious way to account for this is to assume that the context in which (34b) is interpreted contains an assumption such as (35):

(35) An osso-bucco is a main course.

With (35) in the context, the assumption explicitly expressed by Mary's third answer (31b) ('The dessert is ready. I'll make the main course') is contextually implied by her fourth answer (34b), which explains the similarity in relevance of (31b) and (34b).

However, assumption (35) belongs to the encyclopaedic entry of the concept of an osso-bucco. This concept did not occur in the assumptions either expressed or implicated by Peter; it is introduced for the first time by Mary's answer. This is not compatible with the hypothesis that the context for comprehension consists of the assumptions expressed or implicated by preceding utterances, together with the encyclopaedic entries attached to any concepts used in these assumptions.

One might be tempted, then, to formulate a fourth hypothesis to accommodate the fourth version of the dialogue: the context for the comprehension of an utterance consists of the assumptions expressed and implicated by preceding utterances, plus the encyclopaedic entries attached to any concept used in any of these assumptions, plus the encyclopaedic entries attached to any concept used in the new utterance. Note that on this hypothesis the context, though uniquely determined, is not fixed in advance of the comprehension process. This fourth hypothesis implies, instead, that one of the preliminary stages of comprehension consists in identifying the concepts used in the new utterance and adding their encyclopaedic entries to the context. However, there is still no question of a choice of contexts.

With this fourth hypothesis, (35) is part of the context in which Mary's answer (34b) is interpreted, and the relevance of her answer is thus explained.

Consider, however, a fifth version of the dialogue:

(36) (a) *Peter*: I'm tired.
 (b) *Mary*: The dessert is ready. I'll make the speciality of the Capri restaurant.

To establish the relevance of Mary's answer (36b), the hearer would have first to access the encyclopaedic entry for the Capri restaurant and find out that its speciality is osso-bucco, and then to access the entry for osso-bucco and find out that an osso-bucco is a main course, i.e. assumption (35). However, the concept of an osso-bucco occurs neither in Mary's answer, nor in the assumptions expressed or implicated by Peter's initial remark. So, according to our fourth hypothesis, (35) is not part of the context for the interpretation of (36b).

This might lead us, if we still had the stamina, to formulate a fifth hypothesis: the context for the comprehension of an utterance consists of the assumptions expressed and implicated by preceding utterances, plus the encyclopaedic entries attached to any concepts used in these assumptions and in the utterance itself, plus the encyclopaedic entries attached to any concepts used in the assumptions contained in the encyclopaedic entries already added to the context. With our fourth hypothesis, one layer of encyclopaedic entries was added to the context. With our fifth hypothesis, two layers are added.

The defects of this line of speculation are becoming blatant. With the last two hypotheses, we have already assumed that the context is automatically filled with a huge amount of encyclopaedic information, most – and sometimes all – of which fails to increase the contextual effects of the new information being processed. Since each expansion of the context means an increase in processing effort, this method of context formation would lead to a general loss of relevance. Imagine the following dialogue, for instance:

(37) (a) *Peter*: Where does John live?
    (b) *Mary*: John lives next to the Capri restaurant.

If our fourth hypothesis were correct, the context in which Peter interpreted Mary's answer should include the information that the speciality of the Capri restaurant is osso-bucco. If our fifth hypothesis were correct, it should also include the information that an osso-bucco is a main course. This would be of no use – indeed it would be a distraction – in understanding where John lives.

Moreover, it is easy enough to find examples showing that two layers of encylopaedic information may not be enough. Suppose that in answer to Peter's remark that he is tired, Mary says,

(38) The dessert is ready. I'll make the speciality of that restaurant next to where John lives.

First the encyclopaedic entry for John (and the information that he lives next to the Capri restaurant) would be added to the context, which would cause the entry for the Capri restaurant (and the information that its speciality is osso-bucco) to be added. However, the hearer would still need the information that an osso-bucco is a main course, and that information is to be found in the entry for osso-bucco. To ensure that the entry for osso-bucco is part of a uniquely determined context, three layers of encyclopaedic information would have to be automatically added. Other examples would show that more and more layers of encyclopaedic information might be needed. Soon, the context would be shown to consist of the whole of encyclopaedic memory.

If the context included the whole of the hearer's encyclopaedia, virtually any new information that a speaker could express would be relevant, since virtually any new information would have some contextual effects in such an enormous context. On the other hand, given the size of such a context, an enormous processing effort – not to mention processing time – would be needed to achieve these effects. Since relevance decreases as more effort is required, this would mean that, while any new information would easily achieve relevance, no information would ever achieve more than minimal relevance. Furthermore, reminders could never be relevant, since a reminder, on this approach, would merely be repeating information already included in the context. This line is clearly not worth pursuing.

Up to now, we have accepted the widely held view that the context in which a given assumption is to be interpreted is uniquely determined. We have seen the context as being formed either before the comprehension process gets under way, or as a preliminary stage in this process. As we have tried to show, assuming that the context is uniquely determined leads to absurdities. However, there is nothing in the nature of a context, or of comprehension, which excludes the possibility that context formation is open to choices and revisions throughout the comprehension process. In the next section, we explore this possibility further.

4 A choice of contexts

In the last section, we talked rather generally of the context for comprehension. Let us now be more specific and try to add some psychological substance to the notion of a context introduced in chapter 2. The set of assumptions in the memory of the deductive device at the start of a deductive process can be partitioned into two proper subsets, each acting as the context in which the other subset is processed. So far, this is a purely formal move. It enables us to single out those synthetic implications whose derivation actually involves both subsets of assumptions, and describe them as contextual implications of one subset of assumptions in the context of the other. It can then be used to clarify the more psychologically significant distinction between information in the forefront of attention, which is usually new, and information which is taken into account but remains in the background of attention, and which is usually old: a distinction which typically applies to ordinary inferential processes.

We assume that a crucial step in the processing of new information, and in particular of verbally communicated information, is to combine it with an adequately selected set of background assumptions – which then constitutes the context – in the memory of the deductive device. For each item of new information, many different sets of assumptions from diverse sources (long-term memory, short-term memory, perception) might be selected as context. However, this is not to say that any arbitrary subset of the total set of assumptions available to the organism might become a context. The organisation of the individual's encyclopaedic memory, and the mental activity in which he is engaged, limit the class of potential contexts from which an actual context can be chosen at any given time.

For instance, it is generally agreed that encyclopaedic information in long-term memory is organised into chunks of some kind. Such chunks have been discussed in the literature under such names as 'schema', 'frame', 'scenario' and 'prototype'. The encyclopaedic entries we have mentioned are also chunks of a certain size, which may themselves be grouped into larger chunks, and contain smaller chunks. It seems reasonable to assume that the smallest units which can be transferred from encyclopaedic memory to the memory of the deductive device are chunks rather than individual assumptions. For instance, you might be unable to remember and add to the context the information that the speciality of the Capri restaurant is osso-bucco without also remembering and adding other pieces of information about that restaurant: say, that the house's red wine is a Valpolicella.

Moreover, not all chunks of encyclopaedic information are equally accessible at any given time. We have no precise and well-grounded theory of conceptual information retrieval, but various plausible assumptions come to mind. It could well be, for instance, that the encyclopaedic entry of a concept becomes accessible only when that concept appears in an assumption that has already been accessed. For example, you might be unable to recall that the speciality of the Capri restaurant is osso-bucco unless you are already thinking of that restaurant (or of osso-bucco). There will be times, then, when this information will be accessible in a single step, times when it will be accessible in several steps, each involving an extension of the context, and times when the number of steps involved will, in practice, make this information inaccessible.

Consider someone about to process some new information. He still has in mind some of the assumptions he has just been processing. People do not come to the processing of new information with a 'blank mind'; they have some kind of short-term memory store (or several such stores, or devices functionally equivalent to short-term memory stores) whose contents are never simply erased, at least not when the individual is awake.

However, it is not enough to point out that information may be carried over from one conceptual process to the next; one would like to know which information is kept in a short-term memory store, which is transferred to encyclopaedic memory, which is simply erased. Here we have neither formal arguments nor empirical evidence for any particular set of hypotheses. Nevertheless, for the sake of concreteness and explicitness, we will make a few suggestions, in particular about the memory of the deductive device, which are compatible both with the little that is understood and with the theory we are trying to develop.

At the start of each deductive process, the memory of the deductive device contains an initial set of assumptions: that is, a set of premises. Then all the non-trivial implications derivable from this set of premises are derived, and all the strengthenings which can take place do. At the end of the process, if no contradiction has resulted, the memory of the deductive device contains all the original premises, possibly strengthened, and all the newly derived conclusions. What happens now to these assumptions? We will assume that all the newly derived synthetic implications, all the premises which have undergone a synthetic rule, and all the premises which have been strengthened, remain in the memory of the deductive device; other assumptions still in the memory of the deductive device at the end of the deductive process – that is, premises which have not affected the deduction, or been affected by it – are erased from the memory of the device. This is not to say, however, that they are not kept for a time in some other short-term memory store.

There is good reason to think that the memory of the deductive device is not the only short-term memory store available. Consider the fact that someone may divide his attention between two tasks: say, watching television and discussing family affairs at the same time. When this happens, it seems that he may be switching back and forth between two quite different contexts.[5] This strongly suggests the existence of some short-term conceptual memory other than that of the deductive device, in which the context temporarily not in use is stored. We will assume that assumptions erased from the memory of the deductive device are kept for a time in such a general-purpose short-term memory store.

The assumptions left over in the memory of the deductive device from the immediately preceding deductive process then constitute an immediately given context in which the next new item of information may be deductively processed.

More particularly, a hearer who has just interpreted one utterance and is about to interpret the next is characterised by the following distribution of information. He has in the memory of his deductive device the set of assumptions which make up his interpretation of the previous utterance (including the premises actually used in achieving it). Other assumptions which were in the memory of his deductive device, but which have played no role in the interpretation of the previous utterance, have now been transferred to his general short-term memory store. Also in that store, he has the interpretation of some earlier utterances (as well as other items of information and thoughts he may have been attending to in the immediate past). Possibly, part of the interpretation of the previous utterance and of earlier utterances has been copied into encyclopaedic memory. The assumptions left over in the memory of the deductive device, i.e. the interpretation of the previous utterance, constitute an immediately given context in which the next utterance may be processed.

We want to argue, however, that this immediately given context is merely an initial context which can be extended in different directions.

Extensions of the context can be made by 'going back in time' and adding to it assumptions used or derived in previous deductive processes. The fact that such assumptions are easily accessible, which is introspectively and experimentally well established, is a further reason for thinking that they are kept for a time in a general short-term memory store.

In the case of verbal understanding, the hearer may have to include in the context not only the interpretation of the immediately preceding utterance, but also the interpretation of utterances occurring earlier in the exchange. Consider another version of the dialogue between Peter and Mary:

(39) *Mary*: What I would like to eat tonight is an osso-bucco. I'm ravenous. I had a great day in court. How was your day?
Peter: Not so good. Too many patients, and the air conditioning was out of order. I'm tired.
Mary: I'm sorry to hear that. O.K. I'll make it myself.

To understand Mary's concluding remark that she will make 'it' herself, Peter needs information provided by her opening remark that she would like to eat an osso-bucco. However, his interpretation of this opening remark will in the meantime have been transferred from the memory of his deductive device to his general short-term memory, if our above hypotheses are correct. This interpretation must therefore be transferred back to the memory of the deductive device, thus extending the immediately given context (which consists of what is left in the memory of Peter's deductive device after he has interpreted Mary's penultimate remark that she is sorry to hear that he has had a bad day).

A second way of extending the context is to add to it the encyclopaedic entries (or possibly smaller chunks of encyclopaedic information, taken from these entries) of concepts already present either in the context or in the assumption being processed. We have shown the need for such extensions with examples (31)–(38) above. We have also shown that the assumption that such encyclopaedic extensions are automatically made for every concept and in every case leads to absurdities; we used this as an argument against the view that the context is uniquely determined. On the other hand, once the determination of a context is seen as a matter of choice and as part of the interpretation process itself, it seems reasonable to assume that such extensions take place when they appear to be needed – and only then.

A third way of extending the context is to add to it information about the immediately observable environment. People constantly monitor the physical environment while carrying out conceptual tasks which may be partly or totally unrelated to that environment. Where is this sub-attentively monitored information stored? Again, we do not know, but we can speculate: all this information is very briefly retained in specialised short-term perceptual memory stores, from which some of it can be transferred to the general short-term conceptual memory store and to the memory of the deductive device. This happens, in particular, when the interpretation of an utterance leads the hearer to pick up some environmental information and add it to the context. For example, suppose that Mary, holding up a piece of veal, says to Peter,

(40) If you're tired, I'll cook this.

Peter will have to add to the context some description of the object Mary is holding. The very form of Mary's utterance provides an incentive to do so: just as anaphoric pronouns, such as 'it' in (39), suggest going back in discourse, deictic pronouns, such as 'this' in (40), suggest adding environmental information to the context.

We have so far suggested that the choice of a context for inferential processes in general, and for comprehension in particular, is partly determined at any given time by the contents of the memory of the deductive device, those of the general-purpose short-term memory store, and those of the encyclopaedia, and by the information that can be immediately picked up from the physical environment. These factors determine not a single context but a range of possible contexts. What determines the selection of a particular context out of that range? Our answer is that the selection of a particular context is determined by the search for relevance.

In much of the pragmatic literature, events are assumed to take place in the following order: first the context is determined, then the interpretation process takes place, then relevance is assessed. In other words, relevance is seen as a variable to be assessed in function of a pre-determined context. However, from a psychological point of view, this is a highly implausible model of comprehension. Humans are not in the business of simply assessing the relevance of new information. They try to process information as productively as possible; that is, they try to obtain from each new item of information as great a contextual effect as possible for as small as possible a processing effort. The assessment of relevance is not the goal of the comprehension process, but only a means to an end, the end being to maximise the relevance of any information being processed.

If this is true, it suggests a complete reversal of the order of events in comprehension. It is not that first the context is determined, and then relevance is assessed. On the contrary, people hope that the assumption being processed is relevant (or else they would not bother to process it at all), and they try to select a context which will justify that hope: a context which will maximise relevance. In verbal comprehension in particular, it is relevance which is treated as given, and context which is treated as a variable.[6] In this section, we have considered how the domain of this variable is determined.

This change of perspective raises an obvious question: we have defined relevance as a relation between a given assumption and a given context. But when the context is not given, as we are now claiming is the case in human understanding, how is the relevance of an assumption to be defined? In answering this question, we will use our formal definition of *relevance in a context* as the basis for a psychologically more appropriate characterisation of *relevance to an individual*.

5 Relevance to an individual

At the end of each deductive process, the individual has at his disposal a particular set of accessible contexts. This set is partly ordered: each context (apart from the initial context) contains one or more smaller contexts, and each context (apart from the maximal contexts)[7] is contained in one or more larger contexts. The set of accessible contexts is thus partly ordered by the inclusion relation. This formal relation has a psychological counterpart: order of inclusion corresponds to order of accessibility. The initial, minimal context is immediately given; contexts which include only the initial context as a sub-part can be accessed in one step and are therefore the most accessible contexts; contexts which include the initial context and a one-step extension as sub-parts can be accessed in two steps and are therefore the next most accessible contexts, and so on. Notice a point of crucial importance for relevance theory: just as processing an item of information in a context involves some effort, so accessing a context involves some effort. The less accessible a context, the greater the effort involved in accessing it, and conversely.

Consider a new assumption A. This may be relevant in some, all or none of the contexts accessible to an individual at a given time, depending on whether some, all or none of these contexts already contain or imply a token of *A*, and on the relative strength of old and new tokens. Six situations can be distinguished (the list is not exhaustive, but is representative enough for our present purposes):

(41)(a) *A* is already contained in (or implied by) the initial context, at maximal strength. Then the new token of *A* is irrelevant in this context, and in all the other accessible contexts too, since all these contexts include the initial context. In this situation there is no point in searching for relevance beyond the initial context, since the search will be unproductive.

(b) *A* is contained in (or implied by) none of the accessible contexts; however *A* has no contextual effect in any of them either. Then again, *A* is irrelevant in all the accessible contexts, and there is no point in extending the initial context in the search for relevance.

(c) *A* is contained in (or implied by) the initial context and all accessible contexts, at less than maximal strength. Then an independent strengthening of *A* by the new token will ensure its relevance in all the accessible contexts. In this situation an extension of the context will be justified as long as *A* has more contextual effects in the extended context than in the initial context, and the gain in contextual effects is not outweighed by the greater effort needed to process *A* in the extended context.

(d) *A* is contained in (or implied by) none of the accessible contexts, and has some contextual implications in the initial context. Then *A* is relevant in all the accessible contexts in which it retains these contextual implications. Here again an extension of the context will be justified as long as it yields greater contextual effects, and the increase in contextual effects is not outweighed by the increase in processing effort required.

(e) *A* is contained in (or implied by) none of the contexts; it has no contextual effect in the initial context but has some contextual effect in some extensions of the initial context. Then *A* is relevant in some of the accessible contexts. In this situation, no relevance will be achieved unless the context is extended. Extensions should follow the pattern laid down in (c) and (d).

(f) *A* is not contained in (nor implied by) the initial context, but is contained (at maximal strength) in some of the larger accessible contexts; *A* has contextual effects in some of the contexts in which it is not contained (which may or may not include the initial context). Then *A* is relevant in some of the accessible contexts, and its relevance will be that of a reminder. A reminder is relevant only in contexts which do not contain the information in question: its function is to make this information accessible at a smaller processing cost than would be needed to obtain it by successive extensions of the context.

Intuitively, as we will shortly illustrate, an assumption is relevant to an individual in situations (41c), (41d), (41e) and (41f). In situations (41c) and (41d) its relevance is immediately manifest; the difference between the two situations is that relevance is achieved in (41c) by contextual strengthening, and in (41d) by contextual implication. In situation (41e), it takes an extension of the context, and hence some effort, to bring out its relevance, but ordinarily this effort is not consciously felt, and again the relevance is immediately or almost immediately manifest. In situation (41f), the relevance is that of a reminder and is again immediately manifest.

We can now provide a classificatory definition of *relevance to an individual*:[a]

(42) *Relevance to an individual* (classificatory)
    An assumption is relevant to an individual at a given time if and only if it is relevant in one or more of the contexts accessible to that individual at that time.

However, for reasons discussed in section 2, we are less interested in classificatory than comparative definitions of relevance. Just as we did for relevance in a context, we will now characterise the comparative notion of relevance to an individual in terms of effect and effort. On the effort side, what has to be taken into account is not only the effort needed to process an assumption in a given context, but also the effort needed to access that context. For each of the contexts accessible to an individual, the effect and effort involved, and therefore the relevance achieved, will differ. Indeed, the same context can be accessible in different ways, involving different amounts of effort and therefore different relevance values. We might therefore try to characterise the relevance of an assumption to an individual in terms of a set of relevance values, one for each possible way of processing that assumption: i.e. one for each possible context and method of accessing that context.

However, the result of this cumbersome procedure would be of little psychological interest. We assume that the individual automatically aims at maximal relevance, and that it is estimates of this maximal relevance which affect his cognitive behaviour. Achieving maximal relevance involves selecting the best possible context in which to process an assumption: that is, the context enabling the best possible balance of effort against effect to be achieved. When such a balance is achieved, we will say that the assumption has been *optimally processed*. When we talk of the relevance of an assumption to an individual, we will mean the relevance achieved when it is optimally processed. We now define:

(43) *Relevance to an individual* (comparative)

    Extent condition 1: an assumption is relevant to an individual to the extent that the contextual effects achieved when it is optimally processed are large.

    Extent condition 2: an assumption is relevant to an individual to the extent that the effort required to process it optimally is small.

As with definition (10) (the comparative definition of relevance in a context), this definition of relevance to an individual does not make comparisons possible in all cases. Take two unrelated assumptions, each relevant to a different individual at a different time: is assumption $A1$ more relevant to Bill at time $t1$ than assumption $A2$ is to Joan at time $t2$? Our definition does not normally make it possible to answer such a question, nor, from a psychological point of view, is there any reason why it should. The only comparisons of relevance that play a psychological role are those which are subservient to the goal of maximising relevance: relevance to oneself, or, from the point of view of a communicator, relevance to an audience.

Let us illustrate this definition of relevance to an individual with an example somewhat less fragmentary than previous ones (although it still does not come near the complexities of real-life information processing). Suppose that the following exchange has so far taken place:

(44) *Mary*: What I would like to eat tonight is an osso-bucco.
    Peter: I had a long day. I'm tired.

After interpreting Peter's last remark, let us assume that Mary has in the memory of her deductive device an initial context composed of the three assumptions (45a–c), which are strong but not certain:

(45) *Initial context*
    (a) Peter is tired.
    (b) If Peter is tired, he wishes Mary would make the dinner.
    (c) Peter wishes Mary would make the dinner.

(45a) is the assumption expressed by the last utterance to be processed; (45b) is a premise which combined with (45a) to yield the contextual implication (45c). Other assumptions which Mary may have had in the memory of her deductive device when she began interpreting Peter's last remark have failed to yield contextual effects and have therefore been erased at the end of the interpretation process. In real life, the set of assumptions left in the memory of Mary's deductive device after she has interpreted Peter's last remark would presumably be much larger.

Mary can extend this initial context by adding to it various chunks of information, in particular:

Chunk 1. Encyclopaedic information about Peter, including the assumption, *Peter is a surgeon.*

Chunk 2. Encyclopaedic information about Mary.

Chunk 3. Encyclopaedic information about making dinner, including a scenario of looking in the refrigerator to see what is available, and the assumption, *A dinner consists of at least a main course and a dessert.*

Chunk 4. Information about the currently monitored physical environment.

Chunk 5. Assumptions processed at earlier stages in the exchange, including: *Mary would like to eat an osso-bucco.*

Chunks 1–5 are accessible in one step from the initial context. Each of these potential extensions makes further extensions accessible in turn. For instance, the information that Peter is a surgeon makes chunk 6 accessible:

Chunk 6. Encyclopaedic information about surgery.

The scenario of looking in the refrigerator in chunk 3 makes chunk 7 accessible:

Chunk 7. What Mary remembers of what there is in the refrigerator, including the assumption, *There is a chocolate mousse in the refrigerator.*

The concept of an osso-bucco appearing in chunk 5 makes chunk 8 accessible:

Chunk 8. Encyclopaedic information about osso-bucco, including the two assumptions, *An osso-bucco is a main course* and *An osso-bucco is a veal dish.*

Chunks 6, 7 and 8 are accessible only as a result of a two-step extension of the initial context (45). They make other chunks of information accessible in turn. For instance, chunk 9 is accessible as long as the concept of a coronary bypass appears in chunk 6 (information about surgery):

Chunk 9. Encyclopaedic information about coronary bypass, including the assumption, *Performing a coronary bypass is exhausting.*

Similarly, chunk 10 is made accessible by the presence of the concept of a chocolate mousse in chunk 7:

Chunk 10. Encyclopaedic information about chocolate mousse, including the assumption, *A chocolate mousse is a dessert.*

Of course, further levels of extension and many more extensions at each level are possible, but we will stop here and consider what effect various continuations of the dialogue between Peter and Mary might have on context selection.

Case A. Suppose first that Peter stops after saying, 'I'm tired'. Mary might then have a thought which is relevant to her in the context (45). She may for instance decide to make the dinner herself, which contextually implies that she will do what Peter wishes. This contextual implication makes her decision relevant not only to her but also to Peter, so she might decide to inform him of it and say,

(46) *Mary*: If you're tired, I'll make the dinner.

Mary may also extend the context to include chunk 3 (information about making dinner) and chunk 5 (in particular the information that she would like to eat osso-bucco). She can then derive many more contextual effects from her decision, in the form of more specific decisions about what to cook, for instance an osso-bucco, and about the various practical steps to take, like opening the refrigerator, etc.

This case has implications for the role of relevance in thought processes in general, not just in the interpretation of utterances. Each thought process leaves the mind in a state characterised by an initially given context and possible extensions. If we are right in assuming that the train of human thoughts is steered by the search for maximal relevance, then the mind should try to pick out, from whatever sources it has available, including its own internal resources, the information which has the greatest relevance in the initial context: that is, which has the greatest contextual effects and requires the smallest processing effort. Such information is to be sought in accessible extensions of the context, whether they involve encyclopaedic memory, the short-term memory store, or the environment. Thus, relevance theory yields hypotheses about the way thoughts follow one another, and about the points at which the individual might turn to the environment, rather than to his own internal resources, for relevant information.

Case B. Suppose that the dialogue (repeated for convenience with the new development italicised) continues as in (47):

(47) *Mary*: What I would like to eat tonight is an osso-bucco.
   Peter: I had a long day. I'm tired. *I wish you would make the dinner.*

Peter's last remark ('I wish you would make the dinner') achieves relevance in the initial context (45a–c) by strengthening the contextual implication (45c) that Mary had derived from his preceding remark ('I'm tired'). From then on, Mary's train of thought should proceed as it would have if Peter had stopped after saying 'I'm tired': that is, along the lines considered in Case A. The relevance achieved should be greater, though, since all conclusions based on premise (45c) (*Peter wishes Mary would make the dinner*) will be strengthened. This is an illustration, then, of situation (41c): some relevance is achieved in all accessible contexts by the strengthening of an existing assumption.

Case C. Suppose that the dialogue continues as in (48):

(48) *Mary*: What I would like to eat tonight is an osso-bucco.
     Peter: I had a long day. I'm tired. *If we're both tired, I'd like us to go to the Capri restaurant instead of having to make dinner.*

Peter's last remark has a contextual implication in the context (45a–c); it contextually implies (49):

(49) If Mary is tired, Peter would like them to go to the Capri restaurant.

Peter's last remark achieves relevance in all accessible contexts because of this contextual implication. This is therefore an illustration of situation (41d). At the same time, his remark achieves relevance in all accessible contexts in another way: by contradicting, and thereby eliminating, assumptions (45b) (*If Peter is tired, he wishes Mary would make the dinner*) and (45c) (*Peter wishes Mary would make the dinner*).
    Peter's remark also makes accessible an extra chunk of information:

Chunk 11. Encyclopaedic information about the Capri restaurant, in-
    cluding the assumption, *The speciality of the Capri restaurant
    is osso-bucco.*

Now clearly, some possible extensions of the context would diminish overall relevance: for instance there would be no gain in contextual effects from the addition of chunk 6 (information about surgery), and the extra processing costs would lead to a loss of relevance. Other extensions, however, would increase relevance. Suppose, for instance, that chunk 2 contains the assumption (50):

(50) Mary is tired.

With (50) added to the context, Peter's last remark contextually implies (51):

(51) Peter would like them to go to the Capri restaurant.

Adding chunk 5, and in particular the information that Mary would like to eat an osso-bucco, and chunk 11 (information about the Capri restaurant) yields another contextual implication:

(52) Peter would like them to go to a restaurant the speciality of which is what Mary would like to eat.

This leads in turn to many more contextual implications and strengthenings in a context containing information about Mary and Peter (and about osso-bucco).

Case D. Suppose that the dialogue continues as in (53):

(53) *Mary*: What I would like to eat tonight is an osso-bucco.
   Peter: I had a long day. I'm tired. *I've just done a coronary bypass.*

Peter's last remark is not relevant in the initial context (45a–c). However, it is relevant in a context extended to include chunk 9 (information about coronary bypass, including the assumption that performing a coronary bypass is exhausting). This extension, which was accessible in three steps from the initial context, has now become accessible in one step thanks to the presence of the concept of a coronary bypass in Peter's utterance. In a context so extended, the assumption that Peter has just done a coronary bypass contextually strengthens (45a) (*Peter is tired*), and achieves relevance thereby. This, then, is an illustration of situation (41e).

Case E. Suppose that the dialogue continues as in (54):

(54) *Mary*: What I would like to eat tonight is an osso-bucco.
   Peter: I had a long day. I'm tired. *I wish you would make the dinner tonight, and, by the way, there's a dessert, a chocolate mousse, in the refrigerator.*

The first part of Peter's last remark ('I wish you would make the dinner tonight') is relevant as described in the discussion of Case B. It should lead to the addition of chunk 3 (and in particular the assumption that a dinner consists of at least a main course and a dessert) to the context, as described in the discussion of Case A. This one-step extension makes chunk 7 (which contains the information that there is a chocolate mousse in the refrigerator) accessible in one further step, which, in a third step, makes accessible chunk 10 (which contains the information that a chocolate mousse is a dessert).

From the assumptions that would be available in the memory of Mary's deductive device if she carried out this three-step extension of the initial context (45a–c), she would be able to deduce that all she has to do to make the dinner is make a main course. The second part of Peter's last remark ('There's a dessert, a chocolate mousse, in the refrigerator') makes the same conclusion available without her having to extend the context beyond adding chunk 3. It also makes chunk 10 (information about chocolate mousse) accessible in one step, without her having to go through chunk 7 (the contents of the refrigerator).

Case E illustrates situation (41f), and shows how a reminder may be relevant: the effort needed to retrieve some relevant information from memory may be greater than the effort needed to get the same information from the interpretation of an utterance. In these circumstances, a reminder is relevant: the contextual effects it produces could have been produced otherwise, but more slowly and at a greater processing cost. On the other hand, when a reminder comes after the context has been extended to include the very information that the speaker is trying to bring to the hearer's attention, then the extra effort needed to process an utterance which carries no new contextual effects is wasted, and redundancy rather than relevance is the result.

The five cases discussed above show how the rather abstract notion of relevance in a context can help with the construction of a psychologically more significant notion of relevance to an individual. They also show the crucial importance of the organisation of encyclopaedic memory in the pursuit of relevance. In fact, the relation between memory and relevance is so close that relevance theory might well shed new light on the organisation of memory itself. For instance, the way in which information is chunked may in principle help or hinder the search for relevance; plausibly, forms of chunking which are a help rather than a hindrance tend to predominate. Conversely, the pursuit of relevance may lead to the faster building and enrichment of chunks of a certain form.

In this section we have characterised and illustrated a notion of relevance to an individual. We have done this in an attempt to come closer to a psychologically adequate notion of relevance, for use in describing and explaining verbal comprehension and other cognitive processes. So far, we have treated relevance as a property of assumptions. In particular, we have equated the relevance of an utterance with the relevance of the assumption it explicitly expresses. Yet hearers do not simply pick up the assumption expressed by an utterance. More generally, individuals do not simply pick up assumptions from their environment. In either case, a complex cognitive process requiring mental effort is involved.

Conversely, a communicator cannot directly present an audience with an assumption. All a speaker or any other type of communicator can do is present a stimulus, hoping that its perception by members of the audience will lead to a modification of their cognitive environment and trigger some cognitive processes. To the audience, a stimulus is initially just one phenomenon among others: that is, just one perceptible feature of the physical environment. It becomes identifiable as a stimulus only when it is recognised as a phenomenon designed to achieve cognitive effects.

Which phenomena does the individual pay attention to? How does he go about processing the information they make manifest? We want to claim that he tends to pay attention to relevant phenomena, and to process them so as to maximise relevance. However, to do this we have to characterise relevance not just as a property of assumptions in the mind, but also as a property of phenomena (stimuli, e.g. utterances) in the environment which lead to the construction of assumptions. This we will do in the next section.

6 The relevance of phenomena and stimuli

An individual's cognitive environment is the set of all facts which are manifest to him. A phenomenon affects the cognitive environment by making certain facts manifest or more manifest. As a result, the individual can mentally represent these facts as strong or stronger assumptions, and perhaps use them to derive further assumptions which do not correspond to actual facts, but which are nonetheless manifest to him too (see chapter 1, section 8, above).

A phenomenon may make manifest a very large number of assumptions. However, this is not to say that the individual will actually construct any, let alone all, of these assumptions. The house has its usual smells; the individual pays no attention to them and makes no assumptions about them whatsoever. Now suppose there is a distinct smell of gas. The individual is likely to make assumptions (55) and (56):

(55) There is a smell of gas.
(56) There is a gas leak somewhere in the house.

He is less likely to make assumption (57), even though it has become manifest too:

(57) The gas company is not on strike.

Why does he make some assumptions and not others? First, there are certain assumptions he cannot avoid making in a given cognitive environment. Take auditory perception. The faculty of auditory perception handles a great number and variety of noises, few of which reach the level of attention: that is, lead to the construction and manipulation of conceptual representations by the central thought processes. The mechanisms of auditory perception act as a filter, processing and filtering out most acoustic information at a sub-attentive level. These sub-attentively processed phenomena may come to the individual's attention, but only when central thought processes turn to the perceptual mechanisms for information about them.

However, some acoustic phenomena automatically pre-empt attention, automatically give rise to assumptions and inferences at a conceptual level. The perceptual mechanisms are organised so as to let certain types of phenomena impinge on central thought processes. Some of these favoured types of phenomena are probably innately determined: for instance, the automatic attention paid to all sudden loud noises has contributed to the survival of the species and is presumably an outcome of natural selection.

Other types of phenomena pre-empt attention as a result of some form of learning. The crying of a particular baby, even if barely audible, pre-empts the attention of the parents. A smell of gas pre-empts the attention of gas-users. Once the individual has smelled the gas, he cannot help but make assumption (55), the assumption that there is such a smell. The automatic filtering out of some phenomena and the automatic pre-empting of attention by others can be seen as a heuristic device aimed at maximising cognitive efficiency: in general, it is the phenomena which are least likely to be relevant which get filtered out, and those most likely to be relevant which pre-empt attention. In other words, the perceptual mechanisms – and perceptual salience itself – are relevance-oriented.

Assumption (56), the assumption that there is a gas leak, is a contextual implication of assumption (55) in a context containing ordinary encyclo-paedic information about household uses of gas. We want to suggest that assumption (56) is made in an attempt to maximise the relevance of assumption (55); indeed it is particularly useful in this respect, since it gives easy access to many other contextual effects. Precisely because the processing of (55) is governed by the search for relevance, assumption (57) is unlikely to be made: the processing effort needed to derive (57) is greater than the effort needed to derive (56), and moreover (57) does not lead to rich contextual effects achievable at a low processing cost.

A phenomenon can be more or less efficiently processed depending on which, if any, of the assumptions it makes manifest are actually constructed. For some phenomena, the best course is to filter them out at a perceptual level. For others, it is to represent them conceptually and process them in a rich encyclopaedic context. The notion of relevance can thus be extended to phenomena in a straightforward way:

(58) *Relevance of a phenomenon* (classificatory)
      A phenomenon is relevant to an individual if and only if one or more of the assumptions it makes manifest is relevant to him.

A comparative definition is similarly straightforward. As always, we will characterise the comparative notion of relevance in terms of effect and effort. Here, what has to be taken into account on the effort side is not only the effort needed to access a context and process an assumption in that context, but also the effort needed to construct that assumption. The construction and processing of different assumptions will involve diffe-rent effects and amounts of effort, and hence different degrees of relevance. For reasons discussed in the last section, we will characterise the relevance of a phenomenon to an individual as the relevance achieved when it is optimally processed.[8]

We now define:

(59) *Relevance of a phenomenon* (comparative)
    Extent condition 1: a phenomenon is relevant to an individual to the extent that the contextual effects achieved when it is optimally processed are large.
    Extent condition 2: a phenomenon is relevant to an individual to the extent that the effort required to process it optimally is small.

A stimulus is a phenomenon designed to achieve cognitive effects. Relevance for a stimulus is thus the same as relevance for any other phenomenon, and definitions (58) and (59) apply directly. We have argued that the processing of phenomena in general, and hence of stimuli in particular, is geared to the maximisation of relevance. Someone who wants to achieve a specific cognitive effect must therefore try to produce a stimulus which, when optimally processed, will achieve just the intended effect. This effect may be achieved at either the attentive or the sub-attentive level. When a child wants her parents to feel sorry for her, the best course might be to cry in a manifestly sincere way: the parents' attention will be pre-empted, and the most relevant assumption will be that the child is distressed. On the other hand, suppose Peter wants Mary to feel aroused by the manly smell of his after-shave, but is afraid she will be put off if she guesses his intention; his best course would be to use it sparingly, since a strong smell might attract her attention and make his intention all too manifest.

Here we are interested in stimuli used to achieve rather subtler cognitive effects: stimuli used to make an informative intention mutually manifest. *Ostensive stimuli*, as we will call them, must satisfy two conditions: first, they must attract the audience's attention; and second, they must focus it on the communicator's intentions.

Ostensive-inferential communication cannot achieve its effect sub-attentively; this necessarily involves the construction of conceptual representations and the mobilisation of central thought processes. This is why most stimuli used in ostensive communication are attention-pre-empting: they typically involve sudden loud noises such as shouts or doorbell chimes, striking visual stimuli such as hand waves, flashing lights or bright posters, or vigorous tactile stimulation such as prodding or grasping. Most important of all, spoken utterances in one's own native language automatically impinge on the attention: if they are distinctly audible, it is almost impossible to filter them out as background noise. It is only when the audience is likely to pay attention to the ostensive stimulus of its own accord, as you are now doing, that the stimulus, little dark marks on white paper for instance, can be a poor attractor of attention.

The second condition that an ostensive stimulus must meet is to focus the attention of the audience on the communicator's intentions. That is, the assumption that the stimulus is ostensive must be both manifest enough and relevant enough to lead to optimal processing. This condition is generally met by stimuli which both pre-empt the attention and are irrelevant unless treated as ostensive stimuli. This is clearly true of coded signals used in ostensive communication, linguistic utterances in particular, which, unless treated as ostensive stimuli, are mere irrelevant noises or marks on paper. It is also true of non-coded ostensive stimuli.

A non-coded ostensive stimulus may be an ordinary bodily movement, with little intrinsic relevance, made with artificial – and attention-arresting – rigidity: as when Peter leans back ostensively to let Mary see William coming (see chapter 1, section 9). It may be a piece of mimicry: for instance, Mary might mimic the act of driving to communicate to Peter that she wants to leave the party. Most of what such performances make manifest is of little or no relevance. Someone has made some quite ordinary bodily movement: so what? The only *relevant* assumptions made manifest by such behaviour are assumptions about the individual's informative intention.

The best ostensive stimuli are entirely irrelevant unless they are treated as ostensive. Consider a case where an intrinsically highly relevant stimulus is used – or misused – ostensively: say, somebody who is believed to have her arms paralysed mimics the act of driving. Here, the fact that she can move her arms would be so much more relevant than anything she might have wanted to communicate that her informative intention might well go unnoticed. Or to take a political example, acts of terrorism designed to publicise a cause have so many important implications irrespective of the terrorists' informative intention that they are much better at attracting public attention than at conveying the intended message.

However, it is not enough for the ostensive stimulus to attract attention and focus it on the communicator's intentions. It must also *reveal* the communicator's intentions. How can it do this? We will argue that what is crucial here is that an ostensive stimulus comes with the communicator's guarantee of relevance.[b] In general, there is no guarantee that a phenomenon will turn out to be relevant. Some phenomena are not relevant at all, and are therefore not worth processing at a conceptual level; others may be highly relevant, and may set off a whole train of thought. There can be no *a priori* expectation of relevance for phenomena in general.

In the special case of ostensive stimuli, the situation is quite different. By producing an utterance, the speaker requests her hearer's attention. By requesting his attention, she suggests that her utterance is relevant enough to be worth his attention. This applies not just to speech but to all forms of ostensive communication. Ostensive stimuli arouse definite expectations of relevance, of relevance achievable once the communicator's informative intention is recognised. In the next section, we will develop this idea and formalise it as a *principle of relevance*. Then, in the last section of this chapter, we will show how the principle of relevance explains ostensive–inferential comunication.

7 The principle of relevance

We ended chapter 1 with the following definition of ostensive–inferential communication:

(60) The communicator produces a stimulus which makes it mutually manifest to communicator and audience that the communicator intends, by means of this stimulus, to make manifest or more manifest to the audience a set of assumptions I.

As we said, this definition does not explain how ostension works: how the ostensive stimulus makes manifest the communicator's informative intention. We suggested that an answer to this question was to be sought in a principle of relevance, but that such a principle would not be truly explanatory until the notion of relevance had itself been explicitly characterised. Having done this, we can now return to the principle of relevance.

To achieve its effect, an act of ostensive communication must attract the audience's attention. In that sense,[9] an act of ostension is a request for attention. Someone who asks you to behave in a certain way, either physically or cognitively, suggests that he has good reason to think it might be in your own interests, as well as his, to comply with his request. This suggestion may be ill founded or made in bad faith, but it cannot be wholly cancelled. If a request has been made at all, the requester must have assumed that the requestee would have some motive for complying with it. Even a blackmailer has to make it look preferable for his victim to co-operate rather than to refuse; similarly, when a drowning man calls for help, his only chance is that some passer-by will find it morally preferable, however physically inconvenient, to help him.

Less dramatically, the host who asks his guests to eat automatically suggests that what he is offering them is edible, and indeed worth eating. Just as feeding someone normally requires the participation of the recipient in the form of appropriate bodily behaviour, ostensive communication requires the participation of the recipient in the form of appropriate cognitive behaviour, and in particular of attention. If Mary requests Peter's attention by pointing to something in the landscape, or holding something up for him to see, or talking to him, he is entitled to assume that the stimulus being drawn to his attention is relevant to him, or at least that she has reason to think it is; if she gives him something to think about, she must believe that he will find it good food for thought.

There is thus a substantial difference between the frame of mind in which the individual may approach an ostensive stimulus directed at him and the frame of mind in which he approaches other phenomena. When attending to other phenomena, he may have hopes of relevance: if such hopes were totally unwarranted, there would be no point in attending to them at all. However, whether these hopes turn out to be justified depends on a variety of factors, most of which are beyond the individual's control, and which he may not even be aware of. What makes these hopes reasonable is that humans have a number of heuristics, some of them innate, others developed through experience, aimed at picking out relevant phenomena. Even so, hopes of relevance sometimes turn out to be unjustified, and when they are justified, they are justified to a greater or lesser extent: there can be no general expectation of a steady and satisfactory level of relevance.

With an ostensive stimulus, however, the addressee can have not only hopes, but also fairly precise expectations of relevance. It is manifest that an act of ostensive communication cannot achieve its effect unless the audience pays attention to the ostensive stimulus. It is manifest that people will pay attention to a phenomenon only if it seems relevant to them. It is manifest, then, that a communicator who produces an ostensive stimulus must intend it to seem relevant to her audience: that is, must intend to make it manifest to the audience that the stimulus is relevant. Adding a layer of mutuality to this account, let us suppose that it is not merely manifest but mutually manifest to communicator and audience that an ostensive stimulus is being produced. Then it is not merely manifest but mutually manifest that the communicator must intend the stimulus to seem relevant to the audience: that is, must intend it to be manifest to the audience that the stimulus is relevant. By our definition of ostensive-inferential communication, this amounts to saying that an ostensive communicator necessarily communicates that the stimulus she uses is relevant to the audience. In other words, an act of ostensive communication automatically communicates a *presumption of relevance*.

What is the exact content of the presumption of relevance communicated by an act of ostensive communication? As we have said, what is communicated is that to the best of the communicator's knowledge, the ostensive stimulus is relevant enough to be worth the audience's attention. No weaker guarantee would do. But the presumption of relevance is more specific than this. The relevance of a stimulus is determined by two factors: the effort needed to process it optimally, and the cognitive effects this optimal processing achieves. We want to argue that the presumption of relevance is different on the effect and effort sides. On the effect side, the presumption is that the level of effects achievable is never less than is needed to make the stimulus worth processing; on the effort side, it is that the level of effort required is never more than is needed to achieve these effects.

The communicator intends to communicate a set of assumptions I. Of course, it is in the addressee's interest that I should be the most relevant information available to the communicator. However, here the interests of communicator and addressee need not coincide. The communicator may want to keep to herself the most relevant information at her disposal; she may have reasons of her own for communicating information that is less relevant. A communicator wants to communicate not just any arbitrary set of assumptions, but some particular set of assumptions I, which she may have her own reasons for wanting to convey. However, given that she needs the addressee's attention, she cannot but communicate that I is relevant enough to make the stimulus from which I is inferable worth processing. On the effect side, then, the presumption is one of adequacy.

To achieve her communicative intention, the communicator has to choose one of a range of different stimuli which would all make her particular informative intention mutually manifest. We assume that she eliminates any stimuli which would require too much effort on her part (e.g. drawing a map when a verbal indication will do) or which she finds objectionable (e.g. because of cultural rules prohibiting the use of certain words). In most cases, this will still leave a wide range of possible stimuli. It is in the interest of the addressee that the communicator should choose the most relevant stimulus from that range: that is, the one that will call for the least processing effort. Here the interests of communicator and addressee coincide. Unless the communicator is merely pretending to communicate, it is in her interest to be understood, and therefore to make it as easy as possible for the addressee to understand her. An addressee who doubts that the communicator has chosen the most relevant stimulus compatible with her communicative and informative intentions – a hearer, say, who believes that he is being addressed with deliberate and unnecessary obscurity – might doubt that genuine communication was intended, and might justifiably refuse to make the processing effort required. All this is mutually manifest; it is therefore mutually manifest that the communicator intends it to be manifest to the addressee that she has chosen the most relevant stimulus capable of fulfilling her intentions. On the effort side, then, the presumption is of more than mere adequacy.

The level of relevance that will be presumed to exist takes into account the interests of both communicator and audience. Let us call it a level of *optimal* relevance. We can now spell out the presumption of optimal relevance communicated by every act of ostensive communication:[c]

(61) *Presumption of optimal relevance*
  (a) The set of assumptions I which the communicator intends to make manifest to the addressee is relevant enough to make it worth the addressee's while to process the ostensive stimulus.
  (b) The ostensive stimulus is the most relevant one the communicator could have used to communicate I.

And here is the principle of relevance:

(62) *Principle of relevance*
  Every act of ostensive communication communicates a presumption of its own optimal relevance.

Let us now comment on the principle of relevance by raising and answering a number of specific questions.

Does the principle of relevance apply to all forms of communication?

No: it applies only to ostensive communication, not to straightforward coded communication. For instance, a telegraph employee who communicates messages by encoding them is expected to be accurate in her encoding; she is not expected to produce particularly relevant stimuli.

To whom is the stimulus presumed to be relevant when there are no definite addressees?

The addressees of an act of ostensive communication are the individuals whose cognitive environment the communicator is trying to modify. They can be specific individuals, as when Mary addresses Peter, or they may be individuals falling under a certain description, as when we address the present paragraph to all individuals who have read the book so far and found it relevant to them. In broadcast communication, a stimulus can even be addressed to whoever finds it relevant. The communicator is then communicating her presumption of relevance to whoever is willing to entertain it.

How reliable is the presumption of relevance?

As we all know, the world is full of bores. The principle of relevance does not say that communicators necessarily produce optimally relevant stimuli; it says that they necessarily intend the addressee to believe that they do. Even bores manifestly intend their audience to believe that they are worth listening to.

The presumption of relevance communicated by an utterance does not have to be accepted as true. The communicator might fail to achieve relevance; the addressee might doubt the communicator's ability to succeed in being relevant. However, from the presumption of relevance there follows a more reliable presumption that relevance has been attempted, if not achieved. A communicator who fails to make it manifest to her audience that she is being optimally relevant may nevertheless succeed in making it manifest that she is trying to be optimally relevant. However, ostensive communication must be seen as communicating more than a mere presumption of attempted relevance. The addressee may be willing to believe that the communicator has tried very hard to be relevant, but if he also believes that she has totally failed, he will not pay attention to her. So, however full of self-doubts she may be, a communicator must intend to make it manifest to the addressee that her ostensive stimulus *is* relevant enough.

Are you claiming that all ostensive communicators at least TRY to be optimally relevant?

This does not follow from the principle of relevance. Theoretically, a communicator can communicate her presumption of relevance in bad faith, just as she can communicate any assumption in bad faith. However, it is generally true that ostensive communicators try to be optimally relevant. When addressees are disappointed in their expectations of relevance, they rarely consider as a possible explanation that the communicator is not really trying to be optimally relevant. It would be tantamount to assuming that the apparent communicator is not really addressing them, and perhaps not communicating at all. This rare situation is illustrated by the case of filibusters.

Filibusterers make long speeches to an assembly merely in order to delay its proceedings. All the usual features of verbal communication are present and even salient, but for one: there is no attempt at optimal relevance. Even if they tried, filibusterers could not hope to remain relevant for the many hours, or even days, that a filibuster may last, and so they do not keep their audience's attention, or even try to keep it. Are filibusterers communicating, albeit defectively, or merely pretending to communicate? For the apparent addressees, at least, it is clear that only a pretence of communication is taking place, and that they are not being genuinely addressed at all. It is like discovering that your host is putting in front of you stuff whose edibility he has not even bothered to check. This is tantamount to discovering that he is only pretending to feed you.

When no satisfactory level of relevance is achieved, a more plausible assumption is that the communicator has tried to be optimally relevant, but failed. Communicators take risks and sometimes fail, and addressees expect such failures to occur occasionally. For example, if Mary knows that Peter buys every book by Iris Murdoch, and she sees the latest one being put on display in the local bookshop, it would be reasonable for her to say to Peter,

(63) Iris Murdoch's new book is in the bookshops.

It may turn out that Peter already has this information, in which case utterance (63) will in fact be irrelevant to him. However, it would still have been perfectly appropriate, and the presumption of relevance would have been communicated in good faith, because Mary has at least *tried* to be optimally relevant. Moreover, the risk she took was reasonable: it was worth taking because of the hope, if she had succeeded, of achieving a high degree of relevance to Peter.

How much effort the addressee can expect the communicator to put into being relevant varies with the circumstances, the communicator, and the relationship between communicator and addressee. Lecturers are expected to try very hard to be relevant; students are allowed, and sometimes even encouraged, to communicate without being hampered by the fear of being irrelevant. A master talking to his servant may say whatever he wishes and merely assume that it will be relevant enough; a servant addressing his master is expected to have made quite sure that he has something relevant to say.

How relevant is 'relevant enough to be worth the addressee's attention'?

We have assumed that an individual's cognitive resources are optimally allocated when they yield the greatest cognitive effects. It might seem, then, that to be worth the individual's attention, a stimulus must be more relevant than any other external phenomenon, or internal representation, that he could have been processing at the time. However, this does not take the time factor into account.

Some phenomena and representations remain relevant and accessible for a long time; others are both accessible and relevant only for a moment. It is sometimes more efficient – that is, conducive to greater overall relevance in the long run – to pay attention to a less relevant stimulus whose cognitive effects might be lost forever if it is not immediately processed, and to ignore some more relevant information which can as well be processed later on. For instance, it may be consistent with the principle of relevance to interrupt someone who is reading a fascinating book in order to ask a mildly relevant but pressing question, or to draw his attention to some moderately interesting incident in the landscape.

Similarly, some stimuli are of little intrinsic relevance but, by being presented at the right time, increase the relevance of subsequent stimuli so that a greater degree of overall relevance is achieved with them than without them. This is generally true of the first sentence in a novel: though of limited relevance in itself, it helps create a context in which subsequent sentences will be more relevant. It is thus relevant enough to be worth the reader's attention.

What counts as relevance enough, then, varies with the way in which information is accessible, or can be made accessible, to the addressee over time. It also varies with the degree of intellectual alertness of the addressee.

Imagine a group of people having a conversation in a café or a pub after work, just a light conversation between friends. Here a modicum of relevance should be enough: nobody will be willing to put in much processing effort, or expect major contextual effects. For that matter, nobody will put enormous effort into producing stimuli that would be worth extensive processing. By contrast, consider what is supposed to happen in a seminar. Here everyone is supposed to be on the alert, ready to put a considerable amount of intellectual effort into producing and processing information. In these circumstances, information relevant enough to be worth the addressee's attention is quite relevant indeed. There is little point, in one set of circumstances, in expecting a level of relevance only normally achieved in quite different circumstances, and a reasonable addressee will adjust his expectations accordingly.

The various factors we have mentioned are commonplace features of everyone's everyday experience. It should not call for too much observation or imagination on the part of the communicator to estimate the minimal level of relevance required. More specific considerations may help. On various social occasions, the expected level of relevance is culturally defined. In the course of a conversation, the level can be adjusted, increased or decreased one step at a time. The addressee may make manifest the minimal level of relevance he expects: by asking a question, for instance. Even so, mistakes can occur. However, as we will show, it is enough that the presumption of relevance should be communicated – and it always is. It does not have to be accepted as true in order to fulfil its most important role: determining the interpretation of the ostensive stimulus.

What are the differences between relevance theory and Grice's approach?

There are many. One is that the principle of relevance is much more explicit than Grice's co-operative principle and maxims. Another is that Grice assumes that communication involves a greater degree of co-operation than we do.

For us, the only purpose that a genuine communicator and a willing audience necessarily have in common is to achieve uptake: that is, to have the communicator's informative intention recognised by the audience. Grice assumes that the communication must have 'a common purpose or set of purposes, or at least a mutually accepted direction' (Grice 1975: 45) over and above the aim of achieving uptake. We do not mean to deny that this is very often true, particularly in conversation.[10] In a talk exchange, a seminar or a book, there may well be a mutually manifest purpose or direction. However, this does not follow from the principle of relevance, and is not automatically conveyed by every ostensive stimulus. Knowledge of such a common purpose, when it exists, is one contextual factor among others, and it is only as such that it can play a role in comprehension.[d]

Achieving optimal relevance, then, is less demanding than obeying the Gricean maxims. In particular, it is possible to be optimally relevant without being 'as informative as is required' by the current purposes of the exchange (Grice's first maxim of quantity): for instance by keeping secret something that it would be relevant to the audience to know. It seems to us to be a matter of common experience that the degree of co-operation described by Grice is not automatically expected of communicators. People who don't give us all the information we wish they would, and don't answer our questions as well as they could, are no doubt much to blame, but not for violating principles of communication.

A more radical difference between Grice's approach and relevance theory is this. Grice's principle and maxims are norms which communicators and audience must know in order to communicate adequately. Communicators generally keep to the norms, but may also violate them to achieve particular effects; and the audience uses its knowledge of the norms in interpreting communicative behaviour.

The principle of relevance, by contrast, is a generalisation about ostensive–inferential communication. Communicators and audience need no more know the principle of relevance to communicate than they need to know the principles of genetics to reproduce. Communicators do not 'follow' the principle of relevance; and they could not violate it even if they wanted to. The principle of relevance applies without exception: every act of ostensive communication communicates a presumption of relevance. It is not the general principle, but the fact that a particular presumption of relevance has been communicated by and about a particular act of communication, that the audience uses in inferential comprehension.[11]

However, the most important difference between Grice's approach and ours has to do with the explanation of communication. Grice's account of conversation starts from a distinction between what is explicitly said and what is implicated. No explanation of explicit communication is given; essentially, the code model, with a code understood as a set of conventions, is assumed to apply. Implicatures are explained as assumptions that the audience must make to preserve the idea that the speaker has obeyed the maxims, or at least the co-operative principle. The principle of relevance is intended to explain ostensive communication as whole, both explicit and implicit. We will show in the next section how it does.

8 How relevance theory explains ostensive–inferential communication

A communicator who produces an ostensive stimulus is trying to fulfil two intentions: first, the informative intention, to make manifest to her audience a set of assumptions I; and second, the communicative intention, to make her informative intention mutually manifest. It is not hard to see how the fulfilment of the communicative intention can lead to the fulfilment of the informative intention: the realisation that a trustworthy communicator intends to make you believe something is an excellent reason for believing it. This explains well enough *why* people engage in ostensive communication. However, it does not explain how ostensive communication works: how the communicative intention itself is fulfilled.

It is not obvious how the production of a stimulus can make the communicator's informative intention mutually manifest, and thus lead to the fulfilment of the communicative intention. As we have seen, with other forms of intentional behaviour, evidence about the underlying intentions is obtained by observing the effects of this behaviour. With ostensive communication, the intended communicative effect is the recognition of the informative intention. However, the intended informative effect does not generally occur, and thus cannot generally be observed, until *after* the underlying informative intention has been recognised. In that case, the informative intention cannot be inferred by observing its independently achieved effects. The question is, how can it be inferred at all?

Several inferential steps are needed if the informative intention is to become mutually manifest. The stimulus has to make manifest, in the mutual cognitive environment of communicator and audience, other assumptions from which the informative intention can be inferred. First, it must be manifest that the stimulus is ostensive. We have shown in section 6 how this can be achieved: by producing a manifestly intentional stimulus which on the one hand attracts attention, and on the other is irrelevant unless treated as evidence about the communicator's intentions. Once the ostensive nature of a stimulus is mutually manifest to communicator and addressee, it is also mutually manifest that the communicator has an informative intention: that is, that she intends to make manifest to the addressee some set of assumptions I. The problem of identifying the communicator's informative intention reduces, then, to the problem of identifying the set of assumptions I.

What the principle of relevance does is identify one member of I: namely, the presumption of relevance. The presumption of relevance is not just a member of I, it is also *about* I. As a result, it can be confirmed or disconfirmed by the contents of I. The possibilities of confirmation and disconfirmation are different for the two different parts (61a) and (61b) of the presumption of relevance, repeated here for

(61) *Presumption of optimal relevance*

    (a) The set of assumptions I which the communicator intends to make manifest to the addressee is relevant enough to make it worth the addressee's while to process the ostensive stimulus.

    (b) The ostensive stimulus is the most relevant one the communicator could have used to communicate I.

For the addressee, every assumption about the contents of I either verifies (61a) – I is relevant enough – or else falsifies it. There may be borderline cases, sets of assumptions on the margin of being relevant enough. However, there cannot be cases for which there is insufficient evidence, sets of assumptions whose relevance cannot be assessed by the addressee: in processing I, he automatically discovers how relevant it is. With the second part of the presumption of relevance, (61b), things need not be so clear-cut. Given an assumption about the contents of I, it may be manifest that the communicator could have used a more relevant stimulus, and this will falsify (61b). However, (61b) may be neither falsified nor verified: after all, in ordinary conditions, the addressee does not know exactly what range of stimuli the communicator had at her disposal, and hence cannot be sure that she has used the most relevant one to communicate I. The presumption of relevance as a whole, then, should either be clearly falsified (in the case where either (61a) or (61b) is falsified), or be merely confirmed, but not verified (in the case where (61a) is verified and (61b) is not falsified).

For some assumptions in I, all the evidence the communicator gives the addressee is indirect: the addressee's only reason for accepting them is the communicator's mutually manifest intention that he should. For other assumptions in I, the communicator also provides direct evidence, as when Peter ostensively leans back to let Mary see who is coming. The status of the presumption of relevance is altered by the comprehension process itself. At the start of the comprehension process, the initial evidence for the presumption of relevance is entirely indirect; it is entirely based on the communicator's guarantee that her stimulus is optimally relevant to the addressee. However, by processing the stimulus, the addressee naturally obtains direct evidence for or against the presumption that it is optimally relevant; and by the end of the comprehension process this direct evidence will have superseded the initial indirect evidence. In intending to make the presumption of relevance manifest, the communicator must realise that she cannot help but provide direct and decisive evidence for or against it. This is the crucial step towards identifying her full informative intention, the set of assumptions I.

In trying to identify this informative intention, the addressee must assume that the communicator is communicating rationally: that is, that she has good reason to think that the stimulus she is producing will have the intended effects. This applies not just to the identification of informative intentions, but to the inferential identification of intentions in general. Intentions are identified by assuming that the agent is rational, and by trying to find a rational interpretation of her actions. It is not that people in general, and communicators in particular, always suit their means to their ends in a fully rational way. It is just that when they do not, it is impossible to infer their intentions from their behaviour alone. In the case of communicative behaviour, this compounds the irrationality, since the success of communication depends on the addressee's ability to infer the communicator's intentions.

A rational communicator, who intends to make the presumption of relevance manifest to the addressee, must expect the processing of the stimulus to confirm it. In other words, she must expect the contents of I to verify (61a) and not to falsify (61b). To recognise the communicator's informative intention, the addressee must discover for which set I the communicator had reason to think that it would confirm the presumption of relevance. We will argue that this is all he has to do.

The task of the addressee, then, is to construct possible interpretive hypotheses about the contents of I, and to choose the right one. In different circumstances and different cognitive domains, the task of constructing and selecting a hypothesis may be carried out in different ways. In some cases, it is best carried out by listing all the possible hypotheses, comparing them, and choosing the best one. In others, it is better carried out by searching for an initial hypothesis, testing it to see if it meets some criterion, accepting it and stopping there if it does, and otherwise repeating the process by searching for a second hypothesis, and so on. To illustrate, suppose that Peter does not know exactly where he left his sunglasses, but knows they are somewhere in the house. In one case, he is away from home and has to telegraph Mary where to look for the sunglasses. He should then make a mental list of all the places where he might have left them, rank them in order of likelihood, and tell Mary the most likely place. In another case, Peter is at home. He will take the first hypothesis which occurs to him and look there; if he finds his sunglasses there, the search stops; otherwise, he will search a second place, and so on.

These two strategies, listing and ranking hypotheses, or searching for hypotheses and testing them one by one, are suited to different types of tasks. The first strategy is ill suited to tasks where it would be impossible or inconvenient to list all possible hypotheses. For instance, if the task is to find a pupil who is neither the tallest nor the shortest in the school, it would be a waste of effort to rank all the pupils by height. The second strategy is ill suited to tasks where there is no decisive criterion that can be applied to isolated hypotheses. For instance, it would be impossible to find out which is the tallest pupil in a school without taking all the pupils into account.

For other tasks, neither the list-and-rank strategy nor the item-by-item testing strategy is appropriate on its own. The search for a true scientific theory cannot be based on an examination of all possible theories, since we do not know what these are; nor can it be based on a criterion which could be used to decide whether an isolated theory is true. The strategy of scientific discovery is much more complex, and involves both comparison and individual testing; its results are, in principle at least, never final. As we have pointed out, in this respect comprehension is unlike scientific discovery: it yields final results almost immediately, which suggests that a rather simple strategy must be involved.

Could comprehension be achieved by listing and ranking all possible hypotheses about the communicator's informative intention? The idea may seem attractive if comprehension is seen as a simple matter of decoding a signal into a small set of possible messages and then choosing among them. It must be rejected, however, because neither the possible figurative interpretations of a coded message, nor its possible implicatures, are enumerable. We will argue that this is true even when unambiguously coded signals are used as stimuli. Moreover, even if it were possible to list all the possible interpretations of an ostensive stimulus, it would still be absurdly inconvenient. As we have seen, one of the factors which makes one interpretation more relevant than others is that it requires less processing effort. If the only way of finding the right interpretation were to list and rank all possible interpretations, then all possible interpretations would require the same amount of effort: namely, the effort needed to construct and compare them. It is hard to think of any ostensive stimulus that would be worth such an absurd amount of effort.

Could comprehension be achieved, then, by constructing an initial hypothesis, testing it, and moving on to a second one if the first is not adequate? At first sight it might seem that here again the answer must be no. Let us say that an interpretation is *consistent with the principle of relevance* if and only if a rational communicator might have expected it to be optimally relevant to the addressee.[e] Suppose now that the addressee tests a possible interpretation and finds it consistent with the principle of relevance. How could it follow that he would be right to select it? Surely there are many other possible interpretations which might be consistent with the principle of relevance too? Since consistency with the principle of relevance is the only test we have, using it in an item-by-item testing strategy will never yield the desired result.

This argument is mistaken. It misses the fact that the order in which hypotheses are tested affects their relevance. As a result, the principle of relevance does not generally warrant the selection of more than one interpretation for a single ostensive stimulus. We will show that the interpretation whose selection it warrants is the first one tested and found to be consistent with the principle.

Consider first how an addressee who realises that an ostensive stimulus has been produced, and hence that a presumption of relevance has been communicated, might construct hypotheses about the communicator's informative intention. First, the plausibility of some hypotheses may already be manifest in the environment. Consider utterance (64):

(64) *Peter* (to Mary): Do you want some coffee?

By uttering (64), Peter makes it manifest that he wants an answer to his question and that an appropriate answer would satisfy his expectations of relevance. It is then plausible that the informative intention behind Mary's next piece of communicative behaviour will be to make manifest an answer to Peter's question.

The stimulus used by the communicator is itself a source of interpretive hypotheses. The description of a non-coded ostensive stimulus (e.g. *Mary is sniffing ecstatically*, or *Mary is pretending to drive a car*) gives immediate access to the encyclopaedic entries of certain concepts and the assumption schemas they contain. A coded stimulus gives immediate access to a highly determinate set of concepts: the code itself determines which concepts are activated, and moreover assembles them into a logical form which can be directly used as an assumption schema. The context provides ways of completing these assumption schemas into full hypotheses.

Once an initial set of hypotheses has been recovered, the addressee can add to it by assuming that the set I includes further assumptions contextually inferable from those already recovered. Moreover, by extending the context, radically different hypotheses may become accessible. The important point is that, given the cognitive environment, given the initial context, and given the stimulus, some hypotheses are more accessible than others, and this means that they require less processing effort.

Let us now reconsider the feasibility of the item-by-item testing strategy. An addressee who is using this strategy, and who wants to maximise cognitive efficiency, will test hypotheses in order of accessibility. Suppose he arrives at a hypothesis which is consistent with the principle of relevance. Should he stop there, or go on and test the next hypothesis on the ground that it might be consistent with the principle of relevance too? It is easy to show that he should stop there. Suppose he does go on, and finds another hypothesis which verifies the first part of the presumption of relevance: the putative set I is relevant enough. In these circumstances, the second part of the presumption of relevance is almost invariably falsified. If it was at all possible, the communicator should have used a stimulus which would have saved the addressee the effort of first accessing two hypotheses consistent with the principle of relevance, and then having to choose between them.

Consider the following utterance, for instance:

(65) George has a big cat.

In an ordinary situation, the first interpretation of (65) to occur to the hearer will be that George has a big *domestic* cat. If it seems possible that the speaker might have expected this interpretation to be optimally relevant to the hearer, then he should stop there. Suppose he does not, decides instead that the speaker might have expected other interpretations to be optimally relevant too, and goes on searching for them. The word 'cat' is ambiguous: it may refer either to the domestic cat or to any animal of the species *Felis*. Thus the hearer arrives at the hypothesis that (65) might be intended to convey that George has a tiger, a lion, a jaguar, etc. Maybe this information would be even more relevant than the fact that George has a big domestic cat, thus verifying the first part of the presumption of relevance. Nonetheless, the second part would automatically be falsified. A manifestly more relevant stimulus would have been something like (66), or, if the speaker lacked the necessary information, something like (67) or (68):

(66) George has a tiger.
(67) George has a tiger or a lion, I'm not sure which.
(68) George has a felid.

These stimuli would have saved the addressee the effort of first accessing and considering the 'domestic cat' interpretation, then accessing the 'felid' interpretation, and then having to compare the two. Hence, the addressee need not have bothered: the first interpretation consistent with the principle of relevance was the best hypothesis. All other interpretations would manifestly falsify the second part of the presumption of relevance.

When the communicator has an unbounded range of stimuli to choose from, it follows from the second part of the presumption of relevance that of all the interpretations of the stimulus which confirm the first part of the presumption, it is the first interpretation to occur to the addressee that is the one the communicator intended to convey. But what if the communicator has a limited range of stimuli to choose from, so that if she had intended to convey something other than the first optimally relevant interpretation to occur to the addressee, she would have had no more adequate stimulus at her disposal? In this case, either the first interpretation consistent with the principle of relevance is communicated, as before, or nothing is communicated at all.

Imagine, for instance, a prisoner handcuffed and silenced. All she can do before she is taken away is smile at her friend. How can he decide whether she intended to convey something other than a sad goodbye, the first plausible interpretation that occurs to him? And if she did, what did she intend to convey? At first sight, there is no way of telling. However, suppose that all the interpretations he can think of include a sad goodbye as a subpart: then he can feel confident that this, at least, has been communicated. By reasoning further, he should be able to see that the prisoner herself can see that he has no way of crediting her with a fuller informative intention, so that even though she may well have *wished* to communicate more, she was not in a position rationally to *intend* to. So, at most a sad goodbye has been communicated.

What if two essentially different interpretations seem to come simultaneously to the mind of the addressee, and they are both consistent with the principle of relevance? In that case the addressee will be unable to decide what the informative intention was, and communication will fail. This is one of the few cases where an ambiguity is consciously perceived during the comprehension process itself.

What if the communicator is mistaken in her presumption of relevance? This will make the addressee's task a little more effort-consuming, and a little more liable to failure, but not essentially different, and certainly not impossible. To be consistent with the principle of relevance, an interpretation does not actually have to be optimally relevant to the addressee; it must merely have seemed so to the communicator. Conversely, the first optimally relevant interpretation may happen to be relevant in a way the communicator could not have foreseen; in this case it is not consistent with the principle of relevance. In every case, the task of the addressee is to find an interpretation consistent with the principle of relevance – that is, an interpretation which the communicator could manifestly have expected to be optimally relevant. This task is of course made easier, but not essentially altered, when the addressee can trust the communicator, and can therefore assume that the intended interpretation is actually the first optimally relevant one to occur to him.

What happens when an unambiguously coded signal is used? Can the criterion of consistency with the principle of relevance still be used? Yes.

Here, by way of illustration, is an anecdote. Two friends were arguing. Paul had decided to emigrate to a new country, which he saw as a land of justice and freedom. He would go and write back to Henry to let him know the beautiful truth. Henry tried to persuade him not to go: there was oppression and misery in that country, he claimed, goods were scarce, and Paul's letters would be censored anyhow. Since Paul would not be moved, Henry persuaded him to accept at least the following convention: if Paul wrote back in black ink, Henry would know he was sincere. If he wrote in purple ink, Henry would understand that Paul was not free to report the truth. Six months after Paul's departure, Henry received the following letter, written in black ink: 'Dear Henry, this is the country of justice and freedom. It is a worker's paradise. In the shops you can find everything you need, with the sole exception of purple ink . . .'

The point is that when a code is used in human communication, what makes a communicated assumption manifest to the addressee is the communicator's manifest intention to make it manifest. There is no way a communicator could bind herself by a code or a convention to such an extent that it would be impossible for her not to have the intention her signal represents. The coded signal, even if it is unambiguous, is only a piece of evidence about the communicator's intentions, and has to be used inferentially and in a context. The hypothesis the signal suggests still has to be tested for consistency with the principle of relevance, and if it fails to meet this criterion, it must be rejected.

Contrary to first appearances, the principle of relevance does make it possible to use an item-by-item testing strategy in comprehension. It warrants the selection of the first accessible interpretation consistent with the principle, if there is one, and otherwise no interpretation at all. In other words, relevance theory explains how ostensive communication is possible, and how it may fail.

Of course there are a lot of unanswered questions. For instance, how exactly are assumption schemas filled out? What exactly determines the order of accessibility of hypotheses? However, such questions are not specific to relevance theory: they apply to cognitive psychology as a whole. Since relevance theory is, among other things, an attempt to ground models of human communication squarely in cognitive psychology, it cannot just take advantage of the insights of cognitive psychology, but must also share its weaknesses. We have tried to show that the relationship is not one way, and that relevance theory has contributions to make to cognitive psychology. Other unanswered questions have more to do with the study of communication proper, and verbal communication in particular. What are the differences and relations between what is explicitly communicated and what is implicitly communicated? How does linguistic form affect interpretation? How are figurative interpretations determined? How is illocutionary force recognised? These questions will be discussed in the next chapter.

4

Aspects of verbal
communication

In this chapter we want to outline some of the implications of relevance theory for the study of verbal communication. What we are offering is simply a sketch: we will not review the literature, we will discuss only selected issues, and will not always justify our conclusions step by step. However, we hope to show that relevance theory offers a pragmatic framework in which serious questions can be raised, and new answers developed.

1 Language and communication

Language and communication are often seen as two sides of a single coin. On this view, the essential feature of language is that it is used in communication, and the essential feature of communication is that it involves the use of a language or code. The relation between language and communication is thought of as like the relation between the heart and the circulation of the blood: neither is properly describable without reference to the other. In chapter 1, we argued that communication can be achieved without the use of a code; in chapter 3, we showed how. In this section, we want to complete the divorce between language and communication by showing that languages, in a reasonably broad sense of the term, can and do exist without being used for communication. Languages are indispensable not for communication, but for information processing; this is their essential function. Having rejected the assumption that there is a necessary link between language and communication, it then becomes interesting to see what happens when, as a matter of contingent fact, they *do* become linked: in verbal communication, for example.

In the broadest sense, a language is a set of well-formed formulas, a set of permissible combinations of items from some vocabulary, generated by a grammar. In a narrower sense, a language is a set of semantically interpreted well-formed formulas. A formula is semantically interpreted by being put into systematic correspondence with other objects: for example, with the formulas of another language, with states of the user of the language, or with possible states of the world. A language in this narrower sense – the one we will use – is a grammar-governed representational system.

It would be possible to define a language even more restrictively: as a set of semantically interpreted well-formed formulas used for communication. It would then be true by definition that language and communication were inextricably linked. However, the definition itself would have to be motivated. In science, a definition is motivated when it groups together properties which are systematically linked in nature. Our point is precisely that the property of being a grammar-governed representational system and the property of being used for communication are not systematically linked. They are found together in the odd case of human natural languages, just as the property of being an olfactory organ and the property of being a prehensile organ, though not systematically linked in nature, happen to be found together in the odd case of the elephant's trunk.

The activities which necessarily involve the use of a language (i.e. a grammar-governed representational system) are not communicative but cognitive. Language is an essential tool for the processing and memorising of information. As such, it must exist not only in humans but also in a wide variety of animals and machines with information-processing abilities. Any organism or device with a memory must be able to represent past states of the world or of itself. Any organism or device with the ability to draw inferences must have a representational system whose formulas stand in both syntactic and semantic relations to each other. Clearly, these abilities are not confined to humans.

The great debate about whether humans are the only species to have language is based on a misconception of the nature of language. The debate is not really about whether other species than humans have languages, but about whether they have languages which they use as mediums of communication. Now the fact that humans have developed languages which can be used to communicate is interesting, but it tells us nothing about the essential nature of language. The originality of the human species is precisely to have found this curious additional use for something which many other species also possess, as the originality of elephants is to have found that they can use their noses for the curious additional purpose of picking things up. In both cases, the result has been that something widely found in other species has undergone remarkable adaptation and development because of the new uses it has been put to. However, it is as strange for humans to conclude that the essential purpose of language is for communication as it would be for elephants to conclude that the essential purpose of noses is for picking things up.

Language is not a necessary medium for communication: non-coded communication exists. Nor is it necessarily a medium for communication: languages exist which are not used for communication. However, language *is* a necessary attribute of communicating devices. Two devices capable of communicating with each other must also be capable of internally representing the information communicated, and must therefore have an internal language. In the case of ostensive–inferential communication, this internal language must be rich enough to represent the intentions of other organisms, and to allow for complex inferential processes.

In fact, for ostensive communication to be possible, the communicating devices must have a richer internal language and more powerful inferential abilities than are generally needed for coded communication. Bees do not have to attribute intentions to one another or engage in inference in order to communicate among themselves by means of their dance-based code: all they need is an internal language capable of representing directions and distances in space. Cognitively simple organisms can engage in coded communication, whereas only cognitively sophisticated organisms can engage in ostensive communication. Arguably, ostensive–inferential communication exists within, and perhaps between, a variety of animal species: for example, within those animal species which engage in threatening behaviour and are able to distinguish threats from attacks; perhaps between dog and human when the dog recognises its owner's intentions.

It is clear that humans have an internal language rich enough for ostensive–inferential communication. They also have external languages such as Swahili or English, which are, of course, used for communication. It might seem, then, that humans can communicate in two different ways: either by ostension and inference, or by coding and decoding. We have suggested a different view, which will be developed at length in this chapter: that human intentional communication is never a mere matter of coding and decoding. The fact is that human external languages do not encode the kind of information that humans are interested in communicating. Linguistically encoded semantic representations are abstract mental structures which must be inferentially enriched before they can be taken to represent anything of interest.

Although the linguistic analysis of an utterance very much underdetermines its interpretation, the most striking feature of linguistic communication is that it can achieve a degree of precision and complexity rarely achieved in non-verbal communication. When Mary sniffs ostensively to draw Peter's attention to the seaside smells, there is no limit to the number of ways he can represent her behaviour to himself: there may be a whole nebula of alternative interpretations, all closely similar in import and comparable in relevance. To varying degrees, all non-verbal communication is weak communication in the sense defined in chapter 1: one can never be sure which of a variety of assumptions made manifest by the communicator she herself actually had in mind. The set of assumptions which have been communicated can be defined in general terms, but the individual members of this set cannot be enumerated.

With verbal communication, the situation is quite different. First, the linguistic description of an utterance is determined by the grammar, and does not vary with the interests or point of view of the hearers. Second, this linguistic description yields a range of semantic representations, one for every sense of the sentence uttered. Each semantic representation is a schema, which must be completed and integrated into an assumption about the speaker's informative intention, and can be as complex as the speaker cares to make it. Moreover, each schematic sense is generally quite different from all the others, and can be completed in quite different ways. The various alternative interpretations of a non-coded ostensive stimulus, of an appreciative sniff for instance, tend to form a continuous range of variants; by contrast, the various possible interpretations of an utterance tend to be radically different from one another, so that when one is chosen, the others are automatically eliminated.

Consider utterance (1), for example:

(1) He's a bastard.

Let us assume that on the basis of a linguistic analysis of (1) and an assignment of contextually accessible referents, the speaker might be taken to be asserting any of (2a–d):

(2) (a) Peter is a nasty man.
   (b) Bob is a nasty man.
   (c) Peter is illegitimate.
   (d) Bob is illegitimate.

It would be quite extraordinary for these various linguistically and referentially possible interpretations of (1) to be equally consistent with the principle of relevance. Because each alternative interpretation is discrete and sharply distinguishable from the others, the hearer can usually know for certain which one the speaker must have intended. Linguistic communication is the strongest possible form of communication: it introduces an element of explicitness where non-verbal communication can never be more than implicit. Of the assumptions conveyed by an utterance, at least those that are explicitly conveyed can be enumerated.

We regard verbal communication, then, as involving two types of communication process: one based on coding and decoding, the other on ostension and inference. The coded communication process is not autonomous: it is subservient to the inferential process. The inferential process is autonomous: it functions in essentially the same way whether or not combined with coded communication (though in the absence of coded communication, performances are generally poorer). The coded communication is of course linguistic: acoustic (or graphic) signals are used to communicate semantic representations. The semantic representations recovered by decoding are useful only as a source of hypotheses and evidence for the second communication process, the inferential one. Inferential communication involves the application, not of special-purpose decoding rules, but of general-purpose inference rules, which apply to any conceptually represented information.

Incidentally, this view of verbal communication has implications about the origin of human languages. The fact that the semantic representations of natural-language expressions are merely tools for inferential communication suggests that inferential communication had to exist before external languages developed: human external languages are of adaptive value only for a species already deeply involved in inferential communication. Remember the old comparison between language and money: words and currencies are similar in that they both derive their value from convention? We would like to push the comparison in a different direction. Money is central to a modern, monetary economy, just as language is central to verbal communication. However, the monetary system could only appear in a pre-existing economic system, and only makes sense as part of such a system. Similarly, human natural language could only appear in a pre-existing inferential communication system, and it only makes sense as part of such a system. Verbal communication is a specifically human enhancement of ostensive–inferential communication.

2 Verbal communication, explicatures and implicatures

An utterance is a perceptible modification of the physical environment. As such, it makes manifest a variety of assumptions. Suppose, for instance, that Mary utters the complex sound transcribed in (3):

(3) [ɪtḻgetkəʊld]

This makes manifest to Peter a set of assumptions **A** which might include, among many others, assumptions (4a–e):

(4) (a) Someone has made a sound.
    (b) There is someone in the house.

(c) Mary is at home.
(d) Mary has spoken.
(e) Mary has a sore throat.

If some of (4a–e) are relevant to Peter, then Mary's behaviour may be relevant simply by making these assumptions manifest to him. In that case, the linguistic, and in particular the semantic properties of the sentence uttered make no contribution to relevance. A clearing of the throat might have been relevant to Peter in just the same way; or rather, it would have been more relevant, since it would have achieved the same effects without needing any linguistic processing at all.

The set **A** of assumptions made manifest by Mary's behaviour also includes (5):

(5) Mary has uttered the sentence 'It will get cold.'

In appropriate conditions, an assumption of the form in (5) will be automatically constructed. Even in poor acoustic conditions, a phonetic stimulus in the hearer's native language is automatically analysed as a token of a particular linguistic structure: [ɪtḷgetkəʊld] is analysed as 'It will get cold.' This information may be filtered out sub-attentively, but as long as minimum standards of acoustic clarity and salience are met, the phonetic signal will be automatically analysed and assigned a semantic representation (or, in the case of ambiguity, several semantic representations), making manifest an assumption of the form in (5).

In other words, a linguistic stimulus triggers an automatic process of decoding. Just as we cannot choose to see the objects around us in black and white rather than in colour, just as we cannot choose not to hear a gun going off nearby, so we cannot choose to hear an utterance in a language we know as merely an unanalysed stream of sounds. We automatically recover its semantic representation, even if we accidentally overhear it and know it was not meant for us, or even (as the evidence on binaural shadowing shows)[1] if we are not conscious of hearing it at all. The linguistic decoding system has all the hallmarks of automatic, reflex perceptual systems such as hearing and vision. In the terms of Fodor (1983), who develops this point at length, it is an input system rather than a central processing system, and this is one reason why it has been so relatively amenable to study. This suggests in turn that if comprehension is defined as a process of identifying the speaker's informative intention, linguistic decoding is not so much a part of the comprehension process as something that precedes the real work of understanding, something that merely provides an input to the main part of the comprehension process.

Verbal communication is never achieved merely by the automatic decoding of linguistic signals. Such decoding occurs even when it is manifest that no attempt at communication is being made: for instance when an actor doing voice exercises is accidentally overheard. It also occurs when an utterance is used to communicate information which bears no relation to its semantic content, as in the following dialogue:

(6) A: Did your treatment for stammering work?
    B: Peter Piper picked a peck of pickled pepper.
    A: How amazing!
    B: Yes, b-b-but th-th-that's not s-s-something I v-v-very often w-w-want to s-s-say.

B's first reply communicates that the treatment worked well, not by saying so, but by producing direct evidence that it did. Properly speaking, this is not a case of verbal communication, and it falls outside the scope of pragmatics. Verbal communication proper begins when an utterance, such as B's second reply, is manifestly chosen by the speaker for its semantic properties.

In other words, verbal communication proper begins when the speaker is recognised not just as talking, not even just as communicating by talking, but as saying something to someone. Most utterances do this, of course, and an adequate account of verbal communication must explain why. One way of explaining it is to assume that people learn, or are innately equipped with, more or less *ad hoc* pragmatic rules to the effect that utterances should be used for communication only in virtue of their semantic properties.[2] However, this leaves exceptions such as (6) to be explained.

A simpler explanation follows from the principle of relevance. According to relevance theory, the correct interpretation of an ostensive stimulus is the first accessible interpretation consistent with the principle of relevance. For most utterances, this will be an interpretation based on semantic properties: the other properties of the utterance are generally not relevant enough to yield an interpretation consistent with the principle of relevance. In odd cases such as (6), the semantic properties of the utterance do not yield an appropriate interpretation and other properties (in this case acoustic properties) do. The principle of relevance thus explains both the usual, semantically based cases of utterance interpretation and the occasional exceptions.

Suppose that Mary's behaviour is an ordinary case of verbal communication – that is, that it makes manifest assumption (7):

(7) Mary has said to Peter 'It will get cold.'

Since saying something to someone is a case of ostensive communication, the set **A** of assumptions made manifest by Mary's utterance includes (8):

(8) There is a set of assumptions I which Mary intends to make manifest to Peter by saying to him 'It will get cold.'

The task of the hearer can now be described in two ways. One is to say that the hearer must find in A a mutually manifest assumption of the form in (9):

(9) The speaker intends to make I manifest.

However, suppose that the speaker achieves not only her communicative intention but also her informative intention – as she will if the hearer both understands her and trusts her enough. Then I, the set of assumptions communicated by the utterance, will be a subset of A, the set of assumptions made manifest by the utterance. The hearer's task can then be described in another way: the hearer must decide which assumptions in A would also, if the speaker were trustworthy, be members of I: that is, he must decide which assumptions made manifest by her utterance are such that it is mutually manifest that the speaker intended to make them manifest.

Typically, the set I might include assumptions such as (10a–e):

(10) (a) Mary's utterance is optimally relevant to Peter.
    (b) Mary has said that the dinner will get cold very soon.
    (c) Mary believes that the dinner will get cold very soon.
    (d) The dinner will get cold very soon.
    (e) Mary wants Peter to come and eat dinner at once.

The goal of pragmatics is to explain how the hearer's task, as described above, can be carried out: how he can identify a set I, e.g. (10), using as premises a description of the speaker's behaviour, e.g. (7), together with contextual information.

The hearer's task involves a variety of inferential sub-tasks. The first is to assign the utterance a unique propositional form. This involves disambiguating the sentence uttered: that is, selecting one of the semantic representations assigned to it by the grammar. Here, a single sense of 'cold' (*experiencing cold* or *inducing cold*) must be selected. However, the recovery of a unique propositional form involves more than disambiguation. A referent must be assigned to each referring expression (e.g. 'It' in our example). The contribution of vague terms such as 'will' must be made more specific (e.g. by the addition of *very soon* in our example). In other words, a semantic representation must be selected, completed and enriched in various ways to yield the propositional form expressed by the utterance. This task is inferential – that much is uncontroversial. However there is very little in the pragmatic literature to explain how it is carried out – apart from the comment that Gricean maxims and mutual knowledge might help.³ Moreover, the complexity of the task is generally underestimated: it is seen as simply a matter of choosing a single sense and reference from a limited set of alternatives. The fact that logical forms must often be enriched is generally ignored; no explanation is given of how such enrichment can be achieved.

Suppose Peter has decided that 'It' refers to the dinner, that 'will' refers to the immediate future, and that 'cold' means *inducing cold*. In other words, he has decided that the propositional form expressed by Mary's utterance is (10d):

(10) (d) The dinner will get cold very soon.

An utterance does more than express an explicit propositional form: it expresses this form in a certain linguistically determined mood. For instance, if Mary's utterance (3) has a falling intonation contour, it will be in a declarative mood: it will be a case of 'saying that'. If it has a rising intonation contour, it will be in an interrogative mood: it will be a case of 'asking whether'. Mood is linguistically encoded, but just as the logical form of an utterance underdetermines the propositional form expressed, so the mood of an utterance underdetermines the propositional attitude expressed. One of the hearer's sub-tasks, again an inferential one, is to identify this propositional attitude.

Having identified the propositional form of an utterance and the mood expressed, the hearer is in a position to identify one further member of I (apart, that is, from the presumption of relevance itself): namely, the assumption that the speaker has expressed this particular propositional form in this particular mood. For instance, suppose that Mary's utterance is in a declarative mood. Then it is mutually manifest that Mary intended (10b) to be manifest to Peter; in other words, it is inferable that (10b) is a member of I:

(10) (b) Mary has said that the dinner will get cold very soon.

However, a hearer can recover (10b) but still not know what propositional attitude Mary intended to communicate; and without knowing this, he will be unable to decide what she intended to communicate apart from (10b) itself. In particular, even though Mary has said that the dinner will get cold very soon, she need not be *asserting* that the dinner will get cold very soon. Asserting that *P* involves communicating that one believes that *P*. However, in the weak sense of 'saying that' which corresponds to the declarative mood, one can say that *P* without communicating that one believes that *P*. For example, in saying that the dinner will get cold very soon, Mary might be speaking metaphorically or ironically, in which case she would not communicate that she believes that the dinner will get cold very soon.

Moreover, asserting that *P* involves more than merely communicating that one believes that *P*. Hence, Mary might communicate that she believes the dinner will get cold very soon, without actually asserting it. Suppose that (10c) is a member of **I**:

(10) (c) Mary believes that the dinner will get cold very soon.

A speaker who communicates that she believes that *P* does not automatically communicate that *P*. For instance, suppose it is mutually manifest that Peter believes that the dinner will stay hot for as long as it takes him to finish what he is doing, and that he has no reason to trust Mary's opinion here more than his own. Then Mary could not have intended her utterance to achieve relevance by making manifest to Peter that the dinner would get cold very soon, but only by making manifest that she believes it will.

We will discuss problems of figurative interpretation and illocutionary force in sections 7–10. Let us suppose, for the moment, that Peter has decided that Mary intended to communicate both that she believes that the dinner will get cold very soon, and that the dinner will get cold very soon. In other words, let us suppose that it is mutually manifest that Mary intended Peter to infer (10d) from (10c):

(10) (d) The dinner will get cold very soon.

An utterance which meets this condition, i.e. which communicates its propositional form, we will call an ordinary assertion.

Suppose now that from (10d), together with mutually manifest information, (10e) is inferable:

(10) (e) Mary wants Peter to come and eat dinner at once.

Suppose, moreover, that it is mutually manifest that it is contextual implication (10e) which makes the whole utterance relevant enough to be worth Peter's while to process. Then it is inferable that (10e) is a member of **I**, and (10e) is communicated by Mary's utterance.

However, there is a striking difference between the way (10b–d) on the one hand, and (10e) on the other, are identified. Assumptions (10b–d) include as sub-parts one of the logical forms encoded by the utterance. They are constructed inferentially, by using contextual information to complete and enrich this logical form into a propositional form, which is then optionally embedded into an assumption schema typically expressing an attitude to it. Let us call this process of assumption construction the *development* of a logical form. (10e), by contrast, is not a development of one of the logical forms encoded by the utterance; it is constructed on the basis of contextual information, and in particular by developing assumption schemas retrieved from encyclopaedic memory. For instance, Peter's encyclopaedic memory might contain a whole scenario of 'dinner at home', including the assumption schema (11):

(11) Mary wants Peter to come and eat dinner at time t. [t = time at which dinner is still hot]

We see the difference between (10b–d) on the one hand and (10e) on the other as a difference between explicit and implicit communication. We define:

(12) *Explicitness*[a]
   An assumption communicated by an utterance U is *explicit* if and only if it is a development of a logical form encoded by U.

On the analogy of 'implicature', we will call an explicitly communicated assumption an *explicature*. Any assumption communicated, but not explicitly so, is implicitly communicated: it is an *implicature*. By this definition, ostensive stimuli which do not encode logical forms will, of course, only have implicatures.

This classificatory concept of explicitness lends itself quite naturally to a comparative interpretation. An explicature is a combination of linguistically encoded and contextually inferred conceptual features. The smaller the relative contribution of the contextual features, the more explicit the explicature will be, and inversely. Explicitness, so understood, is both classificatory and comparative: a communicated assumption is either an explicature or an implicature, but an explicature is explicit to a greater or lesser degree.

This is an unconventional way of drawing the distinction between the explicit and implicit 'content' of an utterance. On a more traditional view, the explicit content of an utterance is a set of decoded assumptions, and the implicit content a set of inferred assumptions. Since we are claiming that no assumption is simply decoded, and that the recovery of any assumption requires an element of inference, we deny that the distinction between the explicit and the implicit can be drawn in this way.

Grice sees things rather differently. For him, recovering the explicit content of an utterance apparently amounts to recovering what we would call the propositional form and mood expressed; any other assumptions communicated by the utterance, whether decoded or inferred, is an implicature. Decoded implicatures are what he calls 'conventional implicatures'; inferred implicatures are 'non-conventional', the most familiar of these being the famous 'conversational implicatures'. We would deny that there are conventional implicatures in Grice's sense, but this is not our main reservation about his way of drawing the distinction between the explicit and the implicit.

The main problem with Grice's distinction has to do not with the characterisation of implicatures, but with the characterisation of the explicit. First, he does not envisage the kind of enrichment of logical form involved, for instance, in interpreting 'will' as *will very soon*; he treats comparable cases, for instance the interpretation of 'and' as *and then* in some contexts, as cases of implicature. Most Gricean pragmatists assume without question that any pragmatically determined aspect of utterance interpretation apart from disambiguation and reference assignment is necessarily an implicature. In fact, recent work has shown that a number of problems with classical implicature analyses are resolved when the 'implicatures' are reanalysed as pragmatically determined aspects of explicit content.[4]

Second, Grice says very little about how propositional attitudes are communicated, and it is unclear what he would regard as 'explicit' and what 'implicit' here. Third, he has no notion of degrees of explicitness. Generally speaking, we see the explicit side of communication as richer, more inferential, and hence more worthy of pragmatic investigation than do most pragmatists in the Gricean tradition.

In the next two sections, we show how relevance theory accounts for the recovery of the propositional form of an utterance (section 3) and its implicatures (section 4). For simplicity of exposition, we will look only at ordinary assertions, i.e. utterances which communicate their propositional forms. In the final sections of this chapter we will generalise our treatment to other types of utterance.

3 The identification of propositional form

The hearer's first task in recovering the explicatures of an utterance is to identify its propositional form. In this section, we will describe this task in more detail and show how it is carried out. We will restrict our attention to ordinary assertions, in which the propositional form of the utterance is itself an explicature.

The task is, of course, to identify the *right* propositional form, and the right propositional form is the one intended by the speaker. However, this cannot be the criterion the hearer uses to identify the right propositional form: if he already knew the speaker's intention, he would have no task of identification left. What criterion does the hearer use to select the right propositional form? Although there is considerable literature on disambiguation and reference assignment, this question has not been seriously addressed. Experimental studies of disambiguation simply take for granted that there is normally only a single sense of an utterance which looks as if it could have been intended by the speaker; no attempt is made to explain why this is so. The aims of psycholinguists working on disambiguation lie elsewhere: they want to describe not the criterion used in disambiguation, but the procedure by which disambiguation is achieved.

Could the answer simply be that the right propositional form is the one obtained by going through a certain procedure (just as the right result in multiplication is the one obtained by applying a certain algorithm)? The existence of so-called garden-path utterances is strong evidence that this is not so. Consider (13), with the possible interpretations (14a–b):[5]

(13) I saw that gasoline can explode.
(14) (a) I saw that it is possible for gasoline to explode.
    (b) I saw that can of gasoline explode.

When (13) is processed in isolation, the normal disambiguation procedure favours interpretation (14a). However, the continuation in (15) would force a reinterpretation:

(15) And a brand new gasoline can it was too.

What such garden-path utterances strongly suggest is that the outcome of the normal disambiguation procedure is not automatically accepted as the right propositional form. It is rejected if it fails to meet some criterion which has yet to be defined.

At the end of chapter 3, we made a suggestion about what the general criterion for the interpretation of an ostensive stimulus might be: the right interpretation is the one that is consistent with the principle of relevance. This in turn suggests a criterion for identifying the propositional form of an utterance: the right propositional form is the one that leads to an overall interpretation which is consistent with the principle of relevance. Let us say that in this case the propositional form itself is consistent with the principle of relevance.

Whatever regular procedures there are for disambiguation, reference assignment and enrichment, they yield at best a tentative identification of propositional form, an identification which will be rejected if it turns out not to be consistent with the principle of relevance. This is why interpretation (14a) is rejected: the explicatures recovered by regular disambiguation procedures from (13), the first part of the overall utterance, do not lead to an interpretation which is consistent with the principle of relevance once (15), the second part of the utterance, is taken into account.

Our suggestion is, then, that the propositional form the hearer should be interested in recovering is the one that is consistent with the principle of relevance. The next question is, what general procedure might the hearer use to identify propositional forms which meet this criterion? Here again, the outline of an answer is strongly suggested by the principle of relevance. At every stage in disambiguation, reference assignment and enrichment, the hearer should choose the solution involving the least effort, and should abandon this solution only if it fails to yield an interpretation consistent with the principle of relevance.

We will now look separately at the three sub-tasks involved in the identification of propositional form: disambiguation, reference assignment and enrichment. One problem we immediately encounter is that we cannot avoid the use of artificial examples. When an artificial example is produced, say as part of a theoretical discussion or in an experimental situation, it is processed and understood in isolation from any natural context. This is not to say that it is processed and understood in isolation from *any* context. In the first place, it gives access to encyclopaedic information about the objects and events referred to, and hence to a range of potential contexts of the usual type; in the second place, the author or experimenter may provide some elements of a natural context by describing a setting, asking the individual to imagine a previous utterance, and so on.

Even so, artificial examples tend to favour considerations of effort over considerations of effect in the assessment of relevance. In the absence of real-life contextual constraints, or constraints specially set up by the experimenter, hearers automatically construct a context which yields the least effort-consuming conceivable interpretation. It would thus be easy, on the basis of artificial examples, to conclude that the identification of propositional form is entirely determined by a principle of least effort. The existence of garden-path utterances such as (13) should prevent us from making such a mistake.

Though effort is only one of the two factors involved in the assessment of relevance, it is a factor well worth studying, and here there is an advantage in the fact that it is to some extent isolated by artificial examples. We are assuming that the identification of propositional form involves two mental mechanisms: a linguistic input module and a central inferential ability. How are the two mechanisms related, and how does the effort made by each affect the overall processing effort? More specifically, does the linguistic input module construct all the possible semantic representations of a sentence, one of which is then selected by central processes? Or are the semantic representations of a sentence more or less effort-consuming for the input module to construct, so that the easiest one is constructed first, a second representation being constructed only if the first is rejected, and so on? In other words, how are the 'wrong' interpretations filtered out?

These questions are not going to be answered at the purely speculative level of the present discussion. The considerable experimental evidence already available is not conclusive, judging by the debates it has provoked.[6] What can be said at the speculative level is this: the filtering-out of all interpretations but one is not conscious, which strongly suggests that it is a relatively peripheral process. On the other hand, what makes one interpretation 'right' and another 'wrong' is contextual information: mainly general encyclopaedic information in the case of artificial examples.

Consider (16), for instance:

(16) The child left the straw in the glass.

This could mean either that the child left the drinking tube in the glass, or that the child left the cereal stalks in the glass. In the absence of a special context, it is the *drinking-tube* interpretation which is selected. Why? At a purely linguistic level, there is no reason to assume that the *cereal-stalk* sense of 'straw' is less accessible than the *drinking-tube* sense; no reason, then, why one interpretation should be preferred. The selection manifestly involves contextual factors.

A child drinking from a glass with a straw is a stereotypical event which we assume, as do most other people working on the organisation of memory, is recorded in the form of a single chunk, stored at a single location in memory and accessed as a single unit. Such a chunk constitutes a highly accessible encyclopaedic context in which the *drinking-tube* interpretation of (16) can be processed at minimal cost. There is nothing, of course, to prevent a child leaving a bunch of cereal stalks in a glass, or a speaker choosing to report such an event. However, the encyclopaedic context needed to process this information would be less accessible than the context needed to process the *drinking-tube* interpretation of (16): it would not be stored as a chunk, but would have to be derived by collecting together information about children and glasses on the one hand, and cereal stalks on the other. Hence the more easily accessible *drinking-tube* interpretation of (16), once recovered, is also more easily processed.

If we assume, with Fodor (1983), that input modules have no access to general encyclopaedic information, examples such as (16) seem to imply that the input module has to construct all the semantic representations of an utterance, the wrong ones then being filtered out at a central level after all. However, the relationship between input module and central processes need not be that simple: for instance, the input module might construct all the linguistically possible interpretations of the first constituent of the sentence, and submit them to the central mechanism, which would, when possible, choose one of them and inform the linguistic module of its choice. As a result, the module's decoding processes would be partly inhibited; it would retain only those interpretations of the next constituent which are linguistically compatible with the selected interpretation of the first constituent, and so on. With the interaction of input module and central mechanisms so conceived, it remains true that the module has no access to encyclopaedic contextual information; however, contextual factors may affect its processes in a purely inhibitory way.

For example, when (17), the first part of (13), has been decoded, the central mechanism is in a position to choose between an interpretation on which 'that' is a demonstrative determiner, and one on which it is a complementiser:

(17) I saw that . . .
(13) I saw that gasoline can explode.

Demonstrative determiners need a particular type of context: one created by pointing, for instance. In an artificial situation, the complementiser interpretation, which does not need an *ad hoc* context, is less effort-consuming and will be preferred. Assuming that from then on the operations of the input module are restricted accordingly, interpretations of (13) on which 'that' is a demonstrative will be automatically filtered out at the modular level, and 'can' will be interpreted as a verb, not a noun.

Disambiguation hypotheses are recovered by decoding and evaluated inferentially. Hypotheses about the intended reference of referring expressions are not generally recoverable by decoding alone.[7] To construct a hypothesis about the reference of 'It' in (18), the hearer must use not only linguistic but also non-linguistic information:

(18) It will get cold.

Linguistically, the only constraint on the reference of 'It' is that it should not refer to a human. This leaves the hearer an indefinitely large choice of referents.

How should the hearer construct and evaluate referential hypotheses? Given the principle of relevance,[b] he should first consider the immediate context, see if any of the concepts of a non-human entity represented in this context, when substituted for 'It', yields a propositional form consistent with the principle of relevance; if not, he should extend the context and repeat the procedure. This may sound like a cumbersome performance, but in practice it can be quite simple. Suppose the hearer knows that dinner is on the table, and is wondering whether it will stay hot long enough for him to finish a letter he is writing: then all the contextual implications of (18) will already have been worked out, and they only need strengthening to yield an immediately accessible chunk of contextual effects. In this case, the hearer has no difficulty in testing *the dinner* as a possible referent for 'It', or in checking that the resulting overall interpretation is consistent with the principle of relevance. It is in such a situation that (18) would be most appropriate. If the immediate context does not yield an adequate referent for 'It', the hearer might add to the context the encyclopaedic entries of the various concepts which have *cold* as their lexical entry. One highly accessible schema these entries would yield is about meals getting cold. The relevance of the resulting interpretation could be easily checked.

It is widely believed that if all but one of the senses of a sentence are eliminated and referents are assigned to its referential expressions, the resulting combination of sense and reference corresponds to a unique propositional form. We have argued against this view. Consider (19):

(19) The bat is grey.

Suppose that 'bat' is understood in the zoological sense, that 'The bat' refers to a specific bat, and that the present tense of 'is' refers to a specific time. Then it is standardly claimed that (19) is capable of being true or false; it expresses a unique propositional form. Maybe so, but what about (20)–(22)?

(20) Peter's bat is grey.
(21) The bat is too grey.
(22) The bat is big.

'Peter's bat' might refer to the bat owned by Peter, the bat chosen by Peter, the bat killed by Peter, the bat mentioned by Peter, and so on indefinitely. It is hard to believe that the genitive is ambiguous, with as many senses as there are types of relationship it may be used to denote, or that all these relationships fall under a single definition which is the only meaning expressed by use of the genitive on any given occasion. It seems, rather, that the semantic interpretation of a sentence with a genitive from which ambiguities and referential indeterminacies have been eliminated is still something less than fully propositional. Contextual information is needed to resolve what should be seen as the semantic incompleteness, rather than the ambiguity, of the genitive.

It can be similarly argued that an adverb such as 'too' is semantically incomplete. A bat is too grey *for something*. If you do not know what that something is, you do not fully know what 'too grey' is being used to express. (21) is a perfectly grammatical sentence of English. Yet a combination of one of its senses with fixed references corresponds to an indefinite range of propositional forms. Again similar arguments apply – and have often been applied – to scalar adjectives such as 'big' in (22): is the bat big for an adult bat, big for a bat of its age, big for a pet, etc.? And does 'big' without a scale of reference express a complete meaning?

Examples such as (20)–(22) strongly suggest that the gap between semantic representations and propositional forms cannot be closed merely by disambiguation and reference assignment. Quite often, semantic representations must also be enriched. This task is, of course, an inferential one. Consider (23):

(23) It will take some time to repair your watch.

The interpretation recoverable from this utterance by decoding and reference assignment is a truism and thus irrelevant. It goes without saying that watch-repairing is a process with a temporal duration, and a speaker aiming at optimal relevance must have intended to express something more than goes without saying. In general, an utterance of the form in (23) should be interpreted as conveying not the truism that the job in question will take some time, but that it will take an amount of time it would be relevant to remark on: i.e. longer than would otherwise be expected. Suppose I always take my watch to the same watchmaker, and it usually takes about a week to repair. Then if the speaker of (23) is aware of these facts, she must be understood as saying that the repair will take longer than a week. The more precise the expectations, the more precisely the speaker's intentions can be pinned down.

This situation is predicted by relevance theory in the usual way: an utterance, like any other ostensive stimulus, is a piece of evidence about the communicator's informative intention. The fact that it activates certain concepts and, in the case of utterances, a certain logical form, is ground for assuming that at least some of the assumptions which the communicator intends to make manifest contain these concepts or this logical form. The logical form of an utterance, in particular, is an assumption schema. The presence of semantically incomplete or manifestly vague terms is a clear indication of where the schema might be enriched. In the case of 'some time' in (23), it is a matter of finding the first accessible enrichment of the concept which will yield an interpretation relevant enough to be consistent with the principle of relevance. The 'some time' in question might be at least one second, at least one hour, at least one week, and so on, each of these interpretations being an enrichment of the preceding one in the sense that it contains the same information and more. In this case, the first accessible enrichment consistent with the principle of relevance is the one which specifies that the time it will take to repair the watch is at least more than would normally be expected.

Similarly, compare (24) and (25):

(24) I have had breakfast.
(25) I have been to Tibet.

What can be recovered from these utterances by decoding and reference assignment is that the speaker has had breakfast, or been to Tibet, at some point within a period of time preceding her utterance. In real life, a hearer would be expected to make some more or less specific assumption about how long that period was. In this, he is guided by the fact that a presumption of relevance has been communicated. In the case of (24), for example, it would normally go without saying that the speaker had had breakfast at some point in her life. If she intends her utterance to be manifestly relevant, she must intend to make manifest that she has had breakfast recently enough for it to be worth remarking on: for example, recently enough not to be in immediate need of food. In the case of (25), by contrast, the mere fact that the speaker had visited Tibet at some point in her life could well be relevant enough, and in the absence of more specific information this is the interpretation that would be consistent with the principle of relevance.

Let us show informally how disambiguation, reference assignment and enrichment combine, by looking at how (26) might be interpreted as a continuation of (27) and (28):

(26) Peter's bat is too grey.
(27) Your team is disqualified from the baseball game.
(28) We have chosen John's mouse for our breeding experiment.

Suppose (26) is a continuation of (27) in a real-life situation in which the hearer is a member of a baseball team. (27) gives him access to his encyclopaedic entries for baseball games, teams, including his own baseball team, and disqualification. It is also likely to raise in his mind the question of why his team has been disqualified. Suppose his team has a member called Peter, who has been playing with a particular grey baseball bat. In the circumstances, he could scarcely avoid the hypothesis that the speaker has said that the baseball bat his team-mate Peter has been playing with is too grey to be used in a regulation baseball game. This hypothesis would be retroactively strengthened by yielding an adequate range of contextual effects in an easily accessible context: in particular, by explaining why his team has been disqualified. It is this interpretation that would be consistent with the principle of relevance.

Suppose (26) is a continuation of (28) in an artificial situation, say in a disambiguation experiment. (28) gives the hearer access to his encyclopaedic entries for choosing, for mice, for breeding and for experiments; to achieve any degree of relevance, however, he would have to make some assumption about who the speaker was, who John was, what John's relation to the mouse was, and what the breeding experiment was for. If he has a schema for classroom biology experiments, he might have easy access, for example, to the assumption that the speaker is a schoolteacher, that John is a schoolboy, and that he has brought the mouse as a possible subject for a classroom experiment on genetics. The same schema can be reused, at minimal processing cost, to interpret the second part of the utterance, yielding the hypothesis that Peter is another schoolboy who has brought a grey bat as a possible subject for the same classroom experiment on genetics, but that this bat is too grey to be used in this particular experiment. This hypothesis would again be retroactively strengthened by yielding a satisfactory range of contextual effects in this stereotypical context. In particular, suppose that the interpretation of (28) has raised in the hearer's mind the question of why that particular mouse was chosen for that particular experiment; then (26), on this interpretation, would provide an answer to this question. The principle of relevance thus plays a decisive role in the recovery of the propositional form of the utterance, and therefore of its explicatures, in artificial situations as in natural ones.

The above discussion, apart from outlining our particular hypotheses about disambiguation, reference assignment and enrichment, raises a more general question about the role of semantic representations in communication. There is a widespread view that all the thoughts that a human might entertain and want to communicate could in principle be linguistically encoded. Katz incorporates this view in the following 'principle of effability':

(29) Each proposition (thought) is expressible by some sentence in every natural language. (Katz 1981: 226)

What does it mean to say that every thought is *expressible* by some sentence? On a weak interpretation, it means that every thought can be conveyed by *uttering* some sentence. If no limit is placed on the complexity of the sentence, this seems a matter of common sense. It is this commonsense intuition which is the strongest and most obvious argument for the effability principle. However, on this interpretation, the claim made by the effability principle is about utterances in context rather than about sentences: about language use rather than about language in itself. It does not entail that every entertainable thought can be linguistically encoded.

Katz offers a stronger and more interesting interpretation of the principle. According to him, for every thinkable thought there is, in every language, a sentence one of whose senses uniquely corresponds to that thought; if that sentence is used literally and in that sense, then, whatever the context, it expresses that thought. According to this view, every thought is encoded by a sense of some sentence.

On this view it would be possible, at least in principle, to communicate thoughts linguistically without any appeal to inference and context (except, perhaps, for purposes of disambiguation). Why, then, do natural languages contain so many sentences which encode not thoughts but merely incomplete logical forms? Why is it that most sentences actually uttered are schematic, requiring inference as well as decoding for full comprehension? Katz's main answer is that

> it allows speakers to make use of contextual features to speak far more concisely than otherwise. Imagine how lengthy utterances would be if everything we wanted to express had to be spelled out explicitly in the grammar of our sentences. Pragmatics saves us from this wasteful verbosity. Thus, instead of using sentences like [(30)], we can, on occasion, use sentences like [(31)].

> [(30)] The man who just asked the stupid question about the relation between the mental and the physical has, thank God, left the room.
> [(31)] Thank God, he is gone. (Katz 1977: 19–20)

Note, however, that (30) is not fully propositional: it would express different propositional forms in different situations by referring to different individuals. Its interpretation might need fewer contextual clues than that of (31), but it would need some. To eliminate the referential indeterminacy, what would be needed is something like (32), where time and space could be specified in terms of universal co-ordinates:

(32) Thank God, the man x who at time t was in location l has, at time t', left the room which the man x was in at time t.

However, it is open to question whether either (30) or (32) expresses the same thought as (31). That is, I may think what is conveyed by 'Thank God, he is gone' without entertaining any of the senses of (30) or (32) or of any other such sentence; I need not describe to myself the man whose departure I am rejoicing over as 'the man who just asked the stupid question about the relation between the mental and the physical' or as 'the man who at time t was in location l'', or in terms of any external-language definite description. It seems plausible that in our internal language we often fix time and space references not in terms of universal co-ordinates, but in terms of a private logbook and an ego-centred map; furthermore, most kinds of reference – to people or events for instance – can be fixed in terms of these private time and space co-ordinates. Thoughts which contain such private references could not be *encoded* in natural languages but could only be incompletely represented.

What does this imply for the possibility of two people having exactly the same thought, and for the possibility of communication? It implies that two people may be able to think *of* the same man *that* he has gone, without being able to think exactly the same thought, because they might not individuate him in exactly the same way. Similarly, by saying 'He has gone' I may induce in you a thought which is similar to mine in that it predicates the same thing (that he is gone) of the same individual, but which differs from mine in the way you fix the reference of 'He'. It seems to us neither paradoxical nor counterintuitive to say that there are thoughts that we cannot exactly share, and that communication can be successful without resulting in an exact duplication of thoughts in communicator and audience. We see communication as a matter of enlarging mutual cognitive environments, not of duplicating thoughts.[8]

If sentences do not encode thoughts, what *do* they encode? What are the meanings of sentences? Sentence meanings are sets of semantic representations, as many semantic representations as there are ways in which the sentence is ambiguous. Semantic representations are incomplete logical forms, i.e. at best fragmentary representations of thoughts. We have argued that they are incomplete in more than one way: not just because they contain indeterminate referring expressions such as pronouns, but also because they contain underdefined constituents such as 'too', 'some time', or the genitive. What we are suggesting is that the claim that the semantics of natural languages might be too weak to encode all humanly thinkable thoughts is quite compatible with what is known of the role of language in verbal communication.

One entertains thoughts; one does not entertain semantic representations of sentences. Semantic representations of sentences are mental objects that never surface to consciousness. If they did, they would seem entirely uninteresting (except, of course, to semanticists). Semantic representations become mentally represented as a result of an automatic and unconscious process of linguistic decoding. They can then be used as assumption schemas to identify first the propositional form and then the explicatures of an utterance. It is these explicatures alone that have contextual effects, and are therefore worthy of conscious attention.

4 The identification of implicatures

In the last section we showed how the principle of relevance guides the identification of propositional form. In section 10, we will discuss the identification of the speaker's propositional attitude. From the context, the propositional form of the utterance and the propositional attitude expressed, all the explicatures of the utterance can be inferred. For the time being, we will continue to look only at ordinary assertions, where the propositional form is itself an explicature, and indeed the explicature on which most of the contextual effects of the utterance, and therefore most of its relevance, depend. In this section, we will show how the principle of relevance guides the recovery of implicatures. We will argue that the implicatures of an utterance are recovered by reference to the speaker's manifest expectations about how her utterance should achieve optimal relevance.

A speaker may have reason to believe that certain information would be relevant to her hearer, without having the faintest idea what its relevance will be. A passer-by asks you the time; you know it is 5 p.m. The fact that he has asked this question gives you reason to believe that the information that it is 5 p.m. will be relevant to him. However, you have no way of knowing how it will be relevant: in what context it will be processed and what its contextual effects will be. Intuitively, in this situation, the simple answer that it is 5 p.m. will carry no implicatures at all. Your informative intention in giving this answer would merely be to make manifest that it is 5 p.m. This is the first inferable interpretation consistent with the principle of relevance.

Contrast this with a case where the speaker does have manifest expectations about how her utterance will be relevant:

(33) (a) *Peter*: Would you drive a Mercedes?
     (b) *Mary*: I wouldn't drive ANY expensive car.

We assume that (33b) is an ordinary assertion, and hence that its main explicature, the only one we will be concerned with, is simply its propositional form. The propositional form of (33b) does not directly answer the question in (33a). However, it gives Peter immediate access to his encyclopaedic information about expensive cars, which includes, let us suppose, the information in (34):

(34) A Mercedes is an expensive car.

If processed in a context containing assumption (34), (33b) would yield the contextual implication (35):

(35) Mary wouldn't drive a Mercedes.

This should, in turn, have an acceptable range of contextual effects in a context which Peter, by asking whether Mary would drive a Mercedes, has indicated that he has accessible.

We have a situation, then, in which Mary, in producing (33b), has not directly – i.e. explicitly – answered Peter's question, but has made manifest a contextually implied answer. Given that, in normal circumstances, she could not expect her utterance to be relevant unless it made manifest such an answer, it is mutually manifest that this implied answer is intentional: it is an implicature of her utterance. An implicature is a contextual assumption or implication which a speaker, intending her utterance to be manifestly relevant, manifestly intended to make manifest to the hearer. We will distinguish two kinds of implicatures: *implicated premises* and *implicated conclusions*. (34) is an implicated premise of (33b), and (35) an implicated conclusion. All implicatures, we claim, fall into one or the other of these two categories.

Implicated premises must be supplied by the hearer, who must either retrieve them from memory or construct them by developing assumption schemas retrieved from memory. What makes it possible to identify such premises as implicatures is that they lead to an interpretation consistent with the principle of relevance, and that they are manifestly the most easily accessible premises to do so. Implicated conclusions are deduced from the explicatures of the utterance and the context. What makes it possible to identify such conclusions as implicatures is that the speaker must have expected the hearer to derive them, or some of them, given that she intended her utterance to be manifestly relevant to the hearer. Thus, implicated premises and conclusions are both identifiable as parts of the first inferable interpretation consistent with the principle of relevance.

Implicatures (34) and (35) have two properties which many pragmatists think of as shared by all – or at least all theoretically interesting – implicatures. In the first place, they are fully determinate. Mary expects Peter to supply not merely something *like* premise (34) and conclusion (35), but a premise and conclusion with just this logical content. Second, Mary is entirely responsible for their truth. Suppose that before (33b) was produced, Peter had mistakenly thought that Mercedes cars were cheap; then (33b) would provide as much disconfirmation of this assumption as if Mary had explicitly asserted that a Mercedes was an expensive car. Or suppose Peter had merely suspected that Mercedes cars were expensive; then (33b) would strengthen this assumption as much as if Mary had explicitly asserted that a Mercedes was an expensive car. In other words, Mary is just as responsible for the truth of (34) and (35) as if she had asserted them directly.

There has been a tendency in modern pragmatics to treat all implicatures along these lines: as fully determinate assumptions for which the speaker is just as much responsible as if she had asserted them directly. On this approach, utterance comprehension consists in the recovery of an enumerable set of assumptions, some explicitly expressed, others implicitly conveyed, but all individually intended by the speaker.

Grice himself does not regard implicatures as determinate:

> Since, to calculate a conversational implicature is to calculate what has to be supposed in order to preserve the supposition that the Cooperative Principle has been observed, and since there may be various possible specific explanations, a list of which may be open, the conversational implicatum in such cases will be a disjunction of

such specific explanations; and if the list of these is open, the implicatum will have just the kind of indeterminacy that many actual implicata do in fact seem to possess. (Grice 1975: 58)

Other pragmatists,[9] while recognising the existence of indeterminacy, have tended to exclude it from consideration. Thus, Gazdar comments:

> because indeterminacy is hard to handle formally, I shall mostly ignore it in the discussion that follows. A fuller treatment of implicature would not be guilty of this omission, which is only really defensible on formal grounds. (Gazdar 1979: 40)

The proposal to ignore indeterminacy might be seen as a legitimate idealisation, a simplifying assumption of the kind which would pass unquestioned in other domains of scientific inquiry and should need no justification here. It is reasonable, the argument goes, to look first not at the complex, fuzzy reality which we know exists, but at an idealisation from which the fuzziness has been eliminated, and which is amenable to formal treatment. If the implicatures of an utterance are treated as a determinate set of intended inferences, an explicit theoretical model can be set up, which can later be filled out in various ways to account for the fuzziness of the full range of data.

However, not every idealisation is legitimate. An idealisation is not legitimate if, in simplifying the data, it introduces some significant distortion which puts theoretical work on the wrong track. An example of such an illegitimate idealisation is the reduction of a language by pre-Chomskyan linguists to a finite corpus of utterances. We will argue that by concentrating on fully determinate implicatures such as (34) and (35) above, modern pragmatists have obscured an important difference between explicit content and implicit import. As a result, they have perpetuated a mistaken semiotic view of communication and in particular have deprived themselves of the ability to provide an adequate analysis of stylistic and poetic effects.

Notice that although, in producing (33b) above, Mary manifestly expects Peter to derive the conclusion in (35) and all the implications of (35) he might be interested in, if this is *all* she expects, she cannot assume that her utterance is optimally relevant. If the entire relevance of (33b) depends on the recovery of (35), Mary could have spared Peter some unnecessary processing effort by saying (36) instead:

(36) I wouldn't drive a Mercedes.

It follows from the principle of relevance that in giving the indirect answer in (33b), she must have expected to achieve some additional contextual effects not obtainable from (36), which would offset the additional effort needed to process (33b), supply premise (34) and deduce (35) as an implicated conclusion. More generally, it follows from the principle of relevance that the surplus of information given in an indirect answer must achieve some relevance in its own right.

It does not follow, though, that there is any specific implicature, apart from (34) and (35), which Mary must have expected Peter to recover. An act of communication merely makes manifest which assumptions the communicator intends to make manifest, or, equivalently, it merely makes these assumptions manifest on the further assumption that the communicator is trustworthy. It does not necessarily make the audience actually entertain all the assumptions communicated. This is true of implicatures too. Implicatures are merely made manifest by the act of communication (again, on the further assumption that the speaker is trustworthy). Some implicatures are made so strongly manifest that the hearer can scarcely avoid recovering them. Others are made less strongly manifest. It is enough that the hearer should pay attention to some of these weaker implicatures for the relevance of the intended interpretation to become manifest.

As we have seen, utterance (33b) gives Peter access to his encyclopaedic information about expensive cars. One obvious line of interpretation would be to retrieve the names of other expensive cars, and derive the conclusion that Mary would not drive them. It is a stereotypical – and hence highly accessible – item of general knowledge that a Rolls Royce and a Cadillac are expensive cars. Hence it would be reasonable for Peter to add premises (37) and (38) to the context, derive conclusions (39) and (40), and investigate their contextual effects:

(37) A Rolls Royce is an expensive car.
(38) A Cadillac is an expensive car.
(39) Mary wouldn't drive a Rolls Royce.
(40) Mary wouldn't drive a Cadillac.

Or he could construct some premise such as (41), which is plausible enough in their mutual cognitive environment, derive conclusion (42) and investigate the contextual effects of this conclusion:

(41) People who refuse to drive expensive cars disapprove of displays of wealth.
(42) Mary disapproves of displays of wealth.

The indirect answer in (33b) thus opens up a number of possibilities of interpretation not available for its direct counterpart (36). Given the principle of relevance, Mary must have expected some of these possibilities to be fruitful enough to offset the extra processing costs incurred.

Are (37)–(42) implicatures of (33b)? Not under the idealisation described above. In the first place, Mary need not have specifically intended Peter to supply premises (37), (38) and (41) and derive conclusions (39), (40) and (42). (33b) has a number of different contextual implications in an appropriately extended context, any of which might yield enough contextual effects to offset the extra processing effort involved. In the second place, precisely because different subsets of implicated premises and conclusions might be used to establish the optimal relevance of the intended interpretation, none of them need have been specifically intended by Mary. Mary's mutually manifest intention is merely to make manifest some such assumptions. Hence she does not make any of these assumptions more than weakly manifest. She does not guarantee their truth as strongly as she guarantees the truth of (34) and (35). Thus, whereas by producing (33b) Mary provides conclusive evidence that she regards a Mercedes as an expensive car and would refuse to drive in one, she provides rather less than conclusive evidence that she would refuse to drive in a Rolls Royce.

On the other hand, it would be nonsense to say that by producing (33b) Mary has not encouraged Peter to think she would refuse to drive in a Rolls Royce. Short of explicitly asserting it, or of actually forcing him to supply it as an implicature, what clearer encouragement could she have given him than (33b)? Although (39), (40) and (42) cannot be forced into the mould of fully determinate, specifically intended inferences, it would be clearly wrong to regard them as entirely unintended, as derived on Peter's sole responsibility. As we have seen, Mary would not have been justified in communicating her presumption of relevance if she had not expected some of these implicatures to be derived – if she had not intended, therefore, to make all of them weakly manifest.

Let us pursue this line of argument by considering some other premises and conclusions that Peter might be tempted to supply in processing the indirect answer (33b). In an ordinary modern cognitive environment, it is manifest that if Mary regards a Mercedes as expensive she will also regard a Rolls Royce and a Cadillac as expensive, and hence that (37)–(40) are fair reflections of her views. It is also manifest that she will regard as expensive any other car which costs as much as or more than a Mercedes. But which are these? Relatively safe premises and conclusions such as (37)–(42) shade off into those, such as (43)–(46), with rather greater risks attached:

(43) An Alfa Romeo is an expensive car.
(44) A BMW is an expensive car.
(45) Mary wouldn't drive an Alfa Romeo.
(46) Mary wouldn't drive a BMW.

Are these implicatures of (33b)? While in no way forcing Peter to investigate these possibilities, Mary has certainly given him some encouragement to think along these lines, although the conclusions derived must be treated with rather more caution than either the fully determinate implicatures (34) and (35) or the strongly invited inferences (37)–(42).

Imagine now that Peter believes (47) and finds it worth his effort to derive (48) as a contextual implication from (47) and the explicature of (33b):

(47) People who would not drive an expensive car would not go on a cruise either.
(48) Mary would not go on a cruise.

It is very doubtful that Mary has given Peter any encouragement to supply the premise in (47) and derive the conclusion in (48). What examples (33)–(48) show is that there may be no cut-off point between assumptions strongly backed by the speaker, and assumptions derived from the utterance but on the hearer's sole responsibility. The fiction that there is a clear-cut distinction between wholly determinate, specifically intended inferences and indeterminate, wholly unintended inferences cannot be maintained. Relevance theory offers a way of getting rid of this fiction without sacrificing clarity of conceptual framework.

Let us say that the implicatures of an utterance – like assumptions in general – may vary in their strength. To communicate an assumption A is to make mutually manifest one's intention to make A manifest or more manifest. The greater the mutual manifestness of the informative intention to make manifest some particular assumption, the more strongly this assumption is communicated. The strongest possible implicatures are those fully determinate premises or conclusions, such as (34) and (35), which must actually be supplied if the interpretation is to be consistent with the principle of relevance, and for which the speaker takes full responsibility. Strong implicatures are those premises and conclusions, such as (37)–(42), which the hearer is strongly encouraged but not actually forced to supply. The weaker the encouragement, and the wider the range of possibilities among which the hearer can choose, the weaker the implicatures. Eventually, as was illustrated with (47)–(48), a point is reached at which the hearer receives no encouragement at all to supply any particular premise and conclusion, and he takes the entire responsibility for supplying them himself.

On this approach, the indeterminacy of implicatures presents no particular formal problem. An utterance with a fully determinate implicated premise or conclusion forces the hearer to supply just this premise or conclusion and attribute it to the speaker as part of her beliefs. An utterance with a small range of strongly implicated premises or conclusions strongly encourages the hearer to use some subset of these premises or conclusions, and to regard some subset of them – not necessarily the same subset – as part of the speaker's beliefs. An utterance with a wide range of weakly implicated premises or conclusions again encourages the hearer to use some subset of these assumptions, and to regard some subset of them – again not necessarily the same – as part of the speaker's beliefs. Clearly, the weaker the implicatures, the less confidence the hearer can have that the particular premises or conclusions he supplies will reflect the speaker's thoughts, and this is where the indeterminacy lies. However, people may entertain different thoughts and come to have different beliefs on the basis of the same cognitive environment. The aim of communication in general is to increase the mutuality of cognitive environments rather than guarantee an impossible duplication of thoughts.

To conclude this section, we want to contrast our approach with other approaches to implicature. First, in our framework, there is no connection between conveying an implicature and violating a pragmatic principle or maxim. Gricean implicatures fall into two classes: those where there is no violation or where the violation is only apparent, and those where the violation is genuine and even the recovery of an implicature does not restore the assumption that the maxims have been observed. For us, this second class of examples must be reanalysed.

In the second place, we have taken seriously Grice's requirement that implicatures should be calculable: that is, recoverable by an inference process. In Grice's framework, and the framework of most pragmatists, some sort of *ex post facto* justification for the identification of an implicature can be given, but the argument could have worked equally well for quite different assumptions which happen not to be implicated at all. This is particularly true of the second class of implicatures, those resulting from deliberate violation of the maxims; they tend to violate the calculability requirement in a particularly blatant way.

Consider Grice's analysis of irony, for example. Mary says (49), and in doing so patently violates the first maxim of quality (truthfulness):

(49) Jim is a fine friend.

Peter, assuming that Mary must have been trying to convey some true information, looks around for some true assumption related to (49), which she might have wanted to convey. He decides that she must have wanted to convey the opposite of what she has said:

(50) Jim is not a fine friend.

Hence, on Grice's analysis a speaker may deliberately violate the maxim of truthfulness and succeed in implicating the opposite of what she has said.

However, 'looking around for some related assumption which the speaker might have wanted to convey' does not count as an inference process: such a process is virtually free of rational constraints. Why, for instance, should Peter not decide that (49) is to be interpreted as conveying the closely related (51), as long as (51) is something that Mary might have wanted to convey?[10]

(51) Bill is a fine friend.

Relevance theory does not sanction the analysis of (49) as meaning (50) – unless (49) is recognisably a slip of the tongue – if only because a speaker who merely wanted to convey (50) could have spared her hearer some unnecessary processing effort by asserting it directly. In section 9 we will propose an alternative account.

The reason why standard accounts of implicature do not always satisfy the calculability requirement on implicatures is that the calculation of implicatures is a matter of non-demonstrative inference. It involves a partly non-logical process of assumption formation; then the assumption has to be confirmed. Standard accounts impose few if any constraints on the formation of assumptions. In practice, they just take what is the intuitively correct assumption and show that it is consistent with Gricean maxims or with some other principles, constraints or rules of the same kind. Intuitively wrong assumptions, such as the assumption that the speaker of (49) means (51) are, alas, just as easy to 'confirm' in this way.

Relevance theory solves this problem by looking not just at the cognitive effects of an assumption, but also at the processing effort it requires. The psychological processes by which assumptions are formed determine their accessibility, which affects their relevance, which affects their plausibility. Different assumptions are thus predicted to differ in plausibility before any confirmation process takes place. When an initially more plausible interpretation is found to be consistent with the principle of relevance, then it is uniquely confirmed, and all less initially plausible interpretations are disconfirmed.

Another important point to have emerged from this section has to do with the scope of pragmatics. The idea that pragmatics should be concerned purely with the recovery of an enumerable set of assumptions, some explicitly expressed, others implicitly conveyed, but all individually intended by the speaker, seems to us to be a mistake. We have argued that there is a continuum of cases, from implicatures which the hearer was specifically intended to recover to implicatures which were merely intended to be made manifest, and to further modifications of the mutual cognitive environment of speaker and hearer that the speaker only intended in the sense that she intended her utterance to be relevant, and hence to have rich and not entirely foreseeable cognitive effects. Pragmatists and semioticians who look only at the strongest forms of implicature have a badly distorted image of verbal communication. They miss, or at least fail to explain, the subtler effects achieved by much implicit communication. We will return to the role of weak implicatures when we discuss style and tropes in sections 6 to 9. But first we want to consider some of the ways in which linguistic form affects pragmatic interpretation.

5 Propositional form and style: presuppositional effects

A speaker who intends to produce a relevant utterance has two related aims: first, to create some contextual effect in the hearer, and second, to minimise the processing effort this involves. It might seem that two utterances with the same linguistically determined truth conditions must have identical contextual effects. We will show that, on the contrary, they may differ both in their contextual effects and in the processing effort they require, and that this is the key to an explanatory theory of style.

In this section we will look at a range of stylistic effects essentially determined by the linguistic structure of the utterance and achieved in the very process of identifying its propositional form. Since, as before, we are looking only at ordinary assertions, this propositional form is also the main explicature of the utterance. These stylistic effects have been approached in terms of various distinctions: between topic and comment, given and new, theme and rheme, presupposition and focus, presupposition and assertion, and so on, and are illustrated by the following sets of examples:[11]

(52)(a) Bill's twin sister lives in BERLIN.
    (b) Bill has a twin sister who lives in BERLIN.
(53)(a) It rained on MONDAY.
    (b) On Monday it RAINED.
    (c) On MONDAY it rained.
(54)(a) John-Paul the Second is the present POPE.
    (b) The present Pope is John-Paul the SECOND.
    (c) It is John-Paul the SECOND who is the present Pope.

In (52a), the information that Bill has a twin sister is presupposed, or treated as given; in (52b), it is asserted, or treated as new. (53a)–(53c) illustrate a variety of effects obtainable by stress placement and word-order change: thus (53a) or (53c), unlike (53b), would be an appropriate answer to the question 'When did it rain?', whereas (53b), unlike (53a) or (53c), would be an appropriate answer to the question 'What was the weather like on Monday?' In (54a) the topic is intuitively John-Paul the Second, whereas in (54b) and (54c) it is the present Pope.

There is huge descriptive literature in this area, but nothing approaching an explanatory theory of the relation between linguistic structure and pragmatic effects.[12] There are, however, a number of scattered insights which seem to us worth pursuing. One is that it is natural for given information (i.e. information the speaker is treating as known or uncontroversial) to come before new and for focal stress to fall towards the end of the utterance, since this in some way facilitates comprehension. This is to a certain extent common sense, but it is not always true that given information comes before new: new information comes before given in our examples (53c) and (54c) above, and Green (1980) surveys a wide range of falsifying examples. The problem is to produce a theory that accommodates both the 'natural' and the 'marked' examples.

Another idea is that stress is a sort of vocal equivalent of pointing, a natural means of drawing attention to one particular constituent in an utterance. The parallel is reinforced by the fact that stress, like pointing, is inherently ambivalent. In (55), for example, the stressed noun 'FOOT-BALL' is part of the noun phrase 'the football match', the verb phrases 'to see the football match' and 'went off to see the football match', and the sentence 'Susan went off to see the football match':

(55) Susan went off to see the FOOTBALL match.

As is well known, a speaker who puts focal stress on 'football' may be intending to highlight any one of these more inclusive syntactic constituents. Let us call the smallest stressed constituent, in this example the noun 'football', the *focally stressed constituent*, and the constituent that it is used to highlight the *focus*. Then the focally stressed constituent rarely determines a unique focus, and the problem is to show how an actual focus is chosen from a range of potential foci.

A third idea is that the way to find the focus of a declarative utterance is to see what Wh–question it was designed or could be appropriately used to answer. For example, (55) can be interpreted as an answer to a series of related questions, each the result of substituting an appropriate Wh-phrase for one of its possible foci: 'Which match did Susan go off to see?', 'What did Susan go off to see?', 'What did Susan go off to do?', 'What did Susan do?', and 'What happened?' Each possible focus determines a Wh–question, and *vice versa*. Although this intuitive observation is made by virtually everyone working in the area, the problem is to provide some satisfactory explanation of why it should be so.

Finally, it is often suggested that instead of binary distinctions between given and new, focus and presupposition and so on, what is really involved is a gradient or hierarchical structure. Suppose that the focus of (55) above is the verb phrase 'to see a FOOTBALL match', so that all the information carried by this verb phrase is highlighted. Nonetheless it is intuitively clear that it is not all equally highlighted: that the information carried by the word 'football' is more prominent than the information carried by the word 'see'. It is as if the focus consisted of a nested series of foci with varying degrees of prominence, the smallest focus being the most prominent of all. Again, the intuitions are clear, although it is less clear how they should be incorporated into an explicit theory.

What gives these observations explanatory value is the idea that the syntactic and phonological organisation of an utterance may directly affect the way it is processed and understood. What is puzzling is that having seen the possibility of a natural linkage between linguistic form and pragmatic interpretation, so many authors feel the need to interpose intermediate levels of semantic and pragmatic description to link artificially what, if these insights are correct, is already naturally linked. We would like to pursue the idea of a natural linkage between linguistic form and pragmatic interpretation, and show how it might be worked out within the framework of relevance theory.

Consider first what in our framework would be the most uneconomical way of processing an utterance. If processing costs were no object, the hearer could explore all possible parsings, disambiguations, illocutionary forces, reference assignments and enrichments. He could take each resulting explicature, extend the immediate context by adding to it the encyclopaedic entries of all the concepts appearing in the explicature, and systematically explore its contextual effects in that context. He could, moreover, derive all the analytic implications of the explicatures, add to the context the encyclopaedic entries of all their constituent concepts, explore the resulting set of contextual implications, and so on indefinitely. This method of processing would guarantee that no conceivable interpretation would be overlooked, no possible context left unexplored, and no possible contextual effect left underived. Clearly, however, it would also involve a lot of fruitless processing.

Notice, though, that because an utterance is produced and processed over time, the hearer will be in a position to access some of its constituent concepts, with their associated logical and encyclopaedic entries, before others. For a speaker aiming at optimal relevance, efficient exploitation of this temporal sequencing will be crucial. Here we will show briefly how it might help to hold down the costs of disambiguation and reference assignment.

The sooner disambiguation and reference assignment are achieved, the less processing effort will be required. The greater the number of possible interpretations that have to be borne in mind as the utterance proceeds, the greater the processing effort. It follows that a speaker aiming at optimal relevance should phrase her utterance so as to facilitate early – and correct – disambiguation. How might this be achieved?

Much recent work on parsing suggests that parsing is to some extent a 'top-down' process: that the hearer constructs anticipatory hypotheses about the overall structure of the utterance on the basis of what he has already heard.[13] For example, he might not only identify each word and tentatively assign it to a syntactic category, but use his knowledge of its lexical properties and syntactic co-occurrence restrictions to predict the syntactic categories of following words or phrases.

The experimental literature on disambiguation suggests that disambiguation and reference assignment are also to some extent 'top-down' processes: that the hearer makes anticipatory hypotheses about the overall logical structure of the utterance and resolves potential ambiguities and ambivalences on the basis of these.[14] We want to suggest a way of constructing anticipatory logical hypotheses on the basis of the anticipatory syntactic hypotheses whose role in comprehension seems fairly well established.

Let us assume that logical forms, like syntactic forms, are trees of labelled nodes (or, equivalently, labelled bracketings). The syntactic labels are the categories N, NP, V, VP, and so on, where N might be regarded as a variable over nouns, NP as a variable over noun phrases, V as a variable over verbs, VP as a variable over verb phrases, and so on. By parallel arguments, the logical labels should be a set of basic logical categories, perhaps from a fixed range which is part of basic human mental equipment, which might be regarded as variables over conceptual representations of different types. We will use the pro-forms of English to represent them: thus *someone* is a variable over conceptual representations of people, *something* over conceptual representations of things, *do something* over conceptual representations of actions, and so on.

To give the simplest possible illustration, sentence (56) has the underlying tree structure (57), and its logical form has the structure (58):

(56) John invited Lucy

(57)

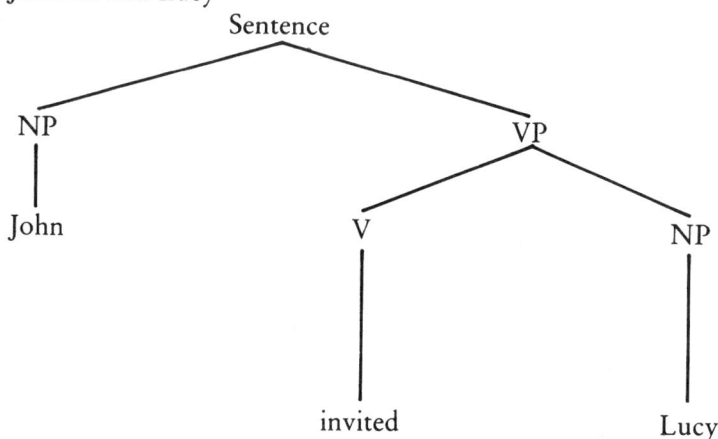

(58)   something is the case

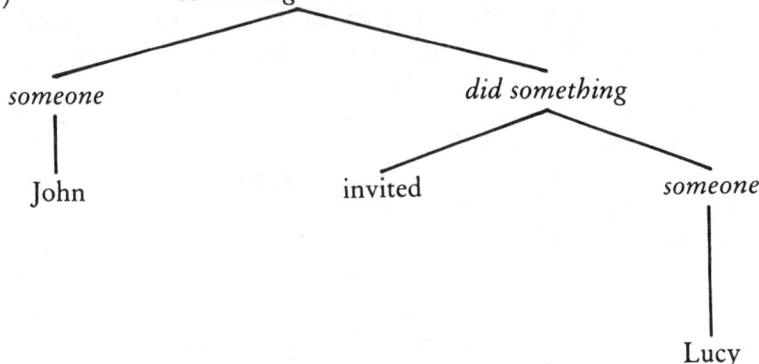

someone   *did something*

John   invited   *someone*

Lucy

A propositional representation of the fact that John invited Lucy would then carry, via the labels on the nodes of its tree structure, the information that someone invited someone, that someone invited Lucy, that John invited someone, that John did something, and so on.

On this approach, there is a clear sense in which the logical category labels correspond to, and are indeed semantic interpretations of, syntactic category labels of natural language (though there need not be a one–one correspondence). As a result, a hearer who has made the anticipatory syntactic hypothesis that, say, the words 'John invited' will be followed by an *NP*, can by semantically interpreting this anticipatory syntactic hypothesis derive the anticipatory logical hypothesis that John invited someone. We see such hypotheses as playing a crucial role in disambiguation and reference assignment.

Let us assume that when he hears the word 'Jennifer' in (59), the hearer accesses a range of possible referents for 'Jennifer' – that is, a set of conceptual addresses with the word 'Jennifer' as part of their lexical entry – and gains access in turn to a range of associated encylopaedic entries:

(59) Jennifer admitted STEALING.

On assigning 'Jennifer' to the syntactic category *NP*, he makes the anticipatory syntactic hypothesis that it will be followed by a *VP*, which yields by variable-substitution the anticipatory logical hypothesis (60):

(60) Jennifer did something.

Let us assume that he knows a Jennifer Smith and a Jennifer O'Hara. Our hypothesis is that he now proceeds to make a tentative assignment of reference to the expression 'Jennifer' by considering whether the information that Jennifer Smith did something or the information that Jennifer O'Hara did something might be relevant to him in some context he currently has accessible.

Suppose, for example, that he has accessible a context in which the information that Jennifer O'Hara did something would be manifestly relevant to him. Then by an argument that should by now be familiar, he should assume that when the speaker said 'Jennifer' she was intending to refer to Jennifer O'Hara. Otherwise she should have rephrased her utterance to eliminate this interpretation. Moreover, he should assume that the context in which he finds relevant the information that Jennifer O'Hara did something will play a further role in the comprehension process: otherwise the effort of accessing it will be wasted.

At this early stage there may be no obvious assignment of reference which would make (60) relevant at all. Nonetheless, on some assignment of reference it may raise a relevant question in the hearer's mind (where a relevant question is a question the answer to which is certain or likely to be relevant). A statement often raises a relevant question. For example, if I tell you that I am unhappy, I will almost certainly make you wonder why. By the same token, there may be some assignment of reference on which (60), while not relevant itself, might raise a question such as (61a) or (61b) which is relevant in some context currently accessible to the hearer:

(61) (a) What did Jennifer Smith do?
     (b) What did Jennifer O'Hara do?

If so, then by a now familiar argument he should assume that this is a question the speaker intended to raise, that the rest of the utterance will answer it, and that the answer will be relevant in the context he has just been encouraged to access.

Let us assume, then, that a reference has been tentatively assigned to the expression 'Jennifer'. The next word to be processed is the verb 'admitted': this has two possible senses, *confess to* and *let in*, on both of which it is transitive. The hearer can thus make the anticipatory syntactic hypothesis that it will be followed by an *NP* and obtain, by variable-substitution, the anticipatory logical hypotheses (62a–b):

(62) (a) Jennifer let someone in.
     (b) Jennifer confessed to something.

The hearer, who now has access to the encyclopaedic entries for *let in* and *confess to*, can proceed to disambiguate the verb 'admit' by asking himself whether one of (62a–b), or one of the related questions (63a–b), is manifestly relevant in some context which he currently has accessible:

(63) (a) Who did Jennifer let in?
     (b) What did Jennifer confess to?

If so, then he should provisionally accept that interpretation and retain the context for further processing.

Finally, if the speaker has achieved optimal relevance, the word 'stealing' should fall into a place already prepared for it during the interpretation process. That is, it should answer any questions that have been raised but left unanswered, and the answers should be relevant in a context that the interpretation process has helped to prepare. For example, if the hearer has accessed a context in which the question 'What did Jennifer confess to?' would be relevant to him on some assignment of reference to the expression 'Jennifer', then the utterance as a whole should be interpretable as an answer to that question on that assignment of reference.

If the speaker has done her job properly, the end of the utterance should confirm all the provisional choices of content and context that have been made along the route. On the other hand, if the end of the utterance does not confirm these provisional choices, then identification of the speaker's informative intention will involve an extra layer of inference in an otherwise unchanged inference pattern. When communication is unproblematic, the hearer just takes for granted that the speaker has an adequate appreciation of what would be relevant to him; when problems arise, the hearer should try to find out under what mistaken image of him the speaker could have thought that her utterance would be optimally relevant.

Notice now that the correct anticipatory hypotheses, the ones that will eventually be confirmed, are logically related to one another. In any pair of such hypotheses, one is necessarily implied by the other. More precisely, the set of anticipatory hypotheses forms a scale, in which each member analytically implies the immediately preceding member and is analytically implied by the immediately succeeding member. For (59), on the interpretation we have just been discussing, the appropriate scale has the three members (64a–c):

(64)(a) Jennifer did something/
         What did Jennifer do?
    (b) Jennifer confessed to something/
         What did Jennifer confess to?
    (c) Jennifer confessed to stealing.

Of these, the most general, (64a), will be recovered first, and as we have seen, if the speaker has achieved optimal relevance, it should either be relevant in its own right or raise a relevant question; the next to be recovered will be (64b), which should either give a relevant answer to a question raised by (64a) or raise a relevant question itself. Finally, (64c) should give a relevant answer to the question raised by (64b), and might itself raise the further question 'Why did Jennifer confess to stealing?', thus preparing the ground for a subsequent utterance. The scale in (64) thus acts as a skeleton around which the whole interpretation is built.

The scale in (64) contains a subset of the analytic implications of (59). This subset is strictly ordered by the relation of analytic implication, as described above. Moreover, given that focal stress in (59) falls on the last word, 'stealing', this subset is related to the set of possible foci of the utterance in an obvious way: take the propositional form of the utterance, replace the focus by its logical label, and you get an implication in the scale; all the implications in the scale, except the propositional form itself, can be obtained in this way. Let us call such a strictly ordered subset of analytic implications, determined by the placement of focal stress, a *focal scale*. When focal stress falls on the last word of an utterance, as it does in (59), the set of anticipatory logical hypotheses made during the interpretation process coincides with the focal scale.

As we have shown, implications in the focal scale of an utterance are not all processed at once. The processing of each implication can contribute to the overall relevance of the utterance in two ways: either by reducing the effort needed to process it, or by increasing its contextual effects. Even if it has no contextual effect in its own right, an implication can contribute to relevance by giving direct access to a context in which effects can be achieved, and thus reducing the processing effort needed to achieve these effects. As for the contextual effects of an utterance, they may be obtained in several steps, via different implications in the focal scale.

Let us say that when an implication in the focal scale of an utterance has contextual effects of its own, and hence is relevant in its own right, it is a *foreground implication*, and that otherwise it is a *background implication*. Then the *focus* of an utterance will be the smallest syntactic constituent whose replacement by a variable yields a background rather than a foreground implication. For example, in (59) above the focus could be the *NP* 'stealing', the *VP* 'admitted stealing' or the sentence as a whole. If (64a) is relevant in its own right, it will be a foreground implication and the focus will be the sentence as a whole; if (64a) is not relevant in its own right but (64b) is, then the focus will be the *VP* 'admitted stealing'; and if (64b) is not relevant in its own right, then the focus will be the *NP* 'stealing' itself.

An implication may contribute to relevance in both of the ways described above: by giving access to a context in which further implications will have contextual effects, and by yielding contextual effects in its own right. It is thus quite possible for the speaker not to know or care exactly where the break between foreground and background will come. In processing (59) above, for example, it might well be that if the hearer accessed enough encyclopaedic information about Jennifer's character and inclinations, he might find it relevant that she has confessed to something. But maybe he is not prepared to put in that much effort. This should make little difference to the speaker. As long as she has reason to believe that at least one member of the focal scale will be relevant in its own right, and in a context to which other members give access, she need not care too much about where the cut-off point between foreground and background will come. That is, she need have no specific intention about which of the implications of her utterance are foreground and which background (which are given and which new), contrary to what is normally accepted in the literature.

We can also shed some light on the intuition that there is a gradient of given and new information. Wherever the cut-off point between foreground and background comes, there is a clear sense in which (64b), for example, simultaneously acts as a foreground implication in relation to (64a), giving a partial answer to the question it raises, and as a background implication in relation to (64c), raising a question to which (64c) gives at least a partial answer. As we have seen, even (64c), which is necessarily a foreground implication, may simultaneously raise a background question which some subsequent utterance (or a continuation of the same utterance) will answer. Our distinction between foreground and background, like our notion of focus itself, is thus a purely functional one, and should play no role in the linguistic description of sentences.

Different stress assignments induce different focal scales. If the focally stressed constituent were 'Jennifer', the focal scale for (59) would be (65):

(65) (a) Someone confessed to stealing/
        Who confessed to stealing?
     (b) Jennifer confessed to stealing.

If the focally stressed constituent were the verb 'admitted', the focal scale would be (66):

(66) (a) Jennifer did something/
        What did Jennifer do?
     (b) Jennifer did something regarding stealing/
        What did Jennifer do regarding stealing?
     (c) Jennifer confessed to stealing.

(65) and (66) have the same logical properties as (64): each consists of a series of logically related members, each member analytically implying the immediately preceding member and being analytically implied by the immediately following member. Moreover, each is obtainable by the same general procedure: take the full propositional form of the utterance and replace by a logical variable, first the interpretation of the focally stressed constituent, then the interpretation of the next smallest syntactic constituent which contains the focally stressed constituent, and so on until there are no more inclusive constituents to be replaced.

However, there is an important difference between (64) on the one hand and (65) and (66) on the other, linked to the fact that, in the two latter cases, the focal stress is not on the last word of the sentence. As a result, the focal scale, which is determined by stress placement, cannot correspond, at least not entirely, to the scale of anticipatory hypotheses, which is determined by word order. It is hard to see how a speaker could lead her hearer step by step, anticipatory hypothesis by anticipatory hypothesis, up the scales in (65) and (66) in the way illustrated above for (64). For example, unless the hearer already knew how the utterance was going to end, he would be unable to make the anticipatory hypothesis (65a) on presentation of the word 'Jennifer', or the anticipatory hypothesis (66b) on presentation of the word 'admitted'. Though (64)–(66) have similar logical properties and a similar relation to the syntactic structure of (59), in normal circumstances only (64) is recoverable by a step-by-step series of anticipatory hypotheses as the utterance proceeds.

The sense in which it is natural for focal stress to fall at the end of the utterance, and hence for the background to be recovered before the foreground, is the sense in which it is natural to raise a question before answering it or to communicate a complex piece of information step by step. However, departures from this pattern do occur, and these, too, may be consistent with the principle of relevance. For example, when a question has been explicitly or implicitly raised by the immediately preceding utterance, it would be a waste of processing effort to repeat it. Responses to explicit questions can thus be very fragmentary, and in a non-fragmentary response the focus may precede the background, as illustrated by the possible responses (67b–d) to the question in (67a):

(67) (a) *Peter*: Who is the greatest English writer?
 (b) *Mary*: SHAKESPEARE is the greatest English writer.
 (c) *Mary*: SHAKESPEARE is.
 (d) *Mary*: SHAKESPEARE.

Each of these responses has the *NP* 'Shakespeare' as focus and the assumption *Someone is the greatest English writer* as background. Only in (67b) is this assumption made fully explicit, and here it follows the focus, acting merely as a reminder, a confirmation of an interpretation which the hearer should have been able to arrive at unaided.

There has been some discussion about whether the contrast between examples such as (68b) and (69b) can be dealt with in purely pragmatic terms:[15]

(68) (a) I'm sorry I'm late. (b) My CAR broke down.
(69) (a) I'm sorry I'm late. (b) My car was BOOBY-trapped.

The issue is whether in these examples stress has lost its natural highlighting function and become subject to arbitrary linguistic constraints, or whether its position can be seen as following in some interesting way from pragmatic principles. If a pragmatic account is possible, we suggest that it might go as follows.

There is a quite deep-rooted intuition that in initially stressed examples such as (68b), the material following the subject noun phrase is predictable in some sense. The appropriate sense, we believe, is derivable from our notions of weak implicature and weak communication. When the speaker of (68a) apologises for being late, the hearer will naturally expect an explanation. At the mention of the words 'my car' he will automatically make the anticipatory hypothesis that something happened to her car which caused her to be late, and access the appropriate part of his encyclopaedic entry for *car*. There he will find the highly accessible and strongly confirmed assumptions that cars can break down, run out of petrol and fail to start, all of which would reasonably account for the speaker's failure to arrive on time.

Notice that the speaker could weakly implicate this range of excuses without ever expressing it explicitly. Thus if she said, 'I'm sorry I'm late. My damned car!' she would be understood precisely to have invoked one of these predictable excuses. Thus, what follows the initial noun phrase in these examples is already weakly communicated by the mention of the initial noun phrase alone, and the contextual effects on which the main relevance of the utterance depends can be calculated on the basis of the resulting anticipatory hypothesis.

Attempts at explaining the contrast between examples like (68b) and (69b) have rarely gone beyond vague appeals to 'relative semantic weight' or 'relative newsworthiness'. In our framework it is possible to do rather better. To the hearer of (69b), even after he has made the anticipatory hypothesis that the speaker is late because something happened to her car, the information that the car was booby-trapped would still be quite relevant. In other words, the material following the initially unstressed noun phrase in (69b) has significant contextual effects in a context created by the processing of the initial noun phrase, whereas the material following the initially stressed noun phrase in (68b) does not. As a result, the material following the initial noun phrase in (69b) should be focally stressed, whereas the material following the initial noun phrase in (68b) should not. Along these lines, the contrast between examples such as (68) and (69) might be approached without appealing to any *ad hoc* stress assignment rules.

At least in the recent literature on generative grammar, contrastive stress has generally been treated as a non-linguistic or paralinguistic phenomenon, not subject to special phonological constraints. This fits well with the view of stress as a purely natural device for pinpointing some noteworthy aspect of an utterance. At first sight, the fact that contrastive stress works differently in different languages presents problems for this approach. It is used much more freely in English than in French: for example, whereas (70) sounds entirely natural, its French counterpart (71b) could only occur naturally as echoing a preceding utterance such as (71a):

(70) YOU must do the washing up.
(71) (a) *He*: Il faut que vous fassiez la vaisselle.
    (b) *She*: Non, il faut que VOUS fassiez la vaisselle.

However, this is not a particularly compelling objection unless it can be shown that variations in contrastive stress can not be accounted for in processing terms. If the same stress pattern may have a higher processing cost in one language than another, or when realised by one expression rather than another, then a speaker aiming at optimal relevance should use the costlier stress pattern more sparingly.

It seems clear that in a language like French, with its relatively flat intonation contour and strongly preferred final placement of focal stress, the non-final use of contrastive stress will cause a much greater disruption to the intonation contour than in a language like English, with its relatively variable intonation contour and freer placement of focal stress. Greater disruption implies greater processing effort and, other things being equal, lowered acceptability. We would predict, then, that utterance-internal contrastive stress in a language like French would be acceptable only in an echoic exchange such as (71) above, where parallelisms in linguistic form and pragmatic interpretation reduce overall processing effort, and where it offers a particularly economical way of pinpointing an intended range of contextual effects.

We are suggesting, then, that stress placement, like other stylistic features, should be looked at in terms of processing effort. The fact that contrastive stress is a natural highlighting device need not prevent it from being more costly to use in some circumstances than in others, just as pointing, another natural highlighting device, may have greater social costs attached to it in some circumstances than in others.[16] This suggests, then, an interesting approach to cross-linguistic variation in stress patterns, and one that we feel might shed light on a range of non-contrastive data which have been the subject of much interesting recent research.[17]

Returning now to our original hypothesis of a natural linkage between linguistic structure and pragmatic effects, let us show how examples (52)–(54) above would be dealt with in the framework sketched in this section. Consider (52a–b):

(52) (a) Bill's twin sister lives in BERLIN.
    (b) Bill has a twin sister who lives in BERLIN.

These examples are standardly described in terms of a presupposition–assertion distinction: (52a) presupposes what (52b) asserts – namely, that Bill has a twin sister. Two types of intuition are called on to justify the distinction. Suppose that Bill has no twin sister and that the hearer knows it. Then there is one intuition we agree with, which indeed seems hardly controvertible: that (52a) would be perceived as much more seriously defective than (52b). It has been claimed that there is a stronger intuition: that if Bill has no twin sister, then regardless of the hearer's belief about the matter, (52a) does not express a proposition at all. This second intuition we dispute, and since it is in any case marginal to pragmatics we do not propose to discuss it here.[18] The first intuition, however, follows directly from our framework.

Let us assume that both (52a) and (52b) analytically imply (72):

(72) Bill has a twin sister.

Then the two utterances share their truth conditions. However, in (52b), (72) is in the focal scale, which in this case corresponds to the scale of anticipatory hypotheses. It acts as a development of the preceding hypothesis, 'Bill has something', or, equivalently, as an answer to the question, 'What does Bill have?'; and it is at least part of a relevant answer to this presumably relevant question. If the only contribution of the information that Bill has a twin sister were to make immediately accessible an existing conceptual address for this twin sister, then the more economical (52a) should be preferred. In (52a), (72) is not an implication in the focal scale, and, correlatively, it does not answer any suggested question. In fact, the first relevant question suggested by the focal scale of (52a) is 'What does Bill's twin sister do?' When should a speaker aiming at optimal relevance prefer (52b) to (52a)? When the information that Bill has a twin sister is relevant enough in its own right. Hence a speaker who regards the assumption that Bill has a twin sister as neither manifest, nor manifestly plausible to the hearer, should choose (52b), and a hearer who rejects this assumption would regard (52a) as much more seriously defective than (52b).

As Strawson (1964b) has noted, there is also a subtler range of intuitions having to do with the presuppositional effects of referential expressions in different syntactic positions. Thus, compare (73a) and (73b):

(73) (a) The King of France visited the EXHIBITION.
      (b) The exhibition was visited by the King of FRANCE.

According to Strawson, if there was an identifiable exhibition but no identifiable King of France, (73b) would succeed in making an assertion, though a mistaken one, whereas (73a) would make no assertion at all. In our framework, these intuitions are predictable in terms of the distinction between foreground and background implications. The strongest presuppositional effects are carried by analytic implications of background implications. Thus, if the focus in (73a) is 'the Exhibition', or 'visited the Exhibition', and the background is *The King of France did something*, or *The King of France visited something*, the information that there is a King of France will be analytically implied by the background, and a hearer who rejects it will be unable to access a context in which the utterance would be relevant at all. By contrast, if the focus in (73b) is 'the King of France', or 'was visited by the King of France', and the background is *The Exhibition had some property*, or *The Exhibition was visited by someone*, then at least the hearer will be able to access the appropriate context and see what sort of contextual effects the speaker must have had in mind. Hence the intuition that in this case the consequences of reference failure are less dramatic.

Turning to examples (53a–c), triples of this type are often seen as showing the need for two separate distinctions, one based on left–right word order and the other on intonational prominence:

(53)(a) It rained on MONDAY.
  (b) On Monday it RAINED.
  (c) On MONDAY it rained.

Thus Halliday (1967–8) distinguishes thematic or textual structure, based on left–right word order, from informational structure, based on intonational prominence. He defines the theme as the leftmost syntactic constituent in the sentence and the rheme as everything that follows. The theme–rheme distinction, like the focus–presupposition distinction, is often seen as genuinely linguistic: thus Brown and Yule (1983: 133) claim that 'theme is a formal category in the analysis of sentences'. In our framework the differences between (53a), (53b) and (53c) can be accounted for without introducing theme as a formal category at all.

We have seen that (53a) has a range of possible foci: 'Monday', 'on Monday' and the sentence as a whole. It is thus construable as an answer to the questions, 'On what day did it rain?', 'When did it rain?' and 'What happened?' The effect of (53b) and (53c) is to modify this range of possible interpretations. By the time the hearer of (53b) has processed the words 'On Monday', he knows that there is some question about what happened on Monday which the speaker thinks is relevant to him. In other words, the effect of fronting the unstressed constituent 'On Monday' is to force it into the background. By the same token, by the time the hearer of (53c) has processed the words 'On Monday', he should know that they give the answer to some question which he should at this point be able to access for himself. In other words, the effect of fronting the stressed constituent 'On Monday' is to select it as focus. Sentences such as (53b) and (53c) may involve slightly greater processing costs than (53a); if so, this would be the price paid for fixing an adverbial expression in the background while retaining utterance-final stress, or of pinpointing the focus more precisely than its normal syntactic position would permit. However, the special effects of such structures arise simply from the interaction between syntax, stress assignment and the principle of relevance. While the theme–rheme distinction may be a valuable way of highlighting intuitions, it has no place in the technical descriptive vocabulary of either linguistics or pragmatics.

The classic paper on the topic–comment distinction is Reinhart (1981). She defines the 'sentence topic' as a syntactic constituent, explicitly present in the sentence, whose referent the sentence is about; many authors also appeal to a vaguer notion of 'discourse topic'. In general, sentence topics will be both unstressed and early in the word order. Thus in (54a) the sentence topic is John-Paul the Second, in (54b) it is the present Pope:

(54)(a) John-Paul the Second is the present POPE.
    (b) The present Pope is John-Paul the SECOND.
    (c) It is John-Paul the SECOND who is the present Pope.

As regards the pragmatic role of topics, there is a general agreement that their function is to provide access to what in our terms would be contextual information crucial to the comprehension process. Thus the classic discourse topics are titles and picture captions, whose role is precisely to give access to encyclopaedic information crucial to the comprehension of the accompanying texts or pictures; by the same token, sentence topics are generally unstressed syntactic constituents occurring early in the utterance, whose function in our framework is to give access to encyclopaedic information which the speaker regards as crucial to the interpretation process.

One reason for looking seriously at the literature on topics is that it is often claimed that the most basic notion of relevance, the one it is most important to define, is that of relevance to a topic. Thus Brown and Yule (1983:68) comment that though the notion of topic is 'very difficult to pin down' it is nonetheless 'essential to concepts such as relevance and coherence'. Given the role of topics in providing access to contexts, these comments are not too surprising. To the extent that an utterance is relevant (in our sense) in a homogeneous context derivable from a single encyclopaedic entry, it will be topic relevant (in a derivative sense), the topic being simply the conceptual address associated with that encyclo-paedic entry. However, in our framework an utterance may also be relevant in a non-homogeneous context – that is, a context derived from a variety of encyclopaedic and environmental sources – in which it should be hard to elicit systematic judgements about its topic relevance. Topic-relevant utterances are only a subset of relevant utterances, and it is the notion of topic relevance which is derivative.[19]

As regards the given–new and focus–presupposition distinctions, we have little to add to what has already been said. In our framework, background information is information that contributes only indirectly to relevance, by reducing the processing effort required; it need be neither given nor presupposed. Foreground information is information that is relevant in its own right by having contextual effects; it need not be new.[20] However, the fundamental difference between our foreground–background distinction and the given–new and focus–presupposition distinctions is in their theoretical status. The given–new and focus–presupposition distinctions are typically regarded as part of the basic machinery of linguistic and/or pragmatic theory. Our foreground–background distinction, by contrast, has no role at all to play in linguistic theory, and in pragmatics it is simply a descriptive label used to distinguish two complementary and independently necessary aspects of the interpretation process. We do not assume, that is, that competent speakers have to have, either built into their grammar or built into their inferential abilities, any notion of background and foreground. Backgrounding and foregrounding arise as automatic effects of the hearer's tendency to maximise relevance, and of the speaker's exploitation of that tendency.

The main argument of this section has been as follows. Given that utterances have constituent structure, internal order and focal stress, and given that they are processed over time, the most cost-efficient way of exploiting these structural features will give rise to a variety of pragmatic effects. There is a natural linkage between linguistic structure and pragmatic interpretation, and no need for any special pragmatic conventions or interpretation rules: the speaker merely adapts her utterance to the way the hearer is going to process it anyhow, given the existing structural and temporal constraints.[21]

6 Implicatures and style: poetic effects

It is sometimes said that style is the man. We would rather say that style is the relationship. From the style of a communication it is possible to infer such things as what the speaker takes to be the hearer's cognitive capacities and level of attention, how much help or guidance she is prepared to give him in processing her utterance, the degree of complicity between them, their emotional closeness or distance. In other words, a speaker not only aims to enlarge the mutual cognitive environment she shares with the hearer; she also assumes a certain degree of mutuality, which is indicated, and sometimes communicated, by her style.

Choice of style is something that no speaker or writer can avoid. In aiming at relevance, the speaker must make some assumptions about the hearer's cognitive abilities and contextual resources, which will necessarily be reflected in the way she communicates, and in particular in what she chooses to make explicit and what she chooses to leave implicit. Compare (74a–c):

(74) (a) Only amateurs could compete in the Olympics in the past.
  (b) The Olympic Games is an international sporting competition held every four years. Only amateurs could compete in the past.
  (c) The Olympic Games is an international sporting competition held every four years. Only amateurs – that is, people who receive no payment for their sporting activities – could compete in the Olympic Games in the past. Professionals – that is, people who receive some payment for their sporting activities – were not allowed to compete in the Olympic Games in the past.

These utterances differ not so much in their import as in the amount of help they give the hearer in recovering it. What the speaker of (74a) trusts the hearer to know about the Olympics is stated explicitly in (74b) and (74c). What the speaker of (74a) and (74b) trusts the hearer to know about amateur status is stipulated explicitly in (74c). The style of (74c) is heavier than that of (74b), which is itself heavier than that of (74a), and this is due to the difference in reliance on the hearer's ability to recover implicit import.

A speaker aiming at optimal relevance will leave implicit everything her hearer can be trusted to supply with less effort than would be needed to process an explicit prompt. The more information she leaves implicit, the greater the degree of mutual understanding she makes it manifest that she takes to exist between her and her hearer. Of course, if she overestimates this degree of mutual understanding, there is a risk of making her utterance harder or even impossible to understand. It is not always easy to strike the correct balance: even a slight mismatch between speaker's estimate and hearer's abilities may make what was merely intended to be helpful seem patronising or positively offensive to the hearer. What is important, however, is that the speaker must choose *some* form in which to convey her intended message, and that the form she chooses cannot but reveal her assumptions about the hearer's contextual resources and processing abilities. There is no entirely neutral style.

Another dimension along which styles may vary is in the degree to which they constrain or guide the hearer's search for relevance. Compare (75b–d) as answers to question (75a):

(75) (a) *Peter*: Is Jack a good sailor?
(b) *Mary*: Yes, he is.
(c) *Mary*: ALL the English are good sailors.
(d) *Mary*: He's English.

As we saw in section 4, whereas a direct answer leaves the hearer free to process the information offered in whatever way he likes, an indirect answer suggests a particular line of processing in the computation of contextual effects. In saying (75c), for example, Mary not only expects Peter to access and use the assumption that Jack is English and infer that Jack is a good sailor; she also encourages him to speculate on, to derive some additional conclusions from, the assumption that the English are good sailors. In saying (75d), by contrast, she behaves as if the assumption that all the English are good sailors were mutually manifest to her and Peter, and more manifest than the assumption that Jack is English. There could be circumstances in which the main relevance of (75d) came not from the strongly implicated conclusion that Jack is a good sailor, but from the fact that Mary, by treating it as mutually manifest that all the English are good sailors, has made mutually manifest her intention to make manifest that she assumes she shares with Peter a sense of national pride.

Style arises, we maintain, in the pursuit of relevance. The classical figures of speech were defined in terms of formal features which may or may not have the expected stylistic effects. Consider epizeuxis or repetition, for example. The effects of repetition on utterance interpretation are by no means constant. Compare the following:

(76) Here's a red sock, here's a red sock, here's a blue sock.
(77) We went for a long, long walk.
(78) There were houses, houses everywhere.
(79) I shall never, never smoke again.
(80) There's a fox, a fox in the garden.
(81) My childhood days are gone, gone.

In circumstances that are easy to imagine, (76) might convey that there are two red socks; (77) that the speaker went for a very long walk; (78) that there were a great many houses, (79) that the speaker will definitely never smoke again, (80) that the speaker was excited about the fox in the garden; and (81) that she was moved by the disappearance of her childhood days. Thus the 'emphatic' effects of repetition are worked out in different ways for different examples. In particular, they may be reflected in the propositional content of the utterance, as in (76)–(78), in the speaker's degree of commitment to that propositional content, as in (79), or in some other expression of the speaker's attitude, as in (80) and (81).

One way of accounting for this variation would be to set up specific principles of semantic or pragmatic intepretation, so that, for example, the first of two repeated scalar adjectives would be interpreted as meaning *very*, the first of two repeated plural nouns would be interpreted as meaning *many*, and so on. However, in the case of (80), and especially (81), it is hard to think of propositional paraphrases that would adequately capture their import. These utterances as it were exhibit rather than merely describe the speaker's mental or emotional state: they give rise to non-propositional effects which would be lost under paraphrase. Thus the idea of *ad hoc* case-by-case semantic or pragmatic treatment of repetition seems to have little to recommend it.

Another possibility would be to show that the effects of repetition follow from more general psychological principles, perhaps from some universal set of cognitive strategies towards repetitive inputs in nature. On the face of it, though, it is hard to see how two sheep, or a flock of sheep, could be construed as a moving, exciting or emphatic version of a single sheep. Moreover, examples (80) and (81) again present problems for such an approach.

From the point of view of relevance theory, both of these approaches are superfluous, anyhow, since the interpretations of (76)–(81) follow automatically from the principle of relevance. Within our framework, the task of the hearer faced with these utterances is to reconcile the fact that a certain expression has been repeated with the assumption that optimal relevance has been aimed at. Clearly, the extra linguistic processing effort incurred by the repetition must be outweighed by some increase in contextual effects triggered by the repetition itself. The different interpretations of (76)-(81) simply illustrate the different ways in which such an increase can be achieved.

With (76) it would be consistent with the principle of relevance to assume that the two occurrences of 'Here's a red sock' refer to numerically distinct objects: hence (76) is naturally understood as meaning that there are two red socks. With (77) it would be consistent with the principle of relevance to assume that the speaker wanted to indicate that the walk was longer than the hearer would otherwise have thought: in other words, that it was a very long walk. With (78) it would be consistent with the principle of relevance to assume that the speaker wanted to indicate that there were more houses than the hearer would otherwise have thought: in other words, that there were a great many houses. In each of these cases the repetition modifies the propositional form and hence the explicatures of the utterance, and achieves extra contextual effects thereby.

None of these lines of interpretation is available for (79). Here it would be consistent with the principle of relevance to assume that the speaker attaches a higher confirmation value to the assumption expressed than the hearer would otherwise have thought. Realising that her utterance will be sceptically received, she repeats the word 'never', the likely target of the scepticism, to convince the hearer that she means what she says. In other words, 'never, never' is here similar in import to 'definitely never', and reflects the speaker's degree of commitment to the assumption expressed. This strengthens the explicature and all its contextual implications, thereby increasing the contextual effects of the utterance.

With (80) and (81), none of the above interpretations works well. No increase in effect is likely to be achieved either by enriching the propositional form, or by strengthening the implicatures. We want to suggest that in these cases, the repetition should yield an increase in contextual effects by encouraging the hearer to extend the context and thereby add further implicatures. The repetition in (80) cannot be accounted for by assuming that there are several foxes in the garden, or by strengthening the assumption that there is a fox. Instead, the hearer of (80) is being encouraged to dig deeper into his encyclopaedic entry for *fox*, with a guarantee that the extra processing effort will be outweighed by a gain in contextual effects: the fact that there's a fox in the garden is presented as more relevant than the hearer would have spontaneously realised.

Similarly, the repetition in (81) cannot be accounted for by assuming that the speaker's childhood days are longer gone, or more definitely gone, than might otherwise have been assumed, so if the presumption of relevance is to be confirmed, then the repetition of 'gone' must be interpreted as an encouragement to expand the context. There is a difference between (80) and (81), though. Paying attention to the fact that there is a fox in the garden, and making the effort to remember basic facts about foxes, is likely to yield some strong and predictable contextual implications, such as 'The chickens are in danger'. These strong implications are likely to be interpreted as strong implicatures of the utterance. In the case of (81), the extra relevance is more likely to be achieved by a more diversified expansion of the context and by a wider array of weaker implicatures. In other words, the hearer is encouraged to be imaginative and to take a large share of responsibility in imagining what it may be for the speaker to be way past her youth.

Compare the interpretation of (81) and (82):

(81) My childhood days are gone, gone.
(82) My childhood days are gone.

Our suggestion is not that, in a given context, (81) has contextual implications that (82) lacks: the hearer of either utterance is free to derive as many consequences as he pleases from the fact that the speaker's childhood days are gone. What (81) has is more *implicatures* than (82): that is, more contextual assumptions and implications which receive some degree of backing from the speaker. To justify the repetition of 'gone', the hearer must think of all the implicatures that the speaker could reasonably have expected him to derive from (82), and then assume that there is a whole range of still further premises and conclusions which the speaker wants to back. For this, the hearer must expand the context. As a result (81) might suggest, say, that the speaker is experiencing a torrent of memories which the hearer is being trusted to imagine for himself. What look like non-propositional effects associated with the expression of attitudes, feelings and states of mind can be approached in terms of the notion of weak implicature developed in section 4.

Let us give the name *poetic effect* to the peculiar effect of an utterance which achieves most of its relevance through a wide array of weak implicatures. Generally, the most striking examples of a particular figure, the ones singled out for attention by rhetoricians and students of style, are those which have poetic effects in this sense. These poetic effects are then attributed to the syntactic or phonological construction in question. However, as the above examples show, a repetitive syntactic pattern does not invariably give rise to noticeable stylistic effects. The same is true of all the figures of style identified by classical rhetoric.

Consider, for example, the syntactic construction that modern syntacticians call gapping and classical rhetoricians call zeugma, as illustrated in (83)–(85):

(83) Mary went on holiday to the mountains, Joan to the sea, and Lily to the country.
(84) Mary lives in Oxford, Joan in York, and Lily in a skyscraper.
(85) Mary came with Peter, Joan with Bob, and Lily with a sad smile on her face.

In each of these examples there are clear syntactic, semantic and phonological parallelisms. These reinforce the hearer's natural tendency to reduce processing effort by looking for matching parallelisms in propositional form and implicatures. In (83), for instance, the missing *VP* in the second and third clause can safely be assumed to be 'went on holiday'. Moreover, the same easily accessible context – scenarios of typical holidays – enables the three clauses to yield parallel contextual effects, with some conclusions true of Mary, Joan and Lily, and others contrasting their respective holidays on fairly standard dimensions of comparison. A speaker aiming at optimal relevance would deliberately introduce such linguistic parallelisms only if she expected them to lead to a reduction in the hearer's processing effort, and in particular, if she thought that the search for parallel contexts and contextual effects would be rewarded. Otherwise, the parallelisms might misdirect the hearer's effort, thus increasing instead of reducing it. Thus, to the extent that it reflects the speaker's deliberate choice, the form of (83)–(85) indicates to the hearer that the search for parallel contexts and contextual implications will be successful.

The parallelism in (83) achieves no striking stylistic effect. In the case of (84), and even more of (85), it does. Here is an explanation: in the case of (83), the syntactic parallelism is matched by semantic parallelism, and parallel contextual effects are easily achieved in a largely common context. The parallelism of (83), therefore, contributes to relevance merely by reducing processing effort, and not by creating special contextual effects. In the case of (84) and (85), the syntactic parallelism is not matched by a similar semantic parallelism in the third clause: 'a skyscraper' does not belong with 'Oxford' and 'York'; 'a sad smile on her face' does not belong with 'Peter' and 'Bob'. The syntactic parallelism, however, is too salient to be accidental or to go unnoticed; it is strong enough to trigger parallel processing in spite of the partial semantic divergence. The problem is then one of finding a context in which all three clauses have parallel contextual effects. This requires an effort of imagination: the hearer has to bring together relatively unrelated encyclopaedic entries and construct non-stereotypical assumptions.

In the case of (84), the hearer's task is to find a set of assumptions in the context of which the facts that Mary lives in Oxford, Joan lives in York and Lily lives in a skyscraper have either identical or directly contrasting implications. Some basic facts about Oxford, York and skyscrapers suggest the conclusion that Mary and Joan do not live in skyscrapers, and that Lily does not live in an old town. Still, these conclusions could have been derived more cheaply if the speaker had named the town where Lily lived, or the type of building where Mary and Joan lived. If the overall interpretation is to be consistent with the principle of relevance, the speaker must be credited with implicating more than that: for example, she might have been trying to convey a variety of weak implicatures showing that the way Mary and Joan live is more affected by the kind of town they live in than by the kind of building they live in, while the reverse is true of Lily's way of life.

In the case of (85), the hearer's task is to find a set of assumptions in the context of which the facts that Mary came with Peter, Joan with Bob, and Lily with a sad smile on her face have either identical or directly contrasting implications. What might be suggested is that Lily had no one to come with, that she was sad because she had no one to come with, that there was a whole story behind her sad smile in which Mary, Peter, Joan and Bob were somehow involved, and which an imaginative hearer could spell out along a whole variety of lines. In this way the required parallelisms of context and contextual effects could be maintained. The result would be a wide range of fairly weak implicatures.

In (83), (84) and (85), because of the form of the utterance, the search for an interpretation consistent with the principle of relevance induces a certain processing strategy; in the case of (83) this strategy yields an unremarkable interpretation; the contribution to relevance made by the form of the utterance is merely to reduce processing effort. In the case of (84), and even more so of (85), this strategy takes the hearer beyond standard contexts and premises, and yields typical poetic effects.

How do poetic effects affect the mutual cognitive environment of speaker and hearer? They do not add entirely new assumptions which are strongly manifest in this environment. Instead, they marginally increase the manifestness of a great many weakly manifest assumptions. In other words, poetic effects create common impressions rather than common knowledge. Utterances with poetic effects can be used precisely to create this sense of apparently affective rather than cognitive mutuality. What we are suggesting is that, if you look at these affective effects through the microscope of relevance theory, you see a wide array of minute cognitive effects.

Poetic effects, we claim, result from the accessing of a large array of very weak implicatures in the otherwise ordinary pursuit of relevance. Stylistic differences are just differences in the way relevance is achieved. One way in which styles may differ is in their greater or lesser reliance on poetic effects, just as they may differ in their greater or lesser reliance on implicature and in the way they exploit the backgrounding and fore-grounding of information in their explicatures.

7 Descriptive and interpretive dimensions of language use

So far, we have restricted our attention to ordinary assertions: utterances whose main explicature is simply their propositional form. In many cases – perhaps most – the propositional form of an utterance is not an explicature at all. This is true of tropes on the one hand, and of non-assertive speech acts on the other. Normally, though, these two kinds of utterance are not regarded as particularly closely related.

The tropes are traditionally analysed as involving the substitution of a figurative for a literal meaning. Consider the ironical (86):

(86) (a) Peter is quite well-read. (b) He's even heard of Shakespeare.

The propositional form of (86a) is the assumption that Peter is quite well-read. However, this is not an assumption that the speaker wants to make manifest; it is not an explicature. The only obvious explicature of (86a) is (87), where as we have already seen, one can say that *P* without asserting or explicating that *P*.

(87) The speaker is saying that Peter is quite well-read.

Similarly, the propositional form of the metaphorical (88) is not an explicature:

(88) This room is a pigsty.

The speaker does not expect her hearer to start looking around for pigs. The only obvious explicature of (88) is (89):

(89) The speaker is saying that this room is a pigsty.

The problem with figurative utterances such as (86a) and (88), which seem to have no other explicatures than reports such as (87) and (89), is to explain how they could be relevant at all.

In the case of speech acts other than assertions, the propositional form of the utterance is not an explicature either. Consider a yes–no question such as (90):

(90) Is Jill coming to the party?

The propositional form of (90) is (91):

(91) Jill is coming to the party.

However, if (90) is a genuine question, the speaker's intention is not to communicate that Jill is coming to the party, but to find out whether she is. The propositional form (91) has to be integrated into an assumption schema such as (92) to yield (93), the explicature of (90):

(92) The speaker is asking whether it is true that ———.
(93) The speaker is asking whether it is true that Jill is coming to the party.

Similarly, the propositional form of the request in (94) is (95):

(94) Close the door, please.
(95) [The hearer] will close the door immediately.

However, the speaker's intention is clearly not to communicate to the hearer that he will close the door immediately. The propositional form (95) has to be integrated into an assumption schema such as (96) to yield (97) as an explicature of (94):

(96) The speaker is telling the hearer to make it true that ———.
(97) The speaker is telling the hearer to make it true that he will close the door immediately.

There is a considerable literature on illocutionary forces and speech acts, and an even more considerable one on tropes. In both cases the central concern has been with problems of classification, and little is offered in the way of explanation. Despite this superficial resemblance, there is very little overlap between work on illocutionary forces and work on tropes, as if it went without saying that they are essentially different aspects of language use. We do not share this view of illocutionary forces and tropes as defining two homogeneous and radically distinct domains. We would like to suggest a different and more integrated approach, based on a fundamental distinction between interpretation and description.[22] This distinction is not an *ad hoc* piece of extra machinery introduced to account for tropes and illocutionary forces. It follows quite naturally from the relevance-based account of ostensive–inferential communication which we have been trying to develop. In this section, we will introduce and illustrate this distinction. We will then use it to explain metaphor in section 8 and irony in section 9, and to look at speech acts and illocutionary forces in a new light in section 10.

Most stimuli used in ostensive communication are representations (public rather than mental representations, of course). This is true not only of linguistic utterances, but of many other kinds of ostensive stimuli as well. Relevance theory provides a straightforward explanation of this fact, and without having to appeal to any *ad hoc* rule, constraint, or principle: for example, a tacit convention to the effect that to represent some state of affairs is to suggest that it exists (to which there are countless counterexamples anyhow).

Identifying a stimulus, an ostensive stimulus in particular, involves entertaining a logical form, a structured set of concepts. As we have seen, concepts give access to encyclopaedic entries, and a logical form can be used as an assumption schema. Given the principle of relevance, and in particular the presumption that on the effort side the stimulus is the best the communicator could have chosen, the addressee of an act of communication is entitled to assume that, to recover the intended interpretation, he must use the assumption schema suggested by the logical form he is entertaining, and the encyclopaedic entries made accessible by its constituent concepts.

A recognisable representation can be used to draw the audience's attention to concepts and assumption schemas which are not instantiated in the immediately perceptible environment. If you want someone to think of a dog when there are no dogs around to point at, use a representation of a dog: a drawing, a dog-like posture, an imitation of a bark, the word 'dog', the word 'chien'. If you want someone to think of a dog biting, use a representation, verbal or visual, of a dog biting. Since this is ostensive behaviour, your addressee will assume that you are communicating, that the information you are communicating is worth his attention, that the stimulus you use is economical, that you are therefore not gratuitously making him entertain the mental representation of a dog biting, and that the first inferable interpretation consistent with these assumptions should be the right one.

In appropriate conditions, any natural or artificial phenomenon in the world can be used as a representation of some other phenomenon which it resembles in some respects. Having climbed the walls of the villa, the first thief silently imitates a dog biting to warn her accomplice at the foot of the wall. You ask me what is the shape of Brazil, and for answer I point to an appropriately shaped cloud in the sky. Mary wants to communicate to Peter that she would like to leave the party, and she mimics the act of driving.

Utterances can be used as representations in another way, too: not in virtue of resembling some phenomenon, but in virtue of having a propositional form which is true of some actual or conceivable state of affairs. In the case of an assertion, for instance, the propositional form of the utterance is used to represent some state of affairs in the real world; in the case of a request, the propositional form of the utterance is used to represent a desirable state of affairs. However, utterances are also phenomena, and like all phenomena they can be used to represent something they resemble. This possibility is often overlooked by theorists, and even when it is not, we want to argue that the role it plays in verbal communication is grossly underestimated.

Consider the following dialogue:

(98) *Peter*: What language did you speak to the inn-keeper?
　　Mary: Bonjour, comment allez-vous, bien, merci, et vous?

Mary communicates that she spoke French to the inn-keeper, not by asserting it but by imitating the fact she wants to make manifest. Her utterance is produced because it resembles the phenomenon of her speaking French to the inn-keeper, even though its propositional form in no way describes this phenomenon. However, as in example (6) of the stammerer showing off, Mary's answer is hardly a case of true linguistic communication.

Now consider dialogue (99):

(99) *Peter*: And what did the inn-keeper say?
　　Mary: Je l'ai cherché partout!

Here again, Mary is not communicating the propositional form of her utterance. She is using this utterance because it resembles the inn-keeper's utterance. It resembles that utterance because it is a token of the same sentence: it is a direct quotation. A direct quotation has a linguistic structure, including a semantic structure, and when it is used to make this semantic structure manifest, it falls within the domain of verbal communication proper. Direct quotations are the most obvious examples of utterances used to represent not what they describe but what they resemble. They are by no means the only examples.

Consider another version of the dialogue between Peter and Mary:

(100) *Peter*: And what did the inn-keeper say?
  Mary: I looked for it everywhere.

This time, Mary's utterance is a translation of the inn-keeper's utterance. Again, it is used to represent what it resembles: it resembles the inn-keeper's utterance because it has the same semantic structure.

Consider now,

(101) *Peter*: And what did the inn-keeper say?
  Mary: He has looked for your wallet everywhere. I don't believe him, though.

In (101), the first sentence of Mary's utterance is a representation of the inn-keeper's utterance, though it is neither a direct quotation nor a translation. How does Mary's utterance resemble the inn-keeper's? The two utterances have different semantic structures, since the inn-keeper used a first-person rather than a third-person pronoun to refer to himself, and a third-person pronoun rather than a definite description to refer to Peter's wallet. What the two utterances have in common is their propositional form.

Now suppose that instead of the single sentence 'Je l'ai cherché partout!', the inn-keeper had produced a long speech which contained neither this nor any closely similar sentence. Consider the following:

(102) *Peter*: And what did the inn-keeper say?
  Mary: That he has looked for your wallet everywhere.

Once more, Mary's utterance is used to represent what it resembles, namely the inn-keeper's speech. But what is the nature of the resemblance this time? The linguistic structures are different, the semantic structures are different, the propositional forms are different. However, if Mary's summary is a faithful one, the propositional forms, though different, must resemble one another: they must share some logical properties, have partly identical contextual implications in some contexts, for instance.

Any representation with a propositional form, and in particular any utterance, can be used to represent things in two ways. It can represent some state of affairs in virtue of its propositional form being true of that state of affairs; in this case we will say that the representation is a *description*, or that it is used *descriptively*. Or it can represent some other representation which also has a propositional form – a thought, for instance – in virtue of a resemblance between the two propositional forms; in this case we will say that the first representation is an *interpretation* of the second one, or that it is used *interpretively*.

How closely must the propositional forms of two representations resemble each other if the one is to be an interpretation of the other? We will show that the answer to this question varies from case to case, but invariably follows from the principle of relevance. What we want to point out here is that while there may be a minimal degree of resemblance below which no interpretive use is possible, there need not be a maximal degree above which resemblance is *replaced* by identity and interpretation by reproduction. Identity is a limiting case of resemblance; reproduction is a limiting case of interpretation. When one representation is used to represent another which has exactly the same propositional form, as in example (101), this is merely a limiting case of interpretation.

The only generally acknowledged interpretive use of utterances is the reporting of speech or thought: when one utterance is used to report another utterance, as in examples (99)–(102), or a thought, as in (103):

(103) *Mary*: We won't bother go to the police, he thinks, and so he can safely keep the wallet.

Here, Mary's utterance, with the exception of the parenthetical 'he thinks', is used to report a thought which Mary attributes to the inn-keeper.

There are other interpretive uses of utterances apart from reports of speech or thought. Consider assumption (104):

(104) There is a prime number greater than 8,364,357 and smaller than 8,366,445.

How plausible does it sound to you? Well, never mind. The point is that we have just used an utterance interpretively, to represent an assumption, without attributing this assumption to anyone: that is, without reporting it. We have already done so many times in this book: many of our numbered examples are used to represent utterances, assumptions or intentions which we did not attribute to anybody, not even to fictitious characters, and which we put forward to illustrate some abstract point.

In speculative thinking, thoughts are often entertained as approximate representations of assumptions one would like to be able to formulate better. This is true of trivial speculation: I don't remember when the party at the Jones's is supposed to be; I try out on myself, 'It's on Tuesday', 'It's on Wednesday', 'It's on Thursday', etc., hoping that when I hit on the right date, I will somehow recognise it. I entertain these successive thoughts as attempts at representing the relevant piece of information in my memory, and this is what makes my hope not entirely unreasonable: a mental match may occur, whereas if these thoughts were to be processed as descriptions, I would have to wait until the event took place to verify one of them and falsify the others. In scientific speculation too, inadequate or incomplete hypotheses are knowingly entertained, not as descriptions of the empirical phenomena under study, but as temporary representations of better hypotheses to come.

Reported speech or thought is thus not the only interpretive use of language. Utterances can be used interpretively to represent utterance types or thoughts which are worth considering for their intrinsic properties, and not because they can be attributed to Peter, Mary, the inn-keeper, or public opinion. But we want to argue that there is an even more essential interpretive use of utterances: on a more fundamental level, *every* utterance is used to represent a thought of the speaker's.

One of the assumptions a speaker intends to make manifest is that she is entertaining some thought with some particular attitude, since it is on this ground that the hearer may be led to entertain a similar thought with a similar attitude. You may well tell me that you will come tomorrow: you will not make me believe it unless you first make me believe that you believe it too. That much is hardly controversial. Actually, an even stronger claim is generally made. Most pragmatists and philosophers of language take for granted that there is a convention, principle or presumption,[23] to the effect that the meaning of the utterance must be a literal expression, i.e. an identical reproduction, of a thought of the speaker's. We believe that this claim is too strong. People certainly do not express themselves literally all the time, and when they do not, there is no intuition that a norm has been transgressed. There is thus no empirical evidence for a convention of literalness or anything of the sort. Such a convention is postulated on purely theoretical grounds: the underlying code model of communication implies that utterances are understood as communicating what they encode; then non-literal uses can be analysed as more or less codified departures from literalness, recoverable by inference.

Our approach is different: we have rejected the code model and we hope to explain how verbal communication is possible without postulating any *ad hoc* constraint apart from strictly grammatical constraints. Code theorists see verbal communication as involving a speaker encoding one of her thoughts in an utterance, which is then decoded by the hearer (with an extra layer of inference in modern versions). We see verbal communication as involving a speaker producing an utterance as a public interpretation of one of her thoughts, and the hearer constructing a mental interpretation of this utterance, and hence of the original thought. Let us say that an utterance is an *interpretive expression* of a thought of the speaker's, and that the hearer makes an *interpretive assumption* about the speaker's informative intention. It follows from our general account of inferential communication that an utterance should be an interpretive expression of a thought of the speaker's. However, we see no reason to postulate a convention, presumption, maxim or rule of literalness to the effect that this interpretation must be a literal reproduction. How close the interpretation is, and in particular when it is literal, can be determined on the basis of the principle of relevance.

We assume, then, that every utterance is an interpretive expression of a thought of the speaker's. What does that thought itself represent, and how? A mental representation, like any representation with a propositional form, can be used descriptively or interpretively. When it is used descriptively, it can be a description of a state of affairs in the actual world,[24] or it can be a description of a desirable state of affairs. When it is used interpretively, it can be an interpretation of some attributed thought or utterance, or it can be an interpretation of some thought which it is or would be desirable to entertain in a certain way: as knowledge, for instance. There may be other possibilities, and one might consider what the thoughts interpreted by thoughts might represent in their turn and how, but let us leave it at that, and use figure 3 (p.232) to show the representations and relationships considered so far.

Any utterance involves at least two relationships: a relationship between its propositional form and a thought of the speaker's, and one of the four possible relationships between that thought and what it represents. All the basic relationships involved in tropes and illocutionary forces are represented in this diagram, as we will show in the next three sections. Our argument may be summarised as follows: metaphor involves an interpretive relation between the propositional form of an utterance and the thought it represents; irony involves an interpretive relation between the speaker's thought and attributed thoughts or utterances; assertion involves a descriptive relation between the speaker's thought and a state of affairs in the world; requesting or advising involves a descriptive relation between the speaker's thought and a desirable state of affairs; interrogatives and exclamatives involve an interpretive relation between the speaker's thought and desirable thoughts. These claims will be discussed in more detail below.

8 Literalness and metaphor

In this section we will consider the relationship at the top of figure 3: between the propositional form of an utterance and the thought this utterance is used to represent. We have argued that in general, the relationship is one of resemblance rather than identity between proposi-

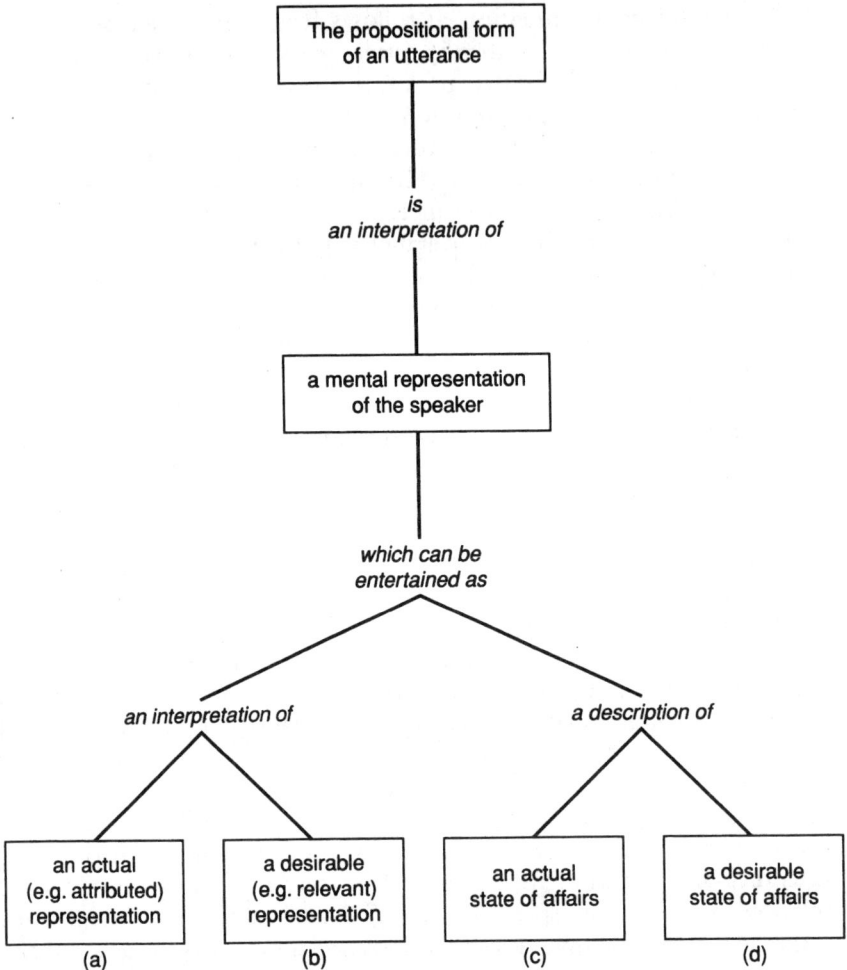

Aspects of verbal communication

```
              ┌─────────────────────┐
              │ The propositional form │
              │   of an utterance    │
              └─────────────────────┘
                          │
                         is
                  an interpretation of

              ┌─────────────────────┐
              │ a mental representation │
              │    of the speaker    │
              └─────────────────────┘
                          │
                    which can be
                   entertained as
                    ╱          ╲
        an interpretation of      a description of
           ╱        ╲              ╱         ╲
```

an actual (e.g. attributed) representation	a desirable (e.g. relevant) representation	an actual state of affairs	a desirable state of affairs
(a)	(b)	(c)	(d)

Figure 3

tional forms. We are treating literalness, or identity of propositional forms, as a limiting case rather than a norm. We will show that this approach, combined with relevance theory, yields a straightforward account of metaphors and related tropes.

It might be thought that in even contemplating a move in this direction we are venturing onto dangerous ground. 'Resemblance' is notoriously not a well-defined term. Anything may resemble anything in at least some respect. When and how a resemblance is perceived is an open question in cognitive psychology; the mechanisms involved are ill understood. However, since we suspect that a proper account of the perception of resemblance in general should be based on a well-developed notion of relevance, we do not feel too dismayed. Moreover, for the time being we are concerned only with resemblances of a very restricted type: logical resemblances among propositional forms (where two propositional forms resemble each other if and only if they share logical properties). We will show that the identification of these resemblances, like every other aspect of comprehension, is governed by the principle of relevance.

Let us say that an utterance, in its role as an interpretive expression of a speaker's thought, is strictly *literal* if it has the same propositional form as that thought. To say that an utterance is less than strictly literal is to say that its propositional form shares some, but not all, of its logical properties with the propositional form of the thought it is being used to interpret. From the standpoint of relevance theory, there is no reason to think that the optimally relevant interpretive expression of a thought is always the most literal one. The speaker is presumed to aim at optimal relevance, not at literal truth. The optimal interpretive expression of a thought should give the hearer information about that thought which is relevant enough to be worth processing, and should require as little processing effort as possible. There are many quite ordinary situations where a literal utterance is not optimally relevant: for example, where the effort needed to process it is not offset by the gain in information conveyed. There are thus many situations where a speaker aiming at optimal relevance should not give a literal interpretation of her thought, and where the hearer should not treat her utterance as literal.

For example, suppose I earn £797.32 a month. You, a friend I have not seen for some years, ask me over a drink how much I am earning now. If I remember the exact figure, I can choose between the strictly literal and truthful answer in (105a), and the less than literal (105b), which I know to be strictly speaking false:

(105) (a) I earn £797.32 a month.
      (b) I earn £800 a month.

In the circumstances, there is no reason to think you need an exact figure. From either reply you will be able to derive exactly the same conclusions about my status, standard of living, purchasing power, life style, and whatever else you are planning to use my salary as an indicator of. Aiming at optimal relevance, I should therefore choose the reply which will convey these conclusions as economically as possible. In other words, I should choose the false but economical (105b) rather than the complex but strictly literal and truthful (105a), and expect you to recognise that I am offering something less than a strictly literal interpretation of my thoughts.

To take a rather more abstract example, suppose I have a complex thought P, which makes manifest to me a set of assumptions I, and I want to communicate I to you. Now suppose that the following conditions are met: *P* is too complex to be represented literally, but the assumptions in I are all straightforwardly derivable as logical or contextual implications of an easily expressed assumption *Q*. The problem is that *Q* is not a thought of mine; it has some logical and contextual implications which I do not accept as true and which I do not want to communicate. What should I do? Given the principle of relevance, as long as you have some way of sorting the implications of *Q* into those I do and those I do not want to endorse, the best way of communicating I may well be to express the single assumption *Q* and leave the sorting to you.

In these circumstances, the utterance which expresses *Q* is an interpretive expression of my complex thought *P*: they share logical properties, more specifically logical and contextual implications. Moreover, the criterion of consistency with the principle of relevance provides a means of distinguishing those contextual implications which are shared from those which are not; that is, it gives you a way of constructing the right interpretive assumption about my informative intention.

We are assuming that all the hearer can take for granted is that an utterance is intended as an interpretation of one of the speaker's thoughts. This does not mean that whenever an assumption is expressed, the hearer has to compute all its logical and contextual implications and sort through them one by one to find out which subset of them are implications of the speaker's thought. In the framework we are proposing, this wasteful manoeuvre is quite unnecessary. If the speaker has done her job correctly, all the hearer has to do is start computing, in order of accessibility, those implications which might be relevant to him, and continue to add them to the overall interpretation of the utterance until it is relevant enough to be consistent with the principle of relevance. At this point, the sorting will have been accomplished as a by-product of the search for relevance, and will require no specific effort of its own.

It follows that the hearer should take an utterance as fully literal only when nothing less than full literality will confirm the presumption of relevance. In general, some looseness of expression is to be expected. For example, if someone says, 'It's 5 p.m.', she should not be taken to task if it turns out to be five minutes or two minutes to, unless the relevance of the utterance depends on that kind of exactitude. If someone says 'I'm exhausted', there is no point in quibbling over whether exhausted is exactly what she is: as long as she can be taken to have conveyed an acceptable range of implications, she will have achieved optimal relevance.

The examples discussed so far would normally be treated as loose uses of language, but would not be regarded as figurative: there is no temptation to invoke the substitution of a figurative for a literal meaning.

We want to claim that there is no discontinuity between these loose uses and a variety of 'figurative' examples which include the most characteristic examples of poetic metaphor. In both cases, the propositional form of the utterance differs from that of the thought interpreted. In both cases, the hearer can proceed on the assumption that these two propositional forms have some identifiable logical and contextual implications in common. In both cases, the same interpretive abilities and procedures are involved.

Consider first an example of hyperbole. The speaker expresses, but does not explicate, the assumption in (106a), and implicates the weaker (106b):

(106) (a) Bill is the nicest person there is.
     (b) Bill is a very nice person.

How can this be consistent with the principle of relevance? Let us assume that by explicating (106b) directly the speaker would not exhaust her thoughts about Bill: its contextual effects would fall short of what she wants to convey. Nor is there any obvious combination of adverbs and adjectives that would exactly express her thoughts. Perhaps they are too vague: there are a lot of aspects of Bill's niceness that she is not thinking about with equal clarity at the time, and to access these thoughts and make them more precise would involve more work than she is prepared to do. She can be sure, on the other hand, that all the assumptions she wants to communicate are among the logical and contextual implications of (106a). (106a) has other implications which she does not want to communicate. As long as she can rely on the hearer to ignore or discard them, (106a) will be a much more adequate interpretation of her thoughts than the weaker (106b).

What exactly does (106a) convey? The speaker is certainly strongly implicating (106b). However, if this were all she had wanted to convey, she could have saved the hearer some processing effort by expressing (106b) directly. As always, the element of indirectness in an utterance must be offset by some increase in contextual effects. By expressing (106a), the speaker thus encourages the hearer to look for a range of further contextual implications not shared, or not equally strengthened, by (106b), and assume that within this range there are some she intends to implicate. He might thus begin running through the names of their common acquaintances and conclude that the speaker prefers Bill to each of these; he might conclude that Bill has behaved in ways that are so admirable that the speaker can find no words to describe them, and so on. The wider the range of possible conclusions, the weaker the implicatures, and the more the hearer must share the responsibility for deriving them. Thus (106a) conveys, on the one hand, a suggestion that the speaker has a certain attitude to Bill, a certain vision of Bill and his niceness, and on the other hand, an incentive to the hearer to develop his own vision of Bill and conclude that it overlaps to some extent with hers.

Let us return, then, to our original example of metaphor:

(88) This room is a pigsty.

This is a very standardised metaphor. Typically, such examples give access to an encyclopaedic schema with one or two dominant and highly accessible assumptions. Thus pigsties are stereotypically filthy and untidy. When (88) is processed in this stereotypical context, it will yield the implication that the room is filthy and untidy. If the speaker had not intended this implication to be derived, she should have rephrased her utterance to eliminate it: hence (88) strongly implicates that the room is filthy and untidy. However, the speaker must have intended to convey something more than this if the relative indirectness of the utterance is to be justified: an image, say, of filthiness and untidiness beyond the norm, beyond what could have been satisfactorily conveyed by saying merely 'This room is very filthy and untidy.' Thus even this very standardised example cannot be paraphrased without loss.

Moving to a marginally more creative example, (107) is a fairly conventional metaphor whose interpretation involves bringing together the encyclopaedic entries for *Robert* and *bulldozer*, which do not normally come together in a subject–predicate relationship:

(107) Robert is a bulldozer.

The result will be a wide array of contextual implications, many of which, being contradictory, can be automatically discarded. The relevance of (107) will be established by finding a range of contextual effects which can be retained as weak or strong implicatures. Here there is no single strong implicature that automatically comes to mind, but rather a slightly weaker, less determinate range having to do with Robert's persistence, obstinacy, insensitivity and refusal to be deflected. The hearer thus has to take a slightly greater responsibility for the resulting interpretation than he does with (106a) and (88).

In general, the wider the range of potential implicatures and the greater the hearer's responsibility for constructing them, the more poetic the effect, the more creative the metaphor. A good creative metaphor is precisely one in which a variety of contextual effects can be retained and understood as weakly implicated by the speaker. In the richest and most successful cases, the hearer or reader can go beyond just exploring the immediate context and the entries for concepts involved in it, accessing a wide area of knowledge, adding metaphors of his own as interpretations of possible developments he is not ready to go into, and getting more and more very weak implicatures, with suggestions for still further processing.

The result is a quite complex picture, for which the hearer has to take a large part of the responsibility, but the discovery of which has been triggered by the writer. The surprise or beauty of a successful creative metaphor lies in this condensation, in the fact that a single expression which has itself been loosely used will determine a very wide range of acceptable weak implicatures.

Take, for example, Flaubert's comment on the poet Leconte de Lisle:

(108) His ink is pale. (Son encre est pale.)

A strictly literal construal of this utterance is clearly ruled out: it is hard to see what relevance could attach to knowing the colour of a poet's ink. Nor is there any obvious strong implicature. The only way of establishing the relevance of this utterance is to look for a wide range of very weak implicatures. This requires several extensions of the context. In the most accessible context of encyclopaedic information about ink and handwriting, most implications are irrelevant: after all, Leconte de Lisle's poetry is read not in his handwriting but in print; the only clear implicature in this first context is that he has the character of a man who would use pale ink. Some other implications – that Leconte de Lisle's writing lacks contrasts, that it may fade – have further relevant implications in a context to which has been added the premise that what is true of his handwriting is true of his style. Someone who knows little of Leconte de Lisle's work might conclude, for example, that there is something weak about his poetry, that his writings will not last, that he does not put his whole heart into his work, and so on. Someone who has a deeper acquaintance with the poet would be able to construe the criticism in much more detailed and pointed ways. The resulting interpretation, with its characteristic poetic effect, owes a lot simultaneously to Flaubert, for foreseeing how it might go, and to the reader, for actually constructing it.

On this approach, metaphor and a variety of related tropes (e.g. hyperbole, metonymy, synecdoche) are simply creative exploitations of a perfectly general dimension of language use. The search for optimal relevance leads the speaker to adopt, on different occasions, a more or a less faithful interpretation of her thoughts. The result in some cases is literalness, in others metaphor. Metaphor thus requires no special interpretive abilities or procedures: it is a natural outcome of some very general abilities and procedures used in verbal communication. In the next section, we will show that the same is true of irony.

9 Echoic utterances and irony

We would now like to show that irony and a variety of related tropes (e.g.

meiosis, litotes) fall together with a range of cases which would not normally be regarded as figurative at all. What unites these cases is the fact that the thought of the speaker which is interpreted by the utterance is itself an interpretation. It is an interpretation of a thought of someone other than the speaker (or of the speaker in the past). That is, these utterances are second-degree interpretations of someone else's thought, as illustrated by path (a) in figure 3 above. If we are right, then the same is true of irony as is true of metaphor: whatever abilities and procedures are needed to understand it are independently needed for the interpretation of quite ordinary non-figurative utterances.[25]

We have already considered, in section 7, the case of utterances used to interpret someone else's speech or thought. They are always (at least) second-degree interpretations: like all utterances, they first interpret a thought of the speaker, and it is only because this thought is itself an interpretation of someone else's thought that the utterance ultimately represents someone else's thought. Another way of making the same point is to say that an utterance used as an interpretation of someone else's thought is always, in the first place, an interpretation of one's understanding of that other person's thought. When we talk of utterances used to interpret someone else's thought, it should be clear, then, that we are always talking of second-degree interpretations.

How do interpretations of someone else's thought achieve relevance? In the best-known case, that of 'reported speech', they achieve relevance by informing the hearer of the fact that so-and-so has said something or thinks something. In other cases, these interpretations achieve relevance by informing the hearer of the fact that the speaker has in mind what so-and-so said, and has a certain attitude to it: the speaker's interpretation of so-and-so's thought is relevant in itself. When interpretations achieve relevance in this way, we will say that they are *echoic*, and we will argue that ironical utterances are cases of echoic interpretation.

Here is a simple case of an echoic utterance:

(109) *Peter*: The Joneses aren't coming to the party.
      Mary: They aren't coming, hum. If that's true, we might invite the Smiths.

Mary's first sentence echoes what Peter has just said. It achieves relevance not, of course, by reporting to Peter what he has just said, but by giving evidence that Mary has paid attention to his utterance and is weighing up its reliability and implications.

An echoic utterance need not interpret a precisely attributable thought: it may echo the thought of a certain kind of person, or of people in general. Suppose you tell me to hurry up and I reply as follows:

(110) More haste, less speed.

This utterance is a literal interpretation of a traditional piece of wisdom which achieves relevance by making manifest that I find this piece of wisdom indeed wise in the circumstances. Clearly, however, what makes traditional wisdom traditional is that it is attributable not to any specific source but to people in general.

By representing someone's utterance, or the opinions of a certain type of person, or popular wisdom, in a manifestly sceptical, amused, surprised, triumphant, approving or reproving way, the speaker can express her own attitude to the thought echoed, and the relevance of her utterance might depend largely on this expression of attitude. Sometimes, the speaker's attitude is left implicit, to be gathered only from tone of voice, context and other paralinguistic clues; at other times it may be made explicit. We will argue that verbal irony invariably involves the implicit expression of an attitude, and that the relevance of an ironical utterance invariably depends, at least in part, on the information it conveys about the speaker's attitude to the opinion echoed.

There is no limit to the attitudes that a speaker can express to an opinion echoed. In particular, she may indicate her agreement or disagreement with it. Compare (111) and (112):

(111) (a) *Peter*: It's a lovely day for a picnic.
　　　　[They go for a picnic and the sun shines.]
　　(b) *Mary* (happily): It's a lovely day for a picnic, indeed.
(112) (a) *Peter*: It's a lovely day for a picnic.
　　　　[They go for a picnic and it rains.]
　　(b) *Mary* (sarcastically): It's a lovely day for a picnic, indeed.

In both (111b) and (112b) there is an echoic allusion to be picked up. In the circumstances described, it is clear that the speaker of (111b) endorses the opinion echoed, whereas the speaker of (112b) rejects it with scorn. These utterances are interpreted on exactly similar patterns; the only difference is in the attitudes they express. (111b) has not been thought by rhetoricians to be worthy of special attention; (112b) is, of course, a case of verbal irony.

The attitude expressed by an ironical utterance is invariably of the rejecting or disapproving kind. The speaker dissociates herself from the opinion echoed and indicates that she does not hold it herself. Indeed, it may be obvious in the circumstances that she believes the opposite of the opinion echoed: thus the speaker of (112b) manifestly believes that it is not a lovely day for a picnic. From this it follows that it was wrong of her companion to say that it was a lovely day for a picnic, that his judgement has been unsound, that they should never have set out, that it was his fault that their day has been ruined, and so on. The recovery of these implicatures depends, first, on a recognition of the utterance as echoic; second, on an identification of the source of the opinion echoed; and third, on a recognition that the speaker's attitude to the opinion echoed is one of rejection or dissociation. We would argue that these are common factors in the interpretation of all ironical utterances.

As regards the particular range of rejecting or dissociative attitudes conveyed by verbal irony, there is no need to look for a clear-cut answer. Are anger, outrage and irritation among the attitudes that the ironist can convey? This question, it seems to us, should be of interest only to lexicographers. From the pragmatic point of view, what is important is that a speaker can use an echoic utterance to convey a whole range of attitudes and emotions, ranging from outright acceptance and endorsement to outright rejection and dissociation, and that the recognition of these attitudes and emotions may be crucial to the interpretation process. We doubt very much that there is either a well-defined subset of ironical attitudes or a well-defined subset of ironical utterances which express them. Rather, what exists is a continuum, with different blends of attitude and emotion giving rise to a whole range of borderline cases which do not fit neatly into any existing scheme. Irony is not a natural kind.

Let us briefly compare this account with the classical account of irony as saying one thing and meaning, or implicating, the opposite. The most obvious problem with the classical account – and with its modern variant, the Gricean account – is that it does not explain why a speaker who could, by hypothesis, have expressed her intended message directly should decide instead to say the opposite of what she meant. It cannot be too strongly emphasised what a bizarre practice this would be. Suppose we are out for a drive and you stop to look both ways before joining the main road. The road is clear, but as you are about to drive on I say quietly,

(113) There's something coming.

You slam on your brakes and look both ways, but the road is as clear as before. When you ask me what on earth I was doing, I explain gently that I was merely trying to reassure you that the road was clear. My utterance satisfies the classical definition of irony. I have said something which is patently false, and there is a logically related assumption, namely (114), which I could truthfully have expressed:

(114) There's nothing coming.

Why do you not instantly leap to the conclusion that this is what I was trying to convey?

The classical account of irony notably fails to explain what distinguishes genuine irony from the mere irrationality exhibited by (113). In our framework, the difference is clear. Genuine irony is echoic, and is primarily designed to ridicule the opinion echoed. Let us recast our example so that these conditions are satisfied. You are an over-cautious driver, constantly on the alert for danger, who *never* pulls into a main road in front of oncoming traffic, however far away. When we stop at the junction, the road is straight and entirely clear in both directions except for a just-visible cyclist on the horizon. As you pull onto the main road, I say, reprovingly, (113). In the circumstances, this remark may well be ironical. I am echoing back to you the sort of opinion you are constantly expressing, but in circumstances which make it clearly ridiculous. Thus, all that is needed to make (113) ironical is an echoic element and an associated attitude of mockery or rejection.

Notice how inadequate it would be with this example to say that I was merely trying to implicate the opposite of what I had said. (114) is at most an implicated premise of my utterance, and certainly does not constitute its main point. The main point of the utterance is to express my attitude to the sort of opinions you are constantly expressing, and in doing so to implicate that you are over-cautious, that you are making a fool of yourself by worrying, and so on. If I had merely wanted to convey (114) I would of course have expressed this assumption directly.

In fact there are many examples of irony which fall outside the scope of the classical definition of irony as saying one thing and meaning the opposite. Consider (115a), cited as an example of irony in many of the standard works:[c]

(115) (a) When all was over and the rival kings were celebrating their victory with Te Deums in their respective camps . . . (Voltaire, *Candide*)

To treat this utterance as equivalent to (115b) or (115c) would be not merely lame but positively wrong:

(115) (b) When all was over and the rival kings were not celebrating their victory with Te Deums in their respective camps . . .
    (c) When all was over and the rival kings were bewailing their defeat with Misereres in their respective camps . . .

Voltaire was not suggesting that neither side won the battle and celebrated victory, nor that both sides lost and bewailed their defeat. The point of the utterance lies elsewhere. Our framework explains both the intuition that this is a genuine case of irony and the fact that it does not implicate (115b) or (115c). Voltaire is echoing claims made by the rival kings. Since the claims contradict each other, it is clear that if he is minimally alert he cannot be endorsing them both: that indeed he must believe, and expect his audience to believe, that at least one of them is false. However, there is no need to come to the stronger conclusion that there is some determinate assumption which means the opposite of what has been explicitly said, and which Voltaire wanted to endorse.

In fact (115a), like many of the best examples of irony, is a garden-path utterance, likely to cause the reader momentary processing difficulties later offset by appropriate rewards. One at first reads it as an ordinary assertion, is led to the absurd conclusion that both sides won, and only then reinterprets echoically. By leaving the echo implicit when the addition of some explicit material would have immediately put the reader on the right track, the author opens up a whole new line of interpretation. What sort of hearer would have needed no explicit push towards the echoic interpretation? One who would automatically assume that after a battle both sides invariably claim victory, that this behaviour is always absurd, that the author and reader are not the sort of people to be fooled, and so on. Thus, by leaving the echo implicit, the author manages to suggest that he shares with his readers a whole cynical vision which is absent from the explicitly interpretive version in (115d):

(115) (d) When the battle was over and the rival kings were doing what they described as celebrating their victory with Te Deums in their respective camps . . .

Example (86) in section 7 fits quite straightforwardly into this framework.

(86) Peter is quite well-read. He's even heard of Shakespeare.

To believe (86), one would also have to believe that anyone who has heard of Shakespeare is quite well-read – a patently ludicrous opinion. The speaker of (86) thus makes fun of the idea that Peter is well-read, and strongly implicates that he is not well-read at all. However, the irony would fall flat if, manifestly, neither Peter himself nor any one else had ever entertained the thought that Peter was well-read: in this case there would be no one to echo.

Our accounts of metaphor and irony share two essential features. First, we are arguing that the possibility of expressing oneself metaphorically or ironically and being understood as doing so follows from very general mechanisms of verbal communication rather than from some extra level of competence.[26] Second, we are arguing that there is a continuum of cases rather than a dividing line between metaphorical and literal utterances on the one hand, between ironical utterances and other echoic utterances on the other; we are arguing, in other words, that metaphor and irony involve no departure from a norm, no transgression of a rule, convention or maxim.

If our account is correct, there are two conclusions to be drawn: first, metaphor and irony are not essentially different from other types of 'non-figurative' utterances; and second, they are not essentially similar to one another. Metaphor plays on the relationship between the propositional form of an utterance and the speaker's thought; irony plays on the relationship between the speaker's thought and a thought of someone other than the speaker. This suggests that the notion of a trope, which covers metaphor and irony and radically distinguishes them from 'non-figurative' utterances, should be abandoned altogether: it groups together phenomena which are not closely related and fails to group together phenomena which are.

10 Speech acts

Perhaps the single most uncontroversial assumption of modern pragmatics is that any adequate account of utterance comprehension must include some version of speech-act theory. As Levinson (1983: 226) says,

> speech acts remain, along with presupposition and implicature in particular, one of the central phenomena that any general pragmatic theory must account for.

We would like to question this assumption. The vast range of data that speech-act theorists have been concerned with is of no special interest to pragmatics. What is of interest is their attempt to deal with the interpretation of non-declarative (e.g. interrogative and imperative) sentences, which must indeed be accounted for in any complete pragmatic theory. In this section we will look first at speech-act theory as a general pragmatic programme, and then at the analysis of non-declaratives, for which we will sketch some proposals of our own.

Speech-act theory grew out of a reaction to what was seen as an excessively narrow concentration on the informative use of language. Language can be used to perform actions – speech acts: for example, to create and discharge obligations, to influence the thoughts and actions of others, and more generally, to create new states of affairs and new social relationships. A better understanding of the nature of language, argued Austin (1962), must involve a better understanding of how language is embedded in social institutions, and of the various actions that it can be used to perform.

Speech-act theorists have been much concerned with descriptive questions: how many types of speech act are there, and how should they be grouped together?[27] Searle (1979a) distinguishes assertives (e.g. statements), which commit the speaker to the truth of the assumption expressed; directives (e.g. orders), attempts to get the hearer to do something; commissives (e.g. promises), which commit the speaker to the performance of a future action; expressives (e.g. congratulations), which convey the speaker's emotional attitude to the assumption expressed; and declarations (e.g. declaring the court open), which bring about the state of affairs described in the assumption expressed.

However, there have also been some explanatory attempts to show how utterances are assigned to speech-act types and how indirect or implicit speech acts are performed. The recognition of indirect speech acts is generally seen as proceeding along Gricean lines. Consider (116), for example:

(116) The battery's gone flat.

This might be analysed as a direct assertion that the battery had gone flat. It is easy to think of circumstances in which a speaker who asserted (116) would also implicate (117) or (118):

(117) The hearer shouldn't have let the battery go flat.
(118) The hearer should get the battery recharged.

According to speech-act theory, these implicatures too should be assigned to speech-act types: thus, (117) might be analysed as an accusation or reproof, and (118) as a request or an order. Speech-act theory thus offers itself as a natural complement to Gricean pragmatics, dealing with the classification in speech-act terms of both explicatures and implicatures.

A crucial assumption behind this pragmatic programme is that the assignment of every utterance to a particular speech-act type is part of what is communicated and plays a necessary role in comprehension. What is surprising is how little attention has been paid to justifying this assumption. It is one thing to invent, for one's own theoretical purposes, a set of categories to use in classifying the utterances of native speakers, or to try to discover the set of categories that native speakers use in classifying their own utterances. It is quite another to claim that such a classification plays a necessary role in communication and comprehension. To see the one type of investigation as necessarily shedding light on the other is rather like moving from the observation that tennis players can generally classify strokes as volleys, lobs, approach shots, cross-court backhands and so on, to the conclusion that they are unable to perform or return a stroke without correctly classifying it. The move clearly requires some justification.

Some speech acts do have to be communicated and identified as such in order to be performed. Bidding two no trumps at bridge is an example. In order to perform this speech act, the speaker must ostensively communicate, by linguistic means, via an utterance such as (119a), or by inference, via an utterance such as (119b), an assumption of the form in (120):

(119) (a) I bid two no trumps.
  (b) Two no trumps.
(120) The speaker is bidding two no trumps.

However, the study of bidding is part of the study of bridge, not of verbal communication. Generally speaking, the study of institutional speech acts such as bidding, or declaring war, belongs to the study of institutions.

Many other speech acts, by contrast, can be successfully performed without being identified as such either by the speaker or by the hearer. Take predicting, for example. What makes an utterance a prediction is not the fact that the speaker ostensively communicates that she is making a prediction; it is that she ostensively communicates an assumption with a certain property: that of being about a future event at least partly beyond her control. Thus, (121) could be a prediction without the speaker's ever intending to communicate, or the hearer's ever recovering, the information in (122):

(121) The weather will be warmer tomorrow.
(122) The speaker is predicting that the weather will be warmer tomorrow.

This is not to say that it would never be desirable for the speaker of (121) simultaneously to communicate assumption (122), or that it would never be relevant for the hearer of (121) to recognise it as a prediction. The fact that a prediction is being made is a fact like any other, and as such may be made manifest by a speaker, or recognised by a hearer, in the usual way. Our claim is simply that even where (122) is manifestly true, its recovery is not *essential* to the comprehension of an utterance such as (121), as the recovery of (120) is essential to the comprehension of an utterance such as (119b) above.

Many speech acts which have been regarded as quite central to pragmatics fall into one or other of these two categories. Promising and thanking, for example, fall into the first category: they are institutional acts, which can be performed only in a society with the requisite institutions, and which must be recognised as such in order to be successfully performed.[28] By contrast, asserting, hypothesising, suggesting, claiming, denying, entreating, demanding, warning and threatening (to the extent that they are speech acts at all) fall into the second category: they are acts which do not need to be identified as such in order to be successfully performed, and which, like predicting, can be identified in terms of some condition on their explicit content or implicatures. In neither case does the interpretation of utterances involving such speech acts require any special pragmatic principles or machinery not already needed on independent grounds.

There is, however, a small class of speech acts which fall into neither of these categories, and which are of genuine interest to pragmatics. They include *saying, telling* and *asking.* Consider (123)-(125):

(123) You will finish the work before 6 p.m.
(124) Will you finish the work before 6 p.m.?
(125) Finish the work before 6 p.m.

It is clear that a declarative such as (123), an interrogative such as (124) and an imperative such as (125) exhibit both logical similarities and differences. Their similarities can be accounted for by assuming that they have the same or similar logical forms. Speech-act theory seems to offer a way of accounting for their differences. It is often suggested, for example, that there are systematic correlations between syntactic sentence type and speech-act type, so that a declarative such as (123) is correlated with the speech-act of saying that the hearer will finish the work before 6 p.m., an interrogative such as (124) with the speech act of asking whether the hearer will finish the work before 6 p.m., and an imperative such as (125) with the speech act of telling the hearer to finish the work before 6 p.m. We adopted something like this assumption in earlier chapters, in suggesting that the propositional form P of an ordinary assertion is standardly integrated into an assumption schema of the form *The speaker said that P.*

If we are right, the recovery of such descriptions is an essential part of the comprehension process, and the speech acts of saying, asking and telling do not fall into our second category of speech acts. However, it is also clear that the acts of saying, asking and telling are neither social nor institutional in the way that bidding at bridge, promising and thanking are. It is easy to think of societies which lack the institution of bridge; we would also maintain that there are societies which lack the institutions of promising and thanking. Saying, telling and asking, by contrast, are universal, and appear to be genuinely communicative rather than social–institutional categories.

However, to say that these three generic speech acts have a role to play in pragmatic theory is not to say that a theoretically adequate account of them already exists. It is tempting to assume that *saying that* is simply the most general type of assertive speech act, *telling to* is simply a general, action-requesting type of directive, and *asking whether* is simply a general, information-requesting type of directive. However, if the correlation between syntactic sentence type and speech-act type is to be maintained, *saying that* cannot be a type of assertive at all. An assertive is a speech act which commits the speaker to the truth of the propositional form of her utterance; but as we have seen, not all declarative utterances are assertive in this sense: for example, metaphors and ironies are not. The problem is quite general. If a directive is an attempt to get the hearer to perform the action explicitly described, then the ironical imperative (126) is not a directive:

(126) Go ahead and ruin my carpet.

It is not a genuine attempt to get the hearer to go ahead and ruin the speaker's carpet. Similarly, the rhetorical question (127) is not a genuine request for information:

(127) What monster would dare to harm a sleeping child?

Thus, the correlation between syntactic sentence types and generic speech acts cannot be maintained unless a whole range of utterance types such as (126) and (127) are excluded as 'insincere' or 'defective', or the traditional typology of speech-act types is abandoned.

Even the claim that there is a well-defined range of mutually exclusive syntactic sentence types is open to question. Is (128), which can be used with either assertive or directive force, a declarative or an imperative?

(128) You are to leave tomorrow.

Is (129), said with rising intonation, a declarative or an interrogative?

(129) You won't be needing the car?

Is (130) a declarative or an exclamative?

(130) This book is so interesting.

What undeniably exists is not a well-defined range of syntactic sentence types but a variety of overt linguistic devices – e.g. indicative, imperative or subjunctive mood, rising or falling intonation, inverted or uninverted word order, the presence or absence of Wh–words, or of markers such as 'let's' or 'please' – which can guide the interpretation process in various ways. While it may be possible to build a theory of syntactic sentence types around these devices, as far as we know this work has not yet been done. In what follows, the use of such terms as 'declarative sentence', 'interrogative sentence' and so on should be regarded as nothing more than a convenient shorthand.[29]

Let us define *saying that P*, where *P* is the propositional form of the utterance, as communicating that the thought interpreted by *P* is entertained as a description of an actual state of affairs. It may be entertained as a true description by the speaker, or by the person or type of person whose thought is being interpreted in the second degree. When you say that *P*, you communicate that you are saying that *P*. You may communicate this by means of linguistic indicators such as indicative mood, declarative word order and so on; in the absence of such linguistic indicators, as in telegraphic forms of writing or speech, it is up to the hearer to decide whether the speaker is saying that P or performing one of the other generic speech acts. In this, as in every other aspect of interpretation, he should adopt the first assumption that is consistent with the principle of relevance.

On hearing (131), the hearer should identify the propositional form of the utterance and integrate it into the description in (132):

(131) The bus is leaving.
(132) The speaker has said that the bus is leaving.

As we have seen, this description can be relevant in a variety of ways. For example, it might provide the hearer with evidence for (133), and if he trusts the speaker enough, for (134):

(133) The speaker believes that the bus is leaving.
(134) The bus is leaving.

An utterance which is intended to achieve relevance in this way is, of course, an ordinary assertion. Ordinary assertions are the result of choosing path (c) on figure 3 above, and producing an utterance which is a fully literal interpretation of the speaker's thought.

Utterance (131) could be metaphorical: imagine that it is said, with no bus in sight, to someone hesitating about joining a group of friends who are all ready to go for a walk and are waiting for his decision. In that case (132) would make manifest (135) and, provided that the hearers trust the speaker enough, (136), where (136) is a contextual implication which (131) manifestly shares with the thought it is used to interpret:

(135) The speaker believes that if the hearer does not decide to go immediately, it will be too late.
(136) If the hearer does not decide to go immediately, it will be too late.

A metaphorical utterance of this type would be the result of choosing path (c) on figure 3 above, and producing an utterance which is a less than fully literal interpretation of the speaker's thought.

Or (131) might be put forward as a report of speech: say a report of what the bus driver has just said. In that case, (132) might provide the hearer with evidence for (137) and, if he trusts the speaker and the bus driver enough, for (138) and (139):

(137) The speaker believes the bus driver has said that the bus is leaving.
(138) The bus driver has said that the bus is leaving.
(139) The bus is leaving.

In this case the utterance would be the result of choosing path (a) on figure 3 above.

As we have seen, some acts of saying that *P* achieve relevance not by providing indirect evidence for *P* but by expressing the speaker's attitude to *P*. For example, the speaker of (131) above, in reporting the bus driver's words, may tacitly dissociate herself from them. In this case, (132) might achieve relevance by providing the hearer with evidence for (140) and, if he trusts the speaker enough, for (141) and (142):

(140) The speaker believes it is ridiculous to say that the bus is leaving.
(141) It is ridiculous to say that the bus is leaving.
(142) The bus is not leaving.

Or, to consider a final case, suppose there has been an argument about when the bus would leave, with the speaker of (131) maintaining that it will not leave for ten minutes and the hearer insisting that it will leave immediately. When the bus moves off and the speaker says (131), the assumption expressed by her utterance will be irrelevant to the hearer, who is already aware that the bus is moving off. In these circumstances, the description in (132) would achieve relevance not by providing the hearer with indirect evidence for the assumption expressed, but by providing him with evidence for such higher-level descriptions as (143)–(144):

(143) The speaker acknowledges that the bus is leaving.
(144) The speaker admits that she was wrong.

There are thus a variety of ways in which a description such as (132) can be relevant; some will have the effect of an ordinary assertion, others the effect of a report of speech or thought, others the effect of an irony or dissociation, others the effect of a speech-act classification and so on. A speaker who wants to achieve some particular effect should give whatever linguistic cues are needed to ensure that the interpretation consistent with the principle of relevance is the one she intended to convey. Thus, when an utterance is interpreted as an ordinary assertion, this is not a result of the operation of some maxim of quality or convention of truthfulness, but simply of an interaction between the form of the utterance, the hearer's accessible assumptions and the principle of relevance.[30]

It is tempting to assume that there is an exactly parallel account of imperatives to the one just proposed for declaratives, replacing the terms 'declarative form', 'saying that' and 'belief' by 'imperative form', 'telling to' and 'desire', respectively. On this approach, an imperative utterance such as (145) would be integrated into a description such as (146), which could again be relevant in a variety of ways — for example, by providing the hearer with evidence for assumption (147), on the basis of which he might then form the desire to leave the room:

(145) Leave the room.
(146) The speaker is telling the hearer to leave the room.
(147) The speaker wants the hearer to leave the room.

In fact, the situation is slightly more complicated than these superficial parallels might suggest. The problem is that there are many types of imperative utterance which are used neither to express a desire of the speaker's, nor to report on someone else's expression of desire. Compare (148)–(149) with (150)–(151):

(148) *Driver to traffic warden*: Pretend you didn't see me.
(149) Keep my dog off his garden, he tells me. As if I could.
(150) (a) *He*: Could you tell me the way to the station?
      (b) *She*: Turn right at the traffic lights and keep straight on.
(151) *Recipe for mint sauce*: Mix two tablespoons of mint leaves, two teaspoons of sugar and half a tablespoon of hot water, add two tablespoons of vinegar and leave to stand.

Whereas (148) is plausibly analysed as an expression by the driver of a desire of her own, and (149) is plausibly analysed as a report by the speaker of someone else's expression of desire, no parallel analysis is possible for (150) and (151). There is no need for the hearer of (150b) to assume that the speaker actually cares whether he turns right or not. There is no reason for the reader of (151) to assume that the writer actually wants anyone who sees the recipe to start making mint sauce. In these cases, the correlation between imperative form and the propositional attitude of desire seems to break down.

It might seem that at this point the speech-act framework comes into its own. A speech-act theorist could ignore the possible links between linguistic form and propositional attitudes such as belief and desire, and simply note that the speech acts performed by imperative utterances fall into two broad types: requestive, as in (148)–(149), and advisory, as in (150)–(151). However, there is a problem with this proposal. Speech acts in the advisory class — giving advice and making suggestions, for example — surely do not have to be recognised as such in order to be performed. In that case it is a mistake to offer an analysis on which the assignment of an imperative utterance to the advisory or the requestive class of speech acts would be fundamental to its comprehension.

We would like to suggest that the distinction between requestive and advisory speech acts is itself reducible to something deeper. Intuitively, a requestive speech act is one that represents a certain state of affairs as desirable from the speaker's point of view, whereas an advisory speech act is one that represents a certain state of affairs as desirable from the hearer's point of view. What makes (148) above intuitively requestive is the fact that the speaker is representing as desirable from her own point of view a state of affairs in which the traffic warden pretends he did not see her; what makes (150b) above intuitively advisory is the fact that the speaker is representing as desirable from the hearer's point of view a state of affairs in which the hearer turns right and keeps straight on. What is essential to the comprehension of these utterances is not their assignment to the class of advisory or requestive speech acts, but a recognition that the state of affairs described is being represented as desirable from the speaker's point of view in the first case, and the hearer's in the second.

If we are right, then the interpretation of imperative and declarative utterances might proceed along broadly parallel lines. The hearer, on recovering the propositional form *P* of an imperative utterance would integrate it into a description of the form *The speaker is telling the hearer to P*. *Telling the hearer to P* might be analysed as communicating that the thought that *P* interprets is entertained as a description of a desirable state of affairs. Who entertains this thought in this way: the speaker or someone whose thought the speaker is interpreting? From whose point of view is the state of affairs described desirable? The hearer has to answer these questions inferentially. As usual, the first interpretation consistent with the principle of relevance will be selected, and a speaker who wants to be correctly understood must make sure that the interpretation she intends to convey is the first one consistent with the principle of relevance. We believe that along these lines a satisfactory account of imperative utterances might be constructed. On this account, the most basic, literal, non-attributive imperatives would be the result of choosing path (d) in figure 3 above and producing an utterance which was a literal interpretation of the speaker's thought. Metaphorical but non-attributive imperatives would be the result of choosing the same path but producing an utterance which was a less than fully literal interpretation of the speaker's thought. Attributive imperatives would be the result of choosing path (a).

Speech-act theorists tend to analyse interrogative utterances as a special sub-type of directive speech act: specifically, as requests for information (see Searle 1969: 69; Bach and Harnish 1979: 48). However, exam questions such as (152), rhetorical questions such as (153), expository questions such as (154), self-addressed questions such as (155) and indirect questions such as (156) all present problems for this approach:

(152) What were the causes of the First World War?
(153) When did you say you were going to give up smoking?
(154) What are the main objections to this approach? First . . .

(155) Why do the leaves of different trees go different colours in autumn?
(156) Peter doesn't know who his neighbour is.

When an examiner asks (152) above, it is not because she wants to know the answer, but because she wants to evaluate the candidate's attempt at an answer. A speaker who asks the rhetorical question (153) would not normally be expecting any verbal response at all. A standard expository device of many writers is to ask a question, such as (154), which they then proceed to answer themselves. Many questions, such as (155), are produced in the absence of any audience, as pure intellectual speculations or musings. Indirect questions such as (156) also resist speech-act analysis. It is hard to see what request for information is being made, or even alluded to, in (156): (156) could be true without it ever having occurred to Peter to wonder, let alone ask, who his neighbour is. The standard speech-act approach thus rules out any possibility of a unitary account of direct and indirect questions.

We would like to suggest that an account of interrogative utterances can be built around the notion of an interpretive use introduced in section 7. Our hypothesis is that the hearer of an interrogative utterance recovers its logical form and integrates it into a description of the form *The speaker is asking Wh-P*, where *Wh-P* is an indirect question. Let us distinguish between yes–no questions, which have not only a logical but also a fully propositional form, and Wh-questions, which have a logical form but no fully propositional form. Then we want to analyse *asking Wh-P*, where *Wh-P* is a yes–no question and *P* is the propositional form of the utterance, as communicating that the thought interpreted by *P* would be relevant if true. We want to analyse *asking Wh-P*, where *Wh-P* is a Wh-question and *P* is the less-than-propositional logical form of the utterance, as communicating that there is some completion of the thought interpreted by *P* into a fully propositional thought which would be relevant if true. In other words, interrogative utterances are interpretations of answers that the speaker would regard as relevant if true.

Relevance, like desirability, is a two-place relation: what is relevant to one person may not be relevant to another. Thus, in interpreting a question, the hearer must always make some assumption about who the speaker thinks its answer would be relevant to. Different assumptions yield different types of question. For example, rhetorical questions such as (153) above ('When did you say you were going to give up smoking?') are often reminders, designed to prompt the retrieval of information the speaker regards as relevant to the hearer. Similarly, expository questions such as (154) above ('What are the main objections to this approach? First . . .'), and more generally offers of information, are analysable as questions whose answers the speaker regards as relevant to the hearer. Regular requests for information, by contrast, are analysable as questions whose answers the speaker regards as relevant to her, and believes, moreover, that the hearer might be in a position to supply. In pure speculations such as (155) above ('Why do the leaves of different trees go different colours in autumn?'), again the suggestion is that the answer would be relevant to the speaker, but there is no manifest expectation that the hearer will be in a position to supply it. In exam questions such as (152) above ('What were the causes of the First World War?') the suggestion is that the answer will be relevant to the speaker, not so much for its content as for the indirect evidence it provides about the candidate's mastery of the subject. There are thus a variety of ways in which the relevance of the description *She is asking Wh-P* can be established, the non-attributive forms of which are the result of choosing path (b) in figure 3 above.

Different questions can be relevant in different ways, some of which have been sketched above. There is no need to analyse all questions as requests for information, no need to set up special speech-act categories to handle offers of information, rhetorical questions, expository questions and so on. Questions can be successfully analysed without appeal to the machinery of speech-act theory.

One advantage of this approach is that it suggests a way of explaining the striking syntactic parallelisms between interrogative and exclamative sentences (see Grimshaw 1979). In traditional speech-act terms, since interrogatives are requests for information and exclamatives are emphatic assertions, it is hard to account for the consistent cross-linguistic parallelisms between utterance types which have so little in common in speech-act terms. Let us assume, however, that exclamatives, like interrogatives, are specialised for interpretive rather than descriptive use, and like non-attributive interrogatives are the result of choosing path (b) in figure 3 above. Whereas a speaker who *asks Wh-P* (where *Wh-P* is an indirect question) guarantees the relevance of some true completion of the incomplete thought represented by *P*, a speaker who *says that Wh-P* (where *Wh-P* is an indirect exclamation) guarantees the truth of some relevant completion of the incomplete thought represented by *P*. On this account, interrogatives and exclamatives have a lot in common.

Consider (157) and (158):

(157) Jane is so clever!
(158) How clever Jane is!

What we are suggesting is that the speaker of (157) or (158) guarantees the truth of some relevant completion of the logical form she has expressed: that is, of some assumption which would be relevant to the hearer and which says how clever Jane is. Which assumption would that be? By the general principles outlined above, it must be the first accessible assumption that is consistent with the principle of relevance. On this analysis, the speaker of (157) and (158) is guaranteeing that Jane is cleverer than the hearer would otherwise have expected. Thus, the intuition that exclamatives are emphatic assertions and the striking parallelisms between exclamative and interrogative form are simultaneously explained.

This very sketchy discussion of speech acts illustrates the general relevance of the principle of relevance. The principle of relevance makes it possible to derive rich and precise non-demonstrative inferences about the communicator's informative intention. With the principle, all that is required is that the properties of the ostensive stimulus should set the inferential process on the right track; to do this they need not represent or encode the communicator's informative intention in any great detail. Thus, illocutionary-force indicators such as declarative or imperative mood or interrogative word order merely have to make manifest a rather abstract property of the speaker's informative intention: the direction in which the relevance of the utterance is to be sought.

Postface

1 Introduction

In the nine years since *Relevance* was first published, the theory of communication it proposes has been widely accepted, widely criticised and widely misunderstood. The book has been translated into several languages;[1] its implications for pragmatic theory have been explored in a growing number of books and articles; it has inspired work in neighbouring disciplines, including linguistics, literary studies, psychology and philosophy. In section 2 of this postface, we review briefly the main developments that have taken place since the first edition was published.[2]

Many commentators, to whom we are very grateful, have raised a wide variety of objections to the theory.[3] We have had the opportunity to answer most of them in a series of publications to which interested readers are referred.[4] These criticisms have helped us correct some mistakes in the book; they have also made us aware of the difficulties in comprehension and the many possibilities of misunderstanding it presents. Either because we are dense, or because we have had more time than our commentators to think about these issues, we find that the most serious problems with our theory are those we have discovered ourselves. In section 3 of this Postface, we outline these problems, and propose several significant changes both of formulation and of substance.

2 Developments

There is now a substantial body of work expounding and evaluating the basic ideas of relevance theory. This includes a précis of *Relevance*,[5] two textbooks and large sections of an encyclopaedia of pragmatics,[6] expository articles designed for non-specialist audiences,[7] and several lengthy critiques.[8] The implications of the theory have been explored in mono-graphs and dissertations,[9] there are edited collections including papers in relevance theory,[10] there is an e-mail network for exchange of ideas, and a bibliography for classroom use.[11] Several research projects have been undertaken; informal workshops are held each year in London, and more formal conferences and lecture series have been held around the world. We will not attempt here a survey of this very diverse literature, but merely point out some of the directions in which we feel that particularly interesting and fruitful work is being done.

2.1 *Explicit communication and the explicit–implicit distinction*

Grice seems not to have noticed (or at least not to have developed the idea) that his Co-operative Principle and maxims could help with other aspects of pragmatic interpretation than the recovery of implicatures: with disambiguation and reference assignment, for example, which he saw as contributing not to what is implicated but to what is (explicitly) said. In 'Logic and Conversation', he gives the impression that sentence meaning and contextual factors are enough on their own to account for disambiguation and reference assignment, and most Gricean pragmatists simply followed him on this.[12] This oversight had two important consequences. First, Gricean pragmatists were slow to react to the extensive psycholinguistic work being done on disambiguation and reference assignment.[13] Second, they tended to take for granted that pragmatic principles make no contribution to explicit content, and that any aspect of utterance interpretation in which pragmatic principles play a role is automatically an implicature.[14]

In *Relevance* (chapter 4, section 2), we rejected this view of pragmatics as *de facto* co-extensive with the study of implicatures. We introduced a notion of explicature, parallel to Grice's notion of implicature, and a definition of explicit communication, which we saw as 'richer, more inferential and hence more worthy of pragmatic investigation than do most pragmatists in the Gricean tradition'. A start was made on studying disambiguation and reference assignment from a relevance-theoretic perspective. We also questioned Grice's suggestion (1989: 25) that disambiguation and reference assignment are the only context-dependent processes involved in explicit communication, drawing attention to a range of further inferential processes required to complete the interpretation of semantically incomplete expressions, narrow the interpretation of vague expressions and, more generally, enrich the linguistically encoded meaning to a point where the resulting overall interpretation would be relevant enough.

The distinction between explicit and implicit communication, and the role of pragmatic factors in explicit communication, have been the focus of much recent research. As noted in *Relevance* (chapter 4, section 3), psycholinguists have provided valuable insights into the actual processes of disambiguation and reference assignment by investigating, for example, how many candidate interpretations are activated, and at what point one is selected and the others dismissed. However, they have been less interested in what makes the selected interpretation pragmatically acceptable, and on this point pragmatic theorists have a contribution to make. Relevance theory claims that in disambiguation and reference assignment, as in every other aspect of interpretation, the first interpretation consistent that meets the hearer's expectation of relevance is the one the hearer should choose.[15] This is not the criterion suggested by most psycholinguists, who tend to talk in informal, Gricean terms. While pragmatic theory can contribute to the development of an adequate criterion, it also stands to gain from the fact that disambiguation and reference assignment are more amenable to experimental testing than the recovery of implicatures. Here, collaboration between pragmatists and psycholinguists should be of benefit to both.

Robyn Carston has studied the contribution of enrichment processes to explicatures in a series of important papers;[16] the role of inference in explicit communication is now being actively explored both inside and outside the relevance-theoretic framework.[17] Criteria have been proposed for distinguishing explicatures from implicatures, and a case has been made for reanalysing some of Grice's best-known examples of generalised implicatures (e.g. the temporal implicatures carried by conjoined utterances, the quantity implicatures carried by numerals such as 'two' and 'three') as pragmatically determined aspects of explicit content. Much of this case rests on an intuitive distinction between truth-conditional and non-truth-conditional content which is standard throughout the speech-act and Gricean literature, but which could itself be usefully reassessed.

The claim that pragmatic principles can contribute to explicit content as well as implicatures has been seen as problematic by those who, following Gazdar (1979), thought of the semantics–pragmatics distinction in a rather non-Gricean way. Gazdar imported into pragmatics a picture common enough in formal semantics at the time, which conflated linguistic semantics with truth-conditional semantics and defined pragmatics as 'meaning minus truth conditions'. On this account, pragmatic processes should be 'post-semantic', and should not 'intrude' into the truth-conditional domain.

Relevance theorists have consistently rejected this picture.[18] In *Relevance* (chapter 4, sections 1 and 7), following Fodor (1975), we systematically distinguished between linguistic semantics (the semantics of natural-language sentences) and truth-conditional semantics (the semantics of conceptual representations). On this approach, the pragmatic processes that contribute to explicit truth-conditional content do not 'intrude' into a unitary semantics: they act on the output of linguistic semantics, enriching incomplete logical forms into fully propositional forms which are in turn the bearers of truth conditions. The need for some such distinction – which is not original to relevance theory – is now widely accepted by those working both inside and outside the relevance-theoretic framework.

2.2 *Linguistic semantics*

The implications of relevance theory for linguistic semantics, and in particular for what is traditionally regarded as non-truth-conditional linguistic meaning, have been a second major focus of research. In previous frameworks, non-truth-conditional meaning was typically analysed in speech-act terms. Speech-act semanticists treated a range of non-truth-conditional expressions (mood indicators, discourse adverbials, discourse particles, parentheticals) as indicators of illocutionary force. Grice extended this account to a range of non-truth-conditional discourse connectives, which he treated as conventionally implicating the performance of higher-order illocutionary acts.[19] Within the relevance-theoretic framework, this approach to non-truth-conditional meaning is being reassessed.[20]

Much of this reassessment was inspired by Diane Blakemore (1987), who reanalysed Grice's discourse connectives using a distinction between conceptual and procedural encoding; her account of discourse connectives as encoding procedural constraints on implicatures has provoked a flood of research.[21] A further impetus was provided by our arguments against speech-act accounts of mood indicators in Wilson and Sperber (1988a), and by our more general critique of speech-act theory in *Relevance* (chapter 4, section 10).[22]

In Wilson and Sperber (1993), we argued that mood indicators and discourse particles are best analysed in procedural rather than conceptual terms. In the relevance-theoretic framework, both types of expression contribute to explicatures rather than implicatures. We therefore generalised Blakemore's notion of constraints on implicatures, arguing that procedural meaning can constrain any aspect of the inferential phase of comprehension, whether explicit or implicit. We also questioned the assumption that procedural meaning and non-truth-conditional meaning invariably coincide: some expressions (e.g. discourse adverbials) which are standardly treated as non-truth-conditional may be best seen as encoding concepts; some truth-conditional expressions (e.g. pronouns) may be best seen as encoding procedures. Relevance-theoretic alternatives to speech-act accounts of mood indicators, discourse particles, discourse adverbials and parentheticals sketched in that paper are now being actively explored.[23] It may turn out that the conceptual-procedural distinction will shed more light on linguistic semantics than the traditional distinction between truth-conditional and non-truth-conditional meaning.

2.3 *Interpretive dimensions of language use*

More fundamental than any of the distinctions discussed above is the one drawn in *Relevance* (chapter 4, sections 7–9) between descriptive and interpretive dimensions of language use. We claimed that, on the most basic level, every utterance is a more or less faithful interpretation of a thought the speaker wants to communicate. An utterance is descriptively used when the thought interpreted is itself entertained as a true description of a state of affairs; it is interpretively used when the thought interpreted is entertained as an interpretation of some further thought: say, an attributed or a relevant thought. In the light of this distinction, traditional pragmatic categories, e.g. tropes and speech acts, must be radically rethought: for example, metaphor falls together with descriptive uses of language, while irony, interrogatives and exclamatives fall together as varieties of interpretive use.

Our approach to metaphor and irony, developed in a series of later papers, has been extensively discussed.[24] Perhaps surprisingly, most reactions have come not from Gricean pragmatists, whose analyses we severely criticised, but from psychologists, non-Gricean pragmatists and literary theorists. The range of data now being considered, and the range of explanations on offer, are much richer than those discussed in the rather limited Gricean literature.

The interpretive dimension of language use is not restricted to irony. Translation has been reanalysed from this perspective in a series of interesting works by Ernst-August Gutt.[25] The notion of interpretive use has also shed light on a range of traditional linguistic topics such as interrogatives, exclamatives, echo questions, pseudo-imperatives, hearsay particles and metalinguistic negation, most of which have resisted analysis in purely descriptive terms.[26] There is much more to be done in this area, from both descriptive and theoretical points of view. However, the reorganisation proposed in *Relevance* seems to be bearing fruit.

2.4 *Wider domains*

A start has been made on investigating the implications of relevance theory in wider domains. In literary studies, the suggestions made by

Paul Kiparsky (1987) have been actively pursued.[27] Humour, politeness, advertising, argumentation, political language and language in education have all been investigated from a relevance-theoretic perspective.[28] Ruth Kempson has applied the assumptions of relevance theory to the investigation of generative grammar and issues of linguistic modularity.[29] Foster-Cohen (1994) and Watson (1995) have looked at language development; the broader implications of relevance theory for language acquisition are assessed in Smith (1989), Smith and Tsimpli (1995); theoretical considerations bearing on both evolution and development are discussed in Sperber (1994a).

In psychology, interesting results are being obtained in several domains. Frith (1989) and Happé (1991, 1992, 1993) have applied relevance theory to the analysis of autism. Politzer (1993) has reanalysed several major experimental paradigms in the psychology of reasoning, and shown how considerations of relevance affect the performance of subjects in ways that can explain some of the most striking experimental results. Sperber, Cara and Girotto (forthcoming) have reanalysed the literature on Wason's famous Selection Task, where subjects are asked to select evidence potentially relevant to evaluating the truth of a conditional statement. Sperber *et al.* suggest that the performance of subjects can be explained on the basis of intuitions of relevance developed in the process of comprehending the task. Their analysis yields precise and novel predictions involving the manipulation of effect and effort, which have been experimentally confirmed.

3 Revisions

3.1 *Not one but two Principles of Relevance*

In *Relevance*, we make two fundamental claims, one about cognition, the other about communication:

(1) Human cognition tends to be geared to the maximisation of relevance.
(2) Every act of ostensive communication communicates a presumption of its own optimal relevance.

Claim (2) is what we called the Principle of Relevance. However, many readers, even careful ones, have used the term 'Principle of Relevance' to refer to claim (1). This is a straight misreading, but an understandable one. Claim (1) is more fundamental and general than claim (2), and at least as worthy to be called a principle. We originally called claim (2) a principle to contrast it with other pragmatic 'principles' proposed in the literature: in particular Grice's Co-operative Principle. We failed to foresee that when our book was read and interpreted – as we wanted – in the context of wider cognitive concerns, this use of the term 'principle' would seem rather arbitrary, cause unnecessary effort, and hence (as we should have predicted on relevance-theoretic grounds) lead to misinterpretation.

We have decided to remedy the situation by talking in future of two Principles of Relevance: the First (or Cognitive) Principle is given in (1), and the Second (or Communicative) Principle is given in (2). Throughout this book, the term 'Principle of Relevance' refers to the Second, Communicative Principle. The change is, of course, expository and not substantive, but it is worth spelling out what we hope to highlight by this reformulation.

3.2 *The First Principle of Relevance*

The First Principle of Relevance is less subtle than the Second Principle, but it is still controversial and in need of justification. As stated, it is also too vague, and in need of elaboration.

Relevance is not a commodity; it is a property. What is it a property of? By our definition, it is a property of inputs to cognitive processes. It can be a property of stimuli, for example, which are inputs to perceptual processes, or of assumptions, which are inputs to inferential processes. Stimuli, and more generally phenomena, are found in the environment external to the organism; assumptions, which are the output of cognitive processes of perception, recall, imagination or inference, are internal to the organism. When we claim that human cognition tends to be geared to the maximisation of relevance, we mean that cognitive resources tend to be allocated to the processing of the most relevant inputs available, whether from internal or external sources. In other words, human cognition tends to be geared to the maximisation of the cumulative relevance of the inputs it processes. It does this not by pursuing a long-term policy based on computation of the cumulative relevance achieved over time, but by local arbitrations, aimed at incremental gains, between simultaneously available inputs competing for immediately available resources.

Why assume that human cognition tends to be geared to the maximisation of relevance? The answer comes in two stages, one to do with the design of biological mechanisms in general, the other with efficiency in cognitive mechanisms.

We start from the assumption that cognition is a biological function, and that cognitive mechanisms are, in general, adaptations. As such, they are the result of a process of Darwinian natural selection (although other evolutionary forces may have helped to shape them). We assume, then, that cognitive mechanisms have evolved in small incremental steps, mostly consisting in the selection of a variant that performed better at the time than other variants that were around. There are many ways in which one variant of a biological mechanism can perform better than others. There may be a qualitative difference in the type of benefits that different variants produce; or the difference may be quantitative, as when the same benefit can be achieved to a greater degree, or at a lower energy cost.

Whereas selection pressures for qualitative improvements vary perpetually with changes in the genotype and the environment, selection pressures for quantitative improvements are a relatively stable factor. *Ceteris paribus*, greater benefits or lower costs are always a good thing. In principle, there are many equally satisfactory ways of balancing costs and benefits: many ways, that is, of being efficient (although few, if any, may be genuine alternatives at a given point in the evolution of an adaptation). Hence, it is not possible to predict what exact balance of costs and benefits should be achieved in a given biological mechanism as a result of the pressure towards greater efficiency. What we can expect is that, in general, an enduring biological mechanism with a stable function will have evolved towards a better cost–benefit balance, i.e. towards greater efficiency.

For example, we can expect that the structure, placement and mode of operation of a muscle will *tend* to minimise the energy costs of performing the bodily movement it is its function to produce. Similarly, we can expect to find a *tendency* towards maximal efficiency in the design of cognitive mechanisms.

We assume, too, that human cognition is the joint product of many specialised mechanisms (see Barkow, Cosmides and Tooby 1992; Hirschfeld and Gelman 1994). Each cognitive mechanism contributes its qualitatively different benefits, in the form of cognitive effects. For each, there has been pressure towards cost–benefit optimisation.

All these cognitive mechanisms taken together constitute the cognitive system. The efficiency of the cognitive system as a whole depends on how its various sub-mechanisms are articulated with one another, and how the resources of the system are shared among them. Articulation and allocation of resources must be such as to maximise the likelihood that the most relevant available information will be processed in the most relevant way.

What the First Principle of Relevance says is that human cognition *tends* to be organised so as to maximise relevance. There may be many shortcomings, many cognitive sub-mechanisms that fail to deliver enough effect for the effort they require, many occasions when the system's resources are poorly allocated. The First Principle does not rule these out. Still, for it to be of any use, the tendency towards maximisation of relevance must be strong enough overall to help guide human interaction. After all, The Second, Communicative Principle of Relevance is grounded in the First Principle, and in the further assumption that the First Principle does indeed make the cognitive behaviour of another human predictable enough to guide communication.

3.2.1 *The First Principle of Relevance and truth*   Our definition of the relevance of an assumption in a context takes no account of the objective truth or falsity of the assumption itself, or of the conclusions that may be derived from it in the context. Thus, a false assumption that contextually implies many false conclusions, or a true assumption that combines with a false contextual premise to imply many false conclusions, is, by our definition, as relevant as a true assumption that implies many true conclusions. On the other hand, our rationale for introducing this notion of relevance has to do with considerations of cognitive efficiency, and the notion of cognitive efficiency cannot be divorced from that of truth. The function of a cognitive system is to deliver knowledge, not false beliefs. Does this mean there is something missing from our definition of relevance? Definitely, and it is in need of revision. Note, though, that for most of our purposes our incomplete definition is good enough.

When we use the notion of relevance to help describe how a cognitive system allocates its resources, there is no harm in leaving objective truth or falsity out of account. The system has no other way of distinguishing true from false assumptions than via its own inputs and internal processes. Basically, if an assumption is caused by the environment in the appropriate way (e.g. through perception), the system accepts it; if an assumption is inferentially derived by the system's own computational mechanisms from accepted premises, it again accepts it. When the system is a reflective one, e.g. a human being, it may be aware that it wants real knowledge and not false beliefs; it may be aware of the risk of accepting false assumptions; it may develop some procedures to double-check the outcome of other procedures; but all it can do in the end is trust the sum of its own procedures to deliver knowledge. So the system will take the output of its own mechanisms as cognitively warranted, and will assess relevance in terms of all contextual effects achieved, even though, unbeknownst to it, some of its conclusions may turn out to be false. From this solipsistic point of view (in the sense of Fodor 1980), truth can safely be ignored.

However, this is not the only point of view that needs to be taken into account. A reflective cognitive system may be aware that some of its beliefs are likely to be false, even if it cannot tell which, and it may regard information leading to false beliefs as worse than irrelevant.

Similarly, a reflective cognitive system that communicates with other systems may regard only true information as relevant to them. Take a speaker who wants her audience to think she is married, when in fact she is not. She lies:

(3) I am married.

Does she believe that what she says is relevant to the hearer, or only that it may *seem* relevant to him, since it would have been relevant if true? We suggest the latter.

Relevant information is information worth having. False information is generally not worth having; it detracts from cognitive efficiency. How should we incorporate this epistemic feature into our definitions? There are two possibilities: we might say that inputs to cognitive processes are relevant only if they meet some specific epistemic condition; or we might say that inputs are relevant only if the outputs of their cognitive processing meet some specific epistemic condition.

The most obvious, and apparently simplest, solution is to make truth of the input a necessary condition of relevance. There are three problems with this choice. First, we want to attribute relevance not just to assumptions but also to phenomena, and in particular to ostensive stimuli. These are inputs to cognitive processes, but they are not the sort of things that can be true or false. Utterances, of course, are said to be true or false, and they are a kind of ostensive stimulus; but when we say that an utterance is true, we really mean that its interpretation is true, and this is the output of a cognitive process of comprehension.

Second, truth of the conclusions seems more crucial to relevance than truth of the premises. Consider the following scenarios:

(4) Peter is a jealous husband. He overhears Mary say on the phone to someone, 'See you tomorrow at the usual place.' Peter guesses rightly that she is speaking to a man, and infers, quite wrongly, that she has a lover and does not love him any more.

(5) Peter is a jealous husband. He overhears Mary say on the phone to someone, 'See you tomorrow at the usual place.' Peter guesses wrongly that she is talking to a man, and infers, rightly as it happens, that she has a lover and does not love him any more. (Mary's lover is a woman.)

In (4), Peter's assumption that Mary was talking to a man was true, and led to rich contextual effects. However, these effects were false beliefs. Was Peter's assumption relevant? We would rather say that it seemed relevant, but in fact was not. In (5), by contrast, Peter's assumption that Mary was talking to a man was false, but it led to many true beliefs, so that here we would be willing to say that it was genuinely relevant (though perhaps not as relevant as it seemed, since it also led to some false beliefs).

Take the more general case of fiction. When you hear a parable, or read *War and Peace*, you may gain insight, through some form of analogical thinking, into yourself, your life, and the world as they are. If only true inputs were relevant, we would have to say such fictions were irrelevant. If truth of the output is what matters, then fictions can be relevant after all.

So let us explore the second way of amending our definition of relevance: by treating an input as relevant only if the output of its cognitive processing meets some specific condition. The basic idea is that for an input to be relevant, its processing must lead to cognitive gains. Now recall our strategy in the book. We first defined relevance in a context, and then relevance to an individual. Our definition of relevance in a context can be left unchanged. A context, even coupled with an inference engine, is not yet a cognitive system; it does not have a cognitive function, and does not stand to gain from true representations or lose by false ones. Relevance in a context is a formal property, interesting as such (with possible applications in Artificial Intelligence, for instance), and is best left as it is.

Things change when we move from relevance in a context to relevance to an individual (or more generally, to any cognitive system). Contextual effects in an individual are *cognitive effects* (a phrase we have used in articles written after 1986). They are changes in the individual's beliefs. An individual does stand to gain or lose by the truth or falsity of his beliefs, and he does have cognitive goals. An individual, were he to reflect on it, would not be interested in contextual effects *per se*, but only in so far as they contribute to his cognitive goals. This is easily built into our definition of relevance to an individual. Let us first define a *cognitive effect* as a contextual effect occurring in a cognitive system (e.g. an individual), and a *positive cognitive effect* as a cognitive effect that contributes positively to the fulfilment of cognitive functions or goals. Then we replace definitions (42) and (43) in chapter 3 with (6) and (7):

(6) *Relevance to an individual* (classificatory)
    An assumption is relevant to an individual at a given time if and only if it has some positive cognitive effect in one or more of the contexts accessible to him at that time.
(7) *Relevance to an individual* (comparative)
    Extent condition 1: An assumption is relevant to an individual to the extent that the positive cognitive effects achieved when it is optimally processed are large.
    Extent condition 2: An assumption is relevant to an individual to the

extent that the effort required to achieve these positive cognitive effects is small.

Definitions (58) and (59) of the relevance of a phenomenon to an individual should also be modified accordingly.

These changes in the definition of relevance might seem to raise two questions. First, isn't the notion of a positive cognitive effect far too vague? Well, we could have been more specific and defined a positive cognitive effect as an epistemic improvement, i.e. an increase in knowledge. All the effects we are actually considering in this book are of this relatively well-defined epistemic kind. However, we want to leave open the possibility of taking into account, in the full picture, other possible contributions to cognitive functioning, involving, for instance, the reorganisation of existing knowledge, or the elaboration of rational desires. And, yes, the resulting definition of a positive cognitive effect is vague, but that is a problem not for relevance theory, but for cognitive psychology in general.

The second question that this redefinition of relevance to an individual might seem to raise is this. Doesn't the First Principle of Relevance then become vacuous? If human cognition tends to be geared to the maximisation of relevance, and if relevance is itself defined in terms of positive cognitive effects, aren't we just saying that human cognition tends to be geared towards the production of positive cognitive effects; which, surely, is a truism, and a vague one at that?

In fact, the First Principle is far from a truism. It makes two empirical claims: neither is self-evident, and the second is original to relevance theory. The First Principle might be false: human cognition might achieve a balance of positive versus negative cognitive effects just good enough to avoid being selected out. In fact, human cognition, being an evolved and adapted system, reflects in fine-grained aspects of its design repeated past pressures towards optimisation. Moreover, we claim that there is one general and essential way in which human cognition exhibits good design, and that is by tending to allocate its resources to the processing of available inputs in such a way as to maximise the expected cognitive effects. That said, we ourselves have stressed that what we now call the First Principle of Relevance is indeed vague and general, and that what makes it worth stating are some of its precise and non-trivial consequences: in particular, the Second Principle of Relevance.

3.3 *Revising the presumption of relevance*

The (Second) Principle of Relevance states that every act of ostensive communication communicates a presumption of its own optimal relevance. The presumption of relevance itself was spelled out as follows:

(8) *Presumption of optimal relevance*
    (a) *The set of assumptions I which the communicator intends to make manifest to the addressee is relevant enough to make it worth the addressee's while to process the ostensive stimulus;*
    (b) *The ostensive stimulus is the most relevant one the communicator could have used to communicate I.*

We believe that this formulation should be substantively modified. The modifications will make the presumption of relevance simpler, and we will argue that they not only preserve the predictive power of the earlier version, but significantly increase it.

There are two reasons for crediting a communicator with the intention to convey a presumption of relevance; these are reflected in the two clauses of the presumption. First, the communicator must intend her ostensive stimulus to appear relevant enough to the addressee to be worth his attention. Otherwise, he might not pay it enough attention, and communication would fail. This sets a lower limit on the level of relevance the communicator intends the addressee to expect. A version of this idea is built into clause (a) of the presumption of relevance above. In this version, the level of effort needed to reconstruct the intended interpretation is treated as given, and the presumption is that the effect will be high enough for the overall relevance of the stimulus to be at or above the lower limit (below which the stimulus would not be worth processing). Clause (a) says, in essence, that the level of effect is at least sufficient.

Now suppose we treat the level of effect rather than effort as given. Then by the same reasoning – based on the fact that the communicator must intend her ostensive stimulus to appear relevant enough – the addressee can have legitimate expectations about the level of effort needed to achieve this effect. This level of effort must be low enough for the overall relevance of the stimulus to be at or above the lower limit.

Since there is no principled asymmetry here between effect and effort, clause (a) of the presumption of relevance can be made both simpler and more general, as follows:

(9) The ostensive stimulus is relevant enough for it to be worth the addressee's effort to process it.

Is it ever legitimate for the addressee to expect – and the communicator to intend him to expect – a level of relevance that is not merely at but well above the lower limit? Grice and most of his followers suggest that it is. They assume that speaker and hearer must have a common goal that goes beyond merely understanding and being understood, and are expected to provide whatever information would best further this common goal. What is to be expected is not just relevance enough, but maximal relevance to achieving the common goal.[30]

We have expressed disagreement with this view. It may be true that in most verbal exchanges the participants share a purpose that goes beyond merely understanding one another, but it need not always be the case. Conflictual or non-reciprocal communication, for example, involve no such purpose. It is also true that understanding is made easier by the presence of a common goal. We can account for by this pointing out that a common goal creates a number of mutually manifest contextual assumptions on which the interlocutors can draw. The existence of a common conversational goal need not be built into pragmatic principles. We still believe this is correct.

However, we ourselves have stressed that interlocutors always share at least one common goal, that of understanding and being understood. It is in the communicator's manifest interest both to do her best and to appear to be doing her best to achieve this common goal. This provides a second reason for crediting her with the intention to convey a presumption of relevance, and is reflected in clause (b) of the presumption as stated above. In its current version, however, clause (b) is wholly about effort. The intended effect is treated as given, and clause (b) says that the stimulus used to achieve this effect is the one that requires least effort from the addressee.

The presumption of minimal effort expressed by (b) is at best too vague and at worst too strong. A communicator may well be willing to try to minimise the addressee's effort, since this will make him more likely to attend to her ostensive stimulus and succeed in understanding it. Still, for all sorts of reasons, the particular stimulus she produces may not be the one that would absolutely minimise the addressee's effort. In the first place, there is the communicator's own effort to consider. As speakers, we are prepared to make only so much effort in formulating our thoughts, and as hearers, we know better than to expect flawlessly crafted utterances. Then there may be rules of etiquette or standards of ideological correctness that rule out the utterance that would be easiest to process (which would also be likely to convey unwanted weak implicatures). As speakers, we avoid what we see as objectionable formulations, and as hearers, we expect such restraint.

Clause (b) of the presumption of optimal relevance should in any case have allowed for the speaker's right to be lazy or prudish, i.e. to have her own preferences and take them into account.[31] In later publications or oral presentations, we amended this effort clause to say that no *unjustified* or *gratuitous* effort was to be demanded. In other words, from a range of possible stimuli which were equally capable of communicating the intended interpretation and equally acceptable to the communicator (given both her desire to minimise her own effort and her own moral, prudential, or aesthetic preferences), the communicator should prefer, and appear to prefer, the stimulus that would minimise the addressee's effort.

However, this line of reasoning, which was based on considerations of effort, applies equally to the effect side. Suppose that, from the communicator's point of view, her goals would be equally well served by a number of utterances (or other stimuli), all of which would cause the intended contextual effects, but some of which would cause further contextual effects, and be (or seem) more relevant to the addressee as a result. Which should she choose? She should choose the utterance that would be (or seem) most relevant to the addressee, for just the reasons given above in discussing the minimisation of effort.

Here is an illustration. Mary wants to make it quite manifest to Peter that she will be out from 4 o'clock to 6 o'clock. She might inform him of this by saying any of (10a–c):

(10) (a) I'll be out from 4 to 6.
     (b) I'll be out at the Jones's from 4 to 6.
     (c) I'll be out at the Jones's from 4 to 6 to discuss the next meeting.

Suppose she assumes that any of these utterances would be relevant enough to Peter. Suppose it doesn't matter to her whether she tells him where she is going and why. Suppose the amount of effort needed to produce any of these utterances makes no difference to her. Then it would be rational enough to utter any of (10a–c), since each would achieve her goal at an equally acceptable cost to her. However, it would be most rational to produce the utterance most relevant to Peter, since this would make it most likely that he would attend to her communication, remember it, and so on: in other words, it would maximise the manifestness to Peter of the information that Mary wants him to have. Since (10c) would demand more effort from Peter than (10b), and (10b) than (10a), Mary should choose one of these longer utterances if and only if the extra information conveyed yields enough effect to make it more relevant to Peter. If he doesn't care where she is going, she should choose (10a). If he cares where she is going, but not why, she should choose (10b). If he cares both where and why, she should choose (10c). These choices are rational even if Mary doesn't particularly want to be helpful to Peter by telling him what he may want to know. They are rational as ways of maximising the chances that she will succeed in making manifest to him the one thing she does want to make manifest: that she will be away from 4 o'clock to 6 o'clock.

We can thus make the following generalisation. Take a set of stimuli that meet the following conditions: any of them would be likely to communicate what the communicator wants to communicate; she is capable of producing any of them; and she has no preferences among them, apart from wanting to choose the one that will be most effective in achieving her communicative goal. These stimuli may differ in terms of the effort demanded of the addressee, the effects achieved, or both effect and effort. The communicator should choose the stimulus that appears most relevant to the addressee, since this will make her communication most likely to succeed. For the same reason, she should appear to be choosing the stimulus that is most relevant to the addressee. In normal conditions, appearance and reality are likely to coincide.

The communicator's choice of ostensive stimuli is limited not only by her preferences but by her abilities. On the effort side, there may be stimuli that would be easier for the hearer to process, but that the communicator is unable to think of at the time, as when the best formulation of some thought just fails to come to mind. On the effect side, the limits on the communicator's abilities are even more significant. There may always be information that the hearer would find more relevant than anything the communicator has to offer. She cannot be more relevant than her own knowledge permits. If she decides to communicate in bad faith, and tries to make manifest assumptions that she does not believe, she would still want the addressee to think that what she is trying to communicate is warranted by what she knows.

Again, there is no principled asymmetry between effect and effort. The presumption is that, of all the stimuli that are available to her and acceptable as a means of achieving her particular communicative goal, the communicator will choose one that is as relevant as possible to the addressee. The second clause of the presumption of relevance can be made both simpler and more general, as follows:

(11) The ostensive stimulus is the most relevant one compatible with the communicator's abilities and preferences.

We now have a fully revised presumption of optimal relevance:

(12) *Presumption of optimal relevance (revised)*
   (a) The ostensive stimulus is relevant enough for it to be worth the addressee's effort to process it.
   (b) The ostensive stimulus is the most relevant one compatible with the communicator's abilities and preferences.

This says that the addressee is entitled to expect a level of relevance high enough to warrant his attending to the stimulus, and which is, moreover, the highest level of relevance that the communicator was capable of achieving given her means and goals.

3.3.1 *The Second Principle of Relevance: that the presumption of optimal relevance is ostensively communicated* It would be a mistake to read the presumption of optimal relevance, in either the early or the revised version, as describing a goal that rational communicators should achieve. Unlike Grice's maxims, neither the principle nor the presumption of relevance is presented as a goal to be pursued or a rule to be followed by the communicator. The (Second) Principle of Relevance is a descriptive (as opposed to normative) claim about the content of a given act of ostensive communication. It claims that part of that content is a presumption that this very act of communication is relevant to the addressee.

The addressee's aim in interpreting an utterance is to identify the communicator's informative intention. As with any attribution of an intention to an agent, this is done by observing the means she chooses and assuming that these are appropriate to her goals, given her beliefs. We claim that a presumption of optimal relevance is communicated by any act of ostensive communication. Given our definition of ostensive communication, for this to be true it must be mutually manifest to communicator and addressee that the communicator has the informative intention of making the presumption of relevance manifest to the addressee. We will now show that this is so.

A rational communicator must intend the stimulus she uses to appear relevant enough to the addressee to attract his attention and make him willing to spend the effort needed for comprehension. How relevant is that? There is a limit below which the addressee will be unlikely to attend to the stimulus at all; clearly, the communicator must intend the addressee to expect a level of relevance at least as high as this. Moreover, it is to the communicator's advantage that the addressee should expect a level of relevance well above this lower limit, so that he will be willing to invest the effort needed for comprehension. However, just as the addressee is guided in interpreting the utterance by the assumption that the communicator is rational, so the communicator's intentions are constrained by the assumption that the addressee is rational. A rational addressee will not expect more relevance than the communicator is willing and able to achieve. There is no point in expecting the communicator to give information she doesn't have, or to produce stimuli she is unable to think of at the time. Nor can she be expected to go against her own preferences. So a rational communicator intends her stimulus to appear as relevant as is compatible with her abilities and preferences.

In other words, it is necessary for the first clause of the presumption of relevance to be manifest to the addressee, and it is advantageous for the second clause to be manifest too. A rational communicator should therefore want both clauses of the presumption of relevance to be manifest. We claim that this is not some hidden fact about the psychology of communicators, but is manifest to any competent communicator or addressee. Thus, when a communicator makes it mutually manifest to herself and her addressee that she is trying to communicate by means of a given stimulus, she thereby makes it mutually manifest that she intends a presumption of relevance to be manifest. Given our definition of ostensive communication, this amounts to saying that a presumption of relevance is communicated.

3.3.2 *Some consequences of the revised presumption of relevance* All the analyses we have given in this book and elsewhere on the basis of the old presumption of optimal relevance go through as before. It is still true that the rational way to go about interpreting an utterance, or any other ostensive stimulus, is to follow a path of least effort and stop at the first interpretation that satisfies one's expectation of relevance. However, in the old version, the expected level of relevance was systematically at the lower limit. This did not mean that an utterance could never be more than just relevant enough to be worth the hearer's attention. What it did mean is that in order to achieve a higher level of relevance, the speaker had to formulate her utterance so that the first interpretation that was relevant enough to be worth the hearer's attention would actually be more than relevant enough.

To illustrate, suppose that Mary says to Peter:

(13) You remember I bought that lottery ticket? Well, guess what? I won £10,000!

Mary's statement, taken literally, may well be not only relevant enough to be worth Peter's attention, but much more relevant than he would have expected, given the unrevised presumption of relevance. Still, if this is the first accessible interpretation that is relevant enough (and unless it conflicts with other of his contextual assumptions), he will accept it as the one intended. This, at least, is what an analysis based on the unrevised presumption of relevance would (correctly) predict.

Compare this with the case where Mary says to Peter:

(14) You remember I bought that lottery ticket? Well, guess what? I won a prize!

Here, the first accessible interpretation that is relevant enough will probably represent Mary's prize as just big enough to be worth talking about. If just knowing that she won a prize is relevant enough, then the value of the prize may not be seen as relevant at all. Here again, an analysis based on the unrevised presumption of relevance is adequate.

The revised presumption of relevance yields the same analysis of these and similar examples. In interpreting (13), Peter assumes that Mary had the ability – in this case the knowledge – to say something more than minimally relevant (namely that she had won £10,000), and that she gave this information in the absence of contrary preferences. In interpreting (14), let us assume that Peter accepts clause (b) of the presumption of relevance and expects Mary's utterance to be the most relevant one compatible with her abilities and preferences. Still, he has no reason to think she has a more relevant piece of information that she is reluctant to share with him; so he will assume that the prize is merely big enough to be worth mentioning. Quite often, the lower limit mentioned in clause (a) of the (revised) presumption of relevance will coincide with the higher limit mentioned in clause (b). The speaker has something just relevant enough to be worth saying, and says it.

In some cases, though, the revised presumption yields different, and better, analyses. Here we will consider two. The first is adapted from Grice (1989: 32). Peter and Mary are planning a holiday in France. Peter has just said that it would be nice to visit their old acquaintance Gérard if it would not take them too far out of their way. The dialogue continues:

(15) (a) *Peter*: Where does Gérard live?
      (b) *Mary*: Somewhere in the South of France.

As Grice notes, Mary's answer implicates (16):

(16) Mary does not know where in the South of France Gérard lives

This implicature is easily explained in terms of Grice's maxims. Mary's answer is less informative than the first maxim of Quantity ('Make your contribution as informative as is required') would suggest. 'This infringement [. . .] can be explained only by the supposition that [Mary] is aware that to be more informative would be to say something that infringed the second maxim of Quality, "Don't say what you lack evidence for" ' (Grice 1989: 32–33).

In the unrevised version of relevance theory, we would have to explain this implicature by noting that, in the situation described, it would generally be mutually manifest that Mary is expected and willing to co-operate in planning the holiday in France. From this assumption, together with the fact that her reply is not relevant enough to answer Peter's question, it can be inferred that she does not know exactly where Gérard lives. Then not only is (16) manifest but, given

Mary's co-operativeness, it is mutually manifest that she should want (16) to be manifest. Hence (16) is a proper implicature.

This analysis acknowledges the presence, in this particular situation, of the kind of co-operativeness which Grice regards as there in principle in every conversation. We have argued that Gricean co-operativeness is neither always at work, nor always presumed to be at work. In circumstances where the speaker is not expected to be co-operative, implicatures of the type in (16) do not go through.

Suppose, for example, that it is mutually manifest that Mary is dead against visiting Gérard. Then her answer would not carry the implicature in (16). She may have no more precise information about Gérard's whereabouts, or she may have it but be reluctant to give it, and there is no telling which. Here, a strict Gricean would have to say that Mary is at least partially 'opting out' of the Co-operative Principle and the first maxim of Quantity. Just as we would have had to explain the Gricean implicature in (16) by adding the contextual assumption that the speaker is co-operative, so a Gricean would have to explain the absence of the implicature by adding the assumption that the speaker is unco-operative.

Notice, now, that the same dialogue could carry a different implicature. Suppose it is mutually manifest that Mary knows where Gérard lives. Then her answer in (15b) would implicate not (16) but (17):

(17) Mary is reluctant to say exactly where Gérard lives.

This raises a problem for the Gricean, since it violates both the Co-operative Principle and the first maxim of Quantity, and implicatures are supposed to arise only on the assumption that the Co-operative Principle is in force. With the unrevised version of the presumption of relevance, this example would have raised a problem for us too. Let us suppose that the information that Gérard lives in the South of France is relevant enough to be worth Peter's attention (even though it is less relevant than he would wish). Then, on our unrevised account, Peter should stop short of constructing the implicature in (17).

With the revised presumption of relevance, we can explain both standard Gricean implicatures such as (16), and non-Gricean implicatures such as (17), which are caused by, and express, a refusal to co-operate. In (15), if it is mutually manifest that Mary would like to be more specific about where Gérard lives, then her response, together with clause (b) of the revised presumption of relevance, will imply that she is unable to be more specific. If it is mutually manifest that this implication increases the relevance of her utterance, then it will be not just implied but implicated. On the other hand, if it is mutually manifest that Mary could have been more specific, then her response, together with clause (b) of the presumption of relevance, will imply that she is unwilling to be more specific. Again, if it is mutually manifest that this implication increases the relevance of her utterance, it will be implicated.

Note that here we are making a subtle and non-obvious claim. We are claiming that if it is mutually manifest to communicator and audience that an assumption contextually implied by an utterance increases its overall relevance, then it is (in general) mutually manifest that the communicator intended this implication to be manifest. In other words, this assumption is communicated (as an implicature). This follows from clause (b) of the revised presumption of relevance, which states that the utterance is the most relevant one compatible with the communicator's abilities and preferences. If a mutually manifest implication of the utterance contributes to overall relevance, and thus helps to confirm the presumption of optimal relevance, the inference that the communicator intended it to play this role is sound. It is obvious that the communicator is able to implicate this assumption. There is evidence that she is willing to implicate it, since she has willingly chosen a form of utterance that manifestly carries this implication, which helps to confirm the presumption of relevance that she herself has communicated.

The claim that manifestly relevant implications can be treated as implicatures has one striking consequence. Sometimes, the addressee may justifiably attribute to the communicator an implicature that she never in fact intended to communicate. Sound though it may be, the inference from the mutually manifest fact that an implication is relevant to the conclusion that it is implicated (i.e. intentionally made manifest) is a non-demonstrative one, and it may on occasion be false. Consider a slightly different version of dialogue (15) above. It is mutually manifest to Mary and Peter that Mary is willing to give him all the relevant information she has:

(18) (a) *Peter*: You said you were in touch with Gérard. Where does he live?

    (b) *Mary*: Somewhere in the South of France, I don't know exactly where.

In (18b), Mary says that she doesn't know exactly where Gérard lives. As it stands, this utterance, made without further explanation, contextually implies that she misinformed Peter when she claimed to be in touch with Gérard. She might not have intended to make this implication manifest, and *a fortiori* she might not have wanted to implicate it. However, unless she explicitly cancels the implicature (for instance, by explaining how it is that she doesn't know where Gérard lives despite being in touch with him), she will be taken to have implicitly admitted that she misinformed Peter. As this example shows, just as the choice of words may commit a speaker to unwanted explicatures, so the contextual implications of an utterance may commit her to unwanted implicatures.

The second type of case where the revised presumption of relevance leads to better analyses has been much discussed in the literature under the label 'scalar implicatures'.[32] Here is a typical example. In most situations, the utterance in (19) would implicate (20) or (21):

(19) Some of our neighbours have pets.
(20) Not all of our neighbours have pets.
(21) The speaker doesn't know whether all her neighbours have pets.

These implicatures do not always go through, as witness (22) and (23):

(22) Some of our neighbours certainly have pets; maybe they all do.
(23) (a) *Peter*: Do some of your neighbours have cats, dogs, goldfish, that sort of thing?
    (b) *Mary*: Yes, some of our neighbour do have pets; in fact they all do.

At first blush, these facts are reasonably well explained in Gricean terms. A speaker who knew that *all* her neighbours have pets and who merely said, without the sort of qualifications in (22) and (23), that *some* of her neighbours have pets, would be giving less information than required by the first maxim of Quantity. To preserve the assumption that the speaker is obeying the Gricean maxims, the hearer must take her to implicate that she doesn't know whether all her neighbours have pets, or more strongly, that not all them do.

This Gricean account is not without weaknesses. It leaves open the question of how much information is required on a given occasion by the first maxim of Quantity – and hence of when 'some' actually carries an implicature. Nor does it offer any obvious way of deciding when 'some' implicates 'not all' (which it seems to do most of the time), and when it merely implicates ignorance on the part of the speaker. Still, 'some' conveys 'not all' so often that the implicature from one to the other is considered by most Griceans (e.g. Levinson 1987) to be a case of 'generalised implicature', working as a default inference automatically made, though defeasible in the presence of negative evidence.[33]

In the unrevised version of relevance theory, examples like (19) raise the following problem. Consider a situation where the fact that (at least) some of the speaker's neighbours have pets would be relevant enough to be worth the hearer's attention. Then, having recovered this basic interpretation (on which 'some' is compatible with 'all'), the hearer would have no reason to go further and assume that the speaker meant 'some, but not all'. This is not an altogether undesirable result. In some cases it makes the right prediction, as in the following dialogue:

(24) (a) *Henry*: If you or some of your neighbours have pets, you shouldn't use this pesticide in your garden.
(b) *Mary*: Thanks. We don't have pets, but some of our neighbours certainly do.

Here, it seems to us, the fact that at least some of Mary's neighbours have pets is relevant enough, and there is no reason to assume she meant that not all of them do (or that she doesn't know whether all of them do). Griceans who treat the inference from 'some' to 'not all' as a generalised implicature would have to claim that Mary's utterance does have this implicature, or that the hearer of (24b) would first make this inference and then (for what reason?) cancel it. Neither hypothesis seems plausible to us.

However, in some cases the predictions of the unrevised presumption of relevance are not obviously correct. This happens when the basic interpretation of 'some' (where 'some' is compatible with 'all') is relevant enough to be worth the hearer's attention, but when it would clearly be more relevant to the hearer to know whether 'not all' is the case too. An example is (25):

(25) (a) *Henry*: Do all, or at least some, of your neighbours have pets?
(b) *Mary*: Some of them do.

Here, Henry has made manifest that it would be relevant to him to know not only whether some of Mary's neighbours have pets, but whether all of them do. An unrevised relevance model, applied mechanically to this case, would predict that Henry should stop at the first interpretation that is relevant enough; this is clearly the one on which Mary is taken to communicate that she has at least some neighbours who have pets, and nothing more. This prediction is manifestly wrong. Mary's answer would normally be taken to convey that not all of her neighbours have pets.

It would, of course, be easy enough to apply the relevance model flexibly: one might argue, for instance, that someone who asks a question automatically makes it manifest that what he would consider relevant enough is nothing less than a full answer to his question, or an utterance at least as relevant as that. In that case, Mary's answer in (25b), understood as conveying only that she has at least some neighbours who have pets, would not be relevant enough. Standard relevance considerations would cause it to be interpreted as implicating[34] that not all her neighbours have pets, thereby satisfying Peter's expectation of adequate relevance.

However, we much prefer a model that can be applied mechanically. Isn't this what taking cognitive science seriously is all about? The revised relevance model is much more satisfactory in this respect (by which we mean not that we have a full-fledged, mechanically applicable model, but that at least we don't need to invoke special factors, however plausible, to account for not-so-special cases). With the revised presumption of relevance, the analysis of example (25) goes as follows. Mary's answer makes it manifest that she is either unable or unwilling to inform Peter that all her neighbours have pets. Either implication would increase the relevance of her utterance. In fact, in most circumstances Mary's answer will make it manifest that she is unable (rather than unwilling). This inability can in turn be explained in two ways: either she doesn't know whether all her neighbours have pets, or she knows that not all of them do. If one of these mutually incompatible assumptions is manifest enough, it will (in general) be mutually manifest that Mary intended it to be manifest, since it increases the relevance of her utterance and is compatible with her preferences. The resulting interpretation is the one consistent with the principle of relevance.

Mary's answer in (25) is a case where the speaker has deliberately chosen to express a less informative proposition when a closely related, equally accessible and more informative proposition would have demanded no more effort, either from Mary or from the hearer. All such cases have a similar analysis. If the more informative proposition would not have been more relevant, there is no implicature. If the more informative proposition would have been more relevant, the utterance will be taken to implicate either that the speaker is unwilling, or (more commonly) that she is unable to provide the more relevant information. In the latter case, the communicator's inability may be due either to her not knowing whether the more relevant information is true, or to her knowing it to be false. If either of these two possibilities is manifest and relevant, it will be treated as an implicature.

3.4 *Far too early to conclude*

There are many other aspects of relevance theory that we would like to see developed, and that we or others have begun working on in articles and unpublished lectures. Many involve local revisions of the version of the theory presented in this book. Some open new perspectives that may turn out to be more important in the general balance of the theory than the present revisions.

Experimental studies testing relevance-theoretic hypotheses have just begun, and we hope that they will lead to revisions, new insights, and, perhaps more important, new problems to investigate. Interesting applications of the theory to literary studies suggest that it might be of some relevance, more generally, in the study of various cultural productions.

Novel insights and new problems should come from the formal modelling of the theory, possibly with the use of spreading activation models which seem particularly well suited to representing, on the one hand, the role of accessibility, and, on the other, the way the system's computations can be guided on line by monitoring its efforts and effects. Two important and related domains have hardly been explored at all from a relevance-theoretic perspective: the theory has been developed from the point of view of the audience of communicative acts, and without taking into account the complex sociological factors richly studied by sociolinguistics. The cognitive processes at work in the communicator, and the social character and context of communication are, of course, essential to the wider picture, to the study of which we hope relevance theory can contribute, and from which it stands greatly to benefit.

We ourselves have been working on a revised and more detailed description of inferential comprehension, integrating in particular the processes involved in enrichment and the comprehension of loose talk or metaphor. This work will be presented in our forthcoming *Relevance and Meaning*.

Notes to First Edition

CHAPTER 1 COMMUNICATION

1 See Reddy 1979 for a discussion of these misleading metaphors.
2 For instance, by Jakobson (1960), who uses it as the basis for a classification of the functions of language, and Lyons (1977), who finds the model incomplete but not radically inadequate to account for verbal communication.
3 For an examination of the work of Lévi-Strauss in this light, see Sperber 1985: chapter 3.
4 See Smith and Wilson 1979 for a general assessment.
5 For a discussion of semiotic approaches to cultural and artistic symbolism and suggestions for an alternative approach, see Sperber 1975a, 1980.
6 A rather infelicitous term proposed by C. W. Morris (1938), who defined syntax as the study of the formal relations among signs, semantics as the study of the relation between signs and their denotations, and pragmatics as the study of the relation between signs and their users or interpreters. For a discussion of the current scope of pragmatics, see Searle, Kiefer and Bierwisch (eds) 1980: Introduction; Levinson 1983: chapter 1.
7 See Grice 1975, 1978. For a survey of the Gricean pragmatic literature, see Levinson 1983: chapter 3. Attempts to spell out the Gricean programme in more detail include Bach and Harnish 1979; Leech 1983. In France, Ducrot (1972, 1980a, 1980b and a number of other works) has developed a programme in some ways comparable to Grice's.
8 See Loftus 1979, Neisser 1982.
9 Our discussion in this section applies more directly to Schiffer's version than to Lewis's. See also note 29 below.
10 For further discussion of the mutual-knowledge hypothesis, see Johnson-Laird 1982a; Sperber and Wilson 1982.
11 See Armstrong 1971; Bach and Harnish 1979; Bennett 1976; Blackburn 1984; Davidson 1984a; Davies 1981; Grice 1957, 1968, 1969, 1982; Harman 1968; Lewis 1969; Loar 1976, 1981; McDowell 1980; Patton and Stampe 1969; Recanati 1979, 1987; Schiffer 1972; Searle 1969, 1983; Strawson 1964a, 1969, 1971; Wright 1975; Yu 1979; Ziff 1967.

12 A notable exception being A. H. Gardiner 1932.

13 For ease of exposition, and unless the context indicates otherwise, we will assume that the communicator is female and the audience male.

14 We are considering here Searle's views as expressed in *Speech Acts* (1969), not his more recent and somewhat different views developed in *Intentionality* (1983). One of Searle's arguments was in the form of a purported counterexample to Grice's analysis (Searle 1965: 221–39; 1969: 44–5). This counterexample has been satisfactorily dealt with by Grice 1968: 160–5; and Schiffer 1972: 27–30.

15 For other examples of codeless communication, discussed in greater detail, see section 10.

16 Note that it would not be too difficult to reconcile the strong inferential theory of communication with a modified code theory. The code theorist might concede to the inferential theorist that all codes are sets of conventions and that decoding is an inferential process along the lines described above, and the inferential theorist might concede in return that the inferences involved in communication are decoding inferences. However, the resulting compromise would combine the worst defects of both theories: it would fail to take into account the role of uncoded inference in communication, and it would ignore the non-inferential character of much decoding.

17 We assume that the 'response' involved in intention (27a) is always that the audience should be informed of something (in the broad sense in which we are using 'inform'). This is by no means a commonly accepted view. Grice himself initially had in mind two types of response: belief, in response to a statement, and action, in response to an injunction. He later (Grice 1968, 1969) excluded action in response to an injunction and considered only mental responses: in the case of a statement, the intended response is the recognition by the audience that the communicator has a certain belief and, sometimes, the adoption of the same belief; in the case of an injunction, the intended response is the recognition by the audience that the communicator has a certain intention, and the adoption of the same intention. Others have expressed still different views (see Searle 1969; Armstrong 1971; Bennett 1976). We develop our own view in sections 8 to 12, and more specifically in section 11.

18 For examples and discussion suggesting that this intention is unnecessary, see Schiffer 1972: chapter 3.

19 See for instance Grice 1982; Recanati 1987.

20 One may also, as suggested by Searle (1969: 47), replace the infinity of intentions by a reflexive intention, i.e. a complex intention comprising as one of its sub-intentions the intention that the whole complex intention should be recognised. Such a reflexive intention is 'overt' in much the same way as an ordered infinity of intentions. It might seem that a single reflexive intention is psychologically more plausible than an infinity of intentions, but we doubt this for the following reason. Normally, when a representation contains a definite reference to a representation, this reference can be replaced by a mention of the representation referred to. For instance (a) contains a reference to the representation expressed by Mary and spelled out in (b); hence (c) can validly be inferred from (a)–(b):

(a) Peter believes what Mary said.
(b) Mary said that it is raining.
(c) Hence: Peter believes that it is raining.

Often, understanding a representation such as (a), or establishing its relevance, involves just such a substitution. A case in point is a communicator's intention *I* that her audience should recognise her intention *J*: intention *I* cannot be fulfilled or fully grasped without grasping *J*. With a reflexive intention *I* which includes the sub-intention that the audience recognise *I*, this yields an infinitely long formula. Since infinitely long formulas are not available, let alone intelligible, to the mind, it yields a headache. Reflexive intentions do not, after all, provide a psychologically plausible way of making the notion of 'overtness' more precise.

21 Though the infinity-of-intentions proposal (and its reflexive variant) on the one hand, and the mutual-knowledge proposal on the other, both dispose of examples of the type suggested by Strawson 1964a and developed by Schiffer 1972, it is possible to think of other examples of untypical communication which are handled differently by the two approaches. The infinity-of-intentions approach does not rule out cases where the communicator's intentions, though recognised by the audience, do not become mutually known. The mutual-knowledge approach does not rule out cases where mutual knowledge, and hence communication, is established unintentionally, or at least seems so to the audience. These cases have not been discussed in the literature. Since we are not aware that any definite conclusion against one or the other solution follows from these extra cases, we leave it at that.

22 A notable exception being the psychologist Herbert Clark and his associates. See Clark 1977, 1978; Clark and Lucy 1975; Clark and Haviland 1977; Clark and Marshall 1981; Clark and Schunk 1980; Clark and Carlson 1981.

23 The *William James Lectures, Logic and conversation*, delivered at Harvard in 1967, brought together ideas first put forward in Grice 1957 and 1961. Versions of the second and third lectures were published as Grice 1975, 1978; parts of the fourth lecture are summarised in Grice 1981; many of the ideas in the last three lectures were presented in Grice 1968, 1969; the complete text, with an important 'Retrospective Epilogue', was published in Grice 1989.

24 The role of the Gricean maxims in disambiguation was not discussed by Grice himself, but was dealt with by Katz 1972: 449–50; Walker 1975: 156–7, Wilson and Sperber 1981: 156–9.

25 A temptation to which Leech 1983 might be felt to have yielded.

26 We have tried (Wilson and Sperber 1981) to show that all the maxims can be reduced to a single well-defined maxim of relevance.

27 Kempson 1975, Stalnaker 1974, Wilson 1975 develop Gricean accounts of presuppositional phenomena; Sadock 1979, Levinson 1983 (147–62) look at metaphor and figurative language from a Gricean perspective; Searle 1975, Bach and Harnish 1979 approach indirect speech acts in Gricean terms. See also note 7 above.

28 It has been argued (see Fodor 1983: 102) that conceptual identifications of distal stimuli, which are the output of perceptual processes, need inferential

validation before being accepted by the individual as facts. If this were so, being perceptible would not be a sufficient condition for being manifest. The best evidence for this claim is the fact that one can mistrust one's senses, and hence perceive and yet not believe. However, one can also infer and not believe, as when a validly inferred conclusion contradicts a strongly held belief. It seems to us that the output of perception, just like that of inference, requires no validation in order to be accepted as true. On the other hand, the output of perception (like the output of inference) can be inferentially invalidated. To be more precise, therefore, we might say that to be manifest is to be capable of being perceived or inferred without being immediately invalidated.

29 What, for instance, Lewis (1969: 56) calls a *basis* for common (i.e. mutual) knowledge is roughly equivalent to our mutual manifestness. We part company with him when he goes on to state, as a mere matter of definition, that the existence of such a basis is a sufficient condition for the existence of common knowledge itself. See also Clark and Marshall 1981.

30 It would be unfair not to mention that inferential theorists generally resist the temptation. Grice (1982: 237), who develops an inferential account of how language could have originated, calls it 'a myth'. See also Lewis 1975/1983: 181.

31 See Catherine Kerbrat-Orecchioni 1977 for a survey.

32 This is why we did not analyse the informative intention as an intention to make I *mutually* manifest. This would not be adequate in the cases where the communicator does not herself believe the information she is trying to communicate. There is another way of handling this problem, though: ostensive communication could be described as an attempt to create a genuinely mutual cognitive environment between social personae. When the communicator is sincere (and so is the audience in manifesting its acceptance of the information communicated), then the actual individuals and their social personae coincide, and otherwise they don't. This formulation, which is a notational variant rather than a substantive alternative to the one we follow here, might be more appealing from a sociological point of view.

Chapter 2 Inference

1 Not all conclusions implied by a set of premises can be generated by inference rules alone. For instance, a premise P implies an infinity of conclusions of the form $(P \text{ or } Q)$, where Q is any assumption whatsoever, and some non-inferential means of generating Q would be required. But those conclusions which cannot be generated are cognitively uninteresting; they are 'trivial' in a sense to be discussed below in section 5.

2 Incidentally, there is a paradox in insisting that verbal communication is constrained by the mutual-knowledge requirement while at the same time recognising that non-demonstrative inference is involved. The point of the mutual-knowledge requirement is to make it possible to account for verbal communication by means of a failsafe algorithm; to recognise the role of non-demonstrative inference is to rule out the possibility of such an algorithm.

If the paradox is not more blatant, it is, we fear, because of the general haziness with which these issues are usually discussed.

3 Here we assume only token identity between brain states and mental states. See Fodor 1974.

4 For the role of incomplete logical forms in speculative thinking, see Sperber 1985: chapter 2.

5 Or storage format: the important point being that all representations stored in that store or format are retrievable and processable in the same way, and differently from representations stored otherwise.

6 See Sperber (1985: chapter 2) for elaboration and discussion of this distinction.

7 Because logical forms, propositional forms and factual assumptions are not directly observable, we will have to use natural-language sentences to represent them, despite the lack of any one-to-one correspondence between sentences on the one hand and logical forms, propositional forms and factual assumptions on the other. In practice, this should present no more problem than it does in everyday communication, when hearers or readers normally have no difficulty in identifying the assumption a given utterance was intended to express. We do not mean to imply that natural language reflects the structure of the language of thought more closely than is required by the fact that both are formal objects with semantic properties, and that the one can be successfully used to communicate the other.

8 And, for that matter, even when he is capable of doing so consciously, as evidenced by the work of Kahneman and Tversky.

9 See Kahneman, Slovic and Tversky 1982: especially chapters 1, 34 and 35.

10 In what format are assumption schemas stored in the mind? They could be embedded in factual assumptions which state that some completion of the schema is or might be true. Or they could be stored as fully propositional factual assumptions, but with very weak empirical import, which achieve relevance only when strengthened by the addition of new constituents. For instance, assumption schema (29) below could be stored as (i) or as (ii):

(29) The outside temperature is —— degrees centigrade.
   (i) For some number n, 'the outside temperature is n degrees centigrade' is true.
   (ii) The outside temperature is some number of degrees centigrade.

Since we have no principled argument in favour of either format, or of any of the other formats which could be imagined, we will not pursue this issue.

11 This is not to say that no such system will ever be developed: Johnson-Laird 1983 outlines a research programme designed to develop an alternative to models of inference based on deductive rules.

12 This fits well with the general view of cognitive systems as purely computational that is currently being developed in cognitive psychology. See Fodor 1980.

13 See, for example, Katz 1972; Fodor 1981a; Fodor, Garrett, Walker and Parkes 1980.

14 For discussion of these notions, see Winograd 1977; Minsky 1977; and Schank and Abelson 1977.

15 Kripke 1972; Putnam 1975; see also Fodor 1982.

16 For survey and discussion, see Pulman 1983; Carston 1984a.

17 We have only considered the propositional content of encyclopaedic entries; there is no reason, however, why they should not contain – or give access to – 'images' and whatever types of mental object can be used as sources of information in conceptual thinking.

18 Fodor, Garrett, Walker and Parkes 1980, Fodor 1981a, reacting against classic decompositionalist accounts such as Katz 1972, Miller and Johnson-Laird 1976. For survey and evaluation of the decompositionalist approach, see J. D. Fodor 1977.

19 For interesting discussion of these questions, see Carston (in preparation).

20 For convenience, we will describe the working of the deductive device for assumptions; it works in exactly the same way for all other logical forms.

21 See Rips 1983. This also contains an excellent survey of previous work on the psychology of natural deduction.

22 For discussion and justification of the distinction between 'forwards' and 'backwards' rules, see Rips 1983.

23 And, possibly, to optional constraints inhibiting parts of the derivation which are unlikely to contribute to the pursuit of relevance; see chapter 4, section 5.

24 We are using this hypothetical rule for expository purposes, and without intending thereby to suggest that such a rule exists. It is quite conceivable that the relation of containment, and other transitive relations as well, are handled not by deductive rules, but by mental models *à la* Johnson-Laird.

25 In general, new information is not necessarily information that is new to the organism, but merely information that is being newly processed. Information retrieved from memory could be new information in this broader sense. The organism must have some rationale for deciding, for any newly retrieved item of information *P*, whether it is best added to the context in which some other information *Q* is being processed, or whether to treat *P* as new information and process it in a context containing *Q*. Considerations of relevance should weigh heavily here, as in other aspects of cognition.

26 We might also give a more formal characterisation of the conditions under which a contextualisation has contextual effects: Let **C** be a context and **P** a set of new premises. Let *Conclusions of* **P** be the set of conclusions deducible from **P** alone, *Conclusions of* **C** the set of conclusions deducible from **C** alone, and *Conclusions of* **P** U **C** the set of conclusions deducible from the union of **P** and **C**. Let two assumptions with the same content but with different strengths count as two different assumptions. Then the contextualisation of **P** in **C** has no contextual effect if and only if the two following conditions are met:

   (i) *Conclusions of* **C** is a subset of *Conclusions of* **P** U **C**;
   (ii) the complement of *Conclusions of* **C** with respect to *Conclusions of* **PUC** is a subset of *Conclusions of* **P**.

If conditions (i) and (ii) are not both met, then the contextualisation of **P** in **C** has some contextual effect.

CHAPTER 3   RELEVANCE

1 For the notion of a comparative concept, see above, chapter 2, section 3.
2 As suggested in chapter 2, note 24, it is quite conceivable that at least some of the inferences determined by transitive relationships such as *richer than* are computed not by use of inference rules but by use of 'mental models'. Even if this is so, effort is involved, effects are achieved, and the notion of relevance applies as we have described.
3 A view once attributed to us by Gazdar and Good 1982.
4 See for example Brown and Yule 1983: chapter 2; Levinson 1983: chapter 1.4; Lyons 1977: chapter 14.
5 This is a complication which could be accommodated in a straightforward way within the framework we are proposing, but to do so would involve too much effort for too little effect.
6 Remarks along these lines are made by Johnson-Laird 1967, Stenning 1978, Stalnaker 1978, McCawley 1979, Sag 1981 and most notably by Hobbs 1979. However, what many of these authors have in mind is a restricted subset of implicated contextual assumptions (often analysed as 'pragmatic presuppositions'), rather than the full set of contextual assumptions used in the interpretation of an utterance.
7 We may assume that the memory of the deductive device has a limited, indeed a rather small capacity, so that no extensions beyond that capacity are possible. The maximal contexts accessible are therefore those which, in view of their size, cannot be extended further.
8 In some contexts, say in a study of different processing strategies for the same stimulus, it might be desirable to compare the relevance of the same phenomenon relative to different possible methods of processing. The comparative definition of the relevance of a phenomenon could be adapted for this purpose in an obvious way.
9 And not, of course, in the sense of speech-act theory.
10 It is true that Grice's theory is put forward as a theory of 'conversation'. However, it has invariably been taken as a more general theory of verbal communication, and Grice has done nothing to correct that interpretation.
11 Earlier versions of relevance theory were closer in these respects to Grice's approach. We had generally assumed that there was a presumption of maximal rather than optimal relevance, and that communicator and audience had to have and use knowledge of the principle of relevance. However, the idea that the principle was exceptionless was there from the start.

CHAPTER 4   ASPECTS OF VERBAL COMMUNICATION

1 See Marslen-Wilson 1973; Fodor 1983: 61–64.
2 For example Bach and Harnish (1979: 7) assume that there is a 'linguistic presumption' and a 'communicative presumption' which together have the desired effect.

3 See for example Bach and Harnish 1979: 20–23.

4 See Carston 1984b, 1988a for a reanalysis of the temporal 'implicatures' of 'and' as aspects of explicit content within a relevance-based framework. Kempson 1986 and Carston 1988a propose reanalyses of 'scalar' or 'quantity implicatures'. Cormack 1980 and Travis 1981, 1985 have independently suggested that not all aspects of explicit content are strictly linguistically determined. See also Blakemore 1987, 1988a.

5 The example comes from Winograd 1977.

6 See for example Swinney 1979, Hogaboam and Perfetti 1975, Tyler and Marslen-Wilson 1977, Cairns and Kamerman 1975, Tanenhaus and Lewman 1979, and more generally Marslen-Wilson and Tyler 1980 and Fodor 1983.

7 It is arguable that the referents of at least some proper names, e.g. 'Mt Qomolangma', 'The Eiffel Tower', are recoverable by decoding alone. The greater the range of possible referents, the less appealing pure decoding solutions become.

8 We do not want to deny that there might be what Quine calls 'eternal sentences'. An eternal sentence, as he defines it, is 'a sentence whose truth value stays fixed through time and from speaker to speaker' (Quine 1960: 193). He gives the following (actually less than perfect) example: 'Copper oxide is green' (ibid: 12). An eternal sentence, if used literally, expresses the same proposition in any context, and therefore leads two people who understand that sentence to entertain exactly the same thought. What we do very much doubt is that for every thought there is a corresponding eternal sentence. The fact that some sentences correspond to a single thought is hardly more significant than the fact that some random strings of fifty letters and spaces correspond to a sentence of English. Quite generally, a single sentence, or even a single sense of a sentence, does not correspond to a single thought, and a single thought does not correspond to a single sentence.

9 See for example Green and Morgan 1981: 170–71; Clark 1977: 420.

10 A similar point is made by Harnish (1976: 346), which raises many interesting questions about Grice's account of implicatures; see also Walker 1975, Hugly and Sayward 1979, Sadock 1978 and Wilson and Sperber 1986a.

11 We are using capitalisation to represent both focal (sentential, nuclear) and contrastive stress. For reasons of space, we will largely ignore the effect of secondary stress and tone group on utterance interpretation.

12 For survey and discussion from rather different perspectives, see Rochemont 1986; Taglicht 1984: chapters 1–3; Brown and Yule 1983: chapters 3–5; Reinhart 1981; Prince 1981; Givón (ed.) 1979; Oh and Dinneen (eds) 1979; Clark and Haviland 1977; Lyons 1977: chapter 12.7; Chafe 1976; Jackendoff 1972; Halliday 1967/8.

13 For survey and discussion see Johnson-Laird 1983: chapter 13.

14 For survey and discussion see note 6 above.

15 See for example Rochemont 1986; Allerton and Cruttenden 1979.

16 Nor need it prevent these natural functions being taken over by some purely linguistic device, syntactic, morphological or intonational: indeed the costlier it is to vary the position of stress in a language, the more one would expect to find such things as focusing particles to compensate.

17 See for example Gussenhoven 1983; Rochemont 1986. If an approach

along the lines suggested here could be worked out, a more general consequence would be that there would be no need for a notion of focus in generative grammar. The issues are complicated and have been the subject of some sophisticated syntactic argumentation. What is worrying about this argumentation is that for all its complex machinery it often ends in appeals to pragmatic notions whose nature is left unspecified. We have simply tried to sketch in the lines of a pragmatic account which should serve at least as a supplement to the linguistic notion of focus, and at best as a replacement for it.

18 For discussion, see Wilson 1975; Kempson 1975; Gazdar 1979; J. D. Fodor 1979; and Soames 1979.

19 In the same way, it can be shown that cohesion and coherence are derivative categories, ultimately derivable from relevance. For detailed arguments for this position, see Blass 1986, 1990.

20 Note also a technical difference of some consequence: while new or focused information has invariably been treated as non-propositional, or of less than propositional size, foreground information is, by our definition, propositional: a foreground implication is an analytic implication, not an *NP* or *VP*, or an *NP* intension or a *VP* intension.

21 This is not to say, however, that no arbitrary linkages between linguistic form and pragmatic interpretation exist. It used to be suggested in the presuppositional literature (e.g. in Stalnaker 1974: 212) that there were certain linguistic structures whose function was to impose constraints on the contexts in which utterances containing those structures could occur. Pending an account of the role of context in utterance interpretation, it was hard to see why such structures should exist. Some years ago, however, Diane Blakemore suggested that in a relevance-based framework they might have a significant advantage from a processing point of view. As we have seen, the speaker can use the linguistic form of an utterance to guide the interpretation process. Blakemore's idea was that, just as the natural links between intonational structure and pragmatic interpretation may become grammaticalised, so a language might develop certain structures whose sole function was to guide the interpretation process by stipulating certain properties of context and contextual effects. Clearly, in a relevance-based framework the use of such structures might be highly cost-efficient. This approach appears to shed light on a wide range of apparently disparate phenomena on the borderlines of grammar and pragmatics, and seems to us a particularly promising area for future research. For a detailed development of this approach, see Brockway 1981, 1983; Blakemore 1985, 1987, 1988a. For further interesting work along these lines see MacLaran 1982; Kempson 1984; Smith 1983; and Blass 1990.

22 The distinction between descriptions and interpretations was developed in another context in Sperber 1985: chapter 2.

23 See Searle 1969: chapter 3; Lewis 1975; Bach and Harnish 1979: 10–12, 127–131.

24 Or in some other given world, in the case of fiction for instance.

25 In an earlier paper (Sperber and Wilson 1981), we analysed irony and free indirect speech as varieties of *mention*. We distinguished direct speech,

involving mention of linguistic form, from indirect speech, which we proposed to analyse as involving mention of logical form; we then assimilated irony to the case of indirect speech. The problem with this proposal is that the notion of mention does not really stretch to cover the full range of cases we are now proposing to handle. Mention is a self-referential or self-representational use of language: it requires full linguistic or logical identity between representation and original. One of the implications of section 7 has been that mention is only a special case of a much more general phenomenon: the use of a propositional form to represent not itself but some other propositional form it more or less closely resembles. We have therefore abandoned the term 'mention' in favour of the more general term 'interpretation'.

Apart from this terminological revision, our account of irony has not substantially changed. It has been criticised on a number of counts (Kerbrat-Orecchioni 1981; Clark and Gerrig 1984); some of the criticisms are answered in Sperber 1984. The theory has received some experimental confirmation in Jorgensen, Miller and Sperber 1984.

26 This is not to deny that some people are better than others at producing or understanding metaphor or irony; but then some people are better than others at producing and understanding strictly literal utterances. What is involved here is not competence but talent.

27 For excellent accounts of the speech-act approach to pragmatics, see Bach and Harnish 1979; Recanati 1987. For a more semantic approach to these phenomena, see Katz 1977.

28 We take it that promising is different from merely asserting that one will do something that the hearer wants one to do. In the latter case, someone who fails to do what she said she would and is accused of not keeping her promise would be quick to deny having promised, and would be quite right to do so. A promise is a particular, culturally defined form of commitment. Similarly, thanking is a particular, culturally defined form of expression of gratitude. Many societies have other forms of commitment, more akin to swearing, for instance, and other forms of expressing gratitude, more akin to blessing, for instance, than the typically modern Western promising and thanking. We have no doubt that a cross-cultural study of such speech acts would confirm their cultural specificity and institutional nature.

29 For an interesting cross-linguistic survey of syntactic sentence types, see Sadock and Zwicky 1985.

30 The strength of the assumption explicated also follows from the principle of relevance. Compare the ordinary assertions (i) and (ii):

(i) My name is Janet.
(ii) Belle Etoile will win the 3 p.m. race.

In normal circumstances, the explicature of (i) would be much stronger than that of (ii), which would typically have the force of nothing more than an educated guess. The first part of the presumption of relevance amounts to a guarantee that the information communicated is relevant enough to be worth the hearer's attention. Whereas in (i) the assumption that the speaker is anything less than certain of her own name would normally be inconsistent with manifest assumptions, with (ii), by contrast, an educated guess would be quite relevant enough

Notes to Second Edition

a Our rejection of mutual knowledge in favour of mutual manifestness has been much discussed (see the commentaries by Bach and Harnish, Gibbs, Russell, McCawley, Gerrig and Hinkelman in *The Behavioral and Brain Sciences* 10.4, and our reply in Sperber and Wilson 1987b). In response to continuing commentary by Garnham and Perner (*The Behavioral and Brain Sciences* 1990: 178–9), we tried in Sperber and Wilson 1990a to bring together the rather scattered arguments in *Relevance* and present the differences between mutual knowledge and mutual manifestness in more perspicuous terms.

b Our use of the term 'guarantee of relevance' has sometimes been misunderstood as implying that utterances cannot but be relevant. As this passage makes clear, we are no more committed to the view that utterances cannot but be relevant than to the view that assertions cannot but be true.

c Throughout this book, the term 'principle of relevance' refers to the (communicative) principle that every act of ostensive communication creates a presumption of relevance, rather than the more general (cognitive) principle that human cognition tends to be geared to the maximisation of relevance. In the Postface, we will suggest that two principles of relevance should be distinguished: a First (or Cognitive) Principle and a Second (or Communicative) Principle.

CHAPTER 2   INFERENCE

a We would not now assume such a sharp distinction between input (specialised) and central (unspecialised) systems. In the last ten years, there has been growing evidence that so-called central systems should be analysed in modular terms. See Sperber 1994b for discussion.

b For reservations about the treatment of 'central' systems in the Fodorian framework, see note a above.

c It is worth emphasising that the deductive system presented in this chapter is designed to do no more than illustrate one way in which deductive inferences might be performed. We are a long way from having the sort of evidence that would choose between the huge range of conceivable methods of performing deductive inference.

d It is sometimes suggested that we have overlooked a fourth type of contextual effect, namely weakening of existing assumptions. Weakenings are allowed for in our formal definition of the conditions under which a contextualisation has contextual effects (chapter 2, note 26). We assume, though, that weakening is always a by-product of a more basic contextual effect: for example, contradiction and elimination of an existing assumption weakens all contextual implications which depended on that assumption for some support.

CHAPTER 3   RELEVANCE

a Definitions (42) and (43) of relevance to an individual (and definitions (58) and (59) of relevance of a phenomenon in section 6 below) are discussed and modified in the Postface.

b See chapter 1, note b.

c The presumption of optimal relevance is discussed and modified in the Postface.

d For further discussion of the relation between co-operation and communication, see the Postface. See also Sperber 1994a.

e By 'consistent with the principle of relevance', we mean consistent with the particular instantiation of it communicated on that occasion. See p. 162 above and our reply to Morgan and Green in Sperber and Wilson 1987b: 745.

CHAPTER 4   ASPECTS OF VERBAL COMMUNICATION

a This definition is too strong as it stands. It should be modified to accommodate the fact that someone who says, for example, 'I tell you that P', or 'P despite Q', can explicitly communicate P.

b That is, given the particular instantiation of the principle of relevance communicated on that occasion.

c In preparing the French translation of *Relevance*, we discovered that, in fact, this classic example of irony (discussed by Booth 1974: 10) is not the work of Voltaire but of his English translator. A closer (and duller) translation of the French original would go: 'Finally, while the two kings had Te Deums sung in their respective camps . . .'.

Notes to Postface

1 French (Editions de Minuit, Paris, 1989); Russian (part-translation, Progress Publishers, Moscow, 1989); Japanese (Kenkyusha Shuppan, Tokyo, 1993); Korean (Hanshin Publishing Co, Seoul, 1993); Italian (Edizioni Anabasi, Milan, 1993); Spanish (Visor, Madrid, 1994); Bahasa Malaysia (to appear).

2 This review is far from complete. We have excluded references to working papers, and listed only selected titles for several authors whose contributions we would have liked to acknowledge more fully. Important areas of research, e.g. on style and intonation, have not been given their due. We have done no more than sample the existing literature, and regret the many omissions due to ignorance, oversight or lack of space.

3 A multiple review of *Relevance* appeared in *The Behavioral and Brain Sciences* (10.4, 1987), with continuing commentary by Politzer 1990, Garnham and Perner 1990 and Chiappe and Kukla forthcoming. Major reviews include Fowler 1989; Hirst 1989; Jayez 1986; Leslie 1989; Levinson 1989; Mey and Talbot 1988; Pateman 1986; Seuren 1987; Travis 1990; Walker 1989. See also note 8.

4 See, for example, Sperber and Wilson 1987b, 1990a, forthcoming a; Wilson 1992a; Wilson and Sperber 1987. See also Blakemore 1994a.

5 Sperber and Wilson 1987a.

6 Blakemore 1992; Sinclair and Winckler 1991; Moeschler and Reboul 1994.

7 See, for example, Gutt 1986; Smith and Wilson 1992; Sperber 1994a; Wilson 1994a; Wilson and Sperber 1986b, c. Encyclopaedia articles discussing aspects of relevance theory include Blakemore 1988b, forthcoming; Carston 1988b, 1993a, b; Kempson 1988b; Leech and Thomas 1990; Moeschler and Reboul 1994.

8 For critique and discussion, see note 3 above, and Berg 1991; Burton-Roberts 1985; Chametzky 1992; Charolles 1990; Culpeper 1994; Escandell Vidal 1993; Gibbs 1987; Giora 1988; Gorayska and Lindsey 1993; Grundy 1995; Nebeska 1991; Nishiyama 1992, 1993, 1995; O'Neill 1988; Roberts 1991; Sadock 1986; Sanchez de Zavala 1990; Sinclair 1995; Sun 1993; Taylor and Cameron 1987; Toolan 1992; Wilks and Cunningham 1986; Ziv 1988. For replies, see note 4 above.

9 Published dissertations include Blakemore 1987; Blass 1990; Forceville 1994a; Gutt 1991; Perrin (forthcoming); Tanaka 1994; Vandepitte 1993. Unpublished dissertations include Austin 1989; Campbell 1990; Clark 1991; Espinal 1985; Ferrar 1993; Groefsema 1992a; Happé 1992; Ifantidou 1994; Itani 1995; Jodlowiec 1991; Mao 1992; Matsui 1995; Pilkington 1994; Politzer 1993; Posnanski 1992; Reboul 1990a; Rouchota 1994a; Stainton 1993; Zegarac 1991. Monographs include Moeschler 1989b; Nasta 1991; Reboul 1992a.

10 These include Carston and Uchida forthcoming; Davis 1991; Guijarro Morales 1993; Kasher forthcoming; Kempson 1988a; Moeschler 1989c, Moeschler *et al.* 1994; Smith 1989; two special issues of *Lingua* (Wilson and Smith 1992, 1993) which contain a representative collection of papers; and the annual *University College London Working Papers in Linguistics*, which contain a wide variety of interesting work not all of which can be individually mentioned here.

11 Mitsunobu 1993.

12 An interesting reassessment of Grice's contribution to the philosophy of language can be found in Neale 1992. Neale cites a passage from Grice (1957: 222) where it is suggested that considerations of relevance can help with disambiguation.

13 This included studies of reference assignment within a broadly Gricean framework by the psycholinguist Herb Clark and his associates (see e.g. Clark 1977, Clark and Haviland 1977, Clark and Marshall 1981), in which the notion of a 'bridging implicature' was introduced. The treatment of bridging implicatures within the relevance-theoretic framework is discussed by Matsui 1993, 1995; Wilson 1992b, 1994b; Wilson and Sperber 1986a. See also note 15.

14 Bach and Harnish 1979, an excellent Gricean account of communication, abandons the Co-operative Principle and maxims when it comes to disambiguation, switching instead to informal talk of 'contextual appropriateness'. Levinson 1983, the standard textbook on pragmatics, contains nothing on disambiguation, but discusses the role of 'implicature' in reference assignment on pp. 34–5. More recently, Levinson (1987, 1988) has done important work on reference assignment in a neo-Gricean framework, where he continues to talk of 'implicatures' as contributing to truth conditions not merely in bridging but in reference assignment in general, and in disambiguation too.

15 Various aspects of the relevance-theoretic treatment of reference assignment are discussed in Ariel 1990; Blass 1986; Forget 1989; Foster-Cohen 1994; Fretheim forthcoming a; Gundel forthcoming; Hawkins 1991; Kempson 1988c; Kleiber 1990, 1992; Matsui 1993, 1995; Reboul 1992b, 1994a, forthcoming; Recanati 1993; Rouchota 1992, 1994a, d; Wilson 1992b, 1994b.

16 See, for example, Carston 1988a, 1993c, forthcoming b. For discussion, see Atlas 1989; Bach 1994a, b; Levinson 1987, 1988; Neale 1992; Recanati 1989; Wilson and Sperber 1993, forthcoming.

17 On enrichment, see, for example, Atlas 1989; Bach 1994a, b; Bertolet 1990; Bertuccelli-Papi 1992; Blakemore 1989a; Espinal 1993; Groefsema 1995, forthcoming; Haegeman 1987, 1989; Hirst 1987; Horn 1992; Kandolf 1993;

Klinge 1993; Moeschler 1993b; Recanati 1994, forthcoming; Scancarelli 1986; Stainton 1993, 1994; Taylor 1993; and references in note 16.

18 See, for example, Blakemore 1987; Carston 1988a.

19 See Grice 1989: 121–2, 361–3.

20 For survey and discussion of early work on non-truth-conditional semantics, see Wilson 1975. For important work outside the relevance-theoretic framework, see Ducrot 1980b, 1983, 1984, Ducrot *et al.* 1980.

21 For procedural accounts of discourse connectives, see Ariel 1988; Blakemore 1988a, b, 1990, 1993; Blass 1990, 1993; Ducrot 1984, Ducrot *et al.* 1980; Gutt 1988; Haegeman 1993; Higashimori 1992a, b, 1994; Itani 1995; Jucker 1993; Luscher 1994; Moeschler 1989a, b, 1993a; Smith and Smith 1988; Unger 1994; Vandepitte 1993; Wilson and Sperber 1993. For related accounts of procedural semantics, see Gabbay and Kempson 1991; Jiang 1994; Kempson forthcoming.

22 Relevance-theoretic accounts of mood indicators are developed in Clark 1991, 1993a, b; Lunn 1989; Rouchota 1994a, b, c; Wilson and Sperber 1988a, b, 1993. For discussion of various aspects of the relevance-theoretic approach to speech acts, see Bird 1994; Clark 1991; Groefsema 1992b; Harnish 1994; Moeschler 1991; Reboul 1990b, 1994b; Recanati 1987; see also Kasher 1994.

23 On mood indicators, see note 22. On discourse particles and adverbials, see Blass 1989, 1990; Espinal 1991; Ifantidou 1994; Ifantidou-Trouki 1993; Itani 1995; König 1991a, b; Nølke 1990; Watts 1988; Wilson and Sperber 1993; Yoshimura 1993b. On parentheticals, see Blakemore 1990/1; Espinal 1991; Ifantidou 1994; Wilson and Sperber 1993. On tense and aspect, see Moeschler 1993b; Smith 1993; Zegarac 1991, 1993.

24 For development and applications of the relevance-theoretic accounts of metaphor and irony, see Forceville 1994a, b; Hymes 1987; Pilkington 1992, 1994; Reboul 1990a, 1992a; Song forthcoming; Sperber and Wilson 1985/6, 1990b; Wilson and Sperber 1988b, 1992; Vicente 1992; Yoshimura 1993a. For discussion, see Gibbs 1994; Goatly 1994; Hamamoto forthcoming; Kreuz and Glucksberg 1989; Martin 1992; Perrin forthcoming; Recanati forthcoming; Seto forthcoming.

25 See Gutt 1990, 1991, 1992; Tirkkonen-Condit 1992; Winckler and van der Merwe 1993.

26 On echo questions, see Blakemore 1994b; on reformulations, see Blakemore 1993; on pseudo-imperatives, see Clark 1991, 1993a; on hearsay particles, see Blass 1989, 1990, Ifantidou 1994, Itani 1995; on metalinguistic negation, see Carston forthcoming a, Moeschler 1992; see also Burton-Roberts 1989a, b; Fretheim forthcoming b; Yoshimura 1993b. For interesting application of the related notion of 'polyphonie', see for example Ducrot 1983.

27 The implications of relevance theory for literature are discussed in Durant and Fabb 1990; Fabb forthcoming, in preparation; Green 1993; Kiparsky 1987; Pilkington 1991, 1992, 1994; Reboul 1990a, 1992a; Richards 1985; Sperber and Wilson 1987b: 751; Trotter 1992; Uchida forthcoming.

28 On humour, see Ferrar 1993, Jodlowiec 1991; on politeness, see Austin 1989, Jucker 1988; on advertising, see Forceville 1994a, b, Tanaka 1992,

1989, Jucker 1988; on advertising, see Forceville 1994a, b, Tanaka 1992, 1994; on argumentation, see Campbell 1990, 1992, Moeschler 1989b, c; on political language, see Wilson, J. 1990; on language in education, see Mayher 1990; on cinema, see Nasta 1991.

29 On the implications of relevance theory for linguistics, and steps towards formalisation, see Gabbay and Kempson 1991; Kempson 1988c, forthcoming; Jiang 1994; see also Posnanski 1992.

30 True, Grice's maxim of Relation is just 'be relevant.' His two maxims of Quantity, however, suggest the maximisation of relevance in our sense. The first maxim of Quantity ('Make your contribution as informative as is required') goes towards increasing effect. The second maxim of Quantity ('Do not make your contribution more informative than is required') goes towards minimising effort (as do the maxims of Manner). See Horn 1984, 1988; Levinson 1987, 1988 for discussion.

31 This was noted in *Relevance* in the text surrounding the presumption of relevance, but was not built into the presumption itself.

32 See Carston 1988a, forthcoming b; Harnish 1976; Horn 1984, 1988; Levinson 1987, 1988.

33 See Carston (forthcoming b) for discussion of Levinson's approach from a relevance-theoretic perspective.

34 For expository purposes, we do not question here the standard view that the richer overall interpretation is reached via an implicature. However, as noted above, there is evidence that at least some cases of so-called 'quantity implicature' are cases of enrichment instead.

Bibliography

Allerton, D. and Cruttenden, A. (1979), 'Three reasons for accenting a definite subject'. *Journal of Linguistics* 15.1: 49–53.

Alves, H. O. (ed.) (1986), *Encontro de Linguistas: Acta*. Universidade do Minho, Minho, Portugal.

Anzai, Y. *et al.* (eds) (1992), *Ninchi-kagaku Hando-bukku* (*Handbook of cognitive science*). Kyoritsu Publishing, Tokyo.

Ariel, M. (1988), 'Retrieving propositions from context: Why and how'. *Journal of Pragmatics* 12.5/6: 567–600.

Ariel, M. (1990), *Accessing noun-phrase antecedents*. Routledge, London.

Aristotle (1963), *De interpretatione*, translated by J. L. Ackrill, Clarendon Aristotle Series. Oxford University Press, Oxford.

Armstrong, D. (1971), 'Meaning and communication'. *Philosophical Review*, 80: 427–47.

Arnauld, A. and Lancelot, C. (1968), *Grammaire de Port-Royal*, English translation edited by R. Alston. Scolar Press, Menston, Yorks.

Atlas, J. (1989), *Philosophy without ambiguity*. Clarendon Press, Oxford.

Austin, J. (1962), *How to do things with words*. Clarendon Press, Oxford.

Austin, J. P. M (1989), *The dark side of politeness*: *A pragmatic analysis of non-co-operative communication*. University of Canterbury, New Zealand, Ph.D. thesis.

Bach, K. (1994a), 'Semantic slack: what is said and more', in Tsohatzidis 1994: 267–91.

Bach, K. (1994b), 'Conversational impliciture'. *Mind and Language* 9: 124–62.

Bach, K. and Harnish, R. (1979), *Linguistic communication and speech acts*. MIT Press, Cambridge, MA.

Barkow, J., Cosmides, L. and Tooby, J. (1992), *The adapted mind: Evolutionary psychology and the generation of culture*. Oxford University Press, New York, N.Y.

de Beaugrande, R. and Dressler, W. (1981), *Introduction to text linguistics*. Longman, London.

Bender, J. and Wellbery, D. (eds) (1990), *The ends of rhetoric: History, theory, practice*. Stanford University Press, Stanford, CA.

Bennett, J. (1976), *Linguistic behaviour*. Cambridge University Press, Cambridge.

Berg, J. (1991), 'The relevant relevance'. *Journal of Pragmatics* 16.5: 411–25.

Bertolet, R. (1990), *What is said*. Kluwer, Dordrecht.

Bertuccelli-Papi, M. (1992), 'Determining the proposition expressed by an utterance: The role of "domain adverbs"'. *Textus* V: 123–40.

Bever, T., Katz, J. and Langendoen, T. (eds) (1976), *An integrated theory of linguistic ability*. Crowell, New York.

Bird, G. (1994), 'Relevance theory and speech acts', in Tsohatzidis 1994: 292–311.

Black, M. (ed.) (1965), *Philosophy in America*. Allen & Unwin, London.

Blackburn, S. (ed.) (1975), *Meaning, reference and necessity*. Cambridge University Press, Cambridge.

Blackburn, S. (1984), *Spreading the word*. Oxford University Press, Oxford.

Blakemore, D. (1985), 'Discourse connectives and conjoined utterances'. Paper presented to the Linguistics Association of Great Britain, September.

Blakemore, D. (1987), *Semantic constraints on relevance*. Blackwell, Oxford.

Blakemore, D. (1988a), '"So" as a constraint on relevance', in Kempson 1988a: 183–95.

Blakemore, D. (1988b), 'The organization of discourse', in Newmeyer 1988, vol. IV: 229–50.

Blakemore, D. (1989a), 'Linguistic form and pragmatic interpretation: The explicit and the implicit', in Hickey 1989: 28–51.

Blakemore, D. (1989b), 'Denial and contrast: A relevance-theoretic analysis of "but"'. *Linguistics and Philosophy* 12: 15–37.

Blakemore, D. (1990), 'Constraints on interpretation'. *Proceedings of the 16th annual meeting of the Berkeley Linguistic Society: General session and parasession on the legacy of Grice*: 363–70.

Blakemore, D. (1990/1), 'Performatives and parentheticals'. *Proceedings of the Aristotelian Society* XCI.3: 197–213.

Blakemore, D. (1992), *Understanding utterances: An introduction to pragmatics*. Blackwell, Oxford.

Blakemore, D. (1993), 'The relevance of reformulations'. *Language and Literature* 2.2: 101–20.

Blakemore, D. (1994a), 'Relevance, poetic effects and social goals: A reply to Culpeper'. *Language and Literature* 3.1: 49–59.

Blakemore, D. (1994b), 'Echo questions: A pragmatic account'. *Lingua* 94: 197–211.

Blakemore, D. (forthcoming), 'Relevance theory'. To appear in Verschueren, Östman and Blommaert forthcoming.

Blass, R. (1986), 'Cohesion, coherence and relevance'. *Notes on Linguistics* 34: 41–64.

Blass, R. (1989), 'Grammaticalisation of interpretive use: The case of *ré* in Sissala'. *Lingua* 79: 229–326.

Blass, R. (1990), *Relevance relations in discourse: A study with special reference to Sissala*. Cambridge University Press, Cambridge.

Blass, R. (1993), 'Are there logical relations in a text?' *Lingua* 90.1/2: 91–110.

Booth, W. (1974), *A rhetoric of irony*. Chicago University Press, Chicago.

Brockway, D. (1981), 'Semantic constraints on relevance', in Parret, Sbisà and Verschueren 1981: 57–78.

Brockway, D. (1983), 'Pragmatic connectives'. Paper presented to the Linguistics Association of Great Britain, April.

Brown, G., Malkmjaer, K., Pollitt, A. and Williams, J. (1994), *Language and understanding*. Oxford University Press, Oxford.

Brown, G. and Yule, G. (1983), *Discourse analysis*. Cambridge University Press, Cambridge.

Burkhardt, A. (ed.) (1990), *Speech acts, meaning and intentions: Critical approaches to the philosophy of John Searle*. Walter de Gruyter, Berlin.

Burton-Roberts, N. (1985), 'Utterance, relevance and problems with text grammar'. *Australian Journal of Linguistics* 5.2: 285–96.

Burton-Roberts, N. (1989a), *The limits to debate: A revised theory of semantic presupposition*. Cambridge University Press, Cambridge.

Burton-Roberts, N. (1989b), 'On Horn's dilemma: Presupposition and negation'. *Journal of Linguistics* 25: 95–125.

Cairns, H. and Kamerman, J. (1975), 'Lexical information processing during sentence comprehension'. *Journal of Verbal Learning and Verbal Behavior* 14: 170–9.

Campbell, J. (1990), 'The relevant communication of rhetorical arguments'. *Dissertation Abstracts International* 51.6: 2001A.

Campbell, J. (1992), 'An applied relevance theory of the making and understanding of rhetorical arguments'. *Language and Communication* 12.2: 145–55.

Carnap, R. (1950), *Logical foundations of probability*. Routledge & Kegan Paul, London.

Carston, R. (1984a), Review of Pulman 1983. *Australian Journal of Linguistics* 4.1: 89–99.

Carston, R. (1984b), 'Semantic and pragmatic analyses of "and"'. Paper delivered to the Linguistics Association of Great Britain, April.

Carston, R. (1988a), 'Implicature, explicature and truth-theoretic semantics', in Kempson 1988a: 155–81. Reprinted in Davis 1991: 33–51.

Carston, R. (1988b), 'Language and cognition', in Newmeyer 1988, vol. III: 38–68.

Carston, R. (1993a), 'Syntax and pragmatics', in *The encyclopedia of language and linguistics*. Pergamon Press and Aberdeen University Press, Oxford and Aberdeen.

Carston, R. (1993b), 'Conjunction and pragmatic effects', in *The encyclopedia of language and linguistics*. Pergamon Press and Aberdeen University Press, Oxford and Aberdeen.

Carston, R. (1993c), 'Conjunction, explanation and relevance'. *Lingua* 90.1/2: 27–48.

Carston, R. (forthcoming a), 'Metalinguistic negation and echoic use'. To appear in *Journal of Pragmatics*.

Carston, R. (forthcoming b), 'Quantity maxims and generalised implicature'. To appear in *Lingua*.

Carston, R. and Uchida, S. (forthcoming) *Relevance theory: Applications and implications*. John Benjamins, Amsterdam.

Chafe, W. (1976), 'Givenness, contrastiveness, definiteness, subjects, topics and points of view', in Li 1976: 25–55.

Chametzky, R. (1992), 'Pragmatics, prediction and relevance'. *Journal of Pragmatics* 17.1: 63–81.

Charolles, M. (1990), 'Coût, surcoût et pertinence'. *Cahiers de linguistique française* 11: 127–47.

Chiappe, D. and Kukla, A. (forthcoming), 'Context-selection and the frame problem'. To appear in *The Behavioral and Brain Sciences*.

Clark, B. (1991), *Relevance theory and the semantics of non-declaratives*. University of London, Ph.D. thesis.

Clark, B. (1993a), 'Relevance and "pseudo-imperatives"'. *Linguistics and Philosophy* 16: 79–121.

Clark, B. (1993b), '*Let* and *let's*: Procedural encoding and explicature'. *Lingua* 90.1/2: 173–200.

Clark, H. (1977), 'Bridging', in Johnson-Laird and Wason 1977: 411–20.

Clark, H. (1978), 'Inferring what is meant', in Levelt and Flores d'Arcais 1978: 295–322.

Clark, H. and Carlson, T. (1981), 'Context for comprehension', in Long and Baddeley 1981: 313–30.

Clark, H. and Gerrig, R. (1984), 'On the pretense theory of irony'. *Journal of Experimental Psychology: General* 113.1: 121–6.

Clark, H. and Haviland, S. (1977), 'Comprehension and the given–new contract', in Freedle 1977: 1–40.

Clark, H., and Lucy, P. (1975), 'Understanding what is meant from what is said: A study in conversationally conveyed requests'. *Journal of Verbal Learning and Verbal Behavior* 14: 56–72.

Clark, H. and Marshall, C. (1981), 'Definite reference and mutual knowledge', in Joshi, Webber and Sag 1981: 10–63.

Clark, H. and Schunk, D. (1980), 'Polite responses to polite requests'. *Cognition* 8.2: 111–43.

Cole, P. (ed.) (1978), *Syntax and semantics 9: Pragmatics*. Academic Press, New York.

Cole, P. (ed.) (1981), *Radical pragmatics*. Academic Press, New York.

Cole, P. and Morgan, J. (eds) (1975), *Syntax and semantics 3: Speech acts*. Academic Press, New York.

Collinge, N. (ed.) (1990), *An encyclopedia of language*. Routledge, London.

Cormack, A. (1980), 'Negation, ambiguity and logical form'. University College London.

Culpeper, J. (1994), 'Why relevance theory does not explain "the relevance of reformulations"'. *Language and Literature* 3.1: 43–8.

Dancy, J., Moravcsik, J. and Taylor, C. (1988), *Human agency: Language, duty and value*. Stanford University Press, Stanford, CA.

Davidson, D. (1984a), 'Communication and convention', in Davidson 1984b: 265–80.

Davidson, D. (1984b), *Truth and interpretation*. Clarendon Press, Oxford.

Davidson, D. and Harman, G. (eds) (1972), *The semantics of natural language*. Reidel, Dordrecht.

Davies, M. (1981), *Meaning, quantification, necessity: Themes in philosophical logic*. Routledge & Kegan Paul, London.

Davis, S. (ed.) (1991), *Pragmatics: A reader*. Oxford University Press, Oxford.

Demonte, V. and Garza Cuaron, B. (eds) (1990), *Estudios de linguistica de Espana y Mexico*. Universidad Nacional Autonoma de Mexico, Mexico City.

Dretske, F. (1981), *Knowledge and the flow of information*. Blackwell, Oxford.

Ducrot, O. (1972), *Dire et ne pas dire*. Hermann, Paris.

Ducrot, O. (1980a), 'Analyses pragmatiques'. *Communications* 32: 11–60.

Ducrot, O. (1980b), *Les échelles argumentatives*. Minuit, Paris.

Ducrot, O. (1983), '*Puisque*: essai de description polyphonique', in Herslund *et al*. 1983: 166–85.

Ducrot, O. (1984), *Le dire et le dit*. Minuit, Paris.

Durant, A. and Fabb, N. (1990), *Literary studies in action*. Routledge, London.

Escandell Vidal, M. V. (1993), *Introductión a la pragmática*. Editorial Anthropos, Barcelona.

Espinal, T. (1985), *Anàlysas interpretives i teoria lingüística*. University Autonoma, Barcelona, Ph.D. thesis.

Espinal, T. (1991), 'The representation of disjunct constituents', *Language* 67: 726–62.

Espinal, T. (1993), 'The interpretation of *no pas* in Catalan'. *Journal of Pragmatics* 19.1: 353–69.

Evans, G. and McDowell, J. (eds) (1976), *Truth and meaning*. Oxford University Press, Oxford.

Fabb, N. (forthcoming), *Linguistics and literary theory*. Blackwell, Oxford.

Fabb, N. (in preparation), *Insight and arousal: The cognitive structure of intense aesthetic experience*.

Fabb, N., Attridge, D., Durant, A. and McCabe, C. (eds) (1987), *The linguistics of writing: Arguments between language and literature*. Manchester University Press, Manchester.

Ferrar, M. (1993), *The logic of the ludicrous: A pragmatic study of humour*. University of London, Ph.D. thesis.

Fodor, J. A. (1974), 'Special sciences'. *Synthese* 28: 77–115. Reprinted in Fodor 1981b: 127–45.

Fodor, J. A. (1975), *The language of thought*. Crowell, New York.

Fodor, J. A. (1980), 'Methodological solipsism considered as a research strategy in cognitive psychology'. *The Behavioral and Brain Sciences* 3.1: 63–109. Reprinted in Fodor 1981b: 225–53.

Fodor, J. A. (1981a), 'The present status of the innateness controversy', in Fodor 1981b: 257–316.

Fodor, J. A. (1981b), *Representations*. Harvester Press, Hassocks.

Fodor, J. A. (1982), 'Cognitive science and the twin-earth problem'. *Notre Dame Journal of Formal Logic* 23.2: 98–118.

Fodor, J.A. (1983), *The modularity of mind*. MIT Press, Cambridge, MA.

Fodor, J. A., Garrett, M., Walker, E. and Parkes, C. (1980), 'Against definitions'. *Cognition* 8.3: 263–367.

Fodor, J. D. (1977), *Semantics: Theories of meaning in generative grammar*. Harvester Press, Hassocks.

Fodor, J. D. (1979), 'In defense of the truth-value gap', in Oh and Dinneen 1979: 199–224.

Forceville, C. (1994a), *Pictorial metaphor in advertising*. Vrije Universiteit, Amsterdam.

Forceville, C. (1994b), 'Pictorial metaphor in billboards: Relevance theory perspectives', in Müller 1994: 93–113.

Forget, D. (1989), '*La*: un marqueur de pertinence discursive'. *Revue québecoise de linguistique* 18.1: 57–83.

Foster, M. and Brandes, S. (eds) (1980), *Symbol as sense*. Academic Press, New York.

Foster-Cohen, S. (1994), 'Exploring the boundary between syntax and pragmatics: Relevance and the binding of pronouns'. *Journal of Child Language* 21: 237–55.

Fowler, A. (1989), 'Review of *Relevance: Communication and cognition*'. *London Review of Books*, 30 March.

Freedle, R. (ed.) (1977), *Discourse production and comprehension*. Ablex, Norwood, NJ.

Fretheim, T. (forthcoming a), 'Accessing contexts with intonation'. To appear in Fretheim and Gundel (forthcoming).

Fretheim, T. (forthcoming b), 'Pragmatic implications of "not until" in Norwegian'. To appear in Simonsen, Loedrup and Moen (forthcoming).

Fretheim, T. and Gundel, J. (eds) (forthcoming), *Reference and referent accessibility*. John Benjamins, Amsterdam.

von Frisch, K. (1967), *The dance language and orientation of bees*. Belknap Press of Harvard University Press, Cambridge, MA.

Frith, U. (1989), *Autism: Explaining the enigma*. Blackwell, Oxford.

Frith, U. (ed.) (1991), *Autism and Asperger syndrome*. Cambridge University Press, Cambridge.

Gabbay, D. and Kempson, R. (1991), 'Labelled abduction and relevance reasoning', in *SOAS Working Papers in Linguistics and Phonetics*, 2: 41–84. To appear in *Proceedings of the workshop on non-standard queries and answers* (Toulouse, 1991).

Gardiner, A. H. (1932), *The theory of speech and language*. Oxford University Press, Oxford.

Garnham, A. and Perner, J. (1990), 'Does manifestness solve problems of mutuality?' *The Behavioral and Brain Sciences* 13.1: 178–9.

Gazdar, G. (1979), *Pragmatics: Implicature, presupposition and logical form*. Academic Press, New York.

Gazdar, G. and Good, D. (1982), 'On a notion of relevance', in Smith 1982: 88–100.

Gibbs, R. (1987), 'Mutual knowledge and the psychology of conversational inference'. *Journal of Pragmatics* 11.5: 561–88.

Gibbs, R. (1994), *The poetics of mind: Figurative thought, language and understanding*. Cambridge University Press, Cambridge.

Giora, R. (1988), 'On the informativeness requirement'. *Journal of Pragmatics* 12.5/6: 547–65.

Givón, T. (ed.) (1979), *Syntax and semantics 12: Discourse and syntax*. Academic Press, New York.

Goatly, A. (1994), 'Register and the redemption of relevance theory: The case of metaphor'. *Journal of the International Pragmatics Association* 4.2: 139–81.

Goodman, N. (1955), *Fact, fiction and forecast*. Harvard University Press, Cambridge, MA.

Gorayska, B. and Lindsey, R. (1993), 'The roots of relevance'. *Journal of Pragmatics* 19.4: 310–23.

Gordon, D. and Lakoff, G. (1975), 'Conversational postulates', in Cole and Morgan 1975: 83–106.

Green, G. (1980), 'Some wherefores of English inversions'. *Language* 56: 582–601.

Green, G. and Morgan, J. (1981), 'Pragmatics, grammar and discourse', in Cole 1981: 167–81.

Green, K. (1993), 'Relevance theory and the literary text: Some problems and perspectives.' *Journal of Literary Semantics* 22: 207–17.

Grice, H. P. (1957), 'Meaning'. *Philosophical Review* 66: 377–88. Reprinted in Steinberg and Jakobovits 1971: 53–9 and Grice 1989: 213–23.

Grice, H. P. (1961), 'The causal theory of perception'. *Proceedings of the Aristotelian Society*, Supplementary vol. 35: 121–52. Reprinted in Grice 1989: 224–47.

Grice, H. P. (1967), *Logic and conversation*. William James Lectures, reprinted in Grice 1989: 1–143.

Grice, H. P. (1968), 'Utterer's meaning, sentence meaning and word meaning'. *Foundations of Language* 4: 225–42. Reprinted in Searle 1971: 54–70 and Grice 1989: 117–37.

Grice, H. P. (1969), 'Utterer's meaning and intentions'. *Philosophical Review* 78: 147–77. Reprinted in Grice 1989: 86–116.

Grice, H. P. (1975), 'Logic and conversation', in Cole and Morgan 1975: 41–58. Reprinted in Grice 1989: 22–40.

Grice, H. P. (1978), 'Further notes on logic and conversation', in Cole 1978: 113–28. Reprinted in Grice 1989: 41–57.

Grice, H. P. (1981), 'Presupposition and conversational implicature', in Cole 1981: 183–98. Reprinted in Grice 1989: 269–82.

Grice, H. P. (1982), 'Meaning revisited', in Smith 1982: 223–43. Reprinted in Grice 1989: 283–303.

Grice, H. P. (1989), 'Retrospective epilogue', in Grice 1989: 339–85.

Grice, H. P. (1989), *Studies in the way of words*. Harvard University Press, Cambridge, MA.

Grimshaw, J. (1979), 'Complement selection and the lexicon'. *Linguistic Inquiry* 10.2: 279–326.

Groefsema, M. (1992a), *Processing for relevance: A pragmatically based account of how we process natural language*. University of London, Ph.D. thesis.

Groefsema, M. (1992b), '"Can you pass the salt?": A short-circuited implicature?' *Lingua* 87: 103–35.

Groefsema, M. (1995), '*Can, may, must* and *should*: A relevance-theoretic approach'. *Journal of Linguistics* 31: 53–79.

Groefsema, M. (forthcoming), 'Understood arguments: A semantic–pragmatic approach. To appear in *Lingua*.

Grundy, P. (1995), *Doing pragmatics*. Edward Arnold, London.

Guijarro Morales, J.-L. (ed.) (1993), *Pragmalingüistica* 1. University of Cadiz, Cadiz.

Gundel, J. (forthcoming), 'Relevance theory meets the givenness hierarchy: An account of inferrables'. To appear in Fretheim and Gundel forthcoming.

Gunderson, K. (ed.) (1975), *Language, mind and knowledge*. Minnesota Studies in the Philosophy of Science, VII. University of Minnesota Press, Minneapolis, MN.

Gussenhoven, C. (1983), 'Focus, mode and the nucleus'. *Journal of Linguistics* 19.2: 377–417.

Gutt, E.-A. (1986), 'Unravelling meaning: An introduction to relevance theory'. *Notes on Translation* 112: 10–20.

Gutt, E.-A. (1988), 'Towards an analysis of pragmatic connectives in Silt'i'. *Proceedings of the Eighth International Conference of Ethiopian Studies.* Addis Ababa University: 26–30.

Gutt, E.-A. (1990), 'A theoretical account of translation: Without a translation theory'. *Target* 2.2: 135–64.

Gutt, E.-A. (1991), *Translation and relevance: Cognition and context.* Blackwell, Oxford.

Gutt, E.-A. (1992), *Relevance theory: A guide to successful communication in translation.* Lectures delivered at the Triennial Translation Workshop of UBS, Zimbabwe. Summer Institute of Linguistics, Dallas; United Bible Societies, New York.

Haegeman, L. (1987), 'The interpretation of inherent objects in English'. *Australian Journal of Linguistics* 7.2: 223–48.

Haegeman, L. (1989), '*Be going to* and *will*: A pragmatic account'. *Journal of Linguistics* 25.2: 291–319.

Haegeman, L. (1993), 'The interpretation of the particle *da* in West Flemish'. *Lingua* 90.1/2: 111–28.

Halle, M., Bresnan, J. and Miller, G. (eds) (1978), *Linguistic theory and psychological reality*. MIT Press, Cambridge, MA.

Halliday, M. (1967/8), 'Notes on transitivity and theme in English'. *Journal of Linguistics* 3: 37–81; 4: 179–215.

Hamamoto, H. (forthcoming), 'Irony from a cognitive perspective'. To appear in Carston and Uchida forthcoming.

Happé, F. (1991), 'The autobiographical writings of three Asperger syndrome adults: Problems of interpretation and implications for theory', in Frith 1991: 207–42.

Happé, F. (1992), *Theory of mind and communication in autism.* University of London, Ph.D. thesis.

Happé, F. (1993), 'Communicative competence and theory of mind in autism: A test of relevance theory'. *Cognition* 48.2: 101–19.

Harman, G. (1968), 'Three levels of meaning'. *Journal of Philosophy* LXV: 590–602. Reprinted in Steinberg and Jakobovits 1971: 66–75.

Harnish, R. M. (1976), 'Logical form and implicature', in Bever, Katz and Langendoen 1976: 464–79. Reprinted in Davis 1991: 316–64.

Harnish, R. M. (1994), 'Mood, meaning and speech acts', in Tsohatzidis 1994: 407–59.

Hawkins, J. (1991), 'On (in)definite articles: Implicatures and (un)grammaticality predictions.' *Journal of Linguistics* 27: 405–42.

Herslund, M. *et al.* (eds) (1983), *Analyses grammaticales du français.* Special issue of *Revue romane*, 24.

Hickey, L. (ed.) (1989), *The pragmatics of style.* Routledge, London.

Higashimori, I. (1992a), 'Review of Kempson (ed.) *Mental Representations'. English Linguistics* 9: 335–56.

Higashimori, I. (1992b), '*Except, but* and relevance theory'. *English Literature Review* (Kyoto Women's University) 36: 62–108.

Higashimori, I. (1994), 'A relevance-theoretic analysis of *even, sae/sura/mo/temo/ddemo/datte/made'. English Literature Review* (Kyoto Women's University) 38: 51–80.

Hirschfeld, L. and Gelman, S. (1994), *Mapping the mind: Domain specificity in cognition and culture.* Cambridge University Press, Cambridge.

Hirst, D. (1987), 'Intonation: Syntaxe, sémantique et pragmatique'. *Sigma* 11: 148–70.

Hirst, D. (1989), 'Review of *Relevance.' Mind and Language* 4. 1/2: 138–46.

Hjelmslev, L. (1928), *Principes de grammaire générale.* Akademisk Forlag, Copenhagen.

Hjelmslev, L. (1959), *Essais linguistiques.* Akademisk Forlag, Copenhagen.

Hobbs, J. (1979), 'Coherence and coreference'. *Cognitive Science* 3.1: 67–90.

Hogaboam, T. and Perfetti, C. (1975), 'Lexical ambiguity and sentence comprehension'. *Journal of Verbal Learning and Verbal Behavior* 14: 265–74.

Horn, L. (1984), 'A new taxonomy for pragmatic inference: Q-based and R-based implicature', in Schiffrin 1984: 11–42.

Horn, L. (1988), 'Pragmatic theory', in Newmeyer 1988, vol. I: 113–45.

Horn, L. (1992), 'The said and the unsaid'. *Ohio State University Working Papers in Linguistics* 40: 163–92.

Hugly, P. and Sayward, C. (1979), 'A problem about conversational implicature'. *Linguistics and Philosophy* 3: 19–25.

Hyman, L. and Li, C. (1988), *Language, speech and mind: Essays in honor of Victoria Fromkin.* Routledge, London.

Hymes, D. (1987), 'A theory of verbal irony and a Chinookan pattern of verbal exchange', in Verschueren and Bertuccelli-Papi 1987: 293–337.

Ibsch, E., Schram, D. and Steen, G. (eds) (1991), *Empirical studies of literature: Proceedings of the second IGEL conference* (Amsterdam 1989). Rodopi, Amsterdam.

Ifantidou, E. (1994), *Evidentials and relevance.* University of London, Ph.D. thesis.

Ifantidou-Trouki, E. (1993), 'Sentential adverbs and relevance'. *Lingua* 90.1/2: 65–90.

Itani, R. (1993), 'The Japanese sentence-final particle *ka*: A relevance-theoretic approach'. *Lingua* 90.1/2: 129–47.

Itani, R. (1995), *Semantics and pragmatics of hedges in English and Japanese.* University of London, Ph.D. thesis.

Jackendoff, R. (1972), *Semantic interpretation in generative grammar.* MIT Press, Cambridge, MA.

Jakobson, R. (1960), 'Linguistics and poetics', in Sebeok 1960: 350–77.

Jayez, J. (1986), 'L'analyse de la notion de pertinence d'après Sperber et Wilson'. *Sigma* 10: 7–46.

Jiang, Y. (1994), 'A procedural account of Chinese quantification'. Paper presented to the Third International Conference on Chinese Linguistics, City Polytechnic of Hong Kong. To appear in *Selected Papers of ICCL–3.*

Jodlowiec, M. (1991), *The role of relevance in the interpretation of verbal jokes: a pragmatic analysis*, Jagiellonian University, Krakow, Ph.D. thesis.

Johnson-Laird, P. (1967), *An experimental investigation into one pragmatic factor governing the use of the English language.* University of London, Ph.D. thesis.

Johnson-Laird, P. (1982a), 'Mutual ignorance: Comments on Clark and Carlson's paper', in Smith 1982: 40–5.

Johnson-Laird, P. (1982b), 'Thinking as a skill'. *Quarterly Journal of Experimental Psychology* 34A: 1–29.

Johnson-Laird, P. (1983), *Mental models.* Cambridge University Press, Cambridge.

Johnson-Laird, P. and Wason, P. (eds) (1977), *Thinking: Readings in cognitive science.* Cambridge University Press, Cambridge.

Jorgensen, J., Miller, G. and Sperber, D. (1984), 'Test of the mention theory of irony'. *Journal of Experimental Psychology: General* 113.1: 112–20.

Joshi, A., Webber, B. and Sag, I. (eds) (1981), *Elements of discourse understanding.* Cambridge University Press, Cambridge.

Jucker, A. (1988), 'The relevance of politeness'. *Multilingua* 7.4: 375–84.

Jucker, A. (1993), 'The discourse marker *well*: A relevance-theoretical account'. *Journal of Pragmatics* 19: 435–52.

Just, M. and Carpenter, P. (eds) (1977), *Cognitive processes in comprehension.* Lawrence Erlbaum, Hillsdale, NJ.

Kahneman, D., Slovic, P. and Tversky, A. (1982), *Judgement under uncertainty: Heuristics and biases.* Cambridge University Press, Cambridge.

Kandolf, C. (1993), 'On the difference between explicatures and implicatures in relevance theory'. *Nordic Journal of Linguistics* 16.1: 33–46.

Kasher, A. (1994), 'Modular speech-act theory: Programme and results', in Tsohatzidis 1994: 312–22.

Kasher, A. (ed.) (forthcoming), *Pragmatics: Critical assessment.* Routledge, London.

Katz, J. (1972), *Semantic theory.* Harper & Row, New York.

Katz, J. (1977), *Propositional structure and illocutionary force: A study of the contribution of sentence meaning to speech acts.* Harvester Press, Hassocks.

Katz, J. (1981), *Language and other abstract objects.* Blackwell, Oxford.

Kempson, R. (1975), *Presupposition and the delimitation of semantics*. Cambridge University Press, Cambridge.

Kempson, R. (1984), 'Anaphora, the compositionality requirement and the semantics–pragmatics distinction'. *Proceedings of the North-Eastern Linguistics Society XIV*, University of Massachusetts, Amherst, MA.

Kempson, R. (1986), 'Ambiguity and the semantics–pragmatics distinction', in Travis 1986: 77–103.

Kempson, R. (ed.) (1988a), *Mental representations: The interface between language and reality*. Cambridge University Press, Cambridge.

Kempson, R. (1988b), 'Grammar and conversational principles', in Newmeyer 1988, vol. II: 139–63.

Kempson, R. (1988c), 'Logical form: The grammar–cognition interface'. *Journal of Linguistics* 24.2: 393–431.

Kempson, R. (forthcoming), 'Semantics, pragmatics and natural-language interpretation'. To appear in Lappin forthcoming.

Kerbrat-Orecchioni, C. (1977), *La connotation*. Presses Universitaires de Lyon, Lyon.

Kerbrat-Orecchioni, C. (1981), 'L'ironie comme trope'. *Poétique* 41: 108–27.

Khalfa, J. (ed.) (1994), *What is intelligence?* Cambridge University Press, Cambridge.

Kiparsky, P. (1987), 'On theory and interpretation', in Fabb, Attridge, Durant and McCabe 1987: 185–98.

Kirschner, C. and de Cesaris, J. (eds) (1989), *Studies in Romance linguistics*. John Benjamins, Amsterdam.

Kleiber, G. (1990), 'Marqueurs référentiels et processus interprétatifs: pour une approche "plus sémantique"'. *Cahiers de linguistique française* 11: 241–58.

Kleiber, G. (1992), 'Article défini: unicité et pertinence'. *Revue roumane* 27.1: 61–89.

Klinge, A. (1993), 'The English modal auxiliaries: From lexical semantics to utterance interpretation'. *Journal of Linguistics* 29: 315–57.

König, E. (1991a), 'A relevance-theoretic approach to the analysis of modal particles in German'. *Multilingua* 10. 1/2: 63–77.

König, E. (1991b), *The meaning of focus particles: A comparative perspective*. Routledge, London.

Kreuz, R. and Glucksberg, S. (1989), 'How to be sarcastic: The echoic reminder theory of verbal irony'. *Journal of Experimental Psychology: General* 118: 374–86.

Kripke, S. (1972), 'Naming and necessity', in Davidson and Harman 1972: 253–355. Reprinted as *Naming and necessity*. Blackwell, Oxford (1980).

Lappin, S. (ed.) (forthcoming), *Handbook of contemporary semantics*. Blackwell, Oxford.

Leach, E. (1976), *Culture and communication*. Cambridge University Press, Cambridge.

Leech, G. (1983), *Principles of pragmatics*. Longman, London.

Leech, G. and Thomas, J. (1990), 'Language, meaning and context: Pragmatics', in Collinge 1990: 173–205.

Lemmon, E. (1965), *Beginning logic*. Nelson, London.

Leslie, A. (1989), 'Review of *Relevance*'. *Mind and Language* 4. 1/2: 147–50.

Levelt, W. and Flores d'Arcais, G. (eds) (1978), *Studies in the perception of language*. John Wiley, Chichester.

Levinson, S. (1983), *Pragmatics*. Cambridge University Press, Cambridge.

Levinson, S. (1987), 'Minimization and conversational inference', in Verschueren and Bertuccelli-Papi 1987: 61–129.

Levinson, S. (1988), 'Generalised conversational implicatures and the semantics–pragmatics interface'. Cambridge.

Levinson, S. (1989), 'A review of *Relevance*'. *Journal of Linguistics* 25.2: 455–72.

Lewis, D. (1969), *Convention*. Harvard University Press, Cambridge, MA.

Lewis, D. (1975), 'Languages and language', in Gunderson 1975: 3–35. Reprinted in Lewis 1983: 163–88.

Lewis, D. (1983), *Philosophical papers*, vol. I. Oxford University Press, Oxford.

Li, C. (ed.) (1976), *Subject and topic*. Academic Press, New York.

Loar, B. (1976), 'Two theories of meaning', in Evans and McDowell 1976: 138–61.

Loar, B. (1981), *Mind and meaning*. Cambridge University Press, Cambridge.

Loftus, E. (1979), *Eyewitness testimony*. Harvard University Press, Cambridge, MA.

Long, J. and Baddeley, A. (eds) (1981), *Attention and performance IX*. Lawrence Erlbaum, Hillsdale, NJ.

Lunn, P. (1989), 'The Spanish subjunctive and relevance', in Kirschner and de Cesaris 1989: 249–60.

Luscher, J.-M. (1994), 'Les marques de connexion: des guides pour l'interprétation', in Moeschler *et al.* 1994: 175–227.

Lyons, J. (1977), *Semantics*. Cambridge University Press, Cambridge.

MacLaran, R. (1982), *The semantics and pragmatics of English demonstratives*. Cornell University, Ph.D. thesis.

Mao, L. (1992), *Pragmatic universals and their implications*. University of Minnesota, Ph.D. thesis. *Dissertation Abstracts International* 52.8: 2908A.

Marslen-Wilson, W. (1973), *Speech shadowing and speech perception*. MIT, Ph.D. thesis.

Marslen-Wilson, W. and Tyler, L. (1980), 'The temporal structure of spoken language understanding'. *Cognition* 8.1: 1–72.

Martin, R. (1992), 'Irony and universe of belief'. *Lingua* 87: 77–90.

Matsui, T. (1993), 'Bridging reference and the notions of topic and focus'. *Lingua* 90.1/2: 49–68.

Matsui, T. (1995), *Bridging and relevance*. University of London, Ph.D. thesis.

Mayher, J. (1990), *Uncommon sense: Theoretical practice in language education*. Heinemann, London.

McCawley, J. (1979), 'Presupposition and discourse structure', in Oh and Dinneen 1979: 371–88.

McCawley, J. (1980), *Everything that linguists have always wanted to know about logic but were ashamed to ask*. University of Chicago Press, Chicago, IL.

McDowell, J. (1980), 'Meaning, communication and knowledge', in van Straaten 1980: 117–39.

Mey, J. (ed.) (1986), *Language and discourse: Text and protest*. John Benjamins, Amsterdam.

Mey, J. and Talbot, M. (1988), 'Computation and the soul'. *Journal of Pragmatics* 12: 743–89.

Miller, G. and Johnson-Laird, P. (1976), *Language and perception*. Cambridge University Press, Cambridge.

Minsky, M. (1977), 'Frame system theory', in Johnson-Laird and Wason 1977: 355–76.

Mitsunobu, M. (1993), 'A relevance theory bibliography'. Department of English, Tokyo Metropolitan University.

Moeschler, J. (1989a), 'Pragmatic connectives, argumentative coherence and relevance'. *Argumentation* 3.3: 321–39.

Moeschler, J. (1989b), *Modélisation du dialogue. Représentation de l'inférence argumentative*. Hermès, Paris.

Moeschler, J. (ed.) (1989c), *Argumentation, relevance and discourse. Argumentation* 3.3. Kluwer, Dordrecht.

Moeschler, J. (1991), 'The pragmatic aspects of linguistic negation: Speech acts, argumentation and pragmatic inference'. *Argumentation* 6: 51–75.

Moeschler, J. (1992), 'Une, deux ou trois négations?' *Langue française* 94: 8–25.

Moeschler, J. (1993a), 'Relevance and conversation'. *Lingua* 90. 1/2: 149–71.

Moeschler, J. (1993b), 'Aspects pragmatiques de la référence temporelle: indétermination, ordre temporel et inférence'. *Langages* 112: 39–54.

Moeschler, J. and Reboul, A. (1994), *Dictionnaire encyclopédique de pragmatique*. Seuil, Paris.

Moeschler, J., Reboul, A., Luscher, J.-M. and Jayez, J. (1994), *Langage et pertinence: Référence temporelle, anaphore, connecteurs et métaphore*. Presses Universitaires de Nancy, Nancy.

Morgan, J. (1979), 'Observations on the pragmatics of metaphor', in Ortony 1979: 136–47.

Morris, C. (1938), 'Foundations of the theory of signs', in Neurath, Carnap and Morris 1938: 77–138. Reprinted in Morris 1971.

Morris, C. (1971), *Writings on the general theory of signs*. Mouton, The Hague.

Müller, J. (ed.) (1994), *Towards a pragmatics of the audiovisual*. NODUS, Münster.

Munitz, M. and Unger, P. (eds) (1974), *Semantics and philosophy: Studies in contemporary philosophy*. New York University Press, New York.

Nasta, D. (1991), *Meaning in film: Relevant structures in soundtrack and narrative*. Peter Lang, Bern.

Neale, S. (1992), 'Paul Grice and the philosophy of language'. *Linguistics and Philosophy* 15.5: 509–59.

Nebeska, I. (1991), 'Muze byt relevance postacujicim principem komunikace?' *Slovo a Slovesnost* 52.2: 104–8.

Neisser, U. (ed.) (1982), *Memory observed: Remembering in natural contexts*. W. H. Freeman, San Francisco, CA.

Neurath, O., Carnap, R. and Morris, C. (eds) (1938), *International encyclopaedia of unified science*. University of Chicago Press, Chicago, IL.

312 *Bibliography*

Newmeyer, F. (1988), *Linguistics: The Cambridge Survey*, vols I–IV. Cambridge University Press, Cambridge.

Nishiyama, Y. (1992), 'Hatsuwa-kaishaku to Ninchi: on Kanrensei-riron nitsuite (Utterance interpretation and cognition: On Relevance Theory)', in Anzai *et al.* 1992: 466–76.

Nishiyama, Y. (1993), 'Kontekusuto-kouka to Kanrensei: Kanrensei-riron no Mondai-ten (Contextual effects and relevance: Some problems of relevance theory)'. *Eigo Seinen* 139.5: 14–16.

Nishiyama, Y. (1995), 'Gengai no Imi wo Toraeru (How to read between the lines)'. *Gengo* 24.4: 30–9.

Nølke, H. (1990), 'Pertinence et modalisateurs d'énonciation'. *Cahiers de linguistique française* 11.

Oh, C.-K. and Dinneen, D. (eds) (1979), *Syntax and semantics 11: Presupposition*. Academic Press, New York.

O'Neill, J. (1988), 'Relevance and pragmatic inference'. *Theoretical Linguistics* 15: 241–61.

Ortony, A. (ed.) (1979), *Metaphor and thought*. Cambridge University Press, Cambridge.

Parret, H. (ed.) (1994), *Pretending to communicate*. Walter de Gruyter, Berlin.

Parret, H., Sbisà, M. and Verschueren, J. (1981), *Possibilities and limitations of pragmatics*. John Benjamins, Amsterdam.

Pateman, T. (1986), 'Relevance, contextual effects and least effort'. *Poetics Today* 7.4: 745–54.

Patton, T. and Stampe, D. (1969), 'The rudiments of meaning: Ziff on Grice'. *Foundations of Language* 5.1: 2–16.

Perrin, L. (forthcoming), *L'ironie mise en trope, du sens littéral au sens figuré*. University of Geneva, doctoral dissertation, to be published by Editions Kimé.

Philippaki-Warburton, I., Nicolaides, K. and Sifianou, M. (eds) (1994), *Themes in Greek linguistics. Papers from the 1st international conference on Greek Linguistics* (Reading 1993). John Benjamins, Amsterdam.

Pilkington, A. (1991), 'The literary reading process: A relevance theory perspective', in Ibsch, Schram and Steen 1991: 117–23.

Pilkington, A. (1992), 'Poetic effects'. *Lingua* 87. 1/2: 29–51.

Pilkington, A. (1994), *Poetic thoughts and poetic effects*. University of London, Ph.D. thesis.

Pike, K. (1967), *Language in relation to a unified theory of the structure of human behavior*. Mouton, The Hague.

Politzer, G. (1990), 'Characterizing spontaneous inferences'. *The Behavioral and Brain Sciences* 13.1: 177–8.

Politzer, G. (1993), *La psychologie du raisonnement: Lois de la pragmatique et de la logique formelle*. Thèse de Doctorat d'Etat, University of Paris VIII.

Posnanski, V. (1992), *A relevance-based utterance processing system*. Cambridge University, Ph.D. thesis, University of Cambridge Laboratory, Technical report, No. 246.

Prince, E. (1981), 'Towards a taxonomy of given–new information', in Cole 1981: 223–56.

Pulman, S. (1983), *Word meaning and belief*. Croom Helm, London.

Putnam, H. (1975a), 'The meaning of "meaning"', in Gunderson 1975: 131–93. Reprinted in Putnam 1975b: 215–71.

Putnam, H. (1975b), *Mind, language and reality: Philosophical papers, II*. Cambridge University Press, Cambridge.

Quine, W. (1960), *Word and object*. MIT Press, Cambridge, MA.

Reboul, A. (1990a), *Analyse de la métaphore et de la fiction*. University of Geneva, Ph.D. thesis.

Reboul, A. (1990b), 'The logical status of fictional discourse: What Searle's speaker can't say to his hearer', in Burkhardt 1990: 336–63.

Reboul, A. (1992a), *Rhétorique et stylistique de la fiction*. Presses Universitaires de Nancy, Nancy.

Reboul, A. (1992b), 'How much am *I* I and how much is *she* I?' *Lingua* 87: 169–202.

Reboul, A. (1994a), 'L'anaphore pronominale: le problème de l'attribution des référents', in Moeschler et al. 1994: 105–73.

Reboul, A. (1994b), 'The description of lies in speech-act theory', in Parret 1994: 292–8.

Reboul, A. (forthcoming), 'What (if anything) is accessibility? A relevance-oriented criticism of Ariel's Accessibility Theory of referring expressions'. To appear in *Acts of the 6th international conference on functional grammar* (York, 1994).

Recanati, F. (1979), *La transparence et l'énonciation*. Seuil, Paris.

Recanati, F. (1987), *Meaning and force*. Cambridge University Press, Cambridge.

Recanati, F. (1989), 'The pragmatics of what is said'. *Mind and Language* 4.4: 295–329. Reprinted in Davis 1991: 97–120.

Recanati, F. (1993), *Direct reference: From language to thought*. Blackwell, Oxford.

Recanati, F. (1994), 'Contextualism and anti-contextualism in the philosophy of language', in Tsohatzidis 1994: 156–66.

Recanati, F. (forthcoming), 'The alleged priority of literal interpretation'. To appear in *Cognitive Science*.

Reddy, M. (1979), 'The conduit metaphor – a case of frame conflict in our language about language', in Ortony 1979: 284–324.

Reinhart, T. (1981), 'Pragmatics and linguistics: An analysis of sentence topics'. *Philosophica* 27: 53–94.

Richards, C. (1985), 'Inferential pragmatics and the literary text'. *Journal of Pragmatics* 9: 261–85.

Rips, L. (1983), 'Cognitive processes in propositional reasoning'. *Psychological Review* 90.1: 38–71.

Roberts, L. (1991), 'Relevance as an explanation of communication'. *Linguistics and Philosophy* 14.4: 453–72.

Rochemont, M. (1986), *Focus in generative grammar*. John Benjamins, Amsterdam.

Rouchota, V. (1992), 'On the referential–attributive distinction'. *Lingua* 87.1/2: 137–67.

Rouchota, V. (1994a), *The semantics and pragmatics of the subjunctive in Modern Greek – a relevance-theoretic approach.* University of London, Ph.D. thesis.

Rouchota, V. (1994b), '*Na*-interrogatives in Modern Greek: Their interpretation and relevance.' In Philippaki-Warburton, I., Nicolaides, K. and Sifianou, M. 1994: 177–84.

Rouchota, V. (1994c), 'The subjunctive in Modern Greek: Dividing the labour between semantics and pragmatics'. *Journal of Modern Greek Studies* 12: 185–201.

Rouchota, V. (1994d), 'On indefinite descriptions'. *Journal of Linguistics* 30: 441–75.

Sadock, J. (1978), 'On testing for conversational implicature', in Cole 1978: 281–98.

Sadock, J. (1979), 'Figurative speech and linguistics', in Ortony 1979: 46–63.

Sadock, J. (1986), 'Remarks on the paper by Deirdre Wilson and Dan Sperber', in *Parasession on pragmatics and grammatical theory. Chicago Linguistics Society* 22: 85–90.

Sadock, J. and Zwicky, A. (1985), 'Speech-act distinctions in syntax', in Shopen 1985: 155–96.

Sag, I. (1981), 'Formal semantics and extralinguistic context', in Cole 1981: 273–94.

Sánchez de Zavala, V. (1990), 'Sobre la nueva teoria de la pertinencia', in Demonte and Garza Cuaron 1990: 273–99.

Saussure, F. de (1974), *Course in general linguistics*, translated from the French (1916) by Wade Baskin. Peter Owen, London.

Scancarelli, J. (1986), 'Interpretation in context: A cause of semantic change'. *Cahiers de l'Institut linguistique de Louvain* 12.1/2: 167–82.

Schank, R. and Abelson, R. (1977), 'Scripts, plans and knowledge', in Johnson-Laird and Wason 1977: 421–32.

Schiffer, S. (1972), *Meaning*. Clarendon Press, Oxford.

Schiffrin, D. (ed.) (1984), *Meaning, form and use in context.* Georgetown University Press, Washington, DC.

Searle, J. (1965), 'What is a speech act?', in Black 1965: 221–39.

Searle, J. (1969), *Speech acts.* Cambridge University Press, Cambridge.

Searle, J. (1971a), 'Introduction' to Searle 1971b: 1–12.

Searle, J. (ed.) (1971b), *The philosophy of language.* Oxford University Press, Oxford.

Searle, J. (1975), 'Indirect speech acts', in Cole and Morgan 1975: 59–82.

Searle, J. (1979a), 'The classification of illocutionary acts', in Searle 1979b: 1–29.

Searle, J. (1979b), *Expression and meaning.* Cambridge University Press, Cambridge.

Searle, J. (1983), *Intentionality.* Cambridge University Press, Cambridge.

Searle, J., Kiefer, F. and Bierwisch, M. (eds) (1980), *Speech-act theory and pragmatics.* Reidel, Dordrecht.

Sebeok, T. (ed.) (1960), *Style in language.* MIT Press, Cambridge, MA.

Seto, K.-I. (forthcoming), 'On non-echoic irony'. To appear in Carston and Uchida forthcoming.

Seuren, P. (1987), 'The self-styling of relevance theory'. *Journal of Semantics* 5.2: 123–43.

Shannon, C. and Weaver, W. (1949), *The mathematical theory of communication*. University of Illinois Press, Urbana, IL.

Shopen, T. (ed.) (1985), *Language typology and syntactic description*. Cambridge University Press, Cambridge.

Simonsen, H., Loedrup, H. and Moen, H. (forthcoming), *Selected papers from the XVth Scandinavian Conference of Linguistics* (Oslo, 1995.)

Sinclair, M. (1995), 'Fitting pragmatics into the mind: Some issues in mentalist pragmatics'. *Journal of Pragmatics* 23: 509–39.

Sinclair, M. and Winckler, W. (1991), *Relevance theory: Explaining verbal communication*. Stellenbosch Papers in Linguistics, 18.

Smith, N. (ed.) (1982), *Mutual knowledge*. Academic Press, London.

Smith, N. (1983), 'On interpreting conditionals'. *Australian Journal of Linguistics* 3.1: 1–23.

Smith, N. (1989), *The twitter machine*. Blackwell, Oxford.

Smith, N. (1993), 'Observations sur la pragmatique des temps'. *Langages* 112: 26–38.

Smith, N. and Smith, A. (1988), 'A relevance-theoretic account of conditionals', in Hyman and Li 1988: 322–52.

Smith, N. and Tsimpli, I. (1995), *The mind of a savant*. Blackwell, Oxford.

Smith, N. and Wilson, D. (1979), *Modern linguistics: The results of Chomsky's revolution*. Penguin, Harmondsworth and Indiana University Press.

Smith, N. and Wilson, D. (1992), 'Introduction to the special issue on relevance theory'. *Lingua* 87.1/2: 1–10.

Soames, S. (1979), 'A projection problem for speaker presuppositions'. *Linguistic Inquiry* 10.4: 623–66.

Song, Nam-Sun (forthcoming), 'Metonymy and metaphor'. To appear in Carston and Uchida forthcoming.

Sperber, D. (1975a), *Rethinking symbolism*. Cambridge University Press, Cambridge.

Sperber, D. (1975b), 'Rudiments de rhétorique cognitive'. *Poétique* 23: 389–415.

Sperber, D. (1980), 'Is symbolic thought prerational?' in Foster and Brandes 1980: 25–44.

Sperber, D. (1984), 'Verbal irony: Pretense or echoic mention?' *Journal of Experimental Psychology: General* 113.1: 130–6.

Sperber, D. (1985), *On anthropological knowledge*. Cambridge University Press, Cambridge.

Sperber, D. (1994a), 'Understanding verbal understanding', in Khalfa 1994: 179–98.

Sperber, D. (1994b), 'The modularity of thought and the epidemiology of representations', in Hirschfeld and Gelman 1994: 39–67.

Sperber, D., Cara, F. and Girotto, V. (forthcoming), 'Relevance theory explains the Selection Task'. To appear in *Cognition*.

Sperber, D. and Wilson, D. (1981), 'Irony and the use–mention distinction', in Cole 1981: 295–318. Reprinted in Davis 1991: 550–63.

Sperber, D. and Wilson, D. (1982), 'Mutual knowledge and relevance in theories of comprehension', in Smith 1982: 61–131.

Sperber, D. and Wilson, D. (1985/6), 'Loose talk'. *Proceedings of the Aristotelian Society* LXXXVI: 153–71. Reprinted in Davis 1991: 540–9.

Sperber, D. and Wilson, D. (1987a), 'Précis of *Relevance*'. *The Behavioral and Brain Sciences* 10.4: 697–710.

Sperber, D. and Wilson, D. (1987b), 'Presumptions of relevance'. *The Behavioral and Brain Sciences* 10.4: 736–54.

Sperber, D. and Wilson, D. (1990a), 'Spontaneous deduction and mutual knowledge'. *The Behavioral and Brain Sciences* 3.1: 179–84.

Sperber, D. and Wilson, D. (1990b), 'Rhetoric and relevance', in Bender and Wellbery 1990: 140–56.

Sperber, D. and Wilson, D. (forthcoming a), 'Fodor's frame problem and relevance theory (reply to Chiappe and Kukla)'. To appear in *The Behavioral and Brain Sciences*.

Sperber, D. and Wilson, D. (forthcoming b), *Relevance and meaning*. Blackwell, Oxford.

Stainton, R. (1993), *Non-sentential assertions*. MIT, Ph.D. dissertation.

Stainton, R. (1994), 'Using non-sentences: An application of relevance theory'. *Pragmatics and Cognition* 2.2: 269–84.

Stalnaker, R. (1974), 'Pragmatic presuppositions', in Munitz and Unger 1974: 197–213.

Stalnaker, R. (1978), 'Assertion', in Cole 1978: 315–32.

Steinberg, D. and Jakobovits, L. (eds) (1971), *Semantics: An interdisciplinary reader*. Cambridge University Press, Cambridge.

Stenning, K. (1978), 'Anaphora as an approach to pragmatics', in Halle, Bresnan and Miller 1978: 162–200.

van Straaten, Z. (ed.) (1980), *Philosophical subjects*. Clarendon Press, Oxford.

Strawson, P. (1964a), 'Intention and convention in speech acts'. *Philosophical Review* 73: 439–60. Reprinted in Searle 1971: 170–89.

Strawson, P. (1964b), 'Identifying reference and truth values'. *Theoria* 3: 96–118.

Strawson, P. (1969), 'Meaning and truth'. Inaugural lecture at the University of Oxford. Reprinted in Strawson 1971: 170–89.

Strawson, P. (1971), *Logico-linguistic papers*. Methuen, London.

Sun, Yu (1993), 'Pragmatic inference in relevance theory'. *Waiguoyu* 4.86: 39–43.

Swinney, D. (1979), 'Lexical access during comprehension: (Re)consideration of context effects'. *Journal of Verbal Learning and Verbal Behavior* 18.6: 645–60.

Taglicht, J. (1984), *Message and emphasis: On focus and scope in English*. Longman, London.

Tanaka, K. (1992), 'The pun in advertising: A pragmatic approach'. *Lingua* 87. 1/2: 91–102.

Tanaka, K. (1994), *Advertising language: A pragmatic approach to advertisements in Britain and Japan*. Routledge, London.

Tanenhaus, M. and Lewman, J. (1979), 'Evidence for multiple stages in the processing of ambiguous words in syntactic contexts'. *Journal of Verbal Learning and Verbal Behavior* 18: 427–40.

Taylor, J. (1993), 'Possessives and relevance'. *Stellenbosch Papers in Linguistics* 26: 14–34.

Taylor, T. and Cameron, D. (1987), *Analyzing conversation*. Pergamon Press, New York.

Thomason, R. (1970), *Symbolic logic*. Macmillan, London.

Tirkkonen-Condit, S. (1992), 'A theoretical account of translation: Without translation theory?' *Target* 4.2: 237–45.

Todorov, T. (1977), *Théories du symbole*. Seuil, Paris.

Toolan, M. (1992), 'On relevance theory', in Wolf 1992: 146–62.

Travis, C. (1981), *The true and the false: The domain of the pragmatic*. John Benjamins, Amsterdam.

Travis, C. (1985), 'On what is strictly speaking true'. *Canadian Journal of Philosophy* 15: 187–229.

Travis, C. (ed.) (1986), *Meaning and interpretation*. Blackwell, Oxford.

Travis, C. (1990), 'Critical notice of *Relevance*'. *Canadian Journal of Philosophy* 2.

Trotter, D. (1992), 'Analysing literary prose: The relevance of relevance theory'. *Lingua* 87.1/2: 11–27.

Tsohatzidis, S. (1994), *Foundations of speech act theory: Philosophical and linguistic perspectives*. Routledge, London.

Tyler, L. and Marslen-Wilson, W. (1977), 'The on-line effect of semantic context on syntactic processing'. *Journal of Verbal Learning and Verbal Behavior* 16.6: 683–92.

Uchida, S. (forthcoming), 'Text and relevance'. To appear in Carston and Uchida forthcoming.

Unger, C. (1994), 'The scope of discourse connectives and its relation to the utterance in which it occurs'. University College London, M.A. dissertation, to appear in *Journal of Linguistics*.

Vandepitte, S. (1989), 'A pragmatic function of intonation'. *Lingua* 79: 265–97.

Vandepitte, S. (1993), *A pragmatic study of the expression and the interpretation of causality: Conjuncts and conjunctions in modern spoken British English*. Koninklijke Academie voor Wetenschappen, Letteren en Schone Kunsten van België, Brussels.

Verschueren, J. and Bertuccelli-Papi, M. (eds) (1987), *The pragmatic perspective*. John Benjamins, Amsterdam.

Verschueren, J., Östman, J.-O. and Blommaert, J. (forthcoming), *Handbook of Pragmatics: Manual*. John Benjamins, Amsterdam.

Vicente, B. (1992), 'Metaphor, meaning and comprehension'. *Pragmatics* 2: 49–62.

Vygotsky, L. (1962), *Thought and language*, translated from the Russian (1934). MIT Press, Cambridge, MA.

Walker, R. (1975), 'Conversational implicatures', in Blackburn 1975: 133–81.

Walker, R. (1989), 'Review of *Relevance*'. *Mind and Language* 4.1/2: 151–9.

Watson, R. (1995), 'Relevance and definition'. *Journal of Child Language* 22: 211–22.

Watts, R. (1988), 'A relevance-theoretic approach to commentary pragmatic markers: The case of *actually, really* and *basically'*. *Acta Linguistica Hungarica* 38.1–4: 235–60.

Werth, P. (ed.) (1981), *Conversation and discourse.* Croom Helm, London.

Wilks, Y. and Cunningham, C. (1986), 'A purported theory of relevance', in Mey 1986: 383–418.

Wilson, D. (1975), *Presuppositions and non-truth-conditional semantics.* Academic Press, London. Reprinted in *Gregg Modern Revivals in Philosophy.* Gregg Revivals, Aldershot (1991).

Wilson, D. (1992a), 'Reply to Chametzky'. *Journal of Pragmatics* 17: 73–7.

Wilson, D. (1992b), 'Reference and relevance'. *UCL Working Papers in Linguistics* 4: 165–91.

Wilson, D. (1994a), 'Relevance and understanding', in Brown *et al.* 1994: 35–58. First published in Guijarro Morales 1993.

Wilson, D. (1994b), 'Truth, coherence and relevance'. Paper delivered to the European Society for Philosophy and Psychology, July.

Wilson, D. and Smith, N. (eds) (1992), 'Special issue on relevance theory (volume 1)'. *Lingua* 87.1/2.

Wilson, D. and Smith, N. (eds) (1993), 'Special issue on relevance theory (volume 2)'. *Lingua* 90.1/2.

Wilson, D. and Sperber, D. (1981), 'On Grice's theory of conversation', in Werth 1981: 155–78.

Wilson, D. and Sperber, D. (1986a), 'Inference and implicature', in Travis 1986: 43–75. Reprinted in Davis 1991: 377–93.

Wilson, D. and Sperber, D. (1986b), 'Pragmatics and modularity', in *Parasession on pragmatics and grammatical theory. Chicago Linguistics Society* 22: 67–84. Reprinted in Davis 1991: 583–95.

Wilson, D. and Sperber, D. (1986c), 'An outline of relevance theory', in Alves 1986: 19–42. Reprinted in *Notes on Linguistics* (1987) 39: 5–24.

Wilson, D. and Sperber, D. (1987), 'The self-appointment of Seuren as censor: A reply to Pieter Seuren'. *Journal of Semantics* 5: 145–62.

Wilson, D. and Sperber, D. (1988a), 'Mood and the analysis of non-declarative sentences', in Dancy, Moravcsik and Taylor 1988: 77–101.

Wilson, D. and Sperber, D. (1988b), 'Representation and relevance', in Kempson 1988a: 133–53.

Wilson, D. and Sperber, D. (1992), 'On verbal irony'. *Lingua* 87.1/2: 53–76.

Wilson, D. and Sperber, D. (1993), 'Linguistic form and relevance'. *Lingua* 90.1/2: 1–25.

Wilson, D. and Sperber, D. (forthcoming), 'Pragmatics and time'. To appear in Carston and Uchida forthcoming.

Wilson, J. (1990), *Politically speaking: The pragmatic analysis of political language.* Blackwell, Oxford.

Winckler, W. and van der Merwe, C. (1993), 'Training tomorrow's bible translators: Some theoretical pointers'. *Journal of Northwest Semitic Languages* 19: 41–58.

Winograd, T. (1977), 'A framework for understanding discourse', in Just and Carpenter 1977: 72–86.

Wolf, G. (ed.) (1992), *New departures in linguistics*. Garland, New York.

Wright, R. (1975), 'Meaning$_{NN}$ and conversational implicature', in Cole and Morgan 1975: 363–82.

Yoshimura, A. (1993a), 'Explicature and implicature formation in the modeling of metaphor and metonymy'. *Osaka University Papers in English Linguistics* I: 175–84.

Yoshimura, A. (1993b), 'Pragmatic and cognitive aspects of negative polarity'. *Osaka University Papers in English Linguistics* I: 141–73.

Yu, P. (1979), 'On the Gricean program about meaning'. *Linguistics and Philosophy* 3.2: 273–88.

Zegarac, V. (1991), *Tense, aspect and relevance*. University of London, Ph.D. thesis.

Zegarac, V. (1993), 'Some observations on the pragmatics of the progressive'. *Lingua* 90.1/2: 201–20.

Ziff, P. (1967), 'On H. P. Grice's account of meaning'. *Analysis* 28: 1–8. Reprinted in Steinberg and Jakobovits 1971: 60–5.

Ziv, Y. (1988), 'On the rationality of "Relevance" and the relevance of "Rationality"'. *Journal of Pragmatics* 12.5/6: 535–45.

Index

当代国外语言学与应用语言学文库（升级版）
已出版书目

General Linguistics (Fourth Edition)
《普通语言学概论（第四版）》
R. H. Robins

An Introduction to Linguistics
《语言学入门》
Stuart C. Poole

Language
《语言论》
L. Bloomfield

Language: An Introduction to the Study of Speech
《语言论：言语研究导论》
Edward Sapir

——History of Linguistics 语言学史

A Short History of Linguistics (Fourth Edition)
《语言学简史（第四版）》
R. H. Robins

——Intercultural Communication 跨文化交际

Intercultural Communication: A Discourse Approach (Third Edition)
《跨文化交际：语篇分析法（第三版）》
Ron Scollon, Suzanne Wong Scollon & Rodney H. Jones

Intercultural Interaction: A Multidisciplinary Approach to Intercultural Communication
《跨文化互动：跨文化交际的多学科研究》
Helen Spencer-Oatey & Peter Franklin

——Language Education 语言教育

Approaches and Methods in Language Teaching (Third Edition)
《语言教学的流派（第三版）》
Jack C. Richards & Theodore S. Rodgers

A Course in English Language Teaching (Second Edition)
《语言教学教程：实践与理论（第二版）》
Penny Ur

Experiences of Second Language Teacher Education
《第二语言教师教育经验》
Tony Wright & Mike Beaumont

Principles of Language Learning and Teaching (Sixth Edition)
《语言学习与语言教学的原则（第六版）》
H. Douglas Brown

Teaching by Principles: An Interactive Approach to Language Pedagogy (Fourth Edition)
《根据原理教学：交互式语言教学（第四版）》
H. Douglas Brown & Heekyeong Lee

Usage-inspired L2 Instruction: Researched Pedagogy
《使用驱动的二语教学：实证依据》
Andrea E. Tyler, Lourdes Ortega, Mariko Uno & Hae In Park

——Neurolinguistics 神经语言学

The Handbook of the Neuropsychology of Language (2 Volume Set)
《语言的神经心理学手册》
Miriam Faust

Introduction to Neurolinguistics
《神经语言学导论》
Elisabeth Ahlsén

——Philosophy of Language 语言哲学

How to Do Things with Words
《如何以言行事》
J. L. Austin

——Phonetics and Phonology 语音学与音系学

English Phonetics and Phonology: A Practical Course (Fourth Edition)
《英语语音学与音系学实用教程（第四版）》
Peter Roach

——Pragmatics 语用学

Meaning in Interaction: An Introduction to Pragmatics
《言谈互动中的意义：语用学引论》
Jenny Thomas

Pragmatics: An Introduction (Second Edition)
《语用学引论（第二版）》
Jacob L. Mey

Relevance: Communication and Cognition (Second Edition)
《关联性：交际与认知（第二版）》
　Dan Sperber & Deirdre Wilson

——Psycholinguistics 心理语言学

The Articulate Mammal: An Introduction to Psycholinguistics (Fourth Edition)
《会说话的哺乳动物：心理语言学入门（第四版）》
　Jean Aitchison

Research Methods in Psycholinguistics and the Neurobiology of Language: A Practical Guide
《心理语言学及语言的神经生物学研究方法实用指导》
　Annette M. B. de Groot & Peter Hagoort

——Research Method 研究方法

Projects in Linguistics and Language Studies: A Practical Guide to Researching Language (Third Edition)
《语言学课题：语言研究实用指导（第三版）》
　Alison Wray & Aileen Bloomer

Research Perspectives on English for Academic Purposes
《学术英语的多维研究视角》
　John Flowerdew & Matthew Peacock

——Second Language Acquisition 第二语言习得

Fossilization in Adult Second Language Acquisition
《成人二语习得中的僵化现象》
　韩照红（Zhaohong Han）

Innovative Research and Practices in Second Language Acquisition and Bilingualism
《二语习得与双语现象的创新研究及实践》
　John W. Schwieter

Linguistics and Second Language Acquisition
《语言学和第二语言习得》
　Vivian Cook

Second Language Learning and Language Teaching (Fifth Edition)
《第二语言学习与教学（第五版）》
　Vivian Cook

Second Language Needs Analysis
《第二语言需求分析》
Michael H. Long

Tasks in Second Language Learning
《第二语言学习中的任务》
Virginia Samuda & Martin Bygate

Working Memory in Second Language Acquisition and Processing
《工作记忆与二语习得及加工》
温植胜（Edward）, Mailce Borges Mota & Arthur McNeill

—— Semantics 语义学

Analyzing Meaning: An Introduction to Semantics and Pragmatics (Second Edition)
《意义分析：语义学与语用学导论（第二版）》
Paul R. Kroeger

Meaning in Language: An Introduction to Semantics and Pragmatics (Third Edition)
《语言的意义：语义学与语用学导论（第三版）》
Alan Cruse

Semantics (Fourth Edition)
《语义学（第四版）》
John I. Saeed

—— Sociolinguistics 社会语言学

The Handbook of Sociolinguistics
《社会语言学通览》
Florian Coulmas

An Introduction to Sociolinguistics (Seventh Edition)
《社会语言学引论（第七版）》
Ronald Wardhaugh & Janet M. Fuller

—— Stylistics 文体学

The Bloomsbury Companion to Stylistics
《布鲁姆斯伯里文体学导论》
Violeta Sotirova

A Linguistic Guide to English Poetry
《英诗学习指南：语言学的分析方法》
Geoffrey N. Leech

Patterns in Language: Stylistics for Students of Language and Literature
《语言模式：文体学入门》
　　Joanna Thornborrow & Shân Wareing

Stylistics: A Practical Coursebook
《实用文体学教程》
　　Laura Wright & Jonathan Hope

——Syntax 句法学

Chomsky's Universal Grammar: An Introduction (Third Edition)
《乔姆斯基的普遍语法教程（第三版）》
　　V. J. Cook & Mark Newson

Syntax: A Generative Introduction (Fourth Edition)
《句法学：生成语法导论（第四版）》
　　Andrew Carnie

——Testing 语言测试

Assessing the Language of Young Learners
《少儿和青少年的语言测评》
　　Angela Hasselgreen & Gwendydd Caudwell

Designing Listening Tests: A Practical Approach
《英语听力测试设计指导》
　　Rita Green

Language Testing and Validation: An Evidence-Based Approach
《语言测试与效度验证：基于证据的研究方法》
　　Cyril J. Weir

Second Language Pronunciation Assessment: Interdisciplinary Perspectives
《二语语音评测：跨学科视角》
　　Talia Isaacs & Pavel Trofimovich

Statistical Analyses for Language Assessment
《语言测评中的统计分析》
　　Lyle F. Bachman & Antony J. Kunnan

Writing English Language Tests (Second Edition)
《英语测试（第二版）》
　　J. B. Heaton

——Text Linguistics 语篇语言学

The Language of Evaluation: Appraisal in English
《评估语言：英语评价系统》
　　J. R. Martin & P. R. R. White

Metadiscourse
《元话语》
Ken Hyland

——Translatology 翻译学

Border Crossings: Translation Studies and Other Disciplines
《跨越边界：翻译的跨学科研究》
Yves Gambier & Luc van Doorslaer

In Other Words: A Coursebook on Translation (Third Edition)
《换言之：翻译教程（第三版）》
Mona Baker

The Neurocognition of Translation and Interpreting
《口笔译的认知神经科学研究》
Adolfo M. García